ZEN'S CHINESE HERITAGE

ZEN'S CHINESE HERITAGE

The Masters and Their Teachings

by Andrew Ferguson

Foreword by Reb Anderson

Wisdom Publications • Boston

Wisdom Publications
199 Elm Street
Somerville MA 02144 USA

Library of Congress Cataloging-in-Publication Data
Ferguson, Andrew E.
    Zen's Chinese heritage: the masters and their teachings /
  by Andrew E. Ferguson.
        p.   cm.
    Includes bibliographical references and index.
    ISBN 0-86171-163-7 (alk. paper)
    1. Priests, Zen—China—Biography. 2. Zen Buddhism—
Doctrines. I. Title.
    BQ9298.F47 2000
    294.3'927'0951—dc21   99-088199

ISBN 0-86171-163-7

05 04 03 02 01
6   5   4   3   2

Designed and typeset by Gopa and the Bear
Cover calligraphy by Jing-hua Gao Dalia
Interior calligraphy by Kazuaki Tanahashi

Wisdom Publications' books are printed on acid-free paper
and meet the guidelines for the permanence and durability
of the Committee on Production Guidelines for Book
Longevity of the Council on Library Resources.

Printed in the United States of America

TABLE OF CONTENTS

PART TWO:
THE CLASSICAL PERIOD 755–950

LIST OF ILLUSTRATIONS

CALLIGRAPHY:

Cover: *See one's true nature and become a buddha.*
Title Page and Part I: *Buddha* by Kazuaki Tanahashi
Part II: *Dharma* by Kazuaki Tanahashi
Part III: *Sangha* by Kazuaki Tanahashi

PHOTOGRAPHS:

PUBLISHER'S ACKNOWLEDGMENT

THE PUBLISHER gratefully acknowledges the generous help of the Hershey Family Foundation in sponsoring the publication of this book.

FOREWORD

THANKS TO THE INCOMPARABLY KIND and careful efforts of Andy Ferguson and his skillful collaborators, we now have before us this wonderful collection of sublime Zen stories. These stories are essentially concerned with enlightened compassion, for the ultimate intention of Zen teaching and training is to develop a profound insight that purifies our love and devotion to all living beings. Zen is part of the Mahayana, the Great Vehicle, the universal movement—the movement of the universe—which is fundamentally committed to liberating all living beings from suffering and working to realize their greatest happiness. When our compassion is purified and has no limits we can work together with all beings for the welfare of all.

In order to liberate beings from suffering it is necessary to realize its origin. What is the origin of suffering? Although it has been taught many times and in many different ways, clinging to our deluded stories of who and what we are is the origin of our suffering. Clinging to the idea that we are really separate from each other is our deluded story of the self. Therefore, if we want to work most effectively for the welfare of all beings, we must forget all about our own stories. If we wish to understand Buddha's liberating teaching, we must completely let go of our own narrative about reality.

The stories presented here for our study and inquiry offer virtually endless opportunities to free ourselves from our habitual stories. The shift from our habitual stories of the self to new ones is part of the process of liberation, but it does not stop there; we must even go beyond such liberation. It's not that the old stories are delusion and the new ones are enlightenment; rather it's that clinging to the old stories is deluding and not clinging to them is enlightening. By forgetting our old cherished stories, then each and every story that arrives at our doorstep enlightens us. But if we attach to these enlightening stories, delusion and suffering are reestablished.

What is this story that many of us tell ourselves and hold on to almost all the time? It goes something like this—I'm here and you are over there, my life is separate from yours, the objects of my awareness are external to me. This story is almost instinctive. Once it arises, it is almost impossible not to grasp it as real. Attaching to it as real is the origin of our suffering. With this story we are well equipped with anxiety but not necessarily well equipped to face it, so we embark on a career of trying to avoid anxiety and blaming it on others instead.

Here is another story. All the buddhas throughout space and time are practicing together along with each of us. I'm not really over here separate from you and all the buddhas, and you are not really out there on your own; there really is no here and there; you are not a threat to me, and I'm not a threat to you; we support each other, and we have no separate life; there is nothing out there to be afraid of, and everything that comes brings us our life; our true body is the entire universe; and to have a chance to live is something to be grateful for no matter what form it takes. That's the story.

It's not that one of these stories is true and the other is false, and it's not that one is better than the other. The two are intimately connected, and the one liberates us from the other. Zen practice is not about preferring one of these stories over the other; it's about letting go of both of them.

How can you live today without attachment to your own stories, how can you care for life? The response to this question given by Shakyamuni Buddha and Zen teachers is to train yourself *thus*. This is the teaching and the practice of the way you are, the teaching to simply be the way you have come to be. I propose to the reader of these Zen stories that, in the midst of the practice of *thusness*, you will be relieved of all your old stories and enlightened by these others.

One way to train yourself to be thus is to say to yourself with your whole being, "Thank you very much, I have no complaint whatsoever!" Even if you are in a miserable prison of your old stories you say, "Thank you very much, I have no complaint whatsoever." And no matter what you are, you are grateful for the opportunity to be thus. At this moment, in the middle of whatever is happening, you are grateful for the opportunity to care for what is happening, with no complaint. Even if you are complaining, you are grateful for the opportunity to not complain about your complaints. Even if everyone says they hate you and are disgusted with you or that they love you and admire you, you are grateful in the midst of hearing them. You are not grateful that they hate you or that they love you. You are grateful instead for the opportunity to let what you hear just be what you hear. You don't grasp these words of hatred or love as anything more or less than words of hatred or love. You don't grasp them at all when you let them just be what they are.

My prayer is that readers of these old Zen stories will enter thoroughly into their own stories, and become so intimate with them that they are forgotten.

May your body and mind be open and deeply touched by these stories of liberation without attachment. May your heart gratefully embrace all life, free of prejudice and preference, and be filled with the truth of all things. May your love be purified, and may your wise methods be realized in full.

Tenshin Reb Anderson
Green Dragon Zen Temple
Chinese New Year, Year of the Iron Dragon, 2000

PREFACE

THE COMPLETION OF THIS BOOK depended on the work, wisdom, and scholarship of many people. Its fruition is also unimaginable without the fortunate convergence of streams of endeavor from different times, places, and technologies. Zen master Dachuan Lingyin Puji (1179–1253) at Lingyin Monastery in Hangzhou, China, compiled the *Wudeng Huiyan (Compendium of Five Lamps)*, the primary source for the translations of this volume. Although Puji's work is itself a distillation of previous lamp records, it is a seminal text and an important cornerstone of Zen scholarship. I hereby gratefully acknowledge and remember him and his life. Many other scholars laid foundation stones for this work. No English-language work on Zen should fail to remember and pay tribute to the scholars and teachers who led us to this path and who continue to guide us. Among their contributions must be mentioned the many great works of Daisetz Suzuki, Isshu Miura and Ruth Fuller Sasaki's *Zen Dust*, Chang Chung-yuan's *Original Teachings of Chan Buddhism*, Heinrich Dumoulin's *Zen Buddhism: A History*, the many wonderful and important works of translation and scholarship by Thomas Cleary, the vital works of J. C. Cleary, Sohaku Ogata's the *Transmission of the Lamp: Early Masters*, Nelson Foster and Jack Shoemaker's *The Roaring Stream: A New Zen Reader*, as well as influential books by Alan Watts, Robert Aitken, Burton Watson, Phillip Kapleau, and many others. Special words of remembrance and thanks go to the founder of San Francisco Zen Center, Shunryu Suzuki, and to the late Trudy Dixon, who compiled Suzuki Rōshi's talks into *Zen Mind, Beginner's Mind*. I especially acknowledge the wonderful work of Urs App, Christian Wittern, and others at Hanazono University's International Research Institute for Zen. Their work of digitizing many classical Zen texts has made searching and researching those volumes scandalously easy. Their scholarship cannot be praised too highly. Among a long list of Chinese-language works that helped shape this book, I first and foremost acknowledge the life and work of the great teacher Hsü Yun ("Empty Cloud"), a towering figure of nineteenth- and twentieth-century Chinese Buddhist teaching and scholarship, along with his principal translator, Charles Luk. Next, this book benefits from the life and works of Yin Hsün, the acclaimed contemporary Buddhist teacher and scholar. Among many other Chinese books that served as sources for this volume, I particularly wish to mention the works of a Chinese scholar currently unknown in the West, Yuan Bing, a professor at Shanghai Normal University. Yuan has edited an excellent book on Zen literature and grammar, which served as a valuable resource for my questions about Zen translation. Also, Yuan's own translations of classical Zen discourses into modern Chinese are among the best available.

Among the many individuals who offered assistance, I first thank my lifelong friend Jeffrey Hayden and his teacher, Master Shei, for their ongoing help and encouragement. Thomas Cleary offered early assistance with the addresses of strategic bookstores in Taiwan. Next, I can't overstate the contribution rendered by the talented Buddhist scholar Holger Hoke and his wife Meihua in Beijing. They have, for years, scoured bookstores in mainland China and Taiwan, sending me scores of obscure and otherwise undiscovered books written on Zen, then refusing compensation even for the books themselves. Many of those books have been valuable resources. May all beings have friends of such generosity. I especially acknowledge and thank my friend Kazuaki Tanahashi for his suggestion for the title of this book, and for his critical help with the Lineage Chart of the Zen Ancestors, which ultimately led to this volume's layout and structure. Robert Aitken Rōshi offered wisdom and concrete criticisms that greatly improved the draft manuscript. I humbly thank him for both his direct help and for the entire body of his ongoing and beneficial works. Charlie Pokorney, Charlie Henkel, Susan O'Connell, and other friends at San Francisco Zen Center reviewed the draft manuscript during a winter at Tassajara and provided useful suggestions and editing help. I gratefully acknowledge their assistance. John Daido Loori, the great Zen teacher and abbot of Zen Mountain Monastery at Mt. Tremper, has offered wonderful help and encouragement, as has my friend, the talented Buddhist teacher and writer Taigen Dan Leighton. Particular thanks are extended to my editor, Marsha Calhoun, who patiently corrected my mistakes and made helpful suggestions on style. Appreciation is extended to the many participants of Tenshin Reb Anderson's Monday night *kōan* class at Green Gulch Farm, who have all worked to help me better understand and appreciate the Zen ancients. I offer thanks to my wife, Lisa, and my daughters, Ceann and Sacha, who for many years have endured my work at the computer with scarcely a word of complaint. And finally, my gratitude is extended to my teacher, Tenshin Reb Anderson, whose wisdom has informed any positive contribution this book offers its readers. The book's errors and shortcomings are attributable to me alone.

This book draws from modern Chinese scholarship in mainland China. This may seem unusual, since mainland scholarship through many parts of the twentieth century has withered in the tepid Chinese political climate. The last ten years, however, have seen a new blossoming of Zen scholarship in mainland China, which, while recognizing the work of scholars in Japan and Taiwan, breaks new ground itself. The nineties have produced a great number of new Zen histories and translations of old texts into modern Chinese. In general, I find that the modern Chinese books on Zen accept traditional explanations of events more readily than Western scholars have done. However, mainland sources do not accept events uncritically. Indeed, they back up their views with extensive citations from generally reliable historical sources.

"Zen" is the Japanese pronunciation of the Chinese word "Chan." The two terms are interchangeable. The latter term is generally used in the context of Chinese culture. Because the Zen tradition was made known to Westerners largely through the works of Japanese scholars and religious figures such as Daisetz Suzuki, the term Zen is widely recognized in the West. For this reason, the word Zen is used in this book instead of Chan.

The inspiration for this book came from the public kōan class offered at San Francisco Zen Center's Green Dragon Temple at Green Gulch Farm. For many years, Tenshin Reb Anderson has offered a "Monday night class" on Thomas Cleary's translation of the *Book of Serenity* for the benefit of his students and other serious participants. In the manner of the Zen ancients, Tenshin has raised the ancient cases for public viewing. This is a style of Zen practice whereby students may realize their own personal understandings, and then set them forth for others to see, to taste, and to test.

New shoots grow in Zen's ancient garden. Here at Jia Shan Monastery in Hunan Province, the great work of rebuilding the tangible remnants of Zen history proceeds. New halls have been constructed on the ancient monastery's foundations. The buildings sit grandly in the withering heat of a late summer day. Nearby, at the foot of the Blue Cliff, farmers draw water from cisterns newly built upon the ancient spring.

Andy Ferguson
Mt. Jia (Jia Shan) Monastery,
Hunan Province, China
September 1999

TECHNICAL NOTE

NAMES

IN OLD CHINA the Zen public sometimes referred to Zen masters by their "mountain" or geographic names. "Mountain names" do not necessarily refer to actual mountains, but can refer to cities, temples, or other locations where an individual taught. For example, Zen master Guishan Lingyou taught on Mt. Gui (in Chinese, "Gui Shan"), and was subsequently referred to by that name. When used, mountain names are typically the first word of a name. For clarity, this book compounds the geographic name into one word when refering to a person and not a place. For example, the term "Guishan" refers to an individual, whereas "Gui Shan" refers to a geographic location. To avoid confusion, the book uses English terms such as "Mt. Gui" whenever possible.

Mountain names cause confusion when more than one well-known teacher comes from a single geographic location. For example, Guishan Da'an was another teacher from Mt. Gui. In such cases this book will often use the Dharma name (here, Da'an) instead of the geographic name (Guishan) of the teacher. Various other names were commonly applied to Zen masters, including nicknames and posthumous names. While mountain and Dharma names predominate in the original Chinese texts, any and all possible names were (sometimes ambiguously) used historically. The reader can take some comfort in the fact that names, lacking a clear convention, were sometimes confusing to writers in old China as well.

While the text uses pinyin romanization throughout, I have not used pinyin for words already familiar to the English reading public, such as Kwan Yin, Taoism, and the Yang-tse River.

PRONUNCIATION GUIDE FOR THE PINYIN CHINESE ROMANIZATION SYSTEM

Vowels:
1. "ao" is pronounced "ow." For example, hao = "how."
2. "ou" is pronounced "oe." For example, dou = "doe" (as in female deer).

3. "a" is pronounced "ah." For example, hang = "hong" (rhymes with the English word "song").
4. "o" is pronounced similar to the English sound "oo" in the word "book." For example, song = "soong."
5. "ui" is pronounced "uay." For example, hui = "huay."
6. "e" is pronounced "uh." For example, neng = "nung" (rhymes with English "hung").
7. There is variation in pronunciation for words ending in "i." When "i" follows compound consonants such as "sh," it is pronounced as though followed by an "r." Thus shi = "sure," zhi = "zher," and chi = "cher." However, when "i" follows a single consonant such as "l," "q," or "n," no "r" sound is added. Thus li = "lee,' qi = "chee," and ni = "nee."

Consonants:
1. "x" is pronounced similar to the English letter "s." For example, xuan = "swan," xi = "see," xin = "sin."
2. "q" is pronounced "ch." For example, qi = "chee," qian = "chian."
3. "zh" is pronounced like the English letter "j." For example, zhi = "jer," zhang = "jong," zhen = "jen."
4. "c" is pronounced similar to the English letters "ts." For example, cui = "tsway."

INTRODUCTION

IN RECENT TIMES, writers have used the word Zen in the titles and contents of various books and articles. It is often used in relation to activities, such as in *Zen and the Art of Motorcycle Maintenance*, or *The Zen of Tennis*. Many of these books provide skillful descriptions of ideas and practices that are part of the Zen tradition. As a result, the word Zen evokes certain ideas in the public consciousness, such as "balance," "clarity," or "mindfulness." The word Zen itself, however, remains largely undefined. Many people know that the word is Japanese, and they may also know it is derived from the Chinese word *Chan*, which in turn is derived from the Sanskrit word *dhyana*, meaning meditation. In China, from the sixth century onward, the word *Zen* surpassed this definition and gained additional meaning and color. Tang-dynasty China wove Zen into its culture. Art, philosophy, and politics all enjoyed its influence. Zen spread beyond China to other East Asian societies with great impact and with far-reaching consequences. From one perspective, Zen became a religion in its own right, a school of Buddhism. From another perspective, it became an important cultural force whose influence in East Asian societies can hardly be overstated.

The current wide use of the word Zen notwithstanding, the corpus of Zen history and literature remains mostly unknown in the West (and, regretfully, in the East as well) even among advanced Zen students. An impressive list of writers, including Daisetz Suzuki, Thomas Cleary, Chang Chung-yuan, Ruth Fuller Sasaki, Isshu Miura, Robert Aitken, Gary Snyder, Heinrich Dumoulin, Alan Watts, and many others, have introduced Zen to Western readers in various formats. Despite these wonderful works, the surface of Zen history and teachings has barely been scratched.

This book offers translations of the traditional teachings of Chinese Zen from the time of its introduction to China by the legendary Bodhidharma in the late fifth century up to the mid-thirteenth century, near the end of the Song dynasty. It has been written to harmonize with another Zen publication, the Lineage Chart of the Zen Ancestors. These two publications, as a set, are meant to build a framework whereby teachers, students, and general readers can more readily identify individuals and schools of the Zen tradition. Whenever possible, this book employs the words of the Zen masters themselves rather than secondhand accounts of their teachings. Hundreds of great Zen masters lived in China during the time described, a period that spanned twenty-five generations of enlightened teachers.

Zen existed in China prior to Bodhidharma. Chinese records from as early as the second century reveal the presence of Zen practitioners and Zen texts. The practice of dhyana was a recognized part of Buddhist practice, and was variously emphasized by different individuals and schools. A well-known twentieth-century Chinese practitioner and scholar, Tai Xu, has described Zen before Bodhidharma as "the Zen of cultivating mind according to scripture." The Zen of that early era also appears to have emphasized concentration practice. During the second century, a form of Zen meditation called *an ban* existed. Based on the *Anapana Sutra*, this meditation practice focused the mind on the recitation of the word *an* while inhaling, and *ban* while exhaling.

Some individual Buddhist teachers existed prior to or in the early years of Bodhidharma's Zen who, though outside Bodhidharma's lineage of students, were closely aligned with Bodhidharma's Zen in flavor and spirit. These teachers were well known to later Zen students and were widely cited. An example is the monk Fuxi (497–569), whose life was contemporaneous with Bodhidharma's disciple Huike. Fuxi was an eccentric Zen character who exerted great influence on the court and commoners of the Liang dynasty. A famous poem by Fuxi poses some Zen-flavored contradictions, and is often remembered and repeated in the Chinese Zen tradition.

> *An empty hand grasps the hoe handle,*
> *Walking along, I ride the ox,*
> *The ox crosses the wooden bridge,*
> *The bridge is flowing, the water is still.*

This book will offer only this passing bow to Zen's other ancient roots. It is Bodhidharma and his descendants who occupy the core of the Chinese Zen tradition, and they remain the focus of this book to better establish a clear foundation of traditional Zen history for a new audience.

Zen masters have been included in this book according to their relative importance and appearance in books familiar to the Zen reading public. Most of the Zen masters who appear here are prominently mentioned in the *Book of Serenity*, the *Blue Cliff Record*, or the *Gateless Gate*. This will allow readers already familiar with certain teachers to add to their knowledge. However, no prior familiarity with Zen or any of the Zen ancestors is needed to read this volume.

This book attempts to let the Zen tradition speak for itself. I've tried to minimize parenthetical comments and have also avoided providing secondary interpretations. Some readers will still think I've added too much. Others, too little. My approach does not provide extensive background information about the ages when these masters lived, nor does it reveal the doubts that modern scholarship casts on certain aspects of the Zen tradition. For example, twentieth-century scholarship disputes some crucial connections in the traditional genealogies of Chinese Zen masters. Modern scholarship even questions the existence of some of the Zen teachers included in this book. I am not at all unmindful of these facts, but I propose that understanding how the tradition views itself must be the basis for all later criticism. The traditional view is not yet sufficiently appreciated by Western readers.

It is useful to break the many centuries covered in this book into three periods, which roughly reflect the evolution of Zen literature in China. Different types of Zen writings predominate in each period, and thus provide a (somewhat arbitrary) method for making historical distinctions. These three periods, in order, may be called the "Legendary," "Classical," and "Literary" periods of Zen history.

The Legendary period, stretching from Bodhidharma's arrival in China during the late fifth century until the middle of the Tang dynasty, around 765 C.E., has left us only a sketchy literary record. Modern scholars dismiss many of this era's Zen stories as apocryphal, or at best of dubious origin. Myth, magic, and facts are tightly fused in Zen's early history. The writings handed down to us were recorded long after the events they describe. These are often stories "about" the Zen ancients rather than what was said "by" them. The writings and legends of the First Ancestor, Bodhidharma, fit into this framework. Legends of this Indian sage helped create Zen's mythical ethos, a vital component at the source of the religion. Scholars often do not accept that writings attributed to Bodhidharma were actually written by him, or indeed that Bodhidharma even existed. Luckily, the entertaining legends surrounding Bodhidharma's life are not diminished by the lack of solid evidence about him. Moreover, some stories about Zen's earliest historical period seem to fit well with known historical facts. The gaps in Zen's early record coincide with periods of known suppression of Buddhism by the government or with times of civil unrest and destruction. In such circumstances, it is not surprising that, without a consistent written record, Zen's early history was embellished.

China's true age of enlightenment occurred in the Classical period, stretching roughly from 765 to 950 C.E. In this era, contemporary Zen records exist to describe famous Zen events. From about the time of Zen masters Mazu Daoyi and Shitou Xiqian, Zen students in China commonly recorded their teachers' words and collected them into books called *yulu* ("records" or "discourses"), many of which have survived. Also, the tradition of the *yunshui*, literally "clouds and waters" (meaning itinerant monks on pilgrimage), was now in full force.[1] Traveling monks spread and exchanged news of enlightened teachers throughout the country. Famous Zen teachers of this era were widely recognized and subjected to public and royal adulation. Great Zen masters created public sensations when they traveled from one place to another. Zen now reached all levels of society, as emperors and street peddlers alike became willing students. The unique teaching styles of memorable Zen personalities adorned the culture of Chinese society, as well as the parallel Zen religious culture. Zen possessed a verdant oral, and a developing literary, tradition.

The main Zen literary works of the Classical period served and sustained the oral tradition. But as time passed, successive generations of teachers appended their comments to written accounts of older stories, and thus the origins of the Zen literary culture that flourished in later centuries took root. Several examples of these appended comments have been included in this volume.

The Zen lecture, a main vehicle of the oral tradition, is introduced in Chinese Zen literature by the phrase *shang tang* (literally, "ascend the hall"), meaning that the Zen master "went into the (Dharma) hall," or "ascended the Dharma seat." In this book, the phrase "entered the hall and addressed the monks" often denotes this activity. The lectures often included stories about an ancient teacher's dialogue with a student. The dialogues typically revealed some former teacher's special style and the particular circumstances surrounding a student's enlightenment.

The recorded words of the Classical-period Zen masters reveal their brilliant spiritual clarity. For example, the masters describe each other's ability to "take lives," "trample people to death," or "cut out the tongues of everyone on earth." Such metaphors convey these individuals' awesome posture and presence, and their ability to awaken others to Buddha's truth, causing them to "lose their [previous understanding of] life." The recorded prose and poetry of the Classical teachers is beautifully stark and austere, hardly precedented in tone and depth.

The Classical period was also the era of "Dharma combat," whereby great teachers met and tested each other in a sort of spiritual jousting match. Emperors sought out the greatest teachers and became their students, often bestowing titles and honors upon them (which were usually avoided or declined by the teachers).

The final division set forth in this book, the Literary period of Zen, stretched from about 950 to 1250 C.E. From around the time of the Fayan Zen school (circa 950), and beginning with the Linji school teacher Fenyang Shanzhao (947–1024), Zen stories, known as *gongan* (in Japanese, *kōan*), were compiled and, in a more formal fashion, posed by Zen teachers to their students in the course of their training. This was by no means, however, the first such use of these old stories. Chinese Zen has, from the time of the early masters, incorporated stories as an organic part of the tradition. Moreover, the term gongan itself goes back at least to Baizhang Huaihai in the late eighth century. But in the Song dynasty, as stories of the classical masters had come in some sense to exemplify the essence of the tradition, these stories naturally assumed a more formal role in Zen practice and teaching. (The word gongan means "public case" and relates Zen events well known to the Zen "public.")

In the early part of the Literary period, Fenyang Shanzhao, Hongzhi Zhengjue, Touzi Yiqing, and others compiled traditional Zen gongan into collections, typically of one hundred stories each. These collections were amended with written verses, and this novel literature became the heart of a new literary genre known as *songgu*, meaning "in praise of the ancient."[2] Later, written commentaries were added to the songgu literature, and the result was known as *niansong*, which roughly translates as "held up and praised." The *Blue Cliff Record*, the *Gateless Gate*, and the *Book of Serenity* are the most famous products of this new creative style.

The Literary period had many great and original teachers, but Zen's songgu and niansong literature of the Song dynasty clearly abandoned all pretense of avoiding written words, and instead embraced them. While some teachers opposed this trend, the new literature of enlightenment was too beautiful for most to eschew. During the earlier Tang dynasty, Zen heavily influenced writers and poets. During the Song dynasty, Zen teachers themselves became writers and poets. Also, a tendency to idealize the past infected Zen culture no less than it did other areas of Chinese culture and politics. When the syncretist trends of the Song dynasty diluted Zen's unique flavor, a near mythicization of the earlier classical Zen masters was a natural response. This nostalgia for the earlier masters spawned literature that idealized the earlier Zen era.

As gongan fused more closely into Zen practice, a new modified and contracted form of the gongan, called *huatou*, appeared. This term, literally meaning "speech heads," or essential words, were usually gongan that had been reduced to key phrases or words. For example, the well-known gongan entitled "Zhaozhou's '*Wu!*'" (in Japanese, "Jōshū's '*Mu!*'") is a story about whether or not a dog has buddha nature. When this gongan is contracted to become a huatou, only the word "wu" remains. In some Zen traditions today, this single word is often assigned to new Zen students as an object of study.

Famous gongan, such as "You must show me the face you had before your parents were born," or huatou such as Zhaozhou's "Wu!" have helped shape the modern public perception of Zen. Such stories, which have reached the West mainly through the niansong literary genre, have alternately fascinated and confused public understanding of the tradition. But an understanding of the importance of niansong literature and gongan study is more accessible in the light of the earlier oral and literary tradition from which they began. Niansong literature was distilled from a much larger Zen literary and oral context. This book is an attempt to bring more of that context to light.

Today, the exchanges between the Zen ancients continue to play an important part in Zen study. But applying a system of logic, or nonlogic, to all of these wonderful stories is not the point. They are the recorded examples of expressions of truth and the application of skillful means for the sake of people in an age far removed from our own. They are the exquisite traces of the work of enlightened human beings, and they should inspire us not to mimic them, but to personally realize the source that gave rise to them.

The well-known American Zen teacher Robert Aitken Rōshi comments on the old stories in this manner:

> [In Zen] modern teachers who know what's what do not treat the old stories as history or philosophy or psychology or literature. They do not talk about the old stories, but rather they present them as arcana that require inquiry that is far more profound than academic study or explanation—the very same kind of inquiry that was demanded in the ancient interactions. Koâns are not riddles or riddle-like stories or teaching devices. They are direct expressions of the most profound, perennial facts, and deserve our exacting attention.

THE FIVE HOUSES

According to Zen tradition, there were five main schools ("houses") of Zen that existed during roughly the time I've described as Zen's Classical period. During that era, however, the term *five houses* cannot be found in Zen literature. It was first used during the Literary period, as later generations sought to bring structure to a somewhat chaotic Zen history. Certainly, all five of the traditional houses did exist and were historically prominent. However, other Zen schools also existed, and some of those schools predated and outlived their more famous rivals. Also, Zen schools often grew out of other Zen schools, and demarcating where one school stopped and another began sometimes appears arbitrary.

To a significant degree, the five traditional Zen schools used different teaching methods. At the risk of oversimplifying for the sake of convenience, some features of each school can be mentioned. The Guiyang school employed certain mystical and esoteric symbols that were not generally found in the other schools. Shouts and blows characterized the teaching methods of the early Linji school. The Caodong Zen school became associated with an emphasis on quiet meditation and a pedagogical system known as the *five ranks*. The founder of the Yunmen school distinctively used "one-word barriers" as a method of instruction. Finally, the Fayan school, which arose during the transition from the Classical to the Literary period, made important contributions to the development of Zen literature. Moreover, that school's syncretic tendencies toward non-Zen Buddhist schools signaled a trend that would only intensify later.

The five traditional Zen schools had many similarities. Teachers of one lineage often employed the methods of another. For example, the Linji school teacher Fenyang Shanzhao incorporated the "five ranks" methodology of the Caodong school into his teaching. The formalized use of kōans became a feature of all the schools that existed after 950 C.E., and, of course, Zen meditation was a feature of all schools at all times.

Three of the five houses of Zen passed out of existence within a rather short time. The remaining Linji (in Japanese, *Rinzai*) and Caodong (in Japanese, *Sōtō*) schools are still active throughout the world today. These two schools were, not coincidentally, the most prominent participants in the Zen literary evolution during the Song dynasty.

By our conventional understanding, the Zen ancients lived in a society so far from us in content, space, and time that we risk quickly dismissing their relevance. But Zen, in its greatest definition, is not less relevant today than it was in feudal China. It remains important precisely because the enlightenment of the historical Buddha and his Zen descendants does not depend on considerations of culture, behavior, social relationships, intellect, or gods and goddesses. Buddha's enlightenment is dependent on one thing only—the one thing of the entire universe as it arises in the mind during the present moment. The worn-out phrase "the present moment" is not, on the face of it, very profound, or even very interesting. But there is a profound significance that is dependent on this simple perception. According to all the old masters, this realization is not to be achieved through analysis, but must be directly experienced.

So, Zen enlightenment is "outside of words," but the awesome beauty of Zen literature flows directly from the old masters' breathtaking metaphors of Buddha's realization. That realization moved the Zen ancients to speak the peculiar cant of the awakened, a style of phrase that remains, with a lucky translation, unique and startling these many centuries removed from its origin.

Zen traditionally provides one simple yet grandly genuine metaphor of itself for the sake of people in all times and places. That metaphor is of a beautiful vista of vast mountain peaks, depicted with awesomely precipitous cliffs and crags. The well-known *shanshui* ("mountain and water") paintings from China have conveyed this Zen metaphor most purposefully and sublimely for hundreds of years. Imagination allows us to say that each mountain symbolizes an individual Zen master. After all, great Zen masters typically assumed "mountain names," that is, the names of the mountains upon which they taught. Also, Zen literature's most common metaphors for describing a master's style were great cliffs and lofty pinnacles. Practicing under an accomplished master is described as an arduous climb on a dangerous and slippery slope. Chinese has an abundance of words to convey the varied majesty and danger of high elevations, so many that a translator's resourcefulness is sorely strained to convey their flavor. Each ancient "mountain" is somehow the same, somehow different. A few of these old mountains offer gentle slopes for hiking. But many are composed of deathly, fearsome bluffs and precipices, where Zen students in their multitudes have lost their conventional lives.

In contrast to this grandiose metaphor from Zen's cultural heyday, the simple practice of Zen meditation itself had earlier traveled from ancient India to China with little spiritual baggage. Meditation practice, which is thought to be Zen's basic activity (or nonactivity), was part of many other Buddhist schools and traditions before Zen came into existence as its own institution. Since Zen meditation offers no philosophy to contradict the existing ideas of its practitioners, the practice moved effortlessly into different strata of Chinese society. By about 650, Zen had moved beyond its simple roots to become the pursuit of poets and emperors. Zen's "attaining the Way" was psychologically and linguistically akin to the core teachings of the other two great Chinese traditions, Taoism and Confucianism. Also, Zen's ideal of living in a solitary mountain setting was close to native Chinese Taoist ideas. Partly because Zen generally did not contravene native Chinese ideas, it became and remained the most prominent of the Chinese religions for many centuries.

Now, Zen has entered the consciousness of the West. The parallels between Zen thought and the native religions, philosophies, and sciences are not as evident in the West as in China. But as in China, Zen finds an entrance by advertising an attractive "nonactivity" called meditation. In this age of "pushing the envelope," Zen suggests we turn and look inward to find some refuge from our relentlessly active minds.

Yet, if Zen is just a relaxing activity, then why not go fly-fishing or do aerobics instead? Zen Buddhism is a religion. Its theology, expressed vigorously by the ancient teachers in this book, rests on the teaching that the entire universe is nothing other than one "mind," a mind reborn in every moment of consciousness. A friend once paraphrased a passage to me that said something like "People have the silly idea that their mind is inside their head! Their mind is not inside their head. Their brain is inside their head, and it is just an antenna that receives the field of their mind. The source of their mind is actually outside of their head."

The modern Zen teacher Reb Anderson teaches that the universal "mind" is "without characteristics, and its essence is compassion." The nature of the mind and consciousness remains, fundamentally, unexplained. The findings of modern science, particularly in the fields of quantum mechanics and cosmology, have intriguingly suggested an interpenetration between perception and the perceived, at least on the scales of the extremely small and the extremely large. Science has strongly hinted at dimensions to the nature of mind that are far removed from our usual viewpoints. Similarly, scientific research into a phenomenon called "non-locality" demonstrates an instantaneous, seemingly unmediated intimacy between events separated by huge distances that is vastly deeper than our conventional understanding of the world and of science would allow. Such events, demonstrated in laboratories, command a logic akin to the old masters' saying that "Mt. Sumeru fits inside a mustard seed." In light of the observations of modern science, the Zen ancients' claim of an intuitive insight into the nature of mind takes on special interest and merits our examination, for we currently have no good explanation for this miraculous phenomenon in hand, and none in the offing.

Teachings set forth in this book about concepts like "mind" and "realizing self-nature" might rightfully be dismissed as fanciful by anyone not familiar with the astounding lives of the Zen ancients. The authentic ancient masters, without exception, displayed certain quite remarkable characteristics. Chief among these characteristics was an ineffable sense of total freedom and ease, of peace and equanimity. Such repose is not a "learned" behavior. It appears to be the natural result of truly shedding concern with one's self. It seemed to arise from those ancients' realization of the self's "empty" nature, that is, that the self is not an independent, sovereign entity. The ancients would say, however, that simply realizing genuine self-nature is not enough. The realization must be upheld and sustained with long practice if it is to avoid becoming a mere intellectual understanding.

Another characteristic displayed by those old teachers was the ability to "always act appropriately to circumstances." The mere observation of this wonderful quality inspired (and continues to inspire) countless students to pursue Zen study. Such appropriate behavior was not undertaken according to a prescribed formula. Zen teachers do not act according to a "Zen teacher's manual" or use preordained strategies for helping others. In all ages, such teachers respond to every new circumstance in an unrehearsed yet completely appropriate manner. Their response appears unique and fresh. Nothing sets genuine Zen masters apart from the rest of us more than their ability to speak and act from a place that is unrecognizable to our usual logic and ideas. They act not from some ideological or authoritative religious standpoint, but from a place "before thoughts and words arise." This sort of activity, to the eye of the sensitive observer, cannot be faked. Moreover, in this book are numerous examples of Zen masters testing their students, checking to see if they can truly speak while relying on nothing whatsoever.

Genuine Zen teachers speak the language of liberation, the Dharma. If it is spoken from a lectern or Dharma seat, we may recognize it easily. But where it is most needed and effective, where it provides succor to a suffering world, it is perfectly expressed without any particular sign, in the midst of the world. Although it is the accomplishing work of great peace, it has no particular characteristic. It is the spontaneous response and teachings of buddhas and ancestors to the conditions of our lives. The Zen ancients declared that "all the buddhas in the ten directions can't explain it." The buddhas and ancestors can only speak it. Indeed, they expound it incessantly, so that the rest of us may hear it and wake up.

SOURCES

The *Wudeng Huiyuan (Compendium of Five Lamps)* is the primary source for the translated passages in this book. That text, compiled by the monk Puji at Lingyin Monastery in Hangzhou during the early thirteenth century, is the distillation of five previous "lamp records," which provide traditional accounts of the lives of famous Zen teachers and their teachings (note that the "five lamps" is not a reference to the five traditional Zen schools). Because I have cited the *Wudeng Huiyuan* extensively in this book, I do not cite individual passages translated from that text, to avoid repetition. Unless otherwise indicated, the reader may assume that the *Wudeng Huiyuan* is the source for a translation. I have cited other texts individually either in context or through footnotes.

First and foremost among the five lamp records compiled within the

Compendium of Five Lamps is a text entitled *The Record of the Transmission of the Lamp of the Jingde Era*, commonly called the *Transmission of the Lamp*. I have translated some passages in this book directly from that text. Often, passages from the *Compendium of Five Lamps* and the *Transmission of the Lamp* are the same or quite similar. However, since each text contains material that is omitted from the other, I sometimes cite the *Transmission of the Lamp* separately.

This book also uses many other old Zen source materials. As mentioned above, the students of famous teachers often recorded their teachings for posterity, and these discourses, known as *yulu,* have been invaluable sources.

In China, the ancient style of writing was vastly different from the spoken language. Fortunately, many writers in the Zen tradition did not follow convention, and instead incorporated a vernacular style of writing that was closer to the spoken word. This makes the translation of Zen materials somewhat easier and faster than the translation of other ancient Chinese literature, including the classical Buddhist scriptures. Nevertheless, old Zen texts are sufficiently different from modern Chinese so that translations are needed to make them understandable to modern Chinese readers. Several modern Chinese translations from the older Zen texts have appeared in recent years. The quality of these modern Chinese translations is varied. Some texts demonstrate an intimate understanding and appreciation of the source material by the translator. Other modern texts are fraught with mistakes and seem oblivious to the nuances of style. I have avoided using the modern Chinese translations as primary source material. Modern Chinese translations have often, however, guided me to classical passages most worthy of translation and have informed my own interpretations.

Many passages in this book have previously been translated into English. In some instances, the renderings offered here are virtually the same as found elsewhere, since certain words demand a straightforward translation. However, this book contains differences in interpretation from other translations. Moreover, the lamp records provide more extensive context for some well-known Zen stories than what appears in the *Blue Cliff Record,* the *Book of Serenity,* and other niansong texts. Readers familiar with those books will find some well-known stories repeated in this volume, but often as a part of a larger passage of text.

Although the available selection of English-language translations of old Zen teachings is significant, it remains scattered in many books and not easily accessible to general readers. This book attempts to bring a significant amount of important original material into one volume that is organized chronologically by generation.

The First Four Generations

BODHIDHARMA

DAZU HUIKE

JIANZHI SENGCAN

DAYI DAOXIN

BODHIDHARMA

ACCORDING TO ZEN TRADITION, Bodhidharma, the first Chinese Zen ancestor and twenty-eighth Buddhist master in a lineage starting with the historical Buddha, transmitted Zen from India to China. He is generally thought to have died around 530 C.E. Although history offers no certain evidence about Bodhidharma's life, he remains, before fact and fiction, a preeminent archetype for the profound liberation science called Zen, the crown jewel of Buddhism. In the treasury of Chinese Zen literature the question "Why did the First Ancestor come from the West?" is literally synonymous with the words "What is the essential meaning of Zen?"[3]

Bodhidharma's perilous journey from India to China to transmit the ultimate teaching of the Buddha offers enduring appeal, and is a precedent for the wayfaring spirit that graces Zen history. Traveling first to find, and then to spread, the true teaching is a tangible, breathing part of Zen's tradition and outlook. Zen combines this spirit with an element of rebellious iconoclasm, providing a special appeal to the restless young. As one of the schools of the Mahayana, a Buddhist movement that heralds enlightenment and nirvana for all beings, Zen retains an appeal that has historically crossed divisions of caste, class, and gender.[4]

Born an Indian prince, Bodhidharma became a student of the twenty-seventh Indian ancestor of the Zen lineage, Prajnadhara. His teacher encouraged him to travel to China, and after some time, he set off by ship on a three-year journey to Guangzhou by way of the Straits of Malacca. Arriving in China during the late fifth century, the sage remained in southern China for several years, possibly learning Chinese, before traveling north.

Central to the Bodhidharma legend is his interview with Emperor Liang

Wudi of the Liang dynasty.[5] The legend of their meeting serves as the preeminent example of Zen's uncompromising method of instruction.

The emperor Wudi had attained power through intrigue and murder, but after assuming power he became a great supporter of Buddhism, and in atonement for his past sins, he established many Buddhist temples and provided for the welfare of the Buddhist clergy. But when he asked Bodhidharma what merit he had attained from these activities the sage answered, "No merit."

As recounted in the *Blue Cliff Record*, the emperor then asked Bodhidharma to expound the highest truth of Buddhism, to which he replied, "Emptiness. Nothing holy."

The emperor then asked, "Who is it that faces me?"

Bodhidharma replied "I don't know."

After his encounter with Liang Wudi, Bodhidharma proceeded north, crossing the Yang-tse River "on a single blade of grass," a scene depicted in Chinese paintings and sculpture. At Shaolin Monastery on Mt. Song, Bodhidharma is said to have spent nine years facing the wall of a cave in meditation. Late in life, he may have lived near Luoyang City, which was then a showcase for the splendor of sixth-century Chinese Buddhism. An apparently independent account of Bodhidharma's existence quotes the comments of a monk by his name concerning the grandeur of Luoyang's great temples during this period.[6]

In legends, Bodhidharma's personality is solemn. The enlightened joy and ironic humor that vibrate in many Chinese Zen personalities and stories is not clearly evident in the early years of the sect. Indeed, the artistic paintings and sculptures of Bodhidharma created centuries later depict his legendary seriousness with a sour-looking face, sometimes glaring with what is misconstrued as ill-concealed rage. It is Bodhidharma's scowl, not the placid countenance of a bodhisattva, that announces the Zen of the ancestors. His painful look augurs the fearful enlightenment gates of Linji's shout, Deshan's stick, and Yunmen's one-word barriers.

According to tradition, Bodhidharma gathered at least four disciples. Huike, remembered as the Second Ancestor, received the "mind to mind" transmission that passed in turn to later Zen generations. The *Wudeng Huiyuan*, a classic Zen collection of short biographies and teachings of the Zen ancients, provides the traditional story of this event.[7]

> After nine years, Bodhidharma wanted to return to India. Calling together his disciples he said, "The time for me to return to India is at hand. Can each of you say something to demonstrate your understanding?"
>
> A disciple named Dao Fu said, "As I see it, it is not bound by words and

phrases, nor is it separate from words and phrases. This is the function of Tao."

Bodhidharma said, "You have attained my skin."

The nun Zong Chi said, "According to my understanding, it is like a glorious glimpse of the realm of Akshobhya Buddha. Seen once, it need not be seen again."[8]

Bodhidharma said, "You have attained my flesh."

A disciple named Dao Yu said, "The four elements are all empty and the five *skandhas* are without actual existence. As I see it, there is not a single dharma to be grasped."[9]

Bodhidharma said, "You've attained my bones."

Thereupon Huike bowed and stood up straight.

Bodhidharma said, "You have attained my marrow."

After transmitting the mind-seal of succession to Huike, Bodhidharma is described by various accounts as having either returned to India, or as having been poisoned by jealous rival teachers. One skillful account of his death incorporates both of these possibilities. His work in China complete, Bodhidharma is said to have made no attempt to resist a sixth attempt by his enemies to poison him. Sitting in an upright position, he passed away. The legend then relates that three years later a monk named Song Yun, who was on an official mission to the West, encountered Bodhidharma walking in the Himalayan Mountains carrying one sandal. When Song Yun asked the master where he was going, he replied, "To India." Song Yun returned to China and reported this event to the new emperor, Xiao Chung. Thereupon, Bodhidharma's grave was opened and his body was discovered missing, with only one sandal remaining in the crypt.

Although tradition holds that Bodhidharma brought Zen to China, other teachers taught Zen meditation in China during and prior to Bodhidharma's lifetime. Some scholars argue that Chinese Zen practice prior to Bodhidharma consisted mainly of concentration practice. Bodhidharma's Zen teaching differed from his predecessors because of his emphasis on "pointing directly at mind" to reveal buddha nature. By the time of the fifth Chinese ancestor, Daman Hongren (601–74), Chinese society regarded Bodhidharma's Zen as the true and foremost Zen school.

Zen's essence, the realization and practice of enlightenment, is regarded to be "outside of scriptures." However, Zen teachers use various skillful methods of instruction, including scriptures, depending on an individual student's needs. Bodhidharma is traditionally said to have emphasized the teachings of the *Lankavatara Sutra*. In a text that some scholars ascribe to his disciple Huike, Bodhidharma is quoted as having said, "As I observe the land of the Han (China), there is only this sutra (*Lankavatara*) with which the virtuous will be in accordance, and which will spread widely in the land."[10] In writings most reliably attributed to Bodhidharma, however, no mention of the *Lankavatara Sutra* is found.

Legends about Bodhidharma flourished during the centuries following his life. The "lamp records," the historical biographies about the Zen ancients written mainly in the tenth to twelfth centuries, recorded many popular and pious fictions about him that remain in Chinese and East Asian folklore. However, stories linking Bodhidharma to the Chinese martial arts, or *gongfu*, have no historical basis. No evidence exists of any relationship between Bodhidharma and Chinese martial arts beyond their common connection with Shaolin Temple. A millenium separates the time of Bodhidharma's residence at that temple with the first mention of his supposed link to the martial arts. Thus, the story of this relationship must be seen as a relatively modern invention.

Today, carved figures of Bodhidharma are a common sight throughout East Asia, where his significance as a folk icon remains undiminished. Ironically, his original significance is submerged deeply in the sea of his folklore, and his relationship with Zen is usually only remotely understood and appreciated.

Among the texts traditionally attributed to Bodhidharma, some scholars and Zen practitioners regard a text entitled the *Outline of Practice* as most likely written by Bodhidharma himself.[11]

> The noble enter the Way by many paths, but essentially there are but two of which I speak. One is by principle and one is by practice. Those who enter by principle avail themselves to the teaching of the enlightened doctrine that all beings possess the same true nature, though it is obscured and not apparent due to worldly attachments and delusion. If one forsakes delusion and returns to the true, fixing one's gaze on a wall and forsaking thoughts of self and other, sacred and profane, and so on, then, by not moving and not chasing after scriptures or teachings, one is in accord with principle. [When one undertakes] silent, nondiscriminating nonaction it is called entering the Way through principle.
>
> Entering by practice entails four essential practices that encompass all others. What four types of practice are these? The first is enduring the results of past actions. The second is the practice of acting according to conditions. The third practice is seeking nothing, and the fourth is known as practicing the Dharma.
>
> You ask, "How does one endure the results of past actions?" Those who may be said to practice the Way, upon encountering difficult times, think to themselves, "For endless kalpas without beginning I've forsaken what is essential and pursued the frivolous, tossed by currents and waves, committing sins and

transgressions without end. Now, although I commit no transgressions, it is my accumulated misdeeds, my store of evil karma, which continues to bear fruit. None among the heavens or humankind can see from where it arises. Without rancor or recriminating thoughts I accept this." In the sutra it says, "Upon meeting hardship don't grieve, but just recognize from whence it comes." When one's mind manifests in this manner it is in accord with principle and [even by means of] the body's suffering one enters the Way.

Second is the practice of just acting according to the conditions one encounters. All beings, not having independent existence, transmigrate through time according to conditions. No matter whether a person experiences bitterness or happiness, both arise from conditions. If we attain great achievements and acclaim, then it is due to our past karma. And though we may have it now, if the conditions that brought it to us are exhausted, then it will be gone. Why should one take joy in it? Gain and loss arise due to conditions. Those who remain unmoved by the winds of pleasure are steadfastly in accord with the Way. Therefore this practice is called to "accord with conditions."

Third is the practice of nonseeking. People in the world are always deluded and everywhere covetous. This is known as seeking. The wise awaken to the truth and go against this trend. Pacifying their minds, they do nothing. The myriad forms of the world stir and swirl, all of them empty. But, without any desires or joys, the virtuous remain where forms arise, abiding within the three worlds though they are like a burning house.[12] To have a body is to suffer. Who can arrive at such a state as to bear this with tranquillity? They are the ones who have forsaken all things, stopped discursive thinking, and stopped seeking. The sutra says, "To seek is but bitterness. Nonseeking is joy." To know this and to end seeking is truly practicing the Way. Therefore it is called the practice of nonseeking.

Fourth is called practicing the Dharma. Practicing the Dharma is to perceive the truth of pure nature, the truth that the myriad forms are empty. There is neither "defilement" nor "attachment," neither "this" nor "other." The sutra says, "The Dharma does not have the myriad beings, and thus remains untainted by the myriad beings. The Dharma has no self, and thus remains untainted by self." The wise, if they grasp this truth, should be in accord with the Dharma and live by this understanding. The Dharma-body lacks nothing, so the wise forsake and renounce their bodies, lives, and wealth without regret. They abandon the empty world and, relying on nothing, without attachment, they give up all impurities. They are in accord with evolving life without grasping form. This is their personal practice, which always benefits others. It is, moreover, the majestic way of the bodhisattva—compassionate work. They also practice the other five perfections for the elimination of delusion. Practicing these six perfections in this way is practicing nothing, and is thus practicing the Dharma.

Dazu Huike

THE LIFE OF THE SECOND ANCESTOR, Huike, is also obscured by the currents of time. According to traditional sources he was born in the year 487 to a family with the surname Ji in the city of Wulao, Henan Province. He grew to be an imposing looking individual, with five bumps ("five peaks") upon his head. According to the lamp records, Huike entered monastic life at the Dragon Gate Temple on Fragrant Mountain in Luoyang. There he studied under a Zen master named Baojing ("Precious Peace").[13]

Huike met Bodhidharma and studied with him at Shaolin Temple on Mt. Song for six years.[14] Huike is remembered and extolled in Zen tradition for his determination to realize the great truth of the Zen school. According to legend, Huike stood waiting in the snow outside Bodhidharma's cave, then cut off his left arm to show his sincerity. Recognizing Huike's great resolve, Bodhidharma accepted him as his student. Huike said to Bodhidharma, "My mind is anxious. Please pacify it." To which Bodhidharma replied, "Bring me your mind, and I will pacify it." Huike said, "Although I've sought it, I cannot find it." Bodhidharma then said, "There, I have pacified your mind."

After Bodhidharma's death, Huike traveled to the capital city, Yedu, in the kingdom of Wei. He remained there, except for a period of political turmoil, for the next forty years, upholding and expounding the practice of his teacher. However, religious rivalry and government persecution embroiled Huike in the upheavals of his era. At some time during this period he sought refuge in the mountains. According to tradition, he met and transmitted the lineage of Bodhidharma to his disciple and Dharma heir Sengcan on Wangong Mountain during this period. In the year 579, when political conditions improved, Huike returned to Yedu.

According to the *Continued Biographies of Eminent Monks*, a historical record written in the seventh century, Huike had several prominent disciples and lay students.[15] The lamp records offer a traditional account of Huike's life.

Huike was the Second Ancestor of Zen in China. He came from Wulao and his surname was Ji. His father's name was Jiji.

Before he had children, Huike's father thought, "Our house pays reverence to what is good. How can we not have children?"

They often prayed to Buddha. One night they observed an unnatural light pervade their house, and as a result of this Ji's wife became pregnant. Because of this omen, when the child grew up he was given the name "Light." As a young man, Huike showed uncommon conviction. He was very skilled at poetry but was uninterested in household affairs, preferring to roam among mountains and rivers. Later, when he read the Buddhist sutras, he excelled in his understanding. He then went to Dragon Gate Monastery on Fragrant Mountain in Luoyang, where he began study under Zen master Baojing. He received ordination at Yongmu Temple. He then traveled to various seats of learning for the Buddhadharma, studying the teachings of the Mahayana and Hinayana. At the age of thirty-two, he returned to Fragrant Mountain. There he practiced meditation throughout the day.

Once, while he sat in silent stillness, an apparition appeared to Huike and said, "If you want to be successful, then why are you remaining here? The great way is not far away. Go south!"

Huike then told his teacher about the apparition. His teacher observed Huike's head and saw that there were seven bumps on it that stuck up like small peaks.

His teacher said, "You have seen an auspicious omen. The evidence is here on your head. The apparition said that you should go south. This means that you should study with Bodhidharma at Shaolin Temple."

Huike accepted this instruction and set off for Shaolin.

When Bodhidharma completed the transmission of his Dharma to Huike, Bodhidharma returned to India. Huike then strongly expounded Bodhidharma's teaching and looked far and wide for a Dharma successor.

In the second year of the Tianping era of the Northern Qi dynasty [536], a layman whose name is not known came to Huike and said, "My body has been wracked by a terrible illness. I ask that you help me absolve the transgression I've committed that has caused this."

Huike said, "Bring to me the transgression you've committed and I'll absolve it."

The layman said, "I look for the transgression but I can't find it."

Huike said, "There, I've absolved your transgression. Now you should abide in Buddha, Dharma, and Sangha."

The layman said, "Seeing you here, I know what is meant by 'Sangha,' but I still don't know what are called Buddha and Dharma."

Huike said, "Mind is Buddha. Mind is Dharma. Buddha and Dharma are not two different things. Along with Sangha they comprise the three jewels."[16]

The layman said, "Today, for the first time, I realize that my transgression was not internal, was not external, and was not in between these two states. It was entirely within mind. Buddha and Dharma are not two things."

Huike recognized the layman to be a great Dharma vessel. He received him as a student and shaved his head, saying, "You are a great jewel. I give you the name Sengcan ['Gem Monk']."

On the eighteenth day of the third lunar month of that year, Sengcan underwent ordination. From that time on his illness gradually subsided.

Sengcan spent two years acting as Huike's attendant. Then Huike said to him, "Bodhidharma came from India and transmitted to me the *Treasury of the True Dharma Eye*, along with the robe of the ancestral transmission. I now pass it to you. Uphold and sustain it, and don't allow the lineage to be cut off. Listen to this verse of mine:

Fundamentally, karmic conditions have given rise to the ground
That allows the seeds of flowers to grow.
Fundamentally, nothing has been planted,
And flowers have not grown."

After transmitting Bodhidharma's Dharma and robe to Sengcan, Huike said to him, "You have received my teaching, and now you should live deep in the mountains. Don't circulate in the world, for the country will have a great calamity."

Sengcan said, "Since you know about this calamity in advance, please instruct me about it."

Huike said, "I have no foreknowledge about this. It is a prediction made by [the twenty-seventh Zen ancestor in India] Prajnadhara and transmitted to China by Bodhidharma, wherein he said, 'While it will be auspicious to abide in mind, outside of this there will be evil.' I have studied these times and see that [this calamity] may befall you. Consider the truth of this prediction and don't be ensnared by the world's turmoil. As for me, I have karmic retribution to suffer. You should go and practice what is good. Wait for the time when you can transmit the Dharma to someone else."

After Huike instructed Sengcan in this manner, Huike went to Yedu and expounded the Dharma. His teaching spread widely, and as a result a great number of people from all directions entered monastic life. He continued in this manner for thirty-four years, but then concealed himself and changed his appearance. Sometimes he would go to wine houses, sometimes to butcher shops, and sometimes he would mingle in the bustling lanes of the city. He also was found among the ranks of household servants.

Some people asked him, "The Master is a person of the Way. Why is he acting in this manner?"

But Huike answered them, saying, "I have rectified my mind. Of what concern is this to you?"

On one occasion, Huike expounded the unsurpassed Dharma to a large crowd before the front gate of Kuangqiu Temple in Guangcheng County. At the same time, the Dharma master Bianhe was lecturing on the Nirvana Sutra inside of the temple. As the congregation inside of the temple became aware of Huike's Dharma talk outside, they gradually were drawn outside to listen to him. Bianhe was unable to control his anger, and slandered Huike to the city magistrate, who was named Ti Zhongkan. Ti was confused by Bianhe's slanderous report and charged Huike with a crime. Huike [facing execution because of this criminal charge] remained calmly composed. Those who understand the truth said this episode was the "payment of a debt." The master lived to the age of one hundred and seven. Huike died on the sixteenth day of the third month in the thirteenth year of the Kaihuang era during the reign of Sui Wendi [594]. He was buried seventy *li* [forty-two kilometers] northeast of Fuyang in Ci Province.[17] Later, the Tang dynasty emperor De Zong gave Huike the posthumous name "Dazu" ["Great Ancestor"].

([Later,] a Buddhist patron named Haoyue asked Zen master Changsha Jingcen, "An old worthy said that 'karmic obstacles are fundamentally empty.' I don't understand why, when this is realized, there is still a 'karmic debt' that must be repaid. For example, in the case of the esteemed Second Ancestor, why did he have to repay a karmic debt?" Zen master Changsha replied, "Your Worthiness doesn't understand fundamental emptiness." Haoyue said, "What is fundamental emptiness?" Changsha said, "Karmic obstruction." Haoyue said, "What is karmic obstruction?" Changsha said, "Fundamental emptiness." Haoyue was silent. Changsha then recited a verse:

> If something is fundamental, it doesn't exist.
> If something is annihilated, it doesn't cease.
> Nirvana and karmic retribution
> Are of one inseparable nature.)

Jianzhi Sengcan

Jianzhi Sengcan (d. 606) was a student of Huike and the Third Ancestor of the Zen tradition. Few details are known about his life. According to the *Transmission of the Lamp*, Sengcan was forced by the political persecution of Buddhism during his era to remain out of sight, living inconspicuously among the general population.

With so little reliable evidence about Sengcan's life, some scholars doubt his existence. Yet the lack of evidence may be due to the severe suppression of Buddhism by the government during the years 574–77. According to Chinese historical records, the government of this era attempted to exterminate Buddhism by closing temples, destroying written records and monuments, and defrocking much of the Buddhist clergy.

According to tradition, after receiving Dharma transmission from Huike, Sengcan lived on Mt. Wangong in Shuzhou to avoid the upheaval predicted by the twenty-seventh ancestor in India, Prajnadhara.

Sengcan Jianzhi was the Third Ancestor. His surname is not known. He was a layperson when he first visited the Second Ancestor. After he received ordination and Dharma transmission, he lived in hiding on Wangong Mountain in Shuzhou. Later, when Emperor Zhou Wudi persecuted and destroyed the Buddhadharma, Sengcan lived on Sikong Mountain in Taihu County. Thereafter, for more than ten years, he had no permanent home. During that time people remained unaware of him. During the year Ren Zi, the twelfth year of the Kaihuang era of the Sui dynasty [592], the novice monk Daoxin, only fourteen years old, came to pay respects to Sengcan.

Daoxin said, "I ask for the Master's compassion. Please tell me of the gate of emancipation."

Sengcan said, "Who has bound you?"

Daoxin said, "No one has bound me."

Sengcan said, "Then why are you seeking emancipation?"

Upon hearing these words, Daoxin experienced great enlightenment. Daoxin then acted as Sengcan's attendant for nine years. He later received ordination at Jizhou, then continued attending to Sengcan. Sengcan repeatedly tested Daoxin's understanding of the sublime mystery, and when he knew he was ready, he passed to him the Dharma and robe, reciting this verse:

The flowers are planted when the ground is ready.
From this planting the flower blooms.

If no one plants the seed,
The flowers and ground are both extinguished.

Sengcan then said, "Formerly, Great Teacher Ke passed me his Dharma. He then went to teach in Yedu, passing away after thirty years. Now I have received you as my Dharma successor. To where will it pass from here?"

Sengcan then went to Mt. Luofu, where he spent two years. After that he went back to his former abode. For a period of several months, many nobles and commoners flocked to see him, and the temple received many benefactors. Sengcan expounded the essence of mind to everyone alike, until one day when, as he sat under a tree before a Dharma assembly, he placed his palms together and passed away. This was in the fifteenth day of the tenth month of the year Ding Yan, the second year of the reign of Yangdi Daye in the Sui dynasty [606]. The Tang dynasty emperor Xuan Zong gave the master the posthumous name "Zen Master Jianzhi" ["Mirror Wisdom"].

A poem entitled *Faith in Mind* is attributed to Sengcan by later Zen generations[18] and is included in an appendix to this book. Many phrases of this poem are repeated in the texts and teachings of later masters, and the spirit of the work lies close to the heart of the Caodong Zen school.

DAYI DAOXIN

DAYI DAOXIN (580–651) was a student of the Third Ancestor, Jianzhi Sengcan. He is the Fourth Ancestor of the traditional Chinese Zen line. Daoxin's first meeting with Sengcan, described above, resulted in his great enlightenment. He then served Sengcan for nine years. They parted while Daoxin was still in his early twenties.

The East Mountain school is the name applied to Daoxin, his student Hongren, and their disciples. Some scholars believe that Daoxin made a key contribution to Zen history by introducing the tradition's teachings to a large segment of Chinese society.

Daoxin may have been the first to mix Bodhidharma's Zen with other popular Buddhist traditions, and thus broadened its appeal. The modern Buddhist teacher and scholar Yin Hsun states that Daoxin, influenced in particular by the Sanlun and Tiantai Buddhist schools, made three contributions to Zen that have remained vital parts of the tradition since his time.[19] These contributions were:

1. The unification of Zen practice with acceptance of the Buddhist precepts
2. The unification of the teachings of the *Lankavatara Sutra* with those of the *Mahaprajnaparamita Sutra*, which includes the well-known *Heart* and *Diamond* sutras[20]
3. The incorporation of chanting, including chanting the name of Buddha, into Zen practice

While still in his thirties, Daoxin lived for ten years at Great Woods Temple on Mt. Lu. The founder of that temple, Zhikai, was an adept of the Tiantai and Sanlun schools of Buddhism. Zhikai also used elements of Pure Land practice, especially the chanting of Buddha's name, as a component of his teachings and practice. Yin Hsun points out that Daoxin was thus heavily influenced by these other Buddhist schools. By combining Zen practice with more broadly appealing acts of religious piety, Daoxin created a religion that took root in the broad population of Chinese society. Since his time, acceptance of the precepts, chanting the *Heart Sutra*, and following monastic rules have been widely accepted parts of religious practice in most East Asian Zen temples.

For the broader masses, Zen became a full-featured religion. Its new form and appeal to different levels of society brought it to a foremost position among the schools of Chinese Buddhism.

A measure of Daoxin's association with new practices is found in a traditional story from the lamp records. Daoxin and his disciples once saved a walled city under siege by bandits by teaching its inhabitants to recite the *Mahaprajnaparamita Sutra*. The wondrous powers of the scripture caused the bandits to give up their siege.

Daoxin taught at East Mountain Temple on Potou Shan, "Broken Head Mountain" (later called Shuangfeng, "Twin Peaks"), for thirty years. There he gathered a large number of students, including his prominent disciple and principal Dharma heir, Daman Hongren. Daoxin is believed by some scholars to have created the first monastic home for Bodhidharma's Zen. According to this view, prior to the East Mountain school's existence, Chinese Zen monks did not live in independent and self-supporting monasteries. Instead, they adhered to the itinerant tradition established by Shakyamuni, the historical Buddha. Later, when Zen master Baizhang Huaihai codified the rules of the Zen monastic order, he built upon the monastic foundation already laid down by Daoxin.

According to legend, Daoxin's meeting with a monk named Farong led to the establishment of the Oxhead (in Chinese, *Niutou*) school, a unique school in China's Zen tradition. The Oxhead school is sometimes called the first Zen current with "Chinese characteristics." Controversy exists about whether the meeting between Daoxin and Farong actually occurred. Although not listed among the famous five houses of Zen, the Oxhead school remained prominent in China for the following two centuries.

The Fourth Ancestor was Great Teacher Dayi Daoxin. Originally, his family came from Henei. Later, they moved to Guangqi County in Shanzhou. From the time of his birth, Daoxin displayed highly unusual abilities. When young, he honored all of the various empty gates of liberation, studying them in his home. Upon becoming a successor to the ancestral teaching, he composed his mind and sat upright each night, never lying down in a bed for the next sixty years.

In the thirteenth year of the Daye era of the Sui dynasty [617], Daoxin and his disciples traveled to Ji Province [modern Ji'an City in Jiangxi Province]. There they came upon a town under the siege of bandits. The siege continued for seventy days without letup and the population was terrified. Daoxin took pity on the population and taught them to recite the *Mahaprajnaparamita Sutra*. When the bandits looked at the parapets of the city wall, they thought they saw phantom soldiers, and said to each other, "There are extraordinary people in this city. We shouldn't attack it." The bandits gradually went away. In the year Jia Shen [624] of the reign of Tang Wu De, Daoxin returned to Shanchun, where he resided on Potou Mountain. Students gathered there to study with him.

One day, as Daoxin was walking to Huangmei County, he encountered a young child on the road. The child was unusual looking and fine featured.

Daoxin asked the boy, "What is your name?"

The boy answered, "I have a name, but it isn't a permanent name."

Daoxin said, "What name is it?"

The boy answered, "Buddha."[21]

Daoxin said, "You don't have a name?"

The boy said, "It's empty, so I don't possess it."

Daoxin stared at this young Dharma vessel. He then sent his attendant to call on the boy's mother and requested that she allow him to enter the priesthood.

When the boy's mother realized the great affinity the boy had for the

Dharma, she didn't oppose it. So Daoxin made the boy his disciple, eventually passing to him the ancestral robe and Dharma transmission.

The planted flowers have life's nature.
In fertile earth they bloom and live.
Due to the Great Function and Affinity,
They flourish and live, unborn.

One day Daoxin said to the assembled monks, "During the Wu De era I took a trip to Mt. Lu. I climbed to the very top of the mountain and then looked toward Mt. Potou. There was a layer of purple clouds over the mountain like a cover, but underneath them were several streams of white clouds stretching in six directions. Do you understand the meaning of this?"

The monks were silent. Then Hongren said, "Does it not mean that after the master is gone there will be a branching of the Buddhadharma?"

Daoxin said, "Good."

In the year Gui Mao [643], the emperor Tai Zong, hearing about Daoxin's reputation, invited the master to the capital city. Daoxin declined the invitation. Three times the emperor invited the master and three times he declined. On the fourth occasion, the emperor said to his emissary, "This time if he doesn't come, bring back his head."

When the emissary delivered the emperor's command to the mountain, Daoxin simply exposed and stretched his neck to allow his head to be cut off, and stood there in a dignified manner. This shocked the emissary. When he reported this situation, the emperor changed his intention and honored Daoxin. He presented the master with valuable silk and venerated him as an example. On the fourth day of the ninth month in the year Xin Hai of the Yong Wei era of the Gao Zong reigning period [651], Daoxin suddenly admonished his disciples, saying, "All of the myriad dharmas of the world are to be dropped away. Each of you, protect this understanding and carry it into the future."

Upon saying this, the master sat peacefully and passed away. He was seventy-two years of age. His stupa was built on the mountain where he taught. On the eighth day of the fourth month of the following year, the door of his stupa opened spontaneously and revealed the master sitting inside as though alive. Thereafter, his disciples dared not close the door. The emperor Dai Zong gave Daoxin the posthumous name "Zen Master Dayi" ["Great Healer"]. His stupa was named "Compassionate Cloud."

Fifth Generation

DAMAN HONGREN

NIUTOU FARONG

DAMAN HONGREN

DAMAN HONGREN (601–74) was the disciple and Dharma heir of Dayi Daoxin. His stature and recognition during his own lifetime was probably much greater than the meager historical records we have of him indicate. He was the Fifth Ancestor of the traditional Chinese Zen lineage, and his students spread throughout China, exerting enormous influence on the religious fabric of the society. Hongren's students established three prominent Zen lineages, including the dominant "Southern school" that later encompassed the well-known "five houses" of Zen. Hongren's influence on Zen's historical development is difficult to overstate.

During Hongren's lifetime the phrase "East Mountain school" came into existence to characterize his teachings and those of his teacher, Daoxin. Although acknowledged as one of the "Lankavatara masters," Hongren followed Daoxin's example and did not limit his teaching to the *Lankavatara Sutra*. Instead, he incorporated more diverse currents of Buddhist teaching into the Zen tradition. In particular, he is believed to have included portions of the *Mahaprajnaparamita Sutra*, especially the *Heart* and *Diamond* sutras, as cornerstones of his teaching and practice. But as in the case of the Zen masters who preceded him, few details are certain about Hongren's life and his precise methods of teaching. Also, accounts of Hongren's life are colored by the factional splits that came about in later times. Some sources, possibly influenced by arguments between "Northern" and "Southern" Zen schools that occurred in the eighth century, state that Hongren became learned in practices of both "gradual" and "sudden" enlightenment.

A classical Zen text entitled *Discourse on the Highest Vehicle*, attributed to Hongren, emphasizes the idea of "maintaining the original true mind" that "naturally cuts off the arising of delusion."[22] The maintenance of this original

undefiled mind is described as the "primogenitor of the twelve divisions of scripture and the buddhas of the three worlds."

According to tradition, Hongren left home at the age of seven (some sources say twelve or fourteen) and lived at East Mountain Temple on Twin Peaks, where Daoxin served as abbot. Upon Daoxin's death at the age of seventy-two, Hongren assumed the abbacy. He then moved East Mountain Temple approximately ten kilometers east to the flanks of Mt. Pingmu. Soon, Hongren's fame eclipsed that of his teacher.

The account of Hongren's life that appears in the *Wudeng Huiyuan* and other lamp records offers an example of the fanciful stories passed on about the early generations of Zen masters in China.

The Fifth Ancestor in the East [China], Hongren, was a person from Huangmei County in Qizhou. In his previous life he was a Taoist who planted trees on Twin Peaks. [At that time] he inquired of the Fourth Ancestor, saying, "Can you please explain the Dharma to me?"

The Fourth Ancestor said, "You are already old. If I were to explain it to you, you couldn't use it to save beings. But if you come here again in your next life I'll be waiting for you."

The old man then left. Walking to the bank of a river, he saw a young woman washing clothes. Bowing, he said, "May I pass the night in this place?"

The young woman said, "I have a father and an elder brother, you can go ask them."

The old man said, "You answer me, then I can be on my way."

The young woman nodded her assent, and at this the old man turned and left.

The young woman was a daughter of the Zhou family, and later, after she returned home, she was found to be pregnant. Her father and brother were furious at this news and drove her out of the house. She had no place to live, so during the day she made a living by making garments and at night she would find a guest house to dwell in. Later she gave birth to a son. Regarding him as unlucky, she threw him into the pool of embryonic fluid on the floor and wouldn't care for him. The next day she was startled to see that the child had removed himself from the fluid and his body was now clean and unblemished. She then undertook to raise the child. When he was a little older he would follow his mother as she begged for food. Villagers called him "No-Name Child." One day the mother and son encountered a wise man. He said, "This child lacks only seven marks [of the distinguishing marks of a Buddha]. Only the Tathagata surpasses him." Later the child met Great Teacher Daoxin and, becoming his heir, taught people by expounding the Dharma at Mt. Potou.

The following text, from *Records of the Lankavatara Masters,* is a rare example of Hongren's direct teaching that is recorded in the historical records.[23]

A monk asked Zen master Hongren, "Why can't the study of Buddhadharma take place in cities where there are many people, instead of at places deep in the mountains?"

Hongren answered, "The timbers needed to make a great building originally come from secluded mountain valleys. They can't be grown where many people are congregated. Since they are far from large numbers of people they can't be chopped or harmed by axes and are able to grow into great building material, later to be used to make supporting girders and beams. So in studying Dharma, one should find refuge for the spirit in remote mountain valleys, escaping far from the troubles of the dusty world. People should nourish their nature in the deep mountains, staying away from the affairs of the world for a long time. When not always seeing common affairs the mind will naturally become at ease. Studying Zen in this way is like planting a tree, with the result that later it can bear fruit."

During this era the great teacher Hongren only sat peacefully in an upright position and did not compile writings. He only taught Zen principles by speaking about them, quietly passing on the teaching to other persons.

The Record of the Lankavatara Masters cites ten disciples who inherited and passed on Hongren's teaching. That text quotes him to say, "Of the countless students I have taught, many have passed away. There are only ten remaining who will transmit my teaching." Among the names Hongren then recited are Huineng, Shenxiu, and Zhixian, founders of the Southern, Northern and Sichuan schools of Zen, respectively.

NIUTOU FARONG

ACCORDING TO TRADITION, Niutou Farong (594–657) was a student of the fourth Chinese ancestor, Dayi Daoxin. He founded the Oxhead Zen school on Mt. Niutou (near modern Nanjing City). Later Chinese historians would not acknowledge Niutou's lineage as one of the principal traditional schools of

Chinese Zen, perhaps because he is not known with certainty to have received Dharma transmission from Daoxin, or due to confusion about the origin of his school. Nevertheless, the Oxhead school flourished during the seventh and eighth centuries and continued up until the early years of the Song dynasty (around the end of the tenth century).

The Oxhead school's narrower interpretation of Bodhidharma's Zen is distinct from the East Mountain school of the Fifth Ancestor, Daman Hongren. The Oxhead school is not known to have employed the chanting of sutras or to have emphasized the precepts. The modern scholar Yin Hsun attributes a classical Zen text known as the *Discourse on Cutting Off Perception* to the Oxhead school, pointing out that it is akin linguistically to the period when Niutou lived, and that its theme closely follows Bodhidharma's teachings.

The Oxhead school denied the possibility of objective knowledge more clearly than other Buddhist schools of the era. The fifth-generation Oxhead monk Xuanxu said, "Understanding is not understanding. Doubt is no-doubt." The school also adhered to the Buddhist notion that the world is a creation of the mind. It expressed this theory in the "Wei Ming Lun" ("Only-Mind Doctrine").

Originally located in the area of ancient Jinling (modern Nanjing), the main temples of the school moved south during the eighth century to escape political upheavals. The fifth-generation Oxhead monk Faqin established a temple on Mt. Jing near Hangzhou in 742 that played an important role in Zen's historical development in both China and Japan.

The traditional story of the enlightenment of the Oxhead school's founder, Niutou Farong, is recounted in the *Wudeng Huiyuan:*

> Zen master Farong of Mt. Niutou came from Yanling in Run Province. His surname was Wei. By the age of nineteen he was versed in the classic Confucian histories, but later he read the *Nirvana Sutra* and thereupon penetrated the truth.
>
> One day he exclaimed, "Confucianism is a doctrine of worldly affairs, but it isn't a teaching of the highest truth. When I read the *Nirvana Sutra*, I finally found a vessel for leaving the world behind."
>
> Thereupon Niutou concealed himself on Mao Mountain, where he studied under a teacher and was ordained as a monk. Later, as he sat in meditation in a rock grotto north of Secluded Perch Temple on Mt. Niutou, a hundred birds with flowers in their beaks came to pay homage to him.
>
> During the Zhen Guan era [627–49], the Fourth Ancestor, Zen master Daoxin, saw a strange celestial sign in the distance and realized that an unusual person must be living on Niutou Mountain. He personally climbed the mountain to find the person and pay him a visit.

Seeing a temple monk, he asked, "Is there a monk here?"

The monk responded, "Who among those who've 'left home' is not a monk?"

Daoxin responded, "What one is a [real] monk?"

The temple monk couldn't reply.

Then another monk from the temple said, "About ten miles from here in the mountains there's a hermit. His name is Farong. When he sees people coming he doesn't get up, nor does he pay attention to common courtesy. Is he the one you're looking for?"

Daoxin then traveled into the mountains. There he found Niutou sitting upright in meditation, completely self-absorbed, paying no attention to Daoxin whatsoever.

Daoxin asked him, "What are you doing?"

Farong responded, "Perceiving mind."

Daoxin said, "Who is it who is perceiving mind? And what is 'mind'?"

Farong had no answer. Standing up, he bowed.

Later, he asked, "Where does Your Worthiness reside?"

Daoxin said, "This poor monk has no permanent home. Sometimes I live here, sometimes I live there."

Farong said, "Perhaps you know the master Daoxin."

Daoxin replied, "What would you ask him?"

Farong said, "I've respected his virtue for some time now. I would like to pay my respects to him."

Daoxin said, "I am Zen master Daoxin."

Farong said, "Why have you come here?"

Daoxin said, "I've come here especially to pay you a visit. Do you have someplace we can take a rest?"

Farong pointed and said, "Over there I have a small cottage."

He then led Daoxin to a cottage that was surrounded by wild beasts such as tigers and wolves. Daoxin put both of his hands up in the air as if he were scared.

Farong said, "Are you still like this?"

Daoxin said, "What is 'this'?"

Farong couldn't answer.

Later, Daoxin wrote the word "Buddha" on Farong's meditation seat.

When Farong saw this he was horrified.

Daoxin said, "Are you still like this?"

Farong didn't understand, so he bowed and asked Daoxin to explain his meaning.

Daoxin said, "The hundred thousand gates of the Buddhadharma, they all return to this mind. The source of the countless exquisite sublime practices is this mind. All of the precepts and monastic rules, Zen meditation, Dharma gates of knowledge, and wisdom and every sort of miraculous manifestation are your natural possession, not separate from your mind. Every type of nuisance and karmic impediment is fundamentally empty and without real existence. All causes and effects are but illusions. There are no three worlds that are to be cast off.[24] There is no bodhi that can be attained.[25] The original nature and appearance of what is human and what is nonhuman does not differ. The great way is empty and vast, without a single thought. If you have attained this Dharma, where nothing whatsoever is lacking, what difference is there between yourself and Buddha? When there is not a single teaching left, then you are just left to abide in your own nature; with no need to worry about your behavior; no need to practice cleansing austerities; but just living a life without desires; with a mind without anger, without cares; completely at ease and without impediment; acting according to your own will; without needing to take on any good or evil affairs; just walking, abiding, sitting, and lying down; with whatever meets your eye being nothing other than the essential source; and all of it is but the sublime function of Buddha; blissful and without care. This is called 'Buddha.'"

According to tradition, after Farong received this teaching from Daoxin and fully attained the way of Zen, birds no longer left flowers for him. Farong's enlightenment left no special sign by which it could be recognized.

Beyond this traditional story, a few dialogues involving Zen teacher Niutou are preserved in the classical records.

A monk asked Niutou, "The people known as 'saints'—what dharmas should they cut off and what dharmas should they attain so that they can thus earn this title?"

Niutou said, "Those who don't cut off or attain even a single dharma—they are called 'saints.'"

The monk then asked, "If they don't cut off or attain a single dharma, what difference is there between such people and common people?"

Niutou said, "There is a difference. Do you know why? Because common people try to rid themselves of afflictions and they delusionally scheme for gain. There is nothing that is fundamentally lost or gained by the true mind of a saint. That is why there is a difference."

The monk then asked, "In considering what is attained by common people and what is not attained by saints, where does the difference lie between this attainment and nonattainment?

Niutou said, "The difference lies in that what is attained by common people is delusional, whereas the nonattainment of saints is not delusional. For the deluded, there is a difference in these two viewpoints, whereas saints do not recognize a difference."

The monk then asked, "Please describe the viewpoint of those saints who do not recognize the difference in these two views."

Niutou said, "The terms 'commoner' and 'saint' are but false names. Within these two false names there are actually not two things, and thus there is no difference."[26]

A monk asked, "Just at the moment when someone uses his mind, how can that mind remain composed?"

Niutou said, "Just at the moment when the mind is being used—that is precisely when mind is not being used. Convoluted thinking and speech just cause everyone trouble. But speaking directly and frankly doesn't cause complications. No-mind is exactly the employment of mind, while constantly using the mind is to never employ it. What I've just said about not using mind is no different from using the mind for deliberation."

The monk asked, "When the wise use expedient words they are exactly in accord with mind. But when mind and words diverge, isn't it heresy?"[27]

Niutou said, "Expedient and beneficial speech is the Mahayana way, and it eradicates the mind's disease.[28] Speech that is unconnected to original nature is a hollow fabrication. When one always adheres to no-thought, then one is on the road that cuts off mind. One's nature apart from thoughts is unmoving, and it is without misconceptions concerning birth and death. When there is the sound of an echo in the valley, the reflection in the mirror can turn to hear it."

In the year 656 the magistrate Su Yuanshan invited Niutou to become the abbot of Jianchu Temple. The master tried to decline but was unable to do so. He then gave his genuine Dharma transmission to his great disciple Zhiyan, instructing him to continue the transmission to future generations. When he left Mt. Niutou he said to the congregation, "I'll never return to this mountain!" At that time even the birds and beasts of the mountain wailed in mourning. Four large pauwlonia trees that were in front of Niutou's cottage inexplicably withered and died during [June]. The next year, on the twenty-third day of the first lunar month, although not appearing ill, the master died. He was buried on Jilong Mountain.

Sixth Generation

Dajian Huineng, "Caoxi"

The Sixth Ancestor, Dajian Huineng (638–713), is a preeminent figure of China's Zen heritage. The five traditional schools of Chinese Zen Buddhism all trace their origin through this famous master. The traditional story of Huineng's life reveals an iconoclastic personality whose defiance of religious convention sharpened the unique cultural flavor of Chinese Zen.

The main source of information about Huineng's life is a text of his teaching known as the *Platform Classic*.[29] This work is traditionally regarded as a lecture by Huineng, recorded by his disciple, Fahai. The earliest extant copy of the work, found among papers taken from the Dunhuang caves, dates to about a century after Huineng lived. The events of Huineng's life were central to political intrigues and factional religious struggles that occurred between the Northern and Southern schools of Zen during the eighth century. These facts, plus the dating of the Dunhuang manuscript, have cast serious doubt on the veracity of the main traditional stories about Huineng. The evidence has led many modern scholars, led by the eminent Dr. Hu Shih, to regard the *Platform Classic* as a fabricated document, created by Huineng's spiritual descendant, Shenhui, to provide spiritual legitimacy for his own faction during the turbulent eighth century.

Despite the arguments surrounding the *Platform Classic*, this text of Huineng's teachings contains important and insightful material. From a religious standpoint, the text expounds and supports the "sudden" nature of Zen enlightenment. Strictly speaking, this view does not recognize expedients such as chanting Buddha's name, reading sutras, etc., as being necessary or even useful in realizing enlightenment. In contrast to this view, the Northern school, led by Yuquan Shenxiu, variously emphasized these religious practices as being required to maintain the "original pure mind" that is realized in and not separate from awakening. These contrasting views, in one form or another, have given rise to debates between different Zen schools since at least the time of Huineng.

There is scant solid evidence to support the traditional story of Huineng's life, but his legend remains a cornerstone of Chinese religious culture.

As told in the *Platform Classic*, Huineng lost his father at the age of three and was forced as a youngster to support his widowed mother by selling firewood in ancient Guangzhou City. He is said to have gained enlightenment instantly as he overheard someone reciting the *Diamond Sutra*. Resolving to follow the Dharma, he set off to seek out the Fifth Ancestor, Daman Hongren, who resided at Huangmei. Upon their meeting, the Fifth Ancestor assigned Huineng to work in the kitchen.

Months later, Hongren invited the monks to each write a verse that would display his individual understanding of the Buddha way. In the famous episode that followed, the head monk, Shenxiu, wrote the following verse on a wall in the monastery:

> *The body is the Tree of Wisdom,*
> *The mind but a bright mirror.*
> *At all times diligently polish it,*
> *To remain untainted by dust.*

According to the legend, Huineng, who was illiterate and had not yet gained ordination as a Zen monk, enlisted another monk's help to write his own verse upon the wall. It read:

> *The Tree of Wisdom fundamentally does not exist.*
> *Nor is there a stand for the mirror.*
> *Originally, there is not a single thing,*
> *So where would dust alight?*

Upon reading Huineng's verse, Hongren recognized the author's profound level of spiritual realization. Afraid of the uproar that would result from bestowing authority on someone of such low status, Hongren is said to have met secretly with Huineng at night to pass him the traditional robe and bowl of succession, symbols of the "mind to mind" transmission of Zen. Hongren instructed Huineng to leave the monastery to avoid repercussions from the congregation. Thereafter, Huineng remained in obscurity for, by some accounts, sixteen years, before beginning to teach publicly.

The story cited above is the kernel inside more elaborate legends concerning Huineng's life and teaching. The legend's essence is of an individual, uncultured and unlettered, who injects a strong element of nonconformity into the traditional and structured religious hierarchy. If Bodhidharma's teaching of "directly pointing at mind" was misplaced among the more labored practices that later gained entry into the Zen tradition, the story of Huineng's life moved the scales back toward the direct and simple teaching of immediate awakening.

The *Platform Classic* itself states that fundamentally there is no differentiation to be made between "gradual" and "sudden" as they relate to enlightenment. However, the text also ascribes a lesser standing to the "gradual" idea, associating it with persons of "inferior ability."

Huineng resided as abbot at Baolin ("Precious Woods") Monastery near Shaozhou.[30] According to tradition, he had twenty-six disciples. Among them were Nanyue Huairang and Qingyuan Xingsi, through whom all of the five most famous "houses" of Zen traced their ancestry to Huineng.

Many stories and legends about Huineng's life and teaching remain part of Zen lore. The events offered below are recorded in the Zen classic texts, *The Ancestral Hall Collection* and the *Platform Classic*.

> The monk Yin Zong expounded on the Buddhist sutras. One day during his lecture a storm came up. Seeing a banner waving in the wind, he asked his audience, "Is the wind moving or is the flag moving?"
>
> Someone said, "The wind is moving."
>
> Someone else said, "The flag is moving."
>
> The two people held fast to their viewpoints and asked Yin Zong to say who was right. But Yin Zong had no way to decide, so he asked Huineng, who was standing nearby, to resolve the issue.
>
> Huineng said, "Neither the wind nor the flag is moving."
>
> Yin Zong said, "Then, what is it that is moving?"
>
> Huineng said, "Your mind is moving."

> "Those who would realize the practice of nonaction must arrive at the nonperception of the errors of people. This is non-moving nature. Deluded people simply stop the movement of their bodies, but as soon as they open their mouths they are talking about peoples' rights and wrongs, and contradicting the Way."

"In this school of Buddhism, what is it we call 'sitting in Zen meditation'? In performing this practice no impediments exist. When no thoughts arise with respect to what is external, this is 'sitting.' When one calmly observes original nature, this is 'Zen.' So what is 'sitting meditation'? Detachment from external things is 'Zen.' When internally the mind is composed, this is 'samadhi.'[31] If one clings to external forms, then internally the mind is scattered and confused. If one is unattached to external forms, then internally the mind is composed. Original nature has self-purity and self-composure. It is only when, through causation, some condition is encountered, that confusion arises. Remaining apart from form one remains unperturbed, and samadhi is realized. Externally—Zen; internally—samadhi; together they are called 'sitting Zen.'"

---------- ◆ ----------

"The true thusness of self-nature is the real Buddha.
Perverse views and the three poisons are Mara.[32]
In times of delusion, Mara is in the room.
When right views prevail, then Buddha is in the hall.

If the three poisons are seen in one's nature,
Then Mara there resides.
Right views themselves root out the three poisons,
Demons become buddhas and truth has no falsehoods.

If, in this life, you can realize the Dharma gate of sudden awakening,
Then you can personally see the World-Honored One.[33]
But if you do not grasp this, and go on seeking Buddha,
Who knows when you may finally find true nature?

If you understand that you yourself have buddha nature,
This is the pivotal cause for becoming a buddha.
Those who don't look in their own minds, but seek Buddha externally,
Just waste their effort and are ignorant.

The teaching of sudden awakening formerly was transmitted from India.
To save the people of the world it must be practiced by everyone.
Those of today who endeavor to offer the world the teachings of Buddhism,
But know not this principle, are truly muddle-headed fools."

When Huineng finished speaking these three verses, he said to his disciples,

"Each of you practice this well. Today I say good-bye to you. After I die, don't mourn me in the usual manner of the world. If you receive other people's condolences, offerings, and observances, or you wear mourning clothes, then this is not the true school and you are not my disciples. You should act as though I were still in the world—sitting completely upright, not moving nor resting, without creation or passing away, not going or coming, without positive or negative, not abiding or leaving, but just in solitary peace. This is the great way. After I die, just go on practicing as before, as though I were still here. When I am in the world and you go against my teaching, it is as though my life here as abbot was meaningless."

When he finished saying these words, at the third watch, Huineng suddenly died. He had lived to the age of seventy-six.[34]

Yuquan Shenxiu, "Datong"

Datong Shenxiu (605–706), the founder of the Northern school of Zen, was a student of the Fifth Ancestor, Daman Hongren.

Shenxiu and his students attained widespread fame and stature during the late seventh and first half of the eighth century, when they enjoyed the strong support of China's imperial court. The Northern school thus extended and further popularized the Fifth Ancestor's teachings, moving Zen more securely into the great crucible of Tang dynasty society.

Traditional accounts say that Shenxiu came from ancient Bianzhou (an area near modern Kaifeng City in Hebei Province). He is described as having been abnormally tall (Chinese sources say over nine feet), and to have possessed bushy eyebrows to match his handsome eyes. After studying the traditional Confucian classics and histories, he left home to become a monk. Eventually, he gained the position of senior monk in Hongren's congregation. After his teacher's death in 675, Shenxiu moved to Dangyang Mountain in Jiangling (near modern Jiangling City in Hubei Province). There, a great number of monks gathered to study with him. His fame spread to the capital city of Changan, and soon Empress Wu summoned him to her court to teach the Dharma, paying him special honors. He so impressed the empress that she commissioned the building of a special temple for him at Dangyang. Later, the Chinese emperors Zhong Zong and Rui Zong also honored the master, each becoming his student. Shenxiu was thus known as the "National Teacher of Three Emperors."

According to Zen tradition, Shenxiu competed with the Sixth Ancestor,

Huineng, in a legendary poetry contest at Hongren's monastery at Huangmei. In that competition, the lowly positioned Huineng proved to have superior spiritual insight, despite the fact that Shenxiu was Hongren's most senior student. This famous episode, well known in the religious folklore of East Asia, is the legendary seed of the growth of Zen into Northern (followers of Shenxiu) and Southern (followers of Huineng) schools. Twentieth-century scholarship has, to a large degree, undermined the evidence that this event really occurred. However, the story of the poetry contest at Huangmei remains informative, for it symbolizes the genuine doctrinal differences that many scholars believe divided the Northern and Southern Zen schools.

Because of the historical ascendancy of the Southern school of Zen after 755, the great contemporary influence of Shenxiu and his Northern school was downplayed or overlooked by later generations of scholars and Zennists. The lamp records saved little of the Northern school's detailed history. The evidence that remains describes a Zen current faithful to the expedient practices established by the East Mountain school of Daoxin and Hongren. These practices, including chanting, sutra study, and receiving the Buddhist precepts, were instrumental to Zen's entry into popular Chinese society. These were also the "gradualist" methods that were de-emphasized by the Sixth Ancestor's disciple Shenhui and his followers in the Southern school.

To better understand the doctrinal differences between Shenxiu's "Northern" and Huineng's "Southern" Zen, it would be useful to briefly introduce the Buddhist doctrine of "mind." The concept of "mind" is central to Zen, as well as other schools of Buddhist thought and philosophy. A Zen Buddhist teaching holds that there is but one universal "mind" that is constituted by the mind of all living beings. This universal mind is also called "Buddha," "buddha nature," "true self," and so on.

But different schools of Zen and Buddhism had different interpretations about the teaching of mind and how it may be understood. Shenxiu's Northern school believed and advanced the proposition that there are "impurities" that can cloud the mind. These impurities include an individual's thoughts or intentions, any of which necessarily give rise to the illusion of an individual self. Therefore, a "mirror" analogy is applied to this type of understanding. The individual's small mind is likened to a "mirror" that reflects the entire universe. Delusion is an impurity, the "dust" on the mirror that prevents the individual from maintaining his or her pure, original (and universal) mind.

In contrast, the Southern school advanced the idea that there is no way to realize the nature of mind except through sudden realization, and this must be done quite apart from any ideas of "purity" or "impurity." Even the so-called "dust" on the allegorical mirror must only be part of mind, so how can it be called "impure"? "Polishing" the mirror, or removing impurities through various practices, does not lead to a genuine realization of the nature of mind. This difference was at the heart of the poems attributed to Shenxiu and Huineng in the contest at Huangmei.

But the Northern school did not lose prominence in Chinese society due to its philosophical outlook. Because of its relationship and proximity with the emperor, his court, and the northern capital cities, the school suffered severe damage during the civil war and disturbances that wracked China in the middle of the eighth century. The "twin capital cities" of Luoyang and Changan, showcases of Buddhist culture and architecture during the sixth and seventh centuries, suffered irreparable damage during the An Lushan rebellion and in subsequent social upheavals. These events did not lead to the immediate end of the Northern school, but severely damaged its demographic base.

When writing about the history of the Northern school, Zen scholars cite the well-known maxim that history is written by the victorious. In the dim light we can shine on those times, the alleged differences between the Northern and Southern schools cannot be clearly illuminated. But there is, nonetheless, a believable difference, no less so because the same differences exist today between different Zen groups as well as other Buddhist schools. Also, the practices criticized by Huineng in the *Platform Classic* have been, to a greater or lesser extent, part of virtually all Zen schools since at least the time of the Fourth Ancestor.

Despite the eventual ascendancy of the Southern school, Shenxiu enjoyed widespread prestige and honor in his own lifetime. His practice welcomed the faith of the population and edified China's rulers. The period of Shenxiu's influence corresponded with the "High Tang," widely regarded as the greatest period of Chinese civilization. Shenxiu and his Dharma brothers from Huangmei contributed, in no small measure, to one of the greatest cultural eras in the world's history.

Zen master Shenxiu had a verse that he recited to instruct the congregation.

All Buddhadharmas come forth fundamentally from mind.
If you waste effort seeking it outside,
It's like rejecting your father and running away from home.

Shenxiu died at the age of 102 in the year 706. Among his most famous pupils were Songshan Puji and Jingzhao Yifu. After his death, Shenxiu received the posthumous title "Zen Master of Great Penetration."

Seventh Generation

NANYUE HUAIRANG

QINGYUAN XINGSI

NANYANG HUIZHONG

YONGJIA XUANJUE

HEZE SHENHUI

NANYUE HUAIRANG

NANYUE HUAIRANG (677–744) was the senior student of the Sixth Ancestor, Dajian Huineng. He came from ancient Jinzhou. Two of the five traditional "houses" of Chinese Zen traced their origin to the Sixth Ancestor through Nanyue Huairang and his famous student, Mazu Daoyi.

Nanyue left home at the age of fifteen to study under a Vinaya master named Hongjing.[35] After his ordination he studied the Vinayapitaka, but he became dissatisfied, and then traveled to see a teacher named Hui An on Mt. Song.[36] Although Nanyue made some spiritual progress with Hui An, he soon continued on to Cao Xi in Shaozhou, where he met and studied under the great teacher and Sixth Ancestor of Zen, Dajian Huineng. Their first encounter is described in the *Wudeng Huiyuan*.

> Huineng said to Nanyue, "Where did you come from?"
> Nanyue said, "From Mt. Song."
> Huineng said, "What is it that thus comes?"
> Nanyue couldn't answer.
> After eight years, Nanyue suddenly attained enlightenment. He informed the Sixth Ancestor of this, saying, "I have an understanding."
> The Sixth Ancestor said, "What is it?"
> Nanyue said, "To say it's a thing misses the mark."
> The Sixth Ancestor said, "Then can it be made evident or not?"
> Nanyue said, "I don't say it can't be made evident, but it can't be defiled."
> The Sixth Ancestor said, "Just this that is undefiled is what is upheld and sustained by all buddhas. You are thus. I also am thus.
> "Prajnadhara has foretold that from beneath your feet will come a horse

which will trample to death everyone in the world.[37] Bear this in mind but don't soon repeat it."

Nanyue then served the Sixth Ancestor for fifteen years.

During the Kai Yuan era of the Tang dynasty [713–41] there was a novice monk called Mazu Daoyi who constantly practiced Zen meditation upon Mt. Heng. Nanyue knew that Daoyi was a great vessel for the Dharma, and once walked up to him and said, "What does Your Worthiness intend to do by sitting in meditation?"

Mazu said, "I intend to become a buddha."

Nanyue then picked up a piece of tile from the ground and began grinding it on a rock.

Daoyi then asked, "What are you trying to make by grinding that?"

Nanyue said, "I'm grinding it to make a mirror."

Daoyi said, "How can you make a mirror by grinding a tile on a rock?"

Nanyue said, "If you can't make a mirror by grinding a tile on a rock, how can you become a buddha by sitting in meditation?"

Daoyi said, "What is the correct way?"

Nanyue said, "It can be compared to an ox pulling a cart. If the cart doesn't move, do you strike the cart or strike the ox?"

Daoyi didn't answer.

Nanyue then said, "Are you sitting in order to practice Zen, or are you sitting to be a buddha? If you're sitting to practice Zen, then know that Zen is not found in sitting or lying down. If you're sitting to become a buddha, then know that Buddha has no fixed form.

"With respect to the constantly changing world, you should neither grasp it nor reject it. If you sit to become a buddha, you kill Buddha. If you grasp sitting form then you have not yet reached the meaning."

When Daoyi heard this instruction it was as though he had drunk sweet nectar. He bowed and asked, "How can one cultivate mind to be in accord with formless samadhi?"

Nanyue said, "You are studying the Dharma gate of mind-ground, and this activity is like planting seeds there. The essential Dharma of which I speak may be likened to the rain that falls upon the seeded ground. In this same manner your auspicious karmic conditions will allow you to perceive the Way."

Daoyi then asked, "The Way is without color or form. How can one perceive it?"

Nanyue said, "The Dharma eye of mind-ground can perceive the true way. The formless samadhi is likewise perceived."

Daoyi then asked, "Does it have good and bad, or not?"

Nanyue said, "If the Way is seen in the aggregation and disintegration of good and bad, then it is not the Way. Listen to this verse:

The mind-ground fully sown,
When moisture comes, all seeds sprout
The formless flower of samadhi,
How can it be bad or good?"

At these words Daoyi experienced great enlightenment and unsurpassed realization. He then served Nanyue for ten years, each day embodying the deep mystery.

Six disciples entered Huairang's room [to receive Dharma transmission]. He commended each of them, saying, "The six of you together will represent my body, each in accord with one part of it. One of you (the monk Chang Hao) inherits my eyebrows and their dignified appearance. One of you (Zhida) inherits my eyes and their stern glare. One of you (Danran) inherits my ears and their ability to hear true principle. One of you (Shenzhao) inherits my nose and its ability to perceive *qi*.[38] One of you (Yanxuan) inherits my tongue and its ability for articulate speaking. One of you (Daoyi) inherits my mind and its knowledge of past and present."

Nanyue also said, "All dharmas are born of mind. Mind is unborn. Dharmas are nonabiding. When one reaches the mind-ground, one's actions are unobstructed. Be careful when using this teaching with those not of superior understanding."

---------- ◆ ----------

A great worthy once asked Nanyue, "If an image is reflected in a mirror, where does the light [of the image] go [when it's no longer observed]?"

Nanyue said, "It's similar to remembering when Your Worthiness was a child. Where has your childlike appearance gone [now]?" (Later Fayan said, "What is the image that the worthy one cast in the mirror?")

The worthy one asked, "But afterward, why does the image not remain?"

Nanyue said, "Although it is no longer reflected, it can't be reproved even slightly."

---------- ◆ ----------

Once after Daoyi left Nanyue and was teaching in Jiangxi, Nanyue addressed the monks, saying, "Is Daoyi teaching for the benefit of beings or not?"

Some monks in the congregation replied, "He's been teaching for the benefit of beings."

Nanyue said, "I've never heard any specific news about this."

The congregation couldn't offer any news on this.

Nanyue dispatched a monk to Mazu's place, instructing him, "Wait until he enters the hall to speak, and then ask him 'What's going on?' Take note of his answer and then bring it back and tell it to me."

The monk then carried out Nanyue's instructions. He returned and said, "Master Ma said, 'In the thirty years since the barbarian uprising I've never lacked salt or sauce.'"

Nanyue approved this answer.

On the eleventh day of the eighth month in [the year 744] the master died on Mt. Heng. He received the posthumous name "Zen Master of Great Wisdom." His stupa was named "Most Victorious Wheel."

QINGYUAN XINGSI

QINGYUAN XINGSI (660–740) was an eminent student of the Sixth Ancestor, Huineng. Three of the five traditionally recognized schools of Chinese Zen trace their origins through Qingyuan and his student, Shitou Xiqian. Little is known with certainty about Xingsi's life. He lived in relative obscurity at Quiet Abode Temple on Mt. Qingyuan, near the old city of Luling (modern Ji'an City in southern Jiangxi Province).

Zen master Xingsi of Jingzhu Temple on Qingyuan Mountain in Jizhou was from Ancheng City in the same province. His lay surname was Liu. He left home at a young age. Whenever there was a gathering that discussed the Tao, he always remained quiet.

Upon hearing that [the Sixth Ancestor] was preaching at Cao Xi he traveled there to study with him.

Xingsi asked the Sixth Ancestor, "In all that I do, how can I avoid falling into stages of spiritual development?"

The Sixth Ancestor said, "How do you practice?"

Xingsi said, "I don't even practice the four noble truths."[39]

The Sixth Ancestor said, "What stages have you fallen into?"

Xingsi said, "Without even studying the four noble truths, what stages could I have fallen into?"

The Sixth Ancestor esteemed Xingsi's ability. Although there were many in the congregation, Xingsi was selected as head monk. He is like the Second Ancestor, who, not speaking, attained the marrow.

One day the Sixth Ancestor said to him, "In the past, the robe and teaching have been passed down together, each generation of teacher and student passing them on in turn. The robe has been the evidence of the transmission. The authentic teaching is passed from mind to mind. Now I have suitable heirs. Why worry about not having evidence [of transmission]? Since I received the robe I've encountered innumerable difficulties. Moreover, in future times, the competition for [preeminence between Zen schools] will be even greater. The robe remains at Zhen Mountain Gate.[40] You must establish a separate assembly and expound the teaching. Don't allow my Dharma to be cut off."

After receiving transmission Xingsi returned to live at Mt. Qingyuan.

———————— ◆ ————————

One day, Qingyuan asked his disciple Shitou, "Where have you come from?"
Shitou said, "From Cao Xi."
Qingyuan then held up his whisk and said, "But does Cao Xi have this?"
Shitou said, "Not just Cao Xi, but even India doesn't have it."
Qingyuan said, "You haven't been to India, have you?"
Shitou said, "If I'd been there, then it would have it."
Qingyuan said, "No good! Try again."
Shitou said, "Master, you must say half. Don't rely on your disciple for all of it."
Qingyuan said, "Me speaking to you isn't what matters. What I fear is that there will be no one to carry on my Dharma."

———————— ◆ ————————

Heze Shenhui came to visit the master.
Qingyuan said, "Where have you come from?"
Shenhui said, "From Cao Xi."
Qingyuan said, "What is the essential doctrine of Cao Xi?"
Shenhui suddenly stood up straight.
Qingyuan said, "So, you're still just carrying common tiles."
Shenhui said, "Does the Master not have gold here to give people?"
Qingyuan said, "I don't have any. Where would you go to find some?" ([Later,] Xuansha said, "Just as you'd expect." Yunju Ci said, "Just as Xuansha said. Would you expect gold? Or would you expect tile?")

———————— ◆ ————————

A monk asked Qingyuan, "What is the great meaning of the Buddhadharma?"
Qingyuan said, "What is the price of rice in Luling?"

After the master had passed Dharma transmission to Shitou, on the thirteenth day of the twelfth lunar month in [the year 740], he went into the hall and said good-bye to the congregation. Then, sitting in a cross-legged posture, he passed away. The emperor Xi Zong gave the master the posthumous name "Zen Master Vast Benefit." His burial stupa was named "Return to Truth."

NANYANG HUIZHONG

NANYANG HUIZHONG (675–775), often referred to as the "National Teacher," was an eminent student of the Sixth Ancestor, Dajian Huineng. He came from ancient Zhuji.[41] As a boy, he entered monastic life, first studying under a Vinaya master. During forty years of rigorous practice and study on Baiya mountain, he thoroughly mastered all aspects of scriptural study and meditation practice. Later, Huizhong taught the three Tang dynasty emperors Xuan Zong, Su Zong, and Dai Zong, thus earning the title "National Teacher."

Nanyang's century spanned the golden age of classical Zen. During his youth, the dominant East Mountain school of Hongren branched into the Northern, Southern, and Sichuan schools. Later he witnessed the rise of the Heze, Hongzhou, Shitou, and other Zen schools. But Nanyang was not closely associated with any school, and he attained a stature that transcended the rancorous religious politics of the era.

National Teacher Nanyang Huizhong came from Zhuji in Yuezhou. His surname was Ran. From the time he received Dharma transmission he remained in the Dangzi Valley on Baiya Mountain in Nanyang, not leaving there for forty years. His reputation spread to the capital city.

In the second year of the Shang Yuan era, the emperor, Su Zong, dispatched an envoy to invite the master to the Imperial Capital. He received him there with great ceremony. At first he lived at the Thousand Blessings Temple at the Western Zen Monastery. Toward the end of the Dai Zong era the master was invited to reside at the Luminous Abode Buddha Temple where he stayed for sixteen years, expounding the Dharma in accord with circumstances.

At that time, a famous [Indian monk] named "Big Ears Tripitaka" came from the west to stay at the capital city. He claimed to have telepathic powers. The emperor Su Zong called on the National Teacher to test this monk.

When Tripitaka saw the National Teacher he bowed and stood to his right [in deference].

The National Teacher said, "I hear that you have mind-reading power."

Tripitaka replied, "I don't presume to say so."

The National Teacher said, "Where do you say I am right now?"

Tripitaka said, "The Master is a teacher of the whole nation. So why have you gone to the West River to see a boat race?"

After a while, the National Teacher asked again, saying, "Now where do you say I am?"

Tripitaka said, "The Master is a teacher of the whole nation. So why have you gone to the Tianjin Bridge to see monkeys playing?"

After some time, the National Teacher asked again, saying, "Where do you say I am right now?"

Tripitaka then made a wild guess and the master shouted, saying, "You wild fox spirit! Where is your mind-reading ability?"

Tripitaka couldn't answer.

([Later,] a monk asked [Zen master] Yangshan, "Why couldn't Big Ear Tripitaka see the National Teacher on his third try?" Yangshan said, "On his first two tries he entered the realm of mind. On his third attempt he employed samadhic practices, so he couldn't see the National Teacher." Another monk asked [Zen master] Xuansha about this. Xuansha asked in response, "What do you say Tripitaka saw in his first two attempts?" Yongjia Xuanjue said, "In the first two attempts Tripitaka saw him. Why didn't he see him on his third try? Moreover, what is there in what the National Teacher said that is advantageous or harmful?" A monk asked Zhaozhou, "Big Ear Tripitaka couldn't see the National Teacher on his third attempt. Where did he go?" Zhaozhou said, "On Tripitaka's nose." Later, a monk asked Xuansha Shibei, "Since he was on Tripitaka's nose, why couldn't he see him?" Xuansha said, "Because he was too close.")

--------------- ◆ ---------------

One day the National Teacher called to his attendant. The attendant responded. The National Teacher called three times, and three times the attendant responded.

Then the National Teacher said, "Have I been ungrateful to you, or have you been ungrateful to me?" ([Later], a monk asked Zen master Xuansha Shibei, "What was the meaning of the National Teacher's three calls to his attendant?" Xuansha said, "The attendant understood." Zen master Yunju Ci said, "Do you say that the attendant understood or not? If you say he understood, [remember that] the National Teacher said, 'You've been ungrateful to me.' If you say he didn't understand, [remember that] Xuansha said, 'Only the attendant understood.' How would you explain this?" Zen master Xuanjue queried a monk about this, saying, "What was it that the attendant understood?" The monk said, "If he didn't understand, how could he have answered in that manner?" Xuanjue said, "You understand a little bit." He also said, "If you can explain this then you'll see Xuansha." A monk asked Fayan, "What was the meaning of the National Teacher's three calls to his attendant?" Fayan said, "Get out of here! Come again some other time." Yunju Ci said, "If Fayan spoke that way, did he understand the National Teacher's meaning or not?" A monk asked Zhaozhou, "What was the meaning of the National Teacher's three calls?" Zhaozhou said, "It's as if someone secretly writes a word, and though the word isn't known, the writing style is obvious.")

———— ◆ ————

Zen master Nanquan Puyuan paid a visit to the National Teacher.
The National Teacher said, "Where did you come from?"
Nanquan said, "From Jiangxi."
The National Teacher said, "Then maybe you brought Zen master Mazu's true Dharma along with you?"
Nanquan said, "Here it is."
The National Teacher said, "On your back?"
At these words Nanquan attained awakening, and then he went out. [Changqing Leng said, "It's really like he didn't know." Baofu Zhan said, "It's almost as if he didn't meet the National Teacher on that occasion." Yunju Ci said, "These two great monks, they completely upheld what is on the back. But as to Nanquan comprehending and then going off, was he upholding what was in front of him or what was in back of him?"]

············ ◆ ············

When Mayu Baoche came to practice with the National Teacher, he circled the meditation platform three times, then struck his staff on the ground and stood there upright.
The National Teacher said, "You are thus. I also am thus."
Mayu struck his staff on the ground again.
The National Teacher said, "Get out of here, you wild fox spirit!"

············ ◆ ············

The National Teacher entered the hall and said, "Those who study Zen should venerate the words of Buddha. There is but one vehicle for attaining buddhahood, and that is to understand the great principle that is to connect with the source of mind. If you haven't become clear about the great principle then you haven't embodied the teaching, and you're like a lion cub whose body is still irritated by fleas. And if [in that state] you become a teacher of others, even attaining some worldly renown and fortune, but you are still spreading falsehoods, what good does that do you or anyone else? A skilled axeman does not harm himself with the axe head. What is inside the incense burner can't be carried by a donkey!"

⸻ ◆ ⸻

A monk asked, "How can one become a buddha?"

The National Teacher said, "Cast off the Buddha and all beings, and at that moment you'll be liberated."

⸻ ◆ ⸻

A monk asked, "How can one be in accord with it?"

The National Teacher said, "Don't think of good or evil. Personally see buddha nature."

⸻ ◆ ⸻

A monk asked, "How can one demonstrate the *dharmakaya*?"[42]

The National Teacher said, "Go beyond Vairochana Buddha."[43]

⸻ ◆ ⸻

The monk then asked, "How can one attain the pure dharmakaya?"

The National Teacher said, "Don't beseech Buddha."

A fascinating exchange between Nanyang and a student of the Hongzhou Zen school of Zen master Mazu Daoyi demonstrates the breadth of the National Teacher's ability. Mazu's teaching gained fame through his famous assertion that "mind is Buddha." This passage is taken from an excerpt of *The Record of National Teacher Huizhong* that is preserved in the *Transmission of the Lamp*.

The National Teacher asked a monk, "Where are you from?"

The monk said, "From the South."

The National Teacher said, "Are there any teachers there?"

The monk said, "A great many."

The National Teacher said, "What is it that they teach people?"

The monk said, "In that place, worthies directly impart the teaching 'mind is Buddha' to their students.

"Right now, you completely possess the nature of conscious perception. This benevolent nature can cause the raising of an eyebrow and the twinkling in an eye. It is employed when coming or going, and it pervades the body. If you tap your head, the head knows it. If you stamp the feet, the feet know it. The ancients called it 'pervasive consciousness.' Aside from this, there is no other Buddha. This body is subject to birth and annihilation, but the nature of mind is beginningless, and does not undergo birth and death. The body subject to birth and death is like a dragon that loses and regrows its bones, or a snake that sheds its skin, or a human that leaves his old home. This body is impermanent, but its nature is eternal."

National Teacher Huizhong criticized this, saying, "If that's so, then their teaching is no different from the heretical *Senika* doctrine.[44] Teachers of that doctrine said, 'Within this body is a spirit. Although this spirit can know [the body's] affliction, when the body expires the spirit departs from it. If I am burned up, this spiritual host moves on. Although I am not eternal, this host is eternal.' With such an understanding, true and false can't be distinguished."

Nanyang appears to draw a distinction between an individual eternal mind and a universal mind. Later in the same text, the National Teacher is quoted in the following exchange:

> A monk asked, "What is Buddha?"
> The National Teacher said, "Mind is Buddha."
> A monk asked, "Does mind have defilements?"
> The National Teacher said, "Defilements, by their own nature, drop off."
> A monk asked, "Do you mean that we shouldn't cut them off?"
> The National Teacher said, "Cutting off defilements is called the 'second vehicle.' When defilements do not arise, that is called nirvana."

> A monk asked, "How does one sit in meditation and observe purity?"
> The National Teacher said, "There being neither pollution nor purity, why do you need to assume a posture of observing purity?"

> A monk asked, "When a Zen master observes that everything in the ten directions is empty, is that the dharmakaya?"
> The National Teacher said, "Viewpoints attained with the thinking mind are upside down."

A monk asked, "Aside from 'mind is Buddha,' are there any other practices that can be undertaken?"

The National Teacher said, "All of the ancient sages possessed the two grand attributes, but does this allow them to dispel cause and effect?"[45] Then he said, "The answer I've just given you cannot be exhausted in an incalculable eon. Saying more would be far from the Way. Thus it is said that 'when the Dharma is spoken [with an intention] of gaining, then it is just like a barking fox. When the Dharma is spoken without the intention of gaining, then it is like a lion's roar.'"

When Nanyang Huizhong was near death, he took leave of the emperor Dai Zong.

The emperor said, "After you have gone, how should your disciple memorialize you?"

Nanyang said, "Please build me a seamless monument."

After a long pause, Nanyang said, "Do you understand?"

The emperor said, "No."

Nanyang said, "After I'm gone, my disciple Danyuan will understand about this matter. Please ask him about it.

On the nineteenth day of the second month in [the year 775] the National Teacher laid down on his right side and passed away. His stupa was built in the Dangzi Valley and he received the posthumous name "Zen Master Great Rectitude."

Later, Dai Zong summoned Danyuan and asked about the previous matter.

Danyuan was silent for a long while, and then said, "Do you understand?"

The emperor said, "I don't understand."

Danyuan recited the following verse.

South of Xiang,
North of Tan,
In the middle a unified golden nation,
Beneath a shadowless tree, everyone ferried together,
In the porcelain palace, no worthies are found.

YONGJIA XUANJUE

YONGJIA XUANJUE (665–713) was one of the great disciples of Huineng. He came from Benjun. Yongjia is often remembered by his nickname, the "Overnight Guest," due to his legendary brief encounter with his teacher, Huineng. Yongjia was persuaded by Huineng to stay at Cao Xi only one night. During that night Huineng confirmed Yongjia's enlightenment.

Yongjia Xuanjue was also an adept in the Tiantai school of Buddhism, a sect that originated at Mt. Tiantai in Zhejiang Province. His writings, compiled in a work called the *Yongjia Collection*, compare the Zen practice of *zazen* (sitting meditation) with an equivalent practice of the Tiantai school known as *zhiguan*.

Zen master Yongjia Zhenjue had the given name Xuanjue. He came from Benjun and his lay surname was Dai. He left home as a youth and thoroughly studied the Buddhist scriptures. He also mastered the supreme Tiantai Dharma gate of zhiguan. When he assumed any of the four noble stances he did so with a Zen [meditative] air.[46] Later, at the urging of Zen master Zuo Xilang he traveled with Zen master Dong Yangce. He went to Cao Xi to visit the Sixth Ancestor. Upon first meeting Huineng, Yongjia struck his staff on the ground and circled the Sixth Ancestor three times, then stood there upright.

The Sixth Ancestor said, "This monk possesses the three thousand noble characteristics and the eighty thousand fine attributes. Oh monk! Where have you come from? How have you attained such self-possession?

Yongjia said, "The great matter of birth and death does not tarry."

The Sixth Ancestor said, "Then why not embody what is not born and attain what is not hurried?"

Yongjia said, "What is embodied is not subject to birth. What is attained is fundamentally unmoving."

The Sixth Ancestor said, "Just so! Just so!"

Upon hearing these words, everyone among the congregation of monks was astounded.

Yongjia formally paid his respects to the Sixth Ancestor. He then advised that he was immediately departing.

The Sixth Ancestor said, "Don't go so quickly!"

Yongjia said, "Fundamentally there is nothing moving. So how can something be too quick?"

The Sixth Ancestor said, "How can one know there's no movement?"

Yongjia said, "The distinction is completely of the master's own making."

The Sixth Ancestor said, "You have fully attained the meaning of what is unborn."

Yongjia said, "So, does what is unborn have a meaning?"

The Sixth Ancestor said, "Who makes a distinction about whether there is a meaning or not?"

Yongjia said, "Distinctions are meaningless."

The Sixth Ancestor shouted, "Excellent! Excellent! Now, just stay here a single night!"

Thus people referred to Yongjia as the "Overnight Guest."

The next day Yongjia descended the mountain and returned to Wenzhou, where Zen students gathered to study with him.

In the year 713 Zen master Yongjia passed away peacefully while sitting in meditation. He received the posthumous title "Great Teacher No Form." A stupa named "Shining Purity" was constructed on the south face of West Mountain.

HEZE SHENHUI

HEZE SHENHUI (670–762) was an eminent disciple of the Sixth Ancestor. He strongly supported and promoted Huineng's place in Chinese Zen history. Shenhui championed the Southern school of Zen, and vociferously attacked what became widely known as the Northern school, the school associated with Yuquan Shenxiu.

Shenhui put forward two reasons for his attack on the Northern school. The first was, "The (ancestral) succession is spurious." Attacking Shenxiu's legitimacy as the Dharma heir of Hongren was an extension of Shenhui's proposition that that honor belonged exclusively to Huineng. Obviously, the argument was self-serving as well, since Shenhui could thus make a claim to be the true Seventh Ancestor of the Bodhidharma line.

The second reason for attacking Shenxiu was, "(His) Dharma gate is gradual." By this, Shenhui meant that the various "gradual" spiritual practices employed by Shenxiu, as well as other disciples of Hongren, were fundamentally at odds with what Shenhui regarded as the genuine Zen of his teacher, Huineng.

Shenhui's life and teaching are at the center of the most hotly debated questions of Zen history and thought. He is a controversial figure who set a standard of teaching that emphasized sudden, unmediated enlightenment. This characteristic of Chinese Zen distinguishes it from other Buddhist schools. The idea of nonmediated, sudden enlightenment clearly took solid root as a centerpiece of Chinese Zen during Shenhui's era and suffused the teachings of subsequent generations of the Southern school.

Shenhui's Zen, expounded in the name of the Sixth Ancestor, castigated the idea of "gradual" enlightenment achieved through meditation and religious practices that were meant to realize and maintain "pure original mind." Shenhui's proposition, in effect, attacked not only the Northern school, but many of the practices that were part and parcel of Daoxin and Hongren's East Mountain Zen tradition as well, including their basic outlook on meditation practice.

Scholars have documented that Daoxin, Hongren, and Hongren's disciples variously used "gradualist" practices, practices that set religious life distinctly apart from secular life, in their practice centers. One example was Hongren's disciple Zishou Zhishen, the founder of the Sichuan Zen school, who is believed to have heavily emphasized chanting Buddha's name over all other practices.

Yet Shenhui has been shown to have tampered with, not to say subverted, the historical facts surrounding Huineng's life to gain ascendancy for his "sudden" Zen ideology. Shenhui's account of Huineng's life contains self-serving inconsistencies. Moreover, his writings about earlier Zen development, particularly the succession of Zen ancestors beginning with Shakyamuni Buddha, contain blatant errors and contradictions.

The "Northern" school was the name applied by Shenhui to the most politically dominant and powerful stream of Zen of his era. This stream was a continuation of the East Mountain school of Hongren, as taught by his disciple Shenxiu, and by Shenxiu's own many disciples who were spread through northern areas of the country. Shenxiu obtained unprecedented influence at the imperial court during the late seventh and early eighth centuries. Shenxiu's disciples Puji and Yifu then carried on this influence until events overcame the school around the year 755.

Shenhui's main attack on the Northern school occurred at a conference he staged at Great Cloud Temple in Huatai in the year 734. In that meeting, Shenhui put forth the "Exposition on Determining Right and Wrong [with respect to] Bodhidharma's Southern School." The conference staged a debate between Shenhui and a certain "Dharma master Chongyuan," who defended the Northern school. Although the influence of this conference on the imperial court and public opinion is disputed, the meeting clearly laid out lines of battle between the doctrines of the southern and northern currents of Zen.

After the conference at Huatai, Shenhui proceeded to live in the northern capital city of Luoyang, where he directly confronted the Northern school by inciting opinion in public gatherings. Eventually, Shenhui was banned from Luoyang as a rabble-rouser. During the period of his banishment, historical events transpired that helped his cause. The An Lushan uprising, a catastrophically destructive rebellion against the Tang dynasty, led to the destruction of the twin capital cities of Luoyang and Changan. The areas suffering devastation were important regions of Northern school predominance. This direct destruction of the Northern school led to a vacuum of court influence that Shenhui's followers managed to fill. Thus, the Southern school gained social and political ascendancy not simply due to a preferred religious doctrine, but as the unforeseen result of a civil war that wracked northern China during that era.

Shenhui thus founded what became known as the Heze (in Japanese, *Kataku*) school of Zen. The branch largely died out during the early ninth century and is not remembered as a major school. Nevertheless, the doctrine of sudden enlightenment remained a central characteristic that defined the teaching styles and cultural flavor of later Chinese Zen. In the next Zen generation, Mazu Daoyi's Hongzhou school vigorously adopted a teaching style that expressed the "sudden" Zen outlook. That school displaced Heze's school in influence during the ninth century, but the doctrine espoused by Shenhui had lasting influence on all subsequent generations of Zen teachers.

Zen master Heze Shenhui of the Western Capital came from Xiangyang. His surname was Gao, and he became a novice monk at the age of fourteen.

At their first meeting the Sixth Ancestor asked Shenhui, "You have come on an arduous journey from afar. Did you bring what is fundamental? If you have what is fundamental then you can see the host. Let's see what you have to say."

Shenhui said, "I take no abode as the fundamental. What is seen is the host."

The Sixth Ancestor said, "This novice is talking nonsense!" He then took his staff and struck Shenhui.

As he was being beaten, Shenhui thought, "[This master] is such a great and wise sage. It is difficult to meet such a person even after many kalpas of time. Having met him today how can I lament my life?"

From this time forward Shenhui served as Huineng's attendant.

Once, the Sixth Ancestor addressed the congregation, saying, "I have something which has no head or tail. It is nameless and can't be described. It has no back and no front. Do any of you know what it is?"

Shenhui came forward and said, "It is the source of all things. It is the buddha nature of Shenhui."

The Sixth Ancestor said, "I said that it has no name and no description. How can you say it is the source of buddha nature?"

Shenhui bowed and retreated.

The Sixth Ancestor said, "In the future if this youngster heads a monastery, it will certainly bring forth fully realized disciples of our school." ([Later,] Fayan said, "The record of that time was indeed excellent. Today, if we point to a greatly awakened school, it is the Heze school.")

Before long, Shenhui traveled to the Western Capital [Changan], where he received ordination.

The following passage from the debate between Shenhui and Dharma master Chongyuan is taken from *The Record of the Zen Discourses by the Monk Shenhui.*[47]

Dharma master Yuan asked Shenhui, "Were Zen master Huineng and Zen master Shenxiu not fellow students of Hongren?"

Shenhui said, "They were."

Chongyuan asked, "Since they were fellow students, are their teachings the same or not?"

Shenhui said, "Not the same."

Chongyuan said, "Since they were fellow students, why are their teachings not the same?"

Shenhui said, "I will now explain their difference. It's because Zen master Xiu taught people to 'focus the mind and enter concentration. Stop the mind and observe purity. Give rise to mind that shines outward. Collect the mind inside and bear witness to it.' For this reason their teaching is different."

Chongyuan said, "Why is it that Zen master Neng does not teach [the practices taught by Zen master Xiu]? What are his practices?"

Shenhui said, "The practice of Shenxiu is to harmonize and subdue the mind."

Chongyuan said, "Then should one not [perform the practices taught by Shenxiu]?"

Shenhui said, "These are the methods of the ignorant. Zen master Huineng's practice is found apart from the two methods of 'subduing' or 'not subduing.' This is why is says in the sutra, 'mind does not abide within, nor is it external.' It is in quiet sitting. When one sits in this manner, one realizes buddhahood. In the six generations that have come before, not a single person performed the practices of Shenxiu. They are entirely different."

<hr />

In the year 760 Shenhui passed away while sitting in meditation. His burial stupa is located at Dragon Gate.

Eighth Generation

MAZU DAOYI

SHITOU XIQIAN

DANYUAN YINGZHEN

MAZU DAOYI, "DAJI"

MAZU DAOYI (709–88) was a student of Nanyue Huairang. After Huineng, Mazu is the most famous of the ancient Chinese Zen masters. Two of the traditionally acknowledged major schools of Zen trace their lineage through this renowned Zen ancient. From his home in Sichuan Province, Mazu made his way to Zhongqing, where he initially studied under a second-generation teacher of Daman Hongren (the Fifth Ancestor). There he received ordination as a Buddhist monk. Later, he settled on Mt. Heng, where he met Nanyue Huairang. After ten years of study with Nanyue, he received Dharma transmission, then proceeded to travel as a *yunshui* the length and breadth of China, perfecting his understanding of the Buddha way. Eventually he settled at Zhongling (now Nanchang City), where students from every quarter came to study with him.

Mazu's Zen lineage is remembered as the Hongzhou Zen school. Located in what is now Jiangxi Province, it was the dominant Zen school of the later Tang dynasty (late ninth and early tenth centuries). Mazu was the first Zen teacher acknowledged to use the staff to jolt his students into awakening. The strident style of his Hongzhou school foreshadowed the uncompromising training methods of his famous Zen descendant, Linji Yixuan.

Unlike some other Zen masters of his time, Mazu did not leave an extensive written record of his teachings. Instead, we know of him largely from imaginative legends that reflect the awesome sense of presence that he conveyed.

Like the great Zen masters of all ages, Mazu emphasized the immediacy of Zen enlightenment. He emphasized the teaching that "mind is Buddha" and "This place is itself true thusness." Mazu's "sudden" approach moved the Chinese spiritual scales back toward "pointing directly at mind," the essential teaching of Bodhidharma's Zen.

The acclaimed greatness of a Zen master does not arise simply from his or her message. Equally important is the awesome and bone-chilling presence that such masters demonstrate. This tangible sense of presence reveals an astonishing freedom. Zen students, observing such masters, naturally aspire to gain the remarkable composure, effortless grace, and uncluttered vision that they embody. Later generations gain a sense of what these ancients were like partly through their words, but more intimately through their legends.

The *Wudeng Huiyuan* provides the following account of Mazu's life and teaching.

Zen master Mazu Daoyi of Jiangxi was from Shifang in Hanzhou [about forty kilometers north of the modern city of Chengdu in Sichuan Province]. His surname was Ma. He entered Luohan Temple in his home district. His appearance was most unusual. He strode like an ox and glared like a tiger. His extended tongue covered his nose. On the soles of his feet his veins formed two circles. As a youth he received tonsure under a monk named Tang in Zizhou. He was fully ordained under Vinaya master Yuan in Yu Province.

During the Kai Yuan era [713–41] Mazu met Master Nanyue Huairang while practicing Zen meditation on Mt. Heng. Six others also studied with Nanyue but only Mazu received the secret mind seal. Nanyue Huairang and his student Mazu Daoyi can be compared with Qingyuan Xingsi and his student Shitou Xiqian. Though they came from the same source, they diverged into two branches. The brilliance of ancient Zen arose through these two masters. Liu Ke said, "In Jiangxi is Master Daji. In Hunan is Master Shitou. Anyone traversing the country seeking a teacher who doesn't see these two will remain ignorant."

The record of Prajnadhara of India made a prediction about Bodhidharma, saying, "Although the great land of China is vast, there are no roads where my descendants won't travel. The phoenix, with a single grain, nourishes the saints and monks in the ten directions."

The Sixth Ancestor [also citing an ancient prediction by Prajnadhara] said to Nanyue, "Hereafter, from the area to which you will go, a horse will come forth and trample everyone in the world to death."

Later, the Dharma of Nanyue's spiritual heir was spread across the world. People of that time called him Master Ma.

From Buddha Trace Mountain in Jianyang, Mazu moved to Linchuan. He then moved to Nankang at Gonggong Mountain. In the middle of the Dali era [766–79], Mazu lived at the Kaiyuan Temple in Zhongling. During that time the high official Lu Sigong heard of Mazu's reputation, and personally came to receive instruction. Because of this, students from the four quarters gathered like clouds beneath Mazu's seat.

One day Mazu addressed the congregation, saying, "All of you here! Believe that your own mind is Buddha. This very mind is buddha mind. When Bodhidharma came from India to China he transmitted the supreme vehicle teaching of one mind, allowing people like you to attain awakening. Moreover he brought with him the text of the *Lankavatara Sutra*, using it as the seal of the mind-ground of sentient beings. He feared that your views would be inverted, and you wouldn't believe in the teaching of this mind that each and every one of you possesses. Therefore [Bodhidharma brought] the *Lankavatara Sutra*, which offers the Buddha's words that mind is the essence—and that there is no gate by which to enter Dharma. You who seek Dharma should seek nothing. Apart from mind there is no other Buddha. Apart from Buddha there is no other mind. Do not grasp what is good nor reject what is bad. Don't lean toward either purity or pollution. Arrive at the empty nature of transgressions; that nothing is attained through continuous thoughts; and that because there is no self-nature the three worlds are only mind. The myriad forms of the entire universe are the seal of the single Dharma. Whatever forms are seen are but the perception of mind. But mind is not independently existent. It is co-dependent with form. You should speak appropriately about the affairs of your own life, for each matter you encounter constitutes the meaning of your existence, and your actions are without hindrance. The fruit of the bodhisattva way is just thus, born of mind, taking names to be forms. Because of the knowledge of the emptiness of forms, birth is nonbirth. Comprehending this, one acts in the fashion of one's time, just wearing clothes, eating food, constantly upholding the practices of a bodhisattva, and passing time according to circumstances. If one practices in this manner is there anything more to be done?

"To receive my teaching, listen to this verse:

"The mind-ground responds to conditions.
Bodhi is only peace.
When there is no obstruction in worldly affairs or principles,
Then birth is nonbirth."

A monk asked, "Master, why do you say that mind is Buddha?"

Mazu said, "To stop babies from crying."

The monk said, "What do you say when they stop crying?"

Mazu said, "No mind, no Buddha."

The monk asked, "Without using either of these teachings, how would you instruct someone?"

Mazu said, "I would say to him that it's not a thing."

The monk asked, "If suddenly someone who was in the midst of it came to you, then what would you do?"

Mazu said, "I would teach him to experience the great way."

❖

A monk asked, "What is the essential meaning of Buddhism?"

Mazu said, "What is the meaning of this moment?"

❖

Layman Pang asked, "Would the master please give your esteemed view about the clear-eyed ancestors?"

Mazu looked down.

Layman Pang said, "Other teachers can't play the lute. Only the master does it so sublimely."

Mazu then looked up. Layman Pang bowed. Mazu then returned to the abbot's room. Layman Pang followed him, saying, "Just now something skillful turned awkward."

Layman Pang also asked, "Although water has no muscle or bone, it supports ten-thousand-pound ships. What is the principle this displays?"

Mazu said, "Here there is neither water nor boat. How can you speak of muscle and bone?"

❖

One evening, the monks Xitang, Baizhang, and Nanquan were viewing the moon with Master Mazu.

The master asked them, "At just this moment, what is it?"

Xitang said, "Perfect support."

Baizhang said, "Perfect practice."

Nanquan shook his sleeves and walked away.

Mazu said, "A sutra enters the Buddhist canon. Zen returns to the sea. Only Nanquan has gone beyond things."

Baizhang asked, "What is the essential import of the school?"
Mazu said, "It's just the place where you let go of your body and life."

Mazu asked Baizhang, "What teaching do you offer people?"
Baizhang held his whisk up straight.
Mazu said, "Just this? Nothing more?"
Baizhang threw down the whisk.

A monk asked, "How can one gain accordance with the Way?"
Master Mazu said, "I've never gained accordance with it."
The monk asked, "What is the essential meaning of Zen?"
Mazu struck him and said, "If I didn't hit you, I'd be laughed at from every direction."

The young teacher Danyuan returned from a pilgrimage. He drew a circle in front of Master Mazu, stepped inside it, bowed, and stood there.
Master Mazu said, "So, you don't want to become a buddha?"
Danyuan said, "I can't deceive you."
Master Mazu said, "I'm not like you."
Danyuan was silent.

When Deng Yinfeng was taking his leave, Master Mazu said to him, "Where are you going?"
Yinfeng said, "To Shitou's."
Mazu said, "Shitou's road is slippery."
Yinfeng said, "I'll carry a wooden staff with me. When I encounter such places I'll be ready."
Then he went off.
Upon arriving at Shitou's, he circled the meditation bench, loudly struck his staff on the floor, and asked, "What is the essential doctrine?"

Shitou said, "Blue heavens! Blue heavens!"

Yinfeng didn't speak, but returned and reported this to Master Mazu.

Master Mazu said, "Go there and ask him again. Wait for his answer, then make two roaring sounds."

Yinfeng again went to Shitou and asked the question as before. Shitou made two roaring sounds. Yinfeng again didn't speak. He returned and reported this to Master Ma.

The master said, "Like I told you, 'Shitou's road is slippery.'"

—————— ✦ ——————

A monk drew four lines on the ground in front of the master. The top line was long and the three underneath were short. He said, "It can't be said that the one on top is long and the three underneath are short. Leaving the four descriptions that use these words aside, how does the master describe them?"

Master Ma then drew a line on the ground and said, "Without speaking of long and short, I've answered you." (When National Teacher Nanyang Huizhong heard of this incident, he said, "Why didn't he ask this old monk?")

—————— ✦ ——————

A scholar monk came and asked, "I'd like to know what teaching the master offers."

Master Ma asked the monk, "Professor, what teaching do you offer?"

The scholar monk said, "I lecture upon more than twenty volumes of scripture."

Master Ma said, "Are you a young lion?"[48]

The scholar monk said, "I can't so presume."

Master Ma made a roaring noise.

The scholar monk said, "This is a teaching."

Master Ma said, "What teaching is it?"

The scholar monk said, "The teaching of the lion leaving its den."

Master Ma remained silent.

The scholar monk said, "This also is a teaching."

Master Ma said, "What teaching is it?"

The scholar monk said, "The teaching of the lion in its den."

Master Ma said, "Neither going nor coming, what teaching is it?"

The scholar monk didn't answer.

Baizhang said in his behalf, "Do you see?"

The scholar monk then said good-bye and started to leave.

Master Ma called to him, "Professor!"

The scholar turned his head.

Master Ma said, "What is *it*?"

The scholar again didn't answer.

Master Ma said, "This dull-witted professor!"

------------- ◆ -------------

Magistrate Lian of Hongzhou asked, "Should one drink wine and eat meat or not?"

Master Ma said, "If you consume wine and meat, it is your prosperity. If you don't consume wine and meat, it is your good fortune."

------------- ◆ -------------

The master had one hundred thirty-nine disciples, each becoming a spiritual master in a different place, where each of them ceaselessly conveyed the teaching. In the first month [of the year 788], the master climbed Shimen Mountain in Jianchang. There, as he was walking in the woods, he saw a flat spot in a cave and said to his attendant, "This ruined old body of mine will return to the ground next month."

These words came to pass. He subsequently became ill.

The temple director asked him, "How has the master's honored condition been lately?"

Master Ma said, "Sun-faced buddha. Moon-faced buddha."

On the first day of the second lunar month, the master bathed, sat in a cross-legged position, and passed away. During the Yuan He era [806–20] he received the posthumous name Daji ["Great Stillness"]. His stupa is named "Majestic and Imposing."

SHITOU XIQIAN

SHITOU XIQIAN (700–90) was a disciple of Qingyuan Xingsi. He is a key figure of early Zen development. Three of the five traditional schools of Chinese Zen traced their origins through Shitou and his heirs.

Shitou's Zen lineage is sometimes remembered as the "Hunan school." Along with Mazu's Hongzhou school (in an area corresponding to modern Jiangxi Province), these two comprise the root of all subsequent Zen schools and lineages down to the present day.

Many facets of Shitou's life are obscure or lost. Historical records made little or no mention of a formal "Hunan school" during the years following Shitou's death. He is connected to other great masters of the era mainly through believable anecdotes and claimed succession.

Shitou taught that "what meets the eye is the Way."

Great teacher Shitou Xiqian was from Gaoyao in Duanzhou [west of present-day Guangzhou]. His family name was Chen. When Shitou's mother became pregnant she avoided eating meat, and when he was a small child he was untroublesome. As a young man he was magnanimous. The people where he grew up feared demons and performed debased sacrifices of oxen and wine. This practice was long established. The master would go into the woods and destroy the ceremonial altars, seize the oxen, and drive them away. This went on for ten years and the village elders were never able to stop him.

Later, Xiqian went to Cao Xi. He received tonsure but did not undergo full ordination as a monk. When the Sixth Ancestor died, Xiqian obeyed his request that he go to study under Qingyuan Xingsi. Xiqian then took Zen master Xingsi as his teacher.

One day, Qingyuan said to Shitou, "Someone says there's news from Lingnan."[49]

Shitou said, "Someone doesn't say there's news from Lingnan."

Qingyuan then said, "If that's so, then from where did the sutras and shastras come forth?"

The master said, "They all came from this."

Qingyuan approved this answer.

In the first year of the Tian Bao era [742–55] of the Tang dynasty, the master took up residence at South Temple on Heng Mountain. East of the temple there was a stone outcropping. The master built a thatched hut on top of this spot and was thereafter referred to as "Monk Shitou."[50]

Shitou is recorded to have had a great revelation while reading the *Zhao Lun*.[51] In that text he came upon a passage that said, "The one who realizes that the myriad things are one's own self is no different from the sages." Shitou thereafter dreamed that he, along with the Sixth Ancestor, was riding on the back of a great tortoise that was swimming in the sea. Waking up, he surmised that the tortoise symbolized wisdom and that the sea was the sea of existence.

Shitou took the dream to mean that he, together with the Sixth Ancestor, sat upon wisdom's back, swimming in the sea of existence. This realization inspired Shitou to write a verse entitled *Realizing Unity* (in Chinese, *Cantongjie*), an ode that is widely known and chanted in Zen temples down to the present day.[52]

The *Wudeng Huiyuan* offers examples of Shitou's teachings.

Zen master Xiqian entered the hall and addressed the monks, saying, "My Dharma gate was first taught by former buddhas. I don't say you need to practice some advanced form of meditation. Just see what the Buddha saw. This mind is buddha mind.

"'Buddha mind,' 'all beings,' 'wisdom,' and 'defilement,' the names of these things are different, but actually they are one body. You should each recognize your miraculous mind. Its essence is apart from temporary or everlasting. Its nature is without pollution or purity. It is clear and perfect. Common people and sages are the same. [This mind] reaches everywhere without limit. It is not constrained by the limits of consciousness. The three realms and six realms manifest from this mind.[53] If [this mind] is like the moon reflected on water, where can there be creation and destruction? If you can comprehend this, then there is nothing that you lack."

At this point the monk Tianhuang Daowu asked, "Who is it who has attained the essential principle of Caoxi?"

Shitou said, "The person who has comprehended the Buddhadharma."

Daowu then asked, "Has the master attained it?"

Shitou said, "I haven't attained it."

Daowu said, "Why haven't you attained it?"

Shitou said, "Because I can't comprehend the Buddhadharma."

⸻ ❖ ⸻

A monk asked, "What is liberation?"

Shitou said, "Who has bound you?"

Another monk asked, "What is the Pure Land?"

Shitou said, "Who has polluted you?"

Another monk asked, "What is nirvana?"

Shitou said, "Who has given you birth and death?"

⸻ ❖ ⸻

The master asked a monk who had just arrived, "Where have you come from?"

The monk said, "From Jiangxi."

Shitou said, "Did you see Great Teacher Ma, or not?"

The monk said, "I saw him."

Shitou pointed to a pile of firewood and asked, "Was he like this?"

The monk didn't answer. He then returned to Mazu's place and told him about this encounter with Shitou.

Mazu said, "Did you see how big the stack of wood was?"

The monk said, "It was immeasurably big."

Mazu said, "You're really strong."

The monk said, "Why do you say that?"

Mazu said, "You carried a pile of wood all the way here from Mt. Nanyue. Doesn't that take a lot of strength?"

A monk asked Shitou, "Why did the First Ancestor come from the west?"

Shitou said, "Ask the temple pillar."

The monk said, "I don't understand."

Shitou said, "I don't understand either."

Dadian said, "An ancient said, 'Speaking and not speaking are both slander.' I ask the Master to explain this."

Shitou said, "If there's not a single thing, what could you grasp?"

Shitou also said, "If you take away your throat, your mouth, and your lips, could you still speak?"

Dadian said, "There's nothing left."

Shitou said, "If that's so, then you've entered the gate."

Daowu asked, "What is the great meaning of the Buddhadharma?"

Shitou said, "Not attaining. Not knowing."

Daowu asked, "Is there anything beyond this?"

Shitou said, "The sky does not obstruct the white cloud's flight."

A monk asked, "What is Zen?"

Shitou said, "A piece of tile."

The monk asked, "What is the Way?"

Shitou said, "Wood."

Shitou died in the sixth year of [the year 790]. A stupa was erected in Dongling. Emperor De Zong bestowed upon him the posthumous name "Great Teacher Without Limit."

DANYUAN YINGZHEN

DANYUAN YINGZHEN (n.d.) was an attendant and disciple of National Teacher Nanyang Huizhong. Yingzhen taught at Danyuan Mountain in Qizhou. He is remembered primarily for his role in stories about his famous teacher.

When Zen master Yingzhen of Danyuan Mountain in Qizhou served as attendant for National Teacher Huizhong, one day the National Teacher sat on the meditation platform in the Dharma hall. When Danyuan came in, the National Teacher put down one foot. When Danyuan saw this he immediately went out again. After a while he came back into the hall.

The National Teacher said, "What was that about when you came in a while ago?"

Danyuan said, "To whom do you speak of it?"

The National Teacher said, "I am asking you."

Danyuan said, "Where did you see me?"

On another day Danyuan carried a bamboo basket into the abbot's room.

The National Teacher asked, "What are you carrying in the basket?"

Danyuan said, "Green plums."

The National Teacher said, "Why did you bring them?"

Danyuan said, "To provide you support."

The National Teacher said, "What good are they if they're green?"

Danyuan said, "I just give them as an offering."

The National Teacher said, "Buddha doesn't accept support."

Danyuan said, "When I do something like this, why do you act in this manner?"

The National Teacher said, "I don't give support."

Danyuan said, "Why not?"

The National Teacher said, "I don't have any fruit."

························· ❖ ·························

Mayu asked Danyuan, "Is the twelve-faced Kwan Yin holy or not?"

Danyuan said, "Yes."

Mayu then slapped Danyuan's ears.

Danyuan said, "I didn't imagine that you'd reached this state."

———— ❖ ————

On the anniversary of the death of the National Teacher, Danyuan held a memorial banquet.

A monk asked, "Is the National Teacher coming?"

Danyuan said, "We won't have his mind."

The monk asked, "Then why give this banquet?"

Danyuan said, "To not stop the truth of the world."

Ninth Generation

BAIZHANG HUAIHAI   XITANG ZHIZANG   ZHANGJING HUAIYUN

YANGUAN QI'AN   DAMEI FACHANG   GUIZONG ZHICHANG

LAYMAN PANG   MAYU BAOCHE   PANSHAN BAOJI   LUZU BAOYUN

ZHONGYI HONGEN   WUJIU YOUXUAN   NANQUAN PUYUAN

YAOSHAN WEIYAN   DANXIA TIANRAN   TIANHUANG DAOWU

BAIZHANG HUAIHAI

A FOREMOST DISCIPLE of Mazu, Baizhang Huaihai (720–814) was originally from the city of Changle in Fuzhou. He took his vows as a monk under the Vinaya master Fachao on Mt. Heng. Brilliant and learned as a young man, he traveled to study under the great teacher Mazu Daoyi. The *Wudeng Huiyuan* ranks him, along with Xitang Zhizang and Nanquan Puyuan, as one of the three most illustrious disciples of Mazu.

The story of Baizhang's enlightenment is known by the name "Baizhang's Wild Ducks." The lamp records tell the story as follows:

One day Baizhang accompanied Mazu on a walk. A flock of wild ducks flew past them.

Mazu said, "What's that?"

Baizhang said, "Wild ducks."

Mazu said, "Where'd they go?"

Baizhang said, "They flew away."

Mazu then twisted Baizhang's nose so hard that he cried out.

Mazu said, "So you say they've flown away!"

Upon hearing these words Baizhang attained enlightenment.

Returning to the attendant's room, Baizhang cried loudly.

One of the other attendants asked Baizhang, "Are you homesick?"

Baizhang said, "No."

The attendant said, "Did someone curse at you?"

Baizhang said, "No."

The attendant said, "Then why are you crying?"

Baizhang said, "Master Ma twisted my nose so hard that the pain was unbearable."

The attendant said, "What did you do that offended him?"

Baizhang said, "You go ask him."

The attendant went to Mazu and said, "What did attendant Hai do to offend you? He's in his room crying. Please tell me."

The Great Teacher said, "He himself knows. Go ask him."

The attendant returned to Baizhang's hut and said to him, "The master says that you already know, so I should come here and ask you."

Thereupon Baizhang laughed out loud.

The attendant said, "A moment ago you were crying, so why are you laughing now?"

Baizhang said, "My crying a moment ago is the same as my laughing now."

The attendant was bewildered by Baizhang's behavior.

The next day Mazu went into the hall to address the monks. Just when the monks had finished assembling, Baizhang rolled up his sitting mat. Mazu got down from his chair and Baizhang followed him to the abbot's room.

Mazu said, "Just now I hadn't said a word. Why did you roll up your sitting mat?"

Baizhang said, "Yesterday the master painfully twisted my nose."

Mazu said, "Is there anything special about yesterday that you've noticed?"

Baizhang said, "Today, my nose doesn't hurt anymore."

Mazu said, "Then you really understand what happened yesterday."

Baizhang then bowed and went out.

———— ◆ ————

On another occasion Baizhang was in attendance to Master Ma. He saw the abbot's whisk sitting on its stand and said, "If someone uses this, can he also not use it?"

Mazu said, "In the future if you travel to some other place, how will you help people?"

Baizhang picked up the whisk and held it upright.

Mazu said, "If you use it this way, what other way can it be used?"

Baizhang placed the whisk back on its stand.

Mazu suddenly let out an earth-shaking shout so loud that Baizhang was deaf for three days.

From this thunderclap came a great vibration. Later, a prominent lay supporter invited Baizhang to come to the Xinwu district of Hongzhou and serve as abbot at a temple on Mt. Daxiong.[54] This was a place of high and precipitous peaks. Thus came the name Baizhang ("Hundred Fathoms").

Before Baizhang had even passed a month at the temple, new students seeking his spiritual guidance came from every quarter. Foremost among them were Huangbo and Guishan.

One day Baizhang said to the congregation, "The Buddhadharma is not a trifling matter. Formerly great Master Ma shouted so loudly that I was deaf for three days."

When Huangbo heard this, he stuck out his tongue.

Baizhang said to him, "In the future, will you carry on Mazu's Dharma?"

Huangbo said, "There's no way I could do so. Today, because of what you've said, I've seen Mazu's great function, but I still haven't glimpsed Mazu. If I carry on Mazu's teaching, then our descendants will be cut off."

Baizhang said, "Just so! Just so! The one who is his teacher's equal has diminished his teacher by half. Only a student who surpasses his teacher can transmit his teacher's teaching. So how does the student surpass the teacher?"

Huangbo then bowed.

Baizhang resided and taught as abbot on Daxiong ("Great Hero") Mountain, which was also known as Mt. Bai Zhang, in what is now Fengxin County in Jiangxi Province.

Besides being a Zen master of the first order, Baizhang established the monastic rules of Zen monasteries, partly on the model of the Fourth Ancestor, Dayi Daoxin. Previous to Baizhang's times, many Zen monks followed the Buddhist tradition of begging for support from the community. Influenced by Baizhang's instructions, Zen temples evolved to be more self-supporting and independent. Zen communities upheld Baizhang's famous dictum, "A day without work is a day without eating."

A monk asked, "How can a person gain freedom?"

Baizhang said, "If you attain it at this moment then you've attained it. If you can instantly cut off the emotions of the self, the five desires and winds of attachment, the greed and covetousness, the pollution and purity, that is to say, all delusive thoughts, then you'll be like the sun and the moon hanging in space, purely shining—the mind like wood and stone; thoughts spared from worldly entrapments; like a great elephant crossing a river, engulfed in the rapids but taking no missteps. Heaven and hell can't pull in such a person. When that person reads a sutra or observes a teaching, the words return to the person. The person knows that all teachings with words are only a reflection of the immediacy of self-nature and are just meant to guide you. Such teachings don't penetrate the revolving realms of existence and nonexistence. Only Diamond-Wisdom penetrates the revolving realms of existence and nonexistence, and thus constitutes complete, independent freedom.

"If you don't understand in this manner and just go on chanting the Vedic scriptures, then you're just making matters worse, and moreover you're slandering Buddha.[55] This is not practice.

"But to be separate from all sound and form, though not abiding in the separateness, and not abiding in intellectual comprehension, this is the true practice of reading sutras and observing the teachings. One who lets the world be as it is, always acting in countless situations with clear rectitude, this is one who has truly cut off the passions."

◆

Every day when Zen master Baizhang spoke in the hall, there was an old man who would attend along with the assembly. One day when the congregation had departed, the old man remained.

Baizhang asked him, "Who are you?"

The old man said, "I'm not a person. Formerly, during the age of Kasyapa Buddha, I was the abbot of a monastery on this mountain. At that time a student asked me, 'Does a great adept fall into cause and effect or not?' I answered, saying, 'A great adept does not fall into cause and effect.' Thereafter, for five hundred lifetimes I've been reborn in the body of a fox. Now I ask that the master say a turning phrase in my behalf, so that I can shed the fox's body."

Baizhang said, "Ask the question."

The old man said, "Does a great adept fall into cause and effect or not?"

Baizhang said, "A great adept is not blind to cause and effect."

Upon hearing these words, the old man experienced unsurpassed enlightenment. He then said, "Now I have shed the body of a fox. I lived behind the mountain. Please provide funeral services for a monk who has died."

Baizhang then instructed the temple director to tell the monks to assemble after the next meal for funeral services. The monks were all mystified by this, because there was no one who was ill in the temple infirmary, so how could this be? After the meal, Baizhang instructed the monks to assemble beneath a grotto behind the mountain. He then brought out the body of a dead fox on his staff, and proceeded to cremate it according to established ritual. That evening Baizhang entered the hall to speak, and brought up for discussion what had transpired.

Huangbo asked, "When this ancient spoke a single phrase incorrectly, he fell into rebirth for five hundred lifetimes in the body of a fox. Originally, had he answered correctly, what would have happened?"

Baizhang said, "Come here and I'll tell you."

Huangbo came forward and then hit Baizhang.

Baizhang laughed and clapped his hands, saying, "It's said that the barbarian's beard is red. But there's yet another red-bearded barbarian!" ([Later,] Guishan brought this case up to Yangshan. Yangshan said, "Huangbo always had this ability." Guishan said, "Do you say he had it naturally, or did he get it from other people?" Yangshan said, "Some of it he got from his teacher, and some of it was his own ability." Guishan said, "Just so. Just so." Once, when Guishan was acting as head cook at Baizhang's temple, the mendicant Sima asked him concerning this affair, saying, "What was it about?" Guishan shook the door screen three times. Sima said, "Too crude." Guishan said, "That isn't the meaning of the Buddhadharma.")

Baizhang said, "I want someone to go and tell something to Xitang [Zen master Xitang Zhizang]."

Wufeng said, "I'll go."

Baizhang said, "How will you speak to him?"

Wufeng said, "I'll wait until I see Xitang, then I'll speak."

Baizhang said, "What will you say?"

Wufeng said, "When I come back, I'll tell you."

Zen master Baizhang entered the hall to give a lecture. When the monks had assembled, he suddenly leaped off of the Dharma seat and drove them from the hall with his staff. Just as they were running out of the hall, he called to them. When they turned around he said, "What is it?"[56]

In the everyday work of the monastery, Baizhang always was foremost among the assembly at undertaking the tasks of the day. The monks in charge of the work were concerned about the master. They hid his tools and asked him to rest.

Baizhang said, "I'm unworthy. How can I allow others to work in my behalf?"

He looked everywhere for his tools but was unable to find them. He even forgot to eat [while looking for his tools], and thus the phrase "a day without working is a day without eating" has become known everywhere.

The master died on the seventeenth day of the first month in [the year 814]. He received the posthumous name "Zen Master Great Wisdom." His stupa was named "Great Treasure Victorious Wheel."

XITANG ZHIZANG

XITANG ZHIZANG (735–814) was a student of Mazu Daoyi. He came from Qianhua City in ancient Qian Province.[57] When young, he had an unusually noble appearance. People said that he would likely be an "assistant to the Dharma King" (a servant of Buddha). After receiving ordination at the age of twenty-five, he went traveling, and finally came to study under Mazu Daoyi. A fellow student of Baizhang, they together received Dharma transmission from master Ma.

Among Zhizang's numerous disciples were the Korean monks Jilin Daoyi and Hongshe. These two adepts transmitted Zen to their native country. There, they helped to establish the "Nine Mountains," nine prominent schools of Korean Zen.

One day Mazu dispatched Zhizang to Changan to deliver a letter to the National Teacher [Nanyang Huizhong].

The National Teacher asked him, "What Dharma does your teacher convey to people?"

Zhizang walked from the east side to the west side and stood there.

The National Teacher said, "Is that all?"

Zhizang then walked from the west side to the east side.

The National Teacher said, "This is Mazu's way. What do you do?"

Zhizang said, "I showed it to you already."

———— ◆ ————

One day Mazu asked Zhizang, "Why don't you read sutras?"

Zhizang said, "Aren't they all the same?"

Mazu said, "Although that's true, still you should do so for the sake of people [you will teach] later on."

Zhizang said, "I think Zhizang must cure his own illness. Then he can talk to others."

Mazu said, "Late in your life, you'll be known throughout the world."

Zhizang bowed.

The magistrate Lu Sigong invited Mazu to come to his prefecture for a length of time and convey the teaching. At that time, Zhizang, receiving from Mazu his hundred-sectioned robe, returned to his home province and began receiving students.

A monk asked Zen master Zhizang, "There are questions and there are answers. There is distinguishing guest and host. What about when there are no questions or answers?"

Zhizang said, "I fear it's rotted away!"

After Zhizang became abbot of the Western Hall [in Chinese, Xitang], a lay person asked him, "Is there a heaven and hell?"

Zhizang said, "There is."

The layman then asked, "Is there really a Buddha, Dharma, and Sangha—the three jewels?"

Zhizang said, "There are."

The layman then asked several other questions, and to each Zhizang answered, "There are."

The layman said, "Is the master sure there's no mistake about this?"

Zhizang said, "When you visited other teachers, what did they say?"

The layman said, "I once visited Master Jingshan."

Zhizang said, "What did Jingshan say to you?"

The layman said, "He said that there wasn't a single thing."

Zhizang said, "Do you have a wife and children?"

The layman said, "Yes."

Zhizang said, "Does Master Jingshan have a wife and children?"

The layman said, "No."

Zhizang said, "Then it's okay for Jingshan to say there isn't a single thing."

The layman bowed, thanked Zhizang, and then went away.[58]

Zen master Zhizang died on the eighth day of the fourth month in [the year 814]. The emperor Xuan Zong gave him the posthumous name "Zen Master Great Expounder of the Teaching." The emperor Mu Zong renamed him "Zen Master Great Awakening."

ZHANGJING HUAIYUN

ZHANGJING HUAIYUN (756–815) was a disciple of Mazu. He came from Quanzhou (near modern Fuzhou in Fujian Province). He began study under Mazu and later became his Dharma heir. Thereafter he lived at a succession of mountains and temples. In 808, at the emperor's behest, he took up residence at Zhangjing Temple in Changan, the capital city.

Zen master Zhangjing Huaiyun entered the hall and addressed the congregation, saying, "The true way is not reached without abandoning words. These days, people don't understand this. They diligently study useless things and regard such activity as meritorious. They don't realize that self-nature is fundamentally unblemished. It is a sublime gate of liberation. The mirror of awakening is neither tainted nor pure, but is like a brilliant light, unceasing and undiminished. Through bygone eons down to the present time it is unchanged. It is like the sun, shining near or far, and though appearing in countless shades and forms, it remains apart from conditioned existence. The spiritual light is ethereal and luminous, without need of refinement, existing without explanation, and beyond objects or form.

"But people press on their eyeballs and conjure up fantastic empty illusions, belaboring themselves for numerous eons. If only they would shine the light inward, where there is no 'other' person, cease all activity, and not forsake true emptiness."

———— ◆ ————

A monk asked Zen master Zhangjing Huaiyun, "Please point out the place where mind and Dharma are both gone."

Zhangjing said, "People of Ying don't perspire. You belabor yourself carrying an ax."

The monk said, "Please, Master, don't speak contrarily."

Zhangjing said, "This is not a contrary phrase." ([Later,] the same monk brought up this conversation to Dongshan. Dongshan said, "What speech that was. Seldom does one encounter such an adept!")

———— ◆ ————

As Huaiyun was meditating, Mayu walked up to him carrying his staff, circled his meditation platform three times, shook the staff and then stood still.

Zhangjing said, "Correct, correct."

Mayu then went to Nanquan and circled his seat three times, shook his staff and stood quietly.

Nanquan said, "Wrong, wrong." [Xuedou appended a word here, saying "Wrong."]

Mayu afterward asked Nanquan, "Zhangjing said 'correct.' Why did you say 'wrong'?"

Nanquan replied, "Zhangjing was correct, you are wrong. This is turned on the power of the wind. Finally it turns bad."

———— ◆ ————

A monk asked, "Regarding the mind-ground teaching that has been passed down from the ancestral teachers—is the mind they speak of the true mind, the deluded mind, or neither the true nor the deluded mind? And is it the mind that stands outside the teaching of the Three Vehicles?"[59]

Zhangjing said, "Do you see the emptiness before the eyes?"

The person said, "I believe that knowledge is always before the eyes. People don't see this for themselves."

Zhangjing said, "Don't you see form?"

The person said, "What is your meaning, Master?"

Zhangjing raised his hand and poked the air three times, saying, "What am I doing when I do this?" Then he said, "You'll understand in the future."

.... ◆ ....

A young adept returned from a pilgrimage. Zhangjing asked him, "How long ago did you leave here?"

The monk said, "I left you about eight years ago."

Zhangjing said, "What have you been doing?"

The monk drew a circle on the ground.

Zhangjing said, "Just this? Nothing else?"

The monk then erased the circle and bowed.

Zhangjing said, "No! No!"

.... ◆ ....

Zen master Zhangjing Huaiyun died in [the year 815]. He received the posthumous name "Zen Master Great Awakening."

YANGUAN QI'AN

YANGUAN QI'AN (750–842) was yet another illustrious disciple of Mazu. He came from ancient Haimen prefecture.[60] As a young novice he became accomplished in the teaching of the Vinaya and received ordination on Mt. Heng under the Vinaya master, Zhiyan. Later he moved to Mt. Gonggong, where he first heard Mazu. It is recorded that Yanguan had an unusual appearance, and Mazu, upon seeing him, recognized him as a "great vessel."

After Mazu's death, Yanguan lived at various locales. In the year 820, he assumed the abbacy of Fayao Temple in Yuezhou.

A monk asked Zen master Yanguan Qi'an, "What is the true body of Vairochana Buddha?"

Yanguan said, "Bring me that pitcher of pure water."

The monk brought Yanguan the pitcher.

Yanguan then said, "Now put it back where it was before."

The monk returned the bottle to its former position. Then he asked his previous question again.

Yanguan said, "The ancient buddhas are long gone."

❖

A scholar monk came to visit Zen master Yanguan.

Yanguan asked him, "What do you do?"

The monk said, "I expound the *Flower Garland Sutra*."

Yanguan said, "How many different Dharma realms are there?"

The monk said, "Broadly speaking, there are limitless Dharma realms. But they can be reduced to four types."

Yanguan held his whisk upright and said, "What type of Dharma realm is this?"

The monk sank into reflection.

Yanguan said, "Knowing by thinking, resolving through consideration, these are the strategies of a devil house. A single lamp—when it's put beneath the sun, it really isn't bright." (When Baofu Congzhan heard about this, he said, "If he bows, he'll taste the master's stick." Shushan Kuangren said, "I'm not troubled by this. The master can't be faulted." Fayan, when hearing this, clapped his hands three times.)

❖

Yanguan was told the story of how a monk asked the teacher Damei, "What is the essential meaning of Buddhism?" Damei answered, "There is no essential meaning."

Upon hearing this Yanguan said, "It's one coffin with two corpses." (Xuansha said, "Yanguan was great.")

Yanguan is remembered for a famous exchange with his attendant that is told in case twenty-five of the *Book of Serenity*. The scene is also recorded in the lamp records.

Yanguan called to his attendant, saying "Bring me the rhinoceros fan."
The attendant said, "It's broken."
Yanguan said, "If the fan is broken, then bring me the rhinoceros."
The attendant didn't answer. ([Later,] Touzi answered on behalf of the attendant, saying, "I don't refuse to bring the rhinoceros, but I'm afraid he doesn't have all his horns." Zifu Rubao, answering for the attendant, drew a circle and then wrote the word "ox" in the middle of it. Shishuang answered for the attendant, saying, "If I give it to the master it will be gone." Baoshou Yanzhao said, "The master is of a venerable age. It's proper for him to call on others.")

❖

Master Yanguan said to the congregation, "Vast empty space is the drum. Mt. Sumeru is the mallet. Who can play this drum?"

No one in the congregation spoke. (Someone told this story to Nanquan Puyuan. He said, "Old Teacher Wang doesn't play this broken drum." Later, Fayan said, "Old Teacher Wang (Nanquan) doesn't beat it.")

❖

A Zen master named Fakong came to visit Yanguan and inquired about some ideas expressed in the Buddhist sutras. Yanguan answered each question in turn. When they had finished, Yanguan said, "Since the master arrived here, I haven't been able to play the host."

Fakong said, "I invite the master to take the role of host."

Yanguan said, "It's late today, so let's go back to our quarters and take a rest. Tomorrow come here again."

Fakong then went back to his room.

The next morning, Yanguan sent a novice monk to invite Fakong for another meeting.

When Fakong arrived, Yanguan looked at the novice monk and said, "Aiee!

This novice can't do anything! I told him to go get Zen master Fakong. Instead he went and got this temple maintenance man!"

Fakong was speechless.

---------------- ◆ ----------------

[When Yanguan was ill] the temple director, named Faxin, came to see him. Yanguan said, "Who are you?"

The temple director said, "Faxin."

Yanguan said, "I don't know you."

Later, the master's condition improved, but he suddenly died at a banquet. He received the posthumous name "Zen Master Enlightened Emptiness."

DAMEI FACHANG

DAMEI FACHANG (752–839) was a disciple of Mazu. He came from Xiangyang (now the city of Xiangfan in northern Hubei Province.) His lay surname was Zheng. As a youth he is reported to have left home to live at Yuquan Temple in ancient Xingzhou.[61] As a young man he was extremely well versed in the Buddhist sutras, and possessed the ability to memorize long scriptural passages with one reading. At the age of twenty he received ordination at Longxing Temple.[62] Determined to study Zen, Fachang traveled to study under the great Zen master Mazu Daoyi.

Upon first meeting the great teacher Mazu, Damei asked him, "What is Buddha?"

Mazu said, "Mind is Buddha."

Upon hearing these words, Damei experienced great enlightenment. He soon moved to Mt. Da Mei ["Big Plum"], where he built a cottage and lived in seclusion.

During the Zheng He era [785–820], a monk in Zen master Yanguan Qi'an's congregation was collecting wood for making monks' staffs when he became lost.

Coming upon Zen master Damei Fachang's cottage, he asked, "Master, how long have you been living here?"

Damei said, "I've seen the mountain's green change to brown four times."

The monk then asked, "Where's the road down off of the mountain?"

Damei said, "Follow the flow of the water."

The monk returned to Yanguan and told him about the monk he'd met.

Yanguan said, "When I was at Jiangxi [studying with Mazu] I saw such a monk there. I haven't heard any news about him since then. I don't know if it's him or not."

Yanguan then sent a monk to invite Damei to come for a visit.

Damei responded to the invitation with a poem that said:

A damaged tree stump slumps in the forest.
Mind unchanged as springtimes pass.
A woodcutter passes but still doesn't see it.
Why do you seek trouble by pursuing it?
Limitless lotus leaves on the pool serve as my clothing.
An abundance of pine cones remains for food.
Now people from the world have learned of my home,
So I'll move my hut to a more secluded spot.

When Mazu heard that Damei lived on the mountain, he sent a monk to call upon him and ask the question, "When you saw Master Mazu, what did he say that caused you to come live on this mountain?"

Damei said, "Master Mazu said to me, 'Mind is Buddha.' Then I came here to live."

The monk said, "These days Master Ma's teaching has changed."

Damei said, "What is it?"

The monk said, "Now he says, 'No mind. No Buddha.'"

Damei said, "That old fellow just goes on and on, confusing people. Let him go ahead and say, 'No mind. No Buddha.' As for me, I still say 'Mind is Buddha.'"

The monk returned and reported this to Master Mazu.

Mazu said, "The plum is ripe."

Soon afterward, Damei's reputation spread widely and students traveled into the mountains to receive his instruction.

Zen master Damei Fachang entered the hall and addressed the monks, saying, "All of you must reverse your mind and arrive at its root. Don't pursue its branches! Attaining its source, its end will also be reached. If you want to know the source, then just know your own mind. The source of mind is the entire world. The myriad dharmas are the source of mind. When the mind manifests, the innumerable dharmas are thus manifested. And when the mind passes away, the myriad dharmas pass away. Mind does not, however, dependently arise according to conditions of good and evil. The myriad dharmas arise in their own thusness."

———— ✦ ————

As the monks Jiashan and Dingshan were traveling together they had a discussion.

Dingshan said, "When there is no Buddha within life and death, then there is no life and death."

Jiashan said, "When Buddha is within life and death, there is no confusion about life and death."

The two monks couldn't reach any agreement, so they climbed the mountain to see Damei Fachang.

Jiashan raised their question with Damei and asked, "We'd like to know which viewpoint is most intimate?"

Damei said, "Go now. Come back tomorrow."

The next day Jiashan again came to Damei and raised the question of the previous day.

Damei said, "The one who's intimate doesn't ask. The one who asks isn't intimate." (Years later, when Jiashan was abbot, he said, "At that time I lost my eye.")

———— ✦ ————

One day, Damei suddenly said to his disciples, "When it comes it can't be held back. When it goes it can't be pursued."

When Damei paused, the monks heard the sound of a squirrel.

Damei said, "It's just this thing! Not some other thing! Each of you! Uphold and sustain it well. Now I pass away."

Upon saying these words, Damei left the world.

([Later,] the eminent teacher Yongming Yanshou praised Damei, saying, "When Damei first attained the Way, he said, 'Mind is Buddha.' At the very end he taught the monks, 'It's just this, not something else.' The source of the myriad dharmas penetrates the thousand saints' bones. Truth, though transformed, is unmoving. How would one halt its coming forth and passing away?")

GUIZONG ZHICHANG

GUIZONG ZHICHANG (n.d.) was a disciple of Mazu. He came from ancient Jiangling (located in modern Hubei Province). Almost nothing is recorded of Guizong's early life, nor are the dates of his birth and death known. After leaving Mazu, he lived near Mt. Lu at Guizong Temple.[63] During his lifetime he gained considerable fame as an expounder of Zen. When the famous Tang dynasty poet and statesman Bai Zhuyi served as the magistrate of Jiangzhou, he often visited and paid his respects to Guizong.

Master Zhichang of Guizong Temple of Mt. Lu entered the hall and addressed the monks, saying, "The virtuous of former times were not without knowledge and understanding. Those great adepts were not of the common stream. People these days are unable to be self-empowered, nor can they stand alone. They just idly pass the time. All of you here, don't make the error of employing your mind. No one can do it for you. Moreover, there is no 'place' where the mind can be used. Don't be seeking it somewhere else. Up to now you have been acting in accordance with someone else's understanding. Your own speech is completely obstructed. The light does not shine through. There are obstructions blocking your vision."

◆

A monk asked Zen master Guizong, "What is the essential mystery?"

Guizong said, "No one can understand it."

The monk said, "How about those who seek it?"

Guizong said, "Those who seek it miss it completely."

The monk said, "How about those who don't seek it?"

Guizong said, "Go! There's no place for you to use your mind."

The monk said, "Then, is there no expedient gate through which you can help me to enter?"

Guizong said, "Kwan Yin's sublime wisdom can save the world from suffering."

The monk said, "What is Kwan Yin's sublime wisdom?"[64]

The master struck the top of the incense urn three times with his staff and said, "Did you hear that or not?"

The monk said, "I heard it."

Guizong said, "Why didn't I hear it?"

The monk was silent.

The master then took his staff and got down from the seat.

An unusual story about Guizong is entitled "The Causation of Guizong Chopping the Snake."

One day a scriptural monk came to visit Guizong as he was weeding the garden with a hoe.[65] Suddenly, a snake appeared. Guizong took the hoe and chopped it in two.

The monk said, "Long have I heard that Guizong was a crude-mannered teacher."

Guizong said, "Are you crude or am I crude?"

The monk then asked, "What is 'crude'?"

Guizong held the hoe upright in the air.

The monk said, "What is 'refined'?"

Guizong then assumed a posture to chop the snake.

The monk said, "If you let it, it will go away by itself."

Guizong said, "If I let it go away, how could you see me chop the snake?"

The monk was speechless.

———— ❖ ————

Yunyan came to visit. Guizong assumed a pose of drawing a bow at him. After a long pause, Yunyan assumed a pose of drawing a sword.

Guizong said, "You're too late!"

·············· ❖ ··············

Guizong entered the hall and addressed the monks, saying, "I want to speak about Zen. All of you, gather around."

The monks gathered closely around Guizong.

Guizong said, "Listen to Bodhisattva Kwan Yin's practice. Its goodness extends everywhere."

Someone asked, "What is Kwan Yin's practice?"

Guizong pointed with his finger and said, "Do you still hear it?"

The monks said, "We hear it."

Guizong said, "What is this pack of fools looking for?"

He took his staff and chased the monks out of the hall. With a big laugh he went back to the abbot's quarters.

·············· ❖ ··············

A monk was leaving the monastery.

Guizong asked him, "Where are you going?"

The monk said, "I'm going everywhere to study the five flavors of Zen."

Guizong said, "Everywhere else has five Zen flavors. Here I only have one-flavored Zen."

The monk said, "What is one-flavored Zen?"

Guizong hit him.

The monk said, "I understand! I understand!"

Guizong said, "Speak! Speak!"

The monk hesitated.

Guizong hit him again.

The monk later went to Huangbo and told him about this previous exchange with Guizong.

Huangbo entered the hall and addressed the monks, saying, "Great Teacher Ma brought forth eighty-four people. But if some worthy asks them a question every one of them just wets his pants. Only Guizong is up to snuff!"

———— ◆ ————

Governor Libo of Jiangzhou said to Guizong, "In the scripture it says that a mustard seed fits inside Mt. Sumeru. This I don't doubt. But it also says that Mt. Sumeru fits inside a mustard seed. I'm afraid this is just foolish talk."

Guizong said, "I've heard that Your Excellency has read thousands of scriptures. Is this so or not?"

The governor said, "Yes, it is true."

Guizong said, "From top to bottom your head is about the size of a coconut. Where did all those scriptures go?"

The governor could only bow his head in deference.

On another occasion the governor asked Guizong, "What can someone learn from the great scriptural canon?"

Guizong raised his fist into the air and said, "Do you understand?"

Governor Libo said, "I don't understand."

Guizong said, "There's still a big gap in your understanding! You don't even understand a fist!"

The governor said, "Please, Master, explain it to me."

Guizong said, "If you meet someone on the path, then give it to him. If you don't meet anyone, then just disseminate the world's truth."

———— ◆ ————

Zen master Guizong suffered from cataracts, and he applied a medicine to his eyes that caused them to turn red. Thereafter people called him "Red-eyed Guizong." Later he passed away. He received the posthumous name "Zen Master Arrive at Truth."

Layman Pang, "Pangyun"

Layman Pang (740–808) was the most famous lay Zen Buddhist in Chinese Zen history. He came from Hengyang (in southern Hunan Province). Pangyun studied and gained realization under both of the great teachers of his era, Shitou and Mazu. Pangyun's wife and daughter were also Zen adepts, and stories about this entire lay household's attainment of the Way are unique in the lamp records.

Layman Pang's friends included the famous nonconformist Zen adept, Danxia Tianran. He also was well acquainted with other celebrated Zennists of the era, such as Yaoshan, Luopu, and Yangshan.

In 785, Pangyun began study under Shitou Xiqian. He soon attained a breakthrough recognized by his teacher.

[In the year 785] Pangyun met Zen master Shitou.

He asked him, "Who is the one who is not a companion to the ten thousand dharmas?"

Shitou quickly covered Pangyun's mouth with his hand.

Pangyun suddenly had a realization.

⸭

One day, Shitou asked, "What have you been doing each day since we last saw each other?"

Pangyun said, "If you ask about daily affairs, then nothing can be said."

(Pangyun then recited the verse whose last two lines are widely quoted:)

How miraculous and wondrous,
Hauling water and carrying firewood.

Later, upon meeting Mazu, Pangyun penetrated deeper into the Way.

Layman Pang asked Mazu, "Who is the one who is not a companion to the ten thousand dharmas?"

Mazu said, "When you swallow all of the water in the West River in one gulp, then I'll tell you"

Hearing these words, Layman Pang fully realized the mystery. He then stayed and practiced under Mazu for two years. Pangyun wrote a verse that said:

A man unmarried,
A woman unbetrothed,
Happily they are brought together,
They both speak without saying words.

---◆---

Layman Pang attended a reading of the *Diamond Sutra*. When the speaker reached the phrase, "No self. No other," Layman Pang called out, "Speaker! If there is no self and no other, then who is lecturing and who's listening to it?"

The speaker was dumbstruck.

Layman Pang said, "I'm just a common person, but I'll offer you my crude understanding."

The speaker said, "What is the layman's idea?"

Pangyun answered with this verse:

No self, no other,
Then how could there be intimate and estranged?
I advise you to cease all your lectures.
They can't compare with directly seeking truth.
The Diamond Wisdom nature
Erases even a speck of dust.
"Thus I have heard," and "Thus I believe,"
Are but so many words.

---◆---

Once, Layman Pang asked his daughter, Ling Zhao, "Some ancient said, 'Clear and brilliant are the meadow grasses. Clear and brilliant is the meaning of the ancestral teachers.' How do you understand this?"

Ling Zhao said, "So old and great, and yet you talk like this!"

Layman Pang said, "What would you say?"

Ling Zhao said, "Clear and brilliant are the meadow grasses, clear and brilliant is the meaning of the ancestral teachers."

Layman Pang laughed.

When Pangyun and his family attained the Way, they are said to have taken all their possessions, put them in a boat, and sunk them in a river.

Layman Pang was leaving Yaoshan, so Yaoshan had ten "Zen guests" accompany Pang to the main gate.[66]

The layman pointed to the falling snow and said, "Good snowflakes. Each one not falling any other place."

At that time, a Zen monk named Chuan asked, "Where do they fall?"

The layman struck him.

Chuan said, "Even a layman should not act so rudely."

Pangyun said, "A so-called 'Zen guest' saying such a thing! Yama [the king of hell] will never release you!"

Chuan said, "What do you mean?"

Pangyun hit him again, saying, "You have eyes like a blind man and your mouth speaks like a mute."

[Later] Xuedou said, "When he asked the first question I would have made a snowball and hit him with it."

◆

When Layman Pang was about to die, he said to his daughter, Ling Zhao, "Go look at the sun and see what time it is. Just when it's noon come and tell me."

Ling Zhao went to the door and looked out, saying, "The sun has just reached noon, but there's an eclipse!"

When Layman Pang went to the door and looked out, Ling Zhao went to her father's seat, placed her hands together, and passed away.

Layman Pang smiled and said, "My daughter's deftness!"

He then postponed his departure from the world by seven days.

The governor of Xiangzhou came to visit Pangyun and ask about his illness.

Layman Pang said to him, "I ask that you regard everything that is as empty, nor give substance to that which has none. Farewell. The world is like reflections and echoes."

Then, placing his head on the governor's knee, Layman Pang passed away. His cremated remains were cast upon rivers and lakes. Monks and laity mourned him, saying that he was actually Vimalakirti. Three hundred of Layman Pang's poems were left to spread through the world.

MAYU BAOCHE

MAYU BAOCHE (n.d.) of Puzhou was a famous disciple of Mazu. There is no record of his home province, his surname, or the exact dates of his birth and death. He was a close friend of the famous Zen adept Danxia Tianran. The lamp records provide the following account of Baoche's enlightenment:

> Once, while walking with Mazu, Mayu asked, "What is the great nirvana?"
> Mazu replied, "Hurried."
> Mayu asked, "What is it that's hurried?"
> Mazu said, "See the water!"
> At these words Mayu was awakened.

———— ◆ ————

> Zen master Mayu Baoche was using a fan.
> A monk asked, "The nature of the wind is eternal and there is no place where it doesn't reach. So why does the master use a fan?"
> Baoche said, "You know that the nature of wind is eternal, but you don't know that there's no place it doesn't reach."
> The monk said, "What is the principle of 'there is no place *it* doesn't reach'?"
> Baoche fanned himself.
> The monk bowed.
> Mayu said, "Useless teachers and monks! There are a thousand of them. What are they good for?"

··········· ◆ ···········

> Mayu asked a monk, "Where did you come from?"
> The monk didn't understand.
> Mayu asked again, "Where did you come from? Monk! Hey!"
> Mayu got down from his seat and grabbed the monk, saying, "Look here! When I ask you to demonstrate the Buddhadharma, just give me an answer!"
> The monk said, "Like an eyeless teacher."
> Mayu let go of the monk and said, "I'll spare you your life and let you breathe."
> The monk bowed.
> Mayu tried to grab the monk again, but the monk shook his sleeves and left the hall.
> Mayu said, "Don't pick the three-year bamboo. Get the 10,000-year pine!"

Mayu, Nanquan, and another monk went traveling to Mt. Jing. On their way they encountered an old woman shopkeeper.

They asked her, "What's the way to Mt. Jing?"

She said, "Just go straight ahead."

Mayu said, "Is there water ahead that is too deep to pass through?"

The old woman said, "It won't even soak your feet."

Mayu said, "The rice paddy on the upper terrace is good. The rice paddy on the lower terrace is withered."

The old woman said, "It's all been eaten by crabs."

Mayu said, "The grain is fragrant."

The old woman said, "There's no smell."

Mayu also said, "Where do you live?"

The old woman said, "Right here."

The three monks went into the woman's shop. She boiled a pot of tea and set out three cups.

Then she said, "If you masters have a pervasive spiritual knowledge, then drink some tea."

The three monks looked at each other in surprise, and then the old woman said, "Look at this old crone show her pervasive spirit!" She then grabbed the cups, knocked over the tea pot, and went out.

Once, Baoche and Tianran were hiking in the mountains. Baoche pointed at some fish he saw in a stream.

Tianran said, "Natural. Natural."[67]

Baoche waited until the following day, then asked Tianran, "What did you mean yesterday?"

Danxia then lay down in a prone position.

Baoche said, "Blue heavens!"

A monk asked Baoche, "What is the great meaning of the Buddhadharma?"

Baoche was silent.

Later, a monk asked Zen master Shishuang Qingzhu, "What was Zen master Baoche's meaning?"

Shishuang said, "If the host raises his folded hands in respect, it just does harm. Then you go hauling mud and carrying water."

PANSHAN BAOJI

PANSHAN BAOJI (720–814) was a disciple of the great Zen master Mazu Daoyi. His parents' home was in ancient Youzhou (near present day Beijing). One day as he walked in the market, he overheard a customer speaking to a butcher.

The customer said, "Give me a catty of the best quality."

The butcher put down his chopper, folded his hands before himself and said, "Sir, where is there any that is not the best quality?"

Upon hearing these words Panshan had an awakening.

On another day, Panshan witnessed a funeral and heard one of the mourners wail, "The red orb inevitably sinks in the west. Who knows where the soul goes?"

In the funeral tent, the deceased person's son cried out, "Alas! Alas!"

These words reverberated through Panshan. He then returned to tell his experience to Master Mazu, who confirmed his awakening.

———— ✦ ————

After Panshan assumed the position of abbot at a Zen monastery, a monk asked him, "What is the Way?"

The master cried out, "Aaagh!"

The monk said, "This student doesn't understand your meaning."

The master said, "Go!"

.... ✦ ....

Zen master Panshan addressed the congregation, saying, "When there are no affairs in the mind, the myriad things are not born. In the inconceivable mysterious function, where would a speck of dust alight? The Way itself is formless, but because of form, names are established. The Way itself is nameless, but because of names, there is classification.

"If you say, 'Mind is Buddha,' then you still haven't entered the mystery. If you say, 'No mind, no Buddha,' then you're just pointing at the traces of the ultimate. Even a thousand saints can't transmit the higher road to others. You students are tormented by form. You're like apes grabbing at shadows."

.... ✦ ....

Zen master Panshan entered the hall and addressed the monks, saying, "The great way has no center, so how could it have a front or back? Vast space is endless, so why speak of measuring it? Emptiness being thus, how can one speak of the Way?"

Zen master Panshan addressed the monks, saying, "The moon of mind is solitary and perfect, its light swallowing the myriad forms. Its light does not illuminate realms, for realms do not exist. But when light and realms are both gone, what is it that remains?"

Zen master Panshan entered the hall and addressed the monks, saying, "Zen worthies! To successfully practice the Way is like the earth, which while upholding the mountains, is unaware of the solitary peaks. It is like jade that is concealed within stone. The stone is unaware of the jade's flawless nature. Those who practice in this way may be said to have 'left home.' The ancient teachers said, 'The great way is unimpeded and permeates past, present, and future. Persons without activity or worldly affairs—can golden manacles hold them?' Thus, the brilliant single numinous Way is absolutely unborn. Transcendent wisdom is not clear. True emptiness leaves no trace. 'True thusness,' 'mundane,' and 'sacred,' are all just talk within a dream. 'Buddha' and 'nirvana' are just extra words.

"Zen worthies! Directly observe for yourself! No one can do it for you!"

Panshan addressed the monks, saying, "In the three realms there is not a single dharma, so where will you seek mind? The foundation of the four elements is empty, so where does Buddha abide? The firmament is unmoving. It is still and speechless. If you come face to face with it, then there is nothing left to do.

"Take care."

When Panshan Baoji was near death, he said to the monks, "Is there anyone among you who can draw my likeness?"

Many of the monks made drawings for Panshan, but none were to his liking.

The monk Puhua stepped forward and said, "I can draw it."

Panshan said, "Why don't you show it to me?"

Puhua then turned a somersault and went out.

Panshan said, "Someday, that fellow will teach others in a crazy manner!"

Having said these words, Panshan passed away. He received the posthumous name "Great Teacher Crystallized Silence." His pagoda was named "Truth's Limit."

Luzu Baoyun

Zen master Luzu Baoyun (n.d.) of Chizhou[68] was a disciple of Mazu. He did not leave a record of his origins or fate. Nonetheless, he figures prominently in Zen history for his unorthodox teaching style. When students would come to inquire about Zen, he would often turn and silently face the wall. The story "Luzu faces the wall" has been a kōan for generations of Zen students down to the present.

A monk asked Zen master Luzu Baoyun of Chizhou, "Who are all the buddhas and saints?"

Baoyun said, "Not the ones with crowns on their heads."

The monk said, "Then who are they?"

Baoyun said, "The ones without crowns."

⎯⎯⎯⎯ ◆ ⎯⎯⎯⎯

When Dongshan came to pay his respects, he bowed, stood up, and stood there attentively. After a while he went out and then came back in.

Luzu said, "Just so! Just so! So it's like this."

Dongshan said, "There are many who don't approve."

Luzu said, "Why must you speak contentiously?"

Dongshan then bowed.

⎯⎯⎯⎯ ◆ ⎯⎯⎯⎯

A monk asked, "What is speechless speech?"

Zen master Luzu said, "Where is your mouth?"

The monk said, "I have no mouth."

Luzu said, "Then what do you use to eat?"

The monk didn't answer. ([Later,] Dongshan spoke in the monk's behalf, saying, "He wasn't hungry. What rice would he eat?")

⎯⎯⎯⎯ ◆ ⎯⎯⎯⎯

Whenever Zen master Luzu would see a monk coming he would face the wall. (When Nanquan heard about this he said, "I usually say to the monks, 'You must comprehend what is before the Buddha appears in the world.' But until now there hasn't been a single one, or even a half of one, who understands. If he acts like this he'll keep on going right through the year of the ass!" Xuanjue said, "Is Nanquan going along with Luzu or not?" Baofu asked Changqing, "If everyone was like Luzu, then there'd be no records at all! Isn't this what Nanquan was saying?" Changqing said, "Acceding to people in this way! You can't find one in ten thousand like this!" Luoshan said, "If old teacher Chen [Muzhou Daoming] had seen him he would have given him five hot jabs on the back! Why? Because he lets it out but doesn't take it in." Xuansha said, "If I'd been there, I would have given him five hot jabs on the back too!" Yunju Ci said, "Luoshan and Xuansha talking like this—which one is right? If you can sort it out, then I'll agree that your Dharma skills are proficient." Xuanjue said, "But about these five jabs by Xuansha—can they reach Luzu?")

ZHONGYI HONGEN

ZHONGYI HONGEN (n.d.) was a disciple of Mazu. Little information is available about Zhongyi's life. He taught at Zhongyi Temple in Langzhou (now the city of Nanchang in Jiangxi Province). He is honored as one of the foremost of Mazu's spiritual heirs. Whenever Zhongyi saw a monk coming, he would tap his own mouth with his hand, making a "woo, woo" sound.

The *Wudeng Huiyuan* tells of a meeting between Zhongyi and his student Yangshan shortly after Yangshan received the precepts.

> Yangshan came to the hall to thank Zhongyi [for conferring the precepts upon him]. As Zhongyi sat on the meditation platform, he patted his mouth, making a "woo, woo" sound. Yangshan walked to the east end of the hall and stood there. Then he went to the west end of the hall and stood there. Then Yangshan went to the center of the hall and stood. He then bowed to Zhongyi for having received the precepts. Afterward, he stepped back and stood there.
>
> Zhongyi said, "Where did you receive this samadhi?"
>
> Yangshan said, "I learned it from Tuo Yinzi of Cao Xi."
>
> Zhongyi said, "Are you saying that Caoxi used this samadhi to greet people?"
>
> Yangshan said, "When he received the 'Overnight Guest,' he used this samadhi. Master, where did you learn your samadhi?"
>
> Zhongyi said, "I learned this samadhi at Great Teacher Ma's."
>
> Yangshan said, "How do you see buddha nature?"
>
> Zhongyi said, "Well, let's say there was a room with six windows. Inside the room is a monkey. From the east side another monkey screeches through the window, 'eeeh, eeeh!' The monkey inside then responds, 'eeeh, eeeh!' The monkey outside screeches into each of the six windows and the monkey inside responds each time."
>
> Yangshan bowed and then said, "I understand everything in the metaphor

you've presented, but there's one more thing. What if the monkey inside is asleep and the monkey outside wants it to look at him? Then what?"

Zhongyi got off the platform, grabbed Yangshan's hands, and did a dance, exclaiming, "Eeeh! Eeeh! We see each other! It's like hearing a tiny mite that has a nest in the eyelash of a mosquito calling out in the middle of a busy intersection! In the wasteland people are sparse. You see few of them!" ([Later,] Yunju Ci said, "At that time if Zhongyi had not heard Yangshan's speech, then where would he be?" Chongshou Zhou said, "Are there still people who can confirm what was said? If they can't, then they are just animated ghosts. Where is the essential buddha nature?" Xuansha said, "If not Yangshan, then can Zhongyi be seen? What is the place where Yangshan can see Zhongyi?")

WUJIU YOUXUAN

WUJIU YOUXUAN (n.d.) was a disciple of Mazu. His life is obscure. Wujiu's harsh teaching method, incorporating beatings, provides evidence of the fierce and aggressive style of teaching that Mazu passed to his disciples.

> The monks Xuan and Shao came to practice with Zen master Wujiu.
> The master asked them, "Where have you two Zen guests come from?"
> Xuan said, "Jiangxi."
> Wujiu hit him.
> Xuan said, "Long have I heard of the master's great function."
> Wujiu said, "Since you don't understand, let's see how that monk behind you can do."
> Shao started to come forward when Wujiu suddenly hit him also, saying, "I don't believe that one hole has two kinds of dirt. Go to the monks' hall!"

> Zen master Wujiu asked a monk, "Where have you come from?"
> The monk said, "From Ding Province."
> Wujiu said, "How does the Zen school of Ding Province compare with here?"
> The monk said, "It's the same."
> Wujiu said, "If it's the same then turn around and go back there!"
> Wujiu then hit the monk.
> The monk said, "If the staff has eyes it does not recklessly hit people."
> Wujiu said, "I hit one today."

He then hit the monk three times. The monk then began walking out of the room.

Wujiu said, "People have always received unjust beatings."

The monk stopped and said, "Why is it that the handle is always in the Master's hand?"

Wujiu said, "If you want, this mountain monk will give it to you."

The monk came forward and grabbed the staff, then hit Wujiu three times.

Wujiu said, "No fair! No fair!"

The monk said, "Someone's getting it!"

Wujiu said, "You're recklessly beating someone."

The monk bowed.

Wujiu said, "Give it back."

The monk laughed and went out.

Wujiu said, "Disappearing like this! Disappearing like this!"

NANQUAN PUYUAN, "OLD TEACHER WANG"

NANQUAN PUYUAN (748–835) was a disciple of Mazu Daoyi and the teacher of famous Zhaozhou (in Japanese, Jōshū). His lay surname was Wang, and he came from Xinzheng in Zheng Province.[69] Even before he became an old Zen teacher his students referred to him as "Old Teacher Wang."[70] Before meeting Mazu, he was already widely versed in the various schools and scriptures of Mahayana Buddhism. At their first meeting, he is said to have "instantly forgot the net of delusions and delighted in samadhi."

An incident revealing Nanquan's fully realized Zen independence is found in the lamp records.

> One day, Master Mazu was serving rice gruel to the monks from a bucket. As he gave out portions he asked, "What's in the bucket?"
>
> When Nanquan was so queried he said, "The old monk should close his mouth and say this!"

After gaining transmission from Mazu, Nanquan built a solitary hut on Mt. Nanquan in Chizhou and remained there for more than thirty years practicing Zen. A high-ranking official named Lu Geng invited Nanquan to descend from the mountain and honored him by becoming his student. Due to this event,

Nanquan's reputation spread widely and students numbering in the hundreds came to study under him.

Zen master Nanquan Puyuan entered the hall and addressed the monks, saying, "Dipamkara Buddha said, 'The arising in mind of a single thought gives birth to the myriad things.'[71]

"Why is it that phenomenal existence is empty? If there is nothing within mind, then how does one explain how the myriad things arise? Isn't it as if shadowy forms differentiate emptiness? This question is like someone grasping sound and placing it in a box, or blowing into a net to fill it with air. Therefore some old worthy said, 'It's not mind. It's not Buddha. It's not a thing.' Thus we just teach you brethren to go on a journey.

"It's said that bodhisattvas who have passed through the ten stages of development and attained the Surangama Samadhi and the profound Dharma storehouse of all buddhas naturally realize the pervasive wondrous liberation of Zen samadhi. Throughout all worlds the form-body is revealed, and the highest awakening is manifested. The great Wheel of Dharma is turned, nirvana is entered, and limitless space can be placed in the hole on the point of a feather.

"Although a single phrase of scripture is recited for endless eons, its meaning is never exhausted. It's teaching transports countless billions of beings to the attainment of the unborn and enduring Dharma. And that which is called knowledge or ignorance, even in the very smallest amount, is completely contrary to the Way. So difficult! So difficult!

"Take care!"

❖

Once, Zen master Nanquan said, "Master Mazu of Jiangxi said, 'Mind is Buddha.' But old teacher Wang doesn't talk that way. It's not mind, it's not Buddha, it's not a thing. Is there any error in speaking thus?"

Zhaozhou then bowed and went out.

❖

The monks of the eastern and western halls were arguing about a cat. Nanquan picked it up and said to the monks, "Say the appropriate word and you'll save the cat. If you don't say the appropriate word then it gets cut in two!"

The monks were silent. Nanquan cut the cat in two.

Later, Zhaozhou returned from outside the temple and Nanquan told him what had happened. Zhaozhou then removed his sandals, placed them on his head, and went out.

Nanquan said, "If you had been there, the cat would have been saved."

———— ◆ ————

When Zen master Nanquan Puyuan ascended the Dharma seat in the hall, the official Lu Geng said, "We invite the Master to expound the Dharma for the sake of beings."

Master Nanquan said, "What would you have me say?"

Lu Geng said, "Can the Master offer no expedient method to enter the Way?"

The master said, "What do you say is lacking?"

Lu Geng said, "Why are there six realms and four modes of birth?"[72]

Nanquan said, "I don't teach that."

———— ◆ ————

When the official Lu Geng took his leave from Nanquan to return to his duties as magistrate of Xuancheng City, Nanquan asked him, "When Your Eminence returns to Xuancheng, how will you govern the people there?"

Lu Geng answered, "I will use wisdom to govern them."

Nanquan said, "In that case the people there will meet with great distress."

———— ◆ ————

When Nanquan entered Xuancheng, the official Lu Geng came out of the city to greet him. Pointing at the city gate, Lu Geng said, "Everyone calls this the 'Gate of Harmony.' What would the master call it?"

Nanquan said, "I fear that if I were to speak it would insult Your Eminence's reputation."

———— ◆ ————

Zhaozhou asked Nanquan, "There are no things that are outside of the Way. Outside of things there is no Way. What is the Way outside of things?"

Nanquan hit him with his staff.

Zhaozhou grabbed the staff and said, "Hereafter, don't be hitting people in error!"

Nanquan said, "It's easy to tell dragons from snakes. It's difficult to fool a patch-robed monk!"

———— ◆ ————

When Nanquan was near death, the head monk said, "Master, where will you be a hundred years from now?"

Nanquan said, "I'm going to be an ox living down at the bottom of the mountain."

The monk said, "May I follow you to that place [as an ox]?"

Nanquan said, "If you follow me, you must do so with a single blade of grass in your mouth."

The master then became ill. He said to the monks, "The stars' light is dim but eternal. Don't say that I'm coming or going." When he finished speaking, the master died.

YAOSHAN WEIYAN

YAOSHAN WEIYAN (751–834) was the student of Shitou Xiqian. He came from ancient Jiangzhou (now the city of Xinjiang in Shanxi Province). He left home at the age of seventeen to enter the congregation of Zen master Xishan Huizhao. Later, a Vinaya master named Xicao ordained Yaoshan at Mt. Heng. An earnest student, Yaoshan mastered the sutras and shastras and strictly adhered to the Vinaya rules. But eventually, he grew tired of the repetitive and petty observances of the Vinaya and resolved to find a new teacher. He first went to see Shitou Xiqian, who was then living on Mt. Heng.

Yaoshan first went to Shitou Xiqian's place. He asked, "I have a general understanding of the three vehicles and the twelve divisions of scripture. Now I want to find out about the southern teaching of pointing directly at mind, seeing self-nature, and becoming a buddha. Truly, I'm not clear about this teaching and I ask for the master's compassionate instruction."

Shitou said, "You can't attain it this way. You can't attain it not this way. Trying to attain it this way or not this way, it can't be attained. So what will you do?"

Yaoshan was confused.

Shitou then said, "Your affinity is not at this place. Go to Master Mazu's place."

Yaoshan went and paid his respects to Mazu in accordance with Shitou's instructions. He then posed the same question to Mazu that he had previously presented to Shitou.

Mazu said, "Sometimes I teach it by raising my eyebrows and blinking my eyes. Sometimes I don't teach it by raising my eyebrows and blinking my eyes. Sometimes raising my eyebrows and blinking my eyes is it, sometimes raising my eyebrows and blinking my eyes isn't it. So what will you do?"

At these words Yaoshan was enlightened. He then bowed to Mazu.

Mazu said, "What principle have you observed that makes you bow?"

Yaoshan said, "When I was at Shitou's place, it was like a mosquito on an iron bull."

Mazu said, "Since you are thus, uphold and sustain it well."

Yaoshan then served as Mazu's attendant for three years.

One day, Mazu asked him, "What have you seen lately?"

Yaoshan said, "Shedding the skin completely, leaving only the true body."

Mazu said, "Your attainment can be said to be in accord with the mind-body, spreading through its four limbs. Since it's like this, you should bind your things to your stomach and go traveling to other mountains."

Yaoshan said, "Who am I to speak of being head of a Zen mountain?"

Mazu said, "That's not what I mean. Those who haven't gone on a long pilgrimage can't reside [as an abbot]. There's no advantage to seeking advantage. Nothing is accomplished by seeking something. You should go on a journey and not remain in this place."

Yaoshan then left Mazu and returned to Shitou.

One day, as Yaoshan was sitting, Shitou asked him, "What are you doing here?"

Yaoshan said, "I'm not doing a thing."

Shitou said, "Then you're just sitting leisurely."

Yaoshan said, "If I were sitting leisurely I'd be doing something."

Shitou said, "You say you're not doing anything. What is it that you're not doing?"

Yaoshan said, "A thousand sages don't know."

Shitou then wrote a verse of praise that said:

Long abiding together, not knowing its name,
Just going on, practicing like this,
Since ancient times the sages don't know.
Will searching everywhere now make it known?

Later, Shitou offered an instruction, saying, "Words do not encroach upon it."

Yaoshan said, "No words does not encroach upon it."

Shitou said, "Here, I can't stick a needle into it."

Yaoshan said "Here, it's like I'm growing flowers on a bare rock."

Shitou approved Yaoshan's answer.

Later the master lived on Mt. Yao in Lizhou and a sea of students assembled there.

                ❖

For a long time Yaoshan did not enter the hall to speak.

The temple director said to him, "The monks have been waiting for a long time for the master to give them some instruction."

Yaoshan said, "Ring the bell!"

The monks assembled in the hall.

Yaoshan then got down from the Dharma seat and went back to the abbot's quarters.

The temple director followed him and said, "Master, since you consented to speak to the monks, why didn't you say anything?"

Yaoshan said, "Sutras have sutra teachers. Shastras have shastra teachers. Why are you unhappy with me?"

                ❖

A monk said to Yaoshan, "I have doubt. I ask for the master to resolve it for me."

Yaoshan said, "Wait until I go into the hall tonight to speak. Then I'll resolve it."

That evening, Yaoshan entered the hall. When the assembly was ready, he said, "Where is the monk who asked me today to resolve his doubt?"

The monk came forward and stood there.

Yaoshan got down from the Dharma seat, grabbed the monk, and said, "Everyone! This monk has doubt!"

Yaoshan then released the monk and went back to his room. ([Later,] Xuansha said, "Do you say he resolved the monk's doubt or not? If he resolved it, where was it resolved? If he didn't resolve it, then say whether your own doubts were resolved when he went into the hall.")

                ❖

One night, the lamps remained unlit as the monks assembled to hear Yaoshan speak.

Yaoshan said to the monks, "I have a single phrase. I'll tell it to you when the bull gives birth to a calf."

Then a monk said, "The bull has given birth to a calf. Why don't you say it?"

Yaoshan said, "Bring a lamp!"

But the monk had gone back into the assembly and couldn't be seen. ([Later,] Yunyan brought up this story to Dongshan. Dongshan said, "That monk was enlightened, but he wouldn't allow others to pay him respect.")

Yaoshan asked a monk who had just arrived at the temple, "Where do you come from?"

The monk said, "From Hunan."

Yaoshan then asked, "Is Dongting Lake full or not?"

The monk said, "It's not full."

Yaoshan said, "There's been a lot of rain lately. Why isn't it full?"

The monk didn't answer. ([Later,] Daowu said, "It's full." Yunyan said, "Clear, deep earth." Dongshan said, "In what eon was it ever lacking?" Yunmen said, "It's here.")

In the second month of [the year 834], Zen master Yaoshan called out, "The Dharma hall is collapsing! The Dharma hall is collapsing!"

The monks all grabbed poles and tried to prop up the Dharma hall.

Yaoshan lifted his hand and said, "You don't understand what I mean," and passed away. The master was eighty-four years old and had been a monk for sixty years. His disciples built his memorial stupa on the east side of the hall. He received the posthumous name "Great Teacher Vast Way." His stupa was named "Transforming City."

DANXIA TIANRAN

DANXIA TIANRAN (739–824) was a disciple of Shitou Xiqian. He came from ancient Dengzhou. Spending his youth as an avid scholar, Tianran intended to take the civil service examinations to gain a position in the Chinese government bureaucracy. Traveling to the capital city of Changan before the exams, Tianran stayed at an inn. That night he dreamed that the room filled with white light. A fortuneteller advised him that this was an omen of "resolving emptiness." Tianran then happened to meet a Zen monk who said, "Can being an official compare with practicing Buddhism?" So Danxia went off to see Mazu, who then sent him on to study with Shitou on Mt. Heng.

When Tianran arrived at Mt. Heng he still held his original intention to earnestly undertake study under Shitou.

But Shitou only said, "Go live in the shed."

Tianran bowed and took his leave. He thereafter moved into the monks' quarters and commenced work in the monastery kitchen, where he remained for three years.

Suddenly one day, Shitou informed the monks, "Tomorrow, all of you dig up the wild grass that is growing in front of the Buddha hall."

The next day, the monks and novices all took hoes and began digging out the grass. But Tianran took a basin of water, and, dumping it over his own head, squatted like a barbarian in front of Shitou. Shitou laughed at this, and soon thereafter he shaved Tianran's head. But when Shitou recited the ordination precepts, Tianran covered his ears and left the monastery.

Tianran then again went to see Mazu in Jiangxi, but when he arrived at Mazu's place, before meeting him, he went into the monks' hall and climbed up onto one of the sacred statues there, straddling its neck. The monks were aghast at this behavior and immediately reported it to Mazu. Mazu entered the hall and, taking a look at Tianran, said, "My natural disciple!"

Tianran then removed himself from the statue, bowed to Mazu and said, "Thank you, Master, for giving me this Dharma name." From this time forward, the master had the name Tianran ["natural"].

Mazu then asked, "Where have you come from?"

Tianran said, "From Shitou."

Mazu said, "Shitou's road is slippery. Did you fall down on it?"

Tianran said, "If I had fallen down then I wouldn't have come here."

Later Mazu presented Tianran with a staff and permitted him to go traveling. Tianran then spent three years at Huading Peak on Mt. Tiantai. Later, he traveled to Mt. Jing in Yuhang to pay respects to National Teacher Qin.[73]

During the Yuan He era of the Tang dynasty [around the year 810], Tianran visited Longmen Monastery on Fragrant Mountain in Luoyang. There he became a friend of the monk Funiu.[74] Later, Tianran stayed at Wisdom Woods Temple. During some extremely cold weather, he took a wooden statue of Buddha and burned it in the fire to get warm.

The temple director got extremely upset with Tianran and yelled, "Why are you burning my wooden buddha?"

Tianran pulled some burning embers from the fire and said, "I'm burning this buddha to get the sacred relics from it."[75]

The temple director said, "How can a wooden buddha have sacred relics?"

Tianran said, "Well, if it doesn't have sacred relics, let's burn a couple more of them."

The temple director was so upset that his eyebrows, eyelashes, and beard all fell out.

⸻ ◆ ⸻

Tianran visited the National Teacher [Nanyang Huizhong].

Tianran asked the National Teacher's attendant, "Is the National Teacher here or not?"

The attendant said, "He's here, but he's not seeing guests."

Tianran said, "This is too far off!"

The attendant said, "Even the buddha eye can't see him."

Tianran said, "Dragons give birth to dragons. A phoenix gives birth to a phoenix."

When the National Teacher woke up, the attendant told him of his conversation with Tianran. The National Teacher gave his attendant thirty blows and drove him away.

When Tianran heard about this he said, "Don't tell falsehoods to the National Teacher."

The next day, Tianran went again to pay his respects. When he met the National Teacher he started to spread out his sitting cushion.

The National Teacher said, "Don't! Don't!"

When Tianran stepped back, the National Teacher said, "Just so! Just so!"

Tianran came forward again, and the National Teacher said, "No! No!"

Tianran then circled the National Teacher once and went out.

The National Teacher said, "In this time long removed from the time of the saints, most people are lax. Thirty years from now this fellow will be hard to find!"

◆

Tianran went to pay a visit to Layman Pang. He encountered Layman Pang's daughter Ling Zhao as she was washing vegetables.

Tianran said to Ling Zhao, "Is Layman Pang here?"

Ling Zhao put down the vegetable basket, folded her hands, and stood there.

Tianran again said, "Is Layman Pang here?"

Ling Zhao then picked up the basket and walked away.

Tianran left.

Later, Layman Pang returned. Ling Zhao told him what had gone on before.

Layman Pang said, "You red-soiled ox!"

Another time Tianran came to see Pangyun and they met in front of Pangyun's house.

Tianran said, "Is Layman Pang here?"

Pangyun said, "Starving, but not taking food."

Tianran said, "Is old Yun here or not?"

Pangyun said, "Blue heavens! Blue heavens!" then went into the house.

Tianran said, "Blue heavens! Blue heavens!" and left.

When Tianran was traveling to see Mazu, he encountered an old man with a boy on the road.

Tianran asked the old man, "Where do you live?"

The old man said, "The sky above, the earth below."

Tianran said, 'If suddenly the sky fell down and the earth sank, then what?"

The old man said, "Blue heavens! Blue heavens!"

The boy then roared like a tiger.

Tianran said, "Only you could father such a child!"

The old man then took the boy and went into the mountains.

Zen master Danxia Tianran entered the hall and addressed the monks, saying, "All of you here must take care of the temple and monastery. Things in this place were not made or named by you, and have they not been given as offerings? Formerly I studied with Shitou, and he taught me that I must personally protect these things. This is not to be discussed further.

"Each of you here has a place to put your cushion and sit. Why do you suspect you need something else? Is Zen something you can explain? Is a buddha something you can become? I don't want to hear a single word about Buddhism.

"All of you, look and see! Skillful means and expedience, the unlimited mind of benevolence, compassion, joy, and detachment—these things aren't received from someplace else. Not an inch of these things is evident. Skillful means is Manjushri Bodhisattva.[76] Expedience is Samantabhadra Bodhisattva.[77] Do you still want to go seeking after something? Don't go using the Buddhist scriptures to look for emptiness!

"These days Zen students are all in a tizzy, practicing Zen and asking about Tao. I don't have any Dharma for you to practice here! And there isn't any doctrine to be confirmed. Just eat and drink. Everyone can do that. Don't harbor doubt. It's the same everyplace!

"Just recognize that Shakyamuni was an ordinary old fellow. You must see for yourself. Don't spend your life trying to win some competitive trophy, blindly misleading other blind people, all of you marching right into hell, floundering in duality! I've nothing more to say. Take care!"

During the sixth month of [the year 824], the master said to the monks, "Prepare hot water for a bath. I want to leave."

Tianran then put on his hat, picked up his walking stick, and put on his shoes. Then just as he put down his foot to take a step, he passed away. His monks built his memorial stupa. He was given the posthumous name "Zen Master Wisdom Penetration."

TIANHUANG DAOWU

ACCORDING TO TRADITION, Tianhuang Daowu (748–807) was a student of three different Zen masters, and ultimately received Dharma transmission from Shitou Xiqian. Tianhuang, in turn, imparted Dharma transmission to Longtan Chongxin. The lineage then passed to Deshan, Xuefeng, and on to the two great Zen schools of Yunmen and Fayan.

According to the lamp records, Tianhuang possessed an unusually noble appearance. He left home at the age of fourteen after fasting to demonstrate his resolve to his parents. He first studied under a teacher in Mingzhou (the area of modern Ningbo City). Thereafter, he traveled to Hangzhou, where he underwent ordination at Bamboo Forest Temple. Daowu then studied with and received the Dharma of National Teacher Faqin on Mt. Jing. Later, he studied with the great teacher Mazu Daoyi, who confirmed his attainments. After remaining with Mazu for two years, Daowu traveled on to meet Shitou. According to the lamp records, his experience with Shitou caused his remaining doubts to be dispelled.

His fellow monks regarded Daowu as a most diligent Buddhist practitioner. Accounts say that one night during a fierce storm he defied the elements to sit in immobile meditation in a graveyard.

Lamp records indicate that confusion has existed about Tianhuang's identity because two Zen teachers with similar sounding names lived in the same locale. One monk was named Tianhuang Daowu and the other Tianwang Daowu. Both were students of Mazu Daoyi, and at least one was also a student of Shitou. Mazu and Shitou often sent students back and forth to one another, contributing to the historical uncertainty surrounding Tianhuang's identity.

The record of Tianhuang Daowu's awakening and teaching career is provided in the *Wudeng Huiyuan.*

Upon meeting Shitou, Daowu asked, "By what method do you reveal liberating wisdom to people?"

Shitou said, "There are no slaves here. From what do you seek liberation?"

Daowu said, "How can it be understood?"

Shitou said, "So you're still trying to grasp emptiness?"

Daowu said, "From today I won't do so again."

Shitou then said, "I'd like to know when you came forth from 'that place.'"

Daowu said, "I haven't come from 'that place.'"

Shitou said, "I already know where you've come from."

Daowu said, "Master, how can you slander people in this way?"

Shitou said, "Your body is revealed here now."

Daowu then said, "Although it is thus, how will your teaching be demonstrated to those who come later?"

Shitou said, "Please tell me, who are those who come later?"

Upon hearing these words Daowu instantly experienced great enlightenment, dissolving the mind he had attained from the words of his previous two teachers.

Later, Tianhuang lived on Mt. Ziling at Dangyang City in Xingzhou. The practitioners who came to study under him were pressed shoulder to shoulder, his reputation even reaching to the capital city where he was known among men and women.

At that time, the head of Chongye Temple had told the local garrison commander about Tianhuang. The commander invited Tianhuang into the city for a visit. At the edge of town was Tianhuang Temple. It was quite famous, but because of a bad fire it had been destroyed. The chief monk there, named Lingjian, planned to rebuild it. He said, "If honored master Daowu were to become abbot it would certainly benefit us."

So late at night, Lingjian went to see Daowu, and beseeching him to take the position of abbot, he brought him to the site of the temple by sedan chair.

During this time a duke of the Jiangling region, Pu Shepei, would sometimes come to inquire about Dharma, kowtowing and paying elaborate respects to Daowu. The master would not go out to receive him or accompany him when he departed. Whether noble or mean, guests would all sit with their hands folded in front of them in respect. Duke Pu Shepei returned often to pay respects to Daowu in this manner. Due to this, Daowu's reputation spread and the Dharma of Shitou flourished.

Tianhuang Daowu met Longtan. Longtan asked, "What is the affair that has been passed down through generations?"

Daowu said, "None other than knowing from where you come."

Longtan said, "How many are there who can gain this wisdom eye?"

Daowu said, "Short grasses easily become tall reeds."

A monk asked, "How does one speak of the great mystery?"

Daowu said, "Don't say 'I have realized the Buddhadharma!'"

The monk asked, "How do you deal with students who are stuck?"

Daowu said, "Why don't you ask me?"

The monk said, "I just asked you."

Daowu said, "Go! This isn't the place where you'll find relief."

In the fourth month of the [year 807] Tianhuang became ill. He instructed his disciples to announce that he would soon pass away. At the end of summer, the general public was inquiring about his illness.

Suddenly, the master called for the head cook, who came and sat down before him.

Tianhuang said, "Do you understand?"

The cook said, "I don't understand."

Tianhuang picked up a cushion and threw it down on the ground. He then passed away.

The master was sixty years of age and had been a priest for thirty-five years. On the fifth day of the eighth month of that year, the master's stupa was constructed east of the city.

Tenth Generation

HUANGBO XIYUN WUFENG CHANGGUAN GUISHAN DA'AN

BAIZHANG NIEPAN GUISHAN LINGYOU GUANNAN DAOCHANG

HANGZHOU TIANLONG CHANGSHA JINGCEN ZHAOZHOU CONGSHEN

YUNYAN TANSHENG CHUANZI DECHENG DAOWU YUANZHI

CUIWEI WUXUE LONGTAN CHONGXIN

HUANGBO XIYUN

HUANGBO XIYUN (d. 850) was the disciple of Baizhang and the teacher of Linji Yixuan. He came from ancient Fuzhou. As a youth, he entered a monastery on Mt. Huangbo in his home province. Later, he traveled to the district of Gao'an where he resided at Mt. Huangbo (Xiyun renamed the mountain after his old mountain home in Fuzhou). Huangbo also traveled and lived at Mt. Tiantai, as well as the capital city of Changan, where he received instruction from National Teacher Nanyang Huizhong.

Huangbo's physical appearance was striking. He had a large protruding forehead that was whimsically described as a "large pearl."

Regarded as a teacher with simple methods and few words, Huangbo embodied Mahayana Buddhism's bodhisattva ideal by adhering to the vow to defer the fruit of enlightenment until all other beings can first enjoy it. A famous legend about Huangbo provides a metaphorical teaching on this vow.

While on his journey to Mt. Tiantai, Huangbo met another monk. They talked and laughed, just as though they were old friends who had long known one another. Their eyes gleamed with delight as they then set off traveling together. Coming to the fast rapids of a stream, they removed their hats and took up staffs to walk across. The other monk tried to lead Huangbo across, saying: "Come over! Come over!"

Huangbo said, "If Elder Brother wants to go across, then go ahead."

The other monk then began walking across the top of the water, just as though it were dry land.

The monk turned to Huangbo and said, "Come across! Come across!"

Huangbo yelled, "Ah! You self-saving fellow! If I had known this before I would have chopped off your legs!"

The monk cried out, "You're truly a vessel for the Mahayana, I can't compare with you!" and so saying, the monk vanished.

The *Wudeng Huiyuan* provides this account of Huangbo's initial encounter with Baizhang:

Baizhang asked, "So grand and imposing, where have you come from?"

Huangbo said, "So grand and imposing, I've come from south of the mountains."

Baizhang said, "So grand and imposing, what are you doing?"

Huangbo said, "So grand and imposing, I'm not doing anything else."

Huangbo bowed and said, "From high antiquity, what is the teaching of this order?"

Baizhang remained silent.

Huangbo said, "Don't allow the descendants to be cut off."

Baizhang then said, "It may be said that you are a 'person.'"

Baizhang then arose and returned to his abbot's quarters.

Huangbo followed him there and said, "I've come with a special purpose."

Baizhang said, "If that's really so, then hereafter you won't disappoint me."

❖

One day Baizhang asked Huangbo, "Where have you been?"

Huangbo said, "I've been picking mushrooms at the base of Mt. Great Hero."

Baizhang said, "Did you see a big tiger?"

Huangbo roared.

Baizhang picked up an ax and assumed a pose as if to strike Huangbo. Huangbo then hit him. Baizhang laughed "Ha, ha," and returned to his room.

Later Baizhang entered the hall and said to the monks, "At the base of Great Hero Mountain there's a tiger. You monks should go take a look at it. Just today, I myself suffered a bite from it."

❖

Once, Huangbo was at Nanquan Puyuan's temple and participated in picking vegetables.

Nanquan asked him, "Where are you going?"

Huangbo said, "To pick vegetables."

Nanquan said, "What will you use to pick them?"

Huangbo took his knife and held it straight up.

Nanquan said, "You've only acted as guest. You haven't acted as host."

Huangbo stabbed three holes in the air.

Nanquan said, "Everyone is going to pick vegetables."

⸻ ◆ ⸻

One day, Nanquan said to Huangbo, "I have a song called 'Ode of the Oxherd.' Can you recite it?"

Huangbo said, "I am my own teacher right here."

⸻ ◆ ⸻

Huangbo was taking his leave of Nanquan. Nanquan accompanied Huangbo to the monastery gate. Lifting up Huangbo's hat, Nanquan said, "Elder, your physical size is not large, but isn't your hat too small?"

Huangbo said, "Although that's true, still the entire universe can fit inside it."

Nanquan said, "Teacher Wang!"

Huangbo then put on his hat and left.

⸻ ◆ ⸻

Huangbo was at Yanguan's temple performing rituals. At that time the future emperor Tang Xuan Zong was serving as a novice monk in the temple.

The future emperor asked Huangbo, "Not seeking Buddha; not seeking Dharma; not seeking Sangha—when the master bows, what is it you're seeking?"

Huangbo said, "Not seeking Buddha; not seeking Dharma; not seeking Sangha—one always bows in just this manner."

The novice said, "Then why bow?"

Huangbo hit him.

The novice said, "You're really too crude!"

Huangbo said, "What place is this we're in? Is it for idle chatter?"

He then hit the novice again.

⸻ ◆ ⸻

When Pei Xiangguo was the governing official of Wan Ling Prefecture he built a large Zen monastery and invited Huangbo to become abbot there. Because Huangbo loved his old mountain he used the same name for the new monastery.

One day Pei Xiangguo took a figure of Buddha, placed it in front of Huangbo, and kneeling down, said, "I ask the master to provide me an honorific name."

Huangbo proclaimed, "Pei Xiu!"[78]

Pei Xiangguo responded, "Yes?"

Huangbo said, "I've given you the name."

Pei Xiangguo bowed.

———— ◆ ————

Six new students came to greet Zen master Huangbo. Five of the students bowed, but the other student lifted his meditation cushion and drew a circle in the air with it.

Huangbo said, "I've heard that it's evil to keep a hunting dog."

The monk said, "I'm chasing the sound of the wild sheep."

Huangbo said, "The sheep makes no sound for you to chase."

The monk said, "Then I'll pursue the sheep by seeing its traces."

Huangbo said, "There are no traces for you to pursue."

The monk said, "Then I will track it."

Huangbo said, "There are no tracks for you to follow."

The monk said, "If that's the case, then the sheep is dead."

The next day Huangbo addressed the monks, saying, "I want the monk who was looking for the wild sheep yesterday to come forward."

The monk came forward.

Huangbo said, "The public case we discussed yesterday is not finished. After we finished speaking what did you think?"

The monk remained silent.

Huangbo said, "At first I thought you were a monk of the true teaching, but actually you're a debating instructor."

Huangbo then chased the monk out of the congregation.

———— ◆ ————

One day Huangbo made his hand into a fist and said, "All the teachers under heaven are right here. If I let out a string of words about it, it will just confuse you. If I don't say a single phrase, you'll never get rid of it."

A monk asked, "What happens if you let out a string of words?"

Huangbo said, "Confusion."

The monk said, "If you don't let out a single phrase and it can't be gotten rid of, then what?"

Huangbo said, "Everywhere."

·········· ◆ ··········

One day, the official Pei Xiangguo invited the master to come for a visit at his offices so that he could present him with a book he had written [on his understanding of Zen]. The master received the book and placed it on his chair without looking at it.

After a long pause, Huangbo said, "Do you understand?"

Official Pei said, "I don't understand."

Huangbo said, "If it can be understood in this manner, then it isn't the true teaching. If it can be seen in paper and ink, then it is not the essence of our order."

Official Pei then composed and offered a poem that read:

Since receiving the mind seal from the master,[79]
Pearled forehead and tall,
He dwelt for ten years at the Min waters.[80]
But today the cup overflows past the banks of the Zhang,[81]
A thousand dragons follow his great stride,
And because of ten thousand miles of flowers,
All want to become his student.
Who knows to whom the Dharma will be passed?

Huangbo's stern demeanor remained unchanged. From this event the reputation of his school spread throughout the region south of the Yang-tse River.

———— ✦ ————

One day, Zen master Huangbo entered the hall to speak. When a very large assembly of monks had gathered, he said, "What is it that you people are all seeking here?"

He then used his staff to try and drive them away, but they didn't leave. So Huangbo returned to his seat and said, "You people are all dreg-slurpers. If you go on a pilgrimage seeking in this way you'll just earn people's laughter. When you see eight hundred or a thousand people gathered somewhere you go there. There's no telling what trouble this will cause.

"When I was traveling on pilgrimage and came upon some fellow 'beneath the grass roots' [a teacher], then I'd hammer him on the top of the head and see if he understood pain, and [thus] support him from an overflowing rice bag! If all I ever found were the likes of you here, then how would we ever realize the great matter that's before us today? If you people want to call what you're doing a 'pilgrimage,' then you should show a little spirit! Do you know that today in all the great Tang there are no Zen teachers?"

A monk then asked, "In all directions there are worthies expounding to countless students. Why do you say there are no Zen teachers?"

Huangbo said, "I didn't say there is no Zen, just that there are no teachers. None of you see that although Zen master Mazu had eighty-four Dharma heirs, only two or three of them actually gained Mazu's Dharma eye. One of them is Zen master Guizong of Mt. Lu. Home leavers must know what has happened in former times before they can start to understand. Otherwise you will be like the Fourth Ancestor's student Niutou, speaking high and low but never understanding the critical point. If you possess the Dharma eye, then you can distinguish between true and heretical teachings and you'll deal with the world's affairs with ease. But if you don't understand, and only study some words and phrases or recite sutras, and then put them in your bag and set off on pilgrimage saying 'I understand Zen,' then will they be of any benefit even for your own life and death? If you're unmindful of the worthy ancients you'll shoot straight into hell like an arrow. I know about you as soon as I see you come through the temple gate. How will you gain an understanding? You have to make an effort. It isn't an easy matter. If you just wear a sheet of clothing and eat meals, then you'll spend your whole life in vain. Clear-eyed people will laugh at you. Eventually the common people will just get rid of you. If you go seeking far and wide, how will this resolve the great matter? If you understand, then you understand. If you don't, then get out of here! Take care!"

If a monk asked Huangbo, "Why did the First Ancestor come from the west?" Huangbo would hit him. Through these and other methods, his students realized the highest function. Those of middling or inferior ability have never understood the master's greatness.

Huangbo passed away in [the year 850] on the mountain where he lived and taught. He received the posthumous name "Zen Master Removing Limits."

WUFENG CHANGGUAN

WUFENG CHANGGUAN (n.d.) was a disciple of Baizhang Huaihai. He taught in ancient Yuzhou.[82]

A monk asked Zen master Wufeng Changguan, "What is the situation of the Five Peaks?"[83]
Wufeng said, "Danger."
The monk said, "What about the person there?"
Wufeng said, "Stuck."

A monk was leaving the temple.

Wufeng said, "Your Reverence, where are you going?"

The monk said, "I'm going to Mt. Tai."

Wufeng held up one finger and said, "If you see Manjushri then come back here and show him to me."[84]

The monk didn't answer.

Wufeng asked a monk, "Where are you coming from?"

The monk said, "From the village."

Wufeng asked another monk, "Did you see an ox?"

The monk said, "I saw it."

Wufeng said, "Did you see its left horn or did you see its right horn?"

The monk didn't answer.

Wufeng spoke for him, saying, "I don't see left or right." (Yangshan later said, "Do you still see left and right?")

Another monk was leaving the temple.

Wufeng said, "When you go around everywhere, don't spread slander by saying I'm here."

The monk said, "I won't say the master is here."

Wufeng said, "Where will you say I am?"

The monk held up one finger.

Wufeng said, "You've already slandered me."

GUISHAN DA'AN, "CHANGQING DA'AN," "LAZY AN"

GUISHAN DA'AN (793–883) was a disciple of Baizhang. He grew up and taught in ancient Fuzhou (in modern Fujian Province). At the age of twenty, he went to Mt. Huangbo in Jiangxi and studied the Vinaya. Later he declared, "Despite my hard efforts I still haven't encountered the principle of the great mystery." He thereafter set off in search of the truth. On the advice of an old man he met on the road, he traveled to Nanchang City in Jiangxi and began study under Baizhang Huaihai.

When Da'an met Baizhang, he bowed and asked, "This student seeks to know Buddha. How can I do so?"

Baizhang said, "It's like riding the ox looking for the ox."

Da'an said, "After finding it, then what?"

Baizhang said, "It's like riding the ox and arriving home."

Da'an then asked, "How does one ultimately uphold and sustain this?"

Baizhang said, "It's like an oxherd who, grasping his staff, watches the ox so that he doesn't transgress by eating other people's sprouts and grain."

Upon receiving this instruction Changqing sought nothing further.

Da'an was a Dharma brother of Guishan Lingyou, who had established a temple on Mt. Gui. When Guishan died, Da'an was invited to assume the abbacy there.

Guishan Da'an addressed the monks, saying, "What are you all seeking from me by coming here? If you want to become a buddha, then you should know that you yourself are Buddha. Why are you running around from place to place, like a thirsty deer chasing a mirage? When will you ever succeed?

"You want to be a buddha, but you won't recognize that your topsy-turvy contradictory ideas; your deluded understandings; your mind [which believes in] innumerable beings, purity and pollution; that it is just this mind that is the authentic original awakened mind of Buddha. Where else will you go to find it?

"I've spent the last thirty years here on Mt. Gui, eating Guishan's rice, shitting Guishan's shit, but not practicing Guishan's Zen! I just mind an old water buffalo. If he wanders off the road into the grass then I pull him back by his nose ring. If he eats someone else's rice shoots then I use the whip to move him away. After such a long training period he's become very lovable, and he obeys my words. Now he pulls the Great Vehicle, always staying where I can see him the whole day through, and he can't be driven away.

"Each one of you has a priceless treasure. There is light emanating from your eyes which illuminates mountains, rivers, and the great earth. There is light radiating from your ears which apprehends all good and evil sounds. The six senses—day and night they emanate light and this is called the 'light emanating samadhi.' You yourself can't comprehend it, but it is reflected in the four great bodies.[85] It is completely supported within and without, and never unbalanced. It's like someone with a heavy load on his back, crossing a bridge made from a single tree trunk, but never losing his step. And now if you ask what is it that provides this support and where it is revealed, then I just say that not a single hair of it can be seen. No wonder the monk Zhigong[86] said, 'Searching inside and out you'll find nothing. Actions in the causational realm are a big muddle.'

"Take care!"

A monk asked, "All actions are the function of the dharmakaya. What is the dharmakaya?"

Da'an said, "All actions are the function of the dharmakaya."

A monk asked, "Apart from the five skandhas, what is the original body?"

Da'an said, "Earth, water, fire, wind [the four elements of form], sensation, perception, mental action, and consciousness."

The monk said, "Aren't these the five skandhas?"

Da'an said, "They are not the five skandhas."

Xuefeng came to Mt. Gui. While living there he found an unusual stick shaped like a snake. On the back of it he wrote, "This is natural and was not carved."

Xuefeng gave the stick to Da'an, who said, "Inhabitants of this mountain have no ax with which to carve it."

A monk asked Da'an, "Where is Buddha?"

Da'an said, "Not apart from mind."

The monk said, "Then what were the attainments of the ancestors on Twin Peaks?"

Da'an said, "In the Dharma there is nothing attained. If there is anything to be attained, it is that nothing is attained."

A monk asked, "Where will you flee to if Huang Chao's troops come?"[87]

Da'an said, "Inside Skandhas Mountain."

The monk said, "When they suddenly grab you, then what?"

Da'an said, "Commander Distress."

Da'an taught in Fuzhou. He later returned to Mt. Huangbo and died there. His stupa was constructed on Mt. Lanka and he received the posthumous title "Zen Master Perfect Wisdom."

Baizhang Niepan, "Fazheng"

Baizhang Niepan (n.d.) was a student of Baizhang Huaihai. Little is recorded of Baizhang Niepan's life. It is known that upon the death of his teacher, he assumed the abbacy of his temple. The *Wudeng Huiyuan* offers this short story concerning this teacher.

One day, Zen master Baizhang Niepan spoke to the congregation, saying, "If all of you go and till the field, then I'll lecture on the great meaning."

When the monks had finished plowing the field they returned and asked the master to expound on the great meaning.

Niepan held up his hands before the monks.

The monks were dumbfounded. (In the Song dynasty, Zen master Juefan Hongzhi compiled a text known as *The Record of the Monasteries*. In that record it says, "Fazheng [Baizhang Niepan], a second-generation teacher beneath Baizhang Huaihai, was a great wisdom ancestor. He originally studied the *Nirvana Sutra*. People did not call him by his name, instead referring to him as 'Zen Master Nirvana.' When he ascended the Dharma seat his merit was very great. He was the master who told the monks to first plow the field, and then he would tell them the great meaning." Zen masters Huangbo, Guling, and others all honored him.[88] The Tang dynasty literary figure Huang Wufan recorded the details inscribed on his stupa monument that were originally written by Yang Gongquan, [which revealed the master's] timeless wisdom. The monk Baizhang Weizheng is listed incorrectly in the lamp records as an immediate descendant of Mazu. In the lamp record entitled *The Record of the True School* there are the two names Wei Zheng and Fazheng listed in the generation of Baizhang Huaihai. [The compiler of that record] Zen master Mingzhao did not realize that these two names were the same person and thus saved them both. Now we correct this error in accordance with the record of Yang Gongquan.)

Guishan Lingyou

Zen master Guishan Lingyou (771–853) was a disciple of Baizhang Huaihai. Along with his student, Yangshan, he founded what later generations called the Guiyang school, the first of the five traditional "houses" of Zen. Many kōans in the Zen tradition consist of dialogues between Guishan and Yangshan. Some of these kōans, and the teachings of this school in general, are characterized by the use of symbols, symbolic actions, and metaphors. Although Zen's use of such devices was well established prior to the Guiyang school, there they found their foremost expressions to date within the Chinese Zen tradition. Among the traditional Zen houses, the Guiyang's use of symbols aligned its teaching methods most closely to the practices of Buddhism's esoteric schools.

The *Wudeng Huiyuan* provides this traditional account of Guishan's enlightenment and his subsequent assignment to become the abbot on Mt. Gui.

Zen master Guishan Lingyou had the surname Zhao. He came from the village of Changxi in Fuzhou. He left home to enter Build Goodness Temple in his native province at the age of fifteen. There, he studied under the Vinaya master Fa Chang. Later, Guishan received full ordination at Longxing Temple in Hangzhou, where he also studied the Mahayana and Hinayana scriptures. At the age of twenty-three he traveled to Jiangxi, where he studied under Baizhang Huaihai. Baizhang permitted Guishan to become his disciple upon their first meeting. Later, Guishan attained the position of head of practice among the monks.

Once, while Lingyou was acting as attendant to Baizhang, Baizhang asked him, "Who's there?"

Lingyou said, "Me."

Baizhang then said to him, "Stick a poker in the fire and see if there is any fire left in it."

Lingyou did so and said, "There's no fire left."

Baizhang then took the poker himself and, sticking it deep into the stove, pulled out some hot embers. Showing them to Lingyou he said, "You said there was no fire left, but what about this?"

Upon hearing these words Guishan experienced great enlightenment. He then bowed and made his realization known to Baizhang.

Baizhang said, "What you've experienced is a temporary fork in the road. In the scripture it says, 'If you want to understand the meaning of buddha nature, then you should look in the realm of temporal causation.' When it expresses itself, it is like delusion suddenly turning into enlightenment, like remembering something that was forgotten, and realizing that the self and other things do not come from someplace else. Thus, an ancient teacher said, 'Enlightenment is but the same as nonenlightenment, without mind and without dharmas.' It is just this mind that does not hold to ideas of emptiness, delusion, mundane, or sacred. It is the original mind-Dharma that is, of itself, perfect and complete. Having arrived at this, you must uphold and sustain it."

The next day Lingyou accompanied Baizhang to do work on the mountain. Baizhang said, "Did you bring fire?"

Lingou said, "I brought it."

Baizhang said, "Where is it?"

Guishan then picked up a piece of firewood and whistled twice, then handed the piece of wood to Baizhang.

Baizhang said, "Like a termite eating wood."

———— ◆ ————

A Buddhist pilgrim named Sima came from Hunan. He spoke to Baizhang, saying, "Recently at Hunan, I came upon a mountain named Big Gui where fifteen hundred Buddhist worthies reside."[89]

Baizhang said, "Should I go there [as abbot]?"

The pilgrim said, "It is not where Master Baizhang should reside."

Baizhang said, "Why is that?"

The pilgrim said, "The master is a teacher of bone. That place is the flesh."

Baizhang said, "Is there anyone in my congregation here who could assume that position?"

The pilgrim said, "Let me examine them and see."

At that time the monk Hua Linjue had the position of head monk. Baizhang asked his attendant to summon Hua.

When Hua arrived, Baizhang said to the pilgrim Sima, "How about this fellow?"

Sima asked Hua to speak a few words and walk back and forth. Then he said to Baizhang, "He won't do."

Baizhang then summoned Lingyou. At that time Lingyou served as head cook.

Sima took one look at Guishan and said, "This is the abbot of Mt. Gui."

That night Baizhang summoned Guishan to his room and instructed him, "My fate lies here, but as for glorious Mt. Gui, you will go there as abbot and carry on my teaching for future generations."

When Hua Linjue heard of this, he said to Baizhang, "I'm the one who was promoted to the position of head monk. Why is the chief cook going to attain the position of abbot?"

Baizhang said, "If you can say a special word before all the monks, then I'll appoint you to the position of abbot."

Baizhang then pointed at a water pitcher and said, "Without saying it's a water pitcher, what is it?"

Hua said, "You can't call it a wooden stool."

Baizhang then asked Lingyou the same question.

Lingyou then kicked over the water pitcher and went out.

Baizhang laughed and said, "The head monk loses."

Lingyou then left to travel to Mt. Gui.

———◆———

Zen master Guishan Lingyou entered the hall and addressed the monks, saying, "The mind of a person of the Way is forthright and undevious, with no front or back. It is neither deceitful nor deluded and at all times it is watchful and straightforward, never covering the eyes nor plugging the ears. Such a mind is realized when emotions do not chase after things. All the ancient sages have simply said that by the practice of not giving rise to evil views or thoughts, the difficulties of the corrupted world become like the clear autumn waters, pure and unmoving, tranquil yet unimpeded. A person with such a mind may be called of the Way, a person without worldly affairs."

———◆———

One day, Zen master Guishan addressed the congregation, saying, "There are many who attain the great potential, but few who realize the great function."

Yangshan repeated these words to a hermit who lived below the mountain and said, "What does the master mean when he speaks in this manner?"

The hermit said, "Say it again and we'll see."

When Yangshan began to speak the hermit kicked him and knocked him down.

Yangshan returned and reported this to Guishan. Guishan laughed loudly, "Ha, ha, ha."

———◆———

One day while they were picking tea leaves, Guishan said to Yangshan, "All day today I've heard your voice but I haven't seen your form."

Yangshan then shook the tea tree.

Guishan said, "You attained its function, but you haven't realized its essence."

Yangshan said, "What does the master say?"

Guishan was silent.

Yangshan said, "The master has attained its essence but hasn't realized its function."

Guishan said, "I spare you thirty blows with the staff."

Yangshan said, "If I receive thirty blows of the master's staff, who then will receive thirty blows from me?"

Guishan said, "I spare you thirty blows." (Zen master Xuanjue said, "I ask you, who made the error here?")

Guishan asked Yangshan, "Of the forty sections of the *Nirvana Sutra*, how many were spoken by Buddha and how many were spoken by a devil?"

Yangshan said, "All of them were spoken by a devil!"

Guishan said, "Hereafter, no one will be able to cope with you."

One day Guishan summoned the monastery director. When he came, Guishan said, "I called the monastery director, what are you doing here?"

The director stood there speechless. ([Later,] Caoshan answered on behalf of the monastery director, saying, "I know the master can't call me.")

Guishan also had his attendant summon the head monk. When the head monk came, Guishan said, "I called for the head monk, what are you doing here?"

The head monk also stood there speechless. (Caoshan said on his behalf, "If you ask the attendant to summon him, I'm afraid he won't come.")

Guishan asked Yunyan Tansheng, "I've heard that you've lived on Mt. Yao for a long time. Is that so?"

Yunyan said, "Yes."

Guishan said, "What about the great personage Yaoshan?"

Yunyan said, "There's something after nirvana."

Guishan said, "What is it that's 'after nirvana'?"

Yunyan said, "There are no leaks."

Yunyan then asked Guishan, "What did the great Baizhang look like?"

Guishan said, "Lofty and grand. Brilliantly incandescent. Behind his voice, there was no voice. After his form, there is no form. It's like a mosquito on the back of an iron ox. There's no place to take a bite."

Guishan asked Yangshan, "Where have you just come from?"

Yangshan said, "From the field."

Guishan said, "How many people are in the field?"

Yangshan stuck his hoe in the ground, clasped his hands, and stood there.

Guishan said, "On South Mountain there are a lot of people cutting reeds."

Yangshan pulled his hoe from the ground and walked away.

Guishan asked Yangshan, "All the beings of the great earth have expansive karmic consciousness, without a foundation. How do you know this to be true or not true?"

Yangshan said, "I have a way to show this."

Just then a monk passed by. Yangshan called to him, saying, "Your reverence!"

The monk turned his head.

Yangshan said, "Master, this is expansive karmic consciousness, without a foundation."

Guishan said, "This is a single drop of the milk of teachers and disciples. It dispels six ladles full of donkey milk."

Zen master Guishan Lingyou expounded the teaching for more than forty years, his words reaching countless people. On the ninth day of the first lunar month in [the year 853], Guishan finished bathing, sat in a cross-legged position and peacefully passed away. His age was eighty-three and he had been a monk for sixty-four years. His stupa was constructed on Mt. Gui and named "Clear Purity." He received the posthumous name "Zen Master Great Perfection."

GUANNAN DAOCHANG

GUANNAN DAOCHANG (n.d.) was a disciple of Baizhang Huaihai. He taught students in ancient Xiangzhou (now in Hubei Province).

A student asked, "What is the meaning of Bodhidharma's coming from the west?"

Daochang held up his staff and said, "Do you understand?"

The monk said, "I don't understand."

Guannan hit him.

A monk asked, "What is the source of the great way?"

Guannan struck him.

Whenever the master would see a monk coming to pay respects, he would often take up his staff to strike him and chase him off. Sometimes he'd say

"You're late" or "Beat Guannan's drum." During his time only Beixian was in harmony with him.

HANGZHOU TIANLONG

HANGZHOU TIANLONG (n.d.) was a disciple of Damei Fachang and the teacher of Juzhi (one-fingered Zen). The lamp records provide little information about Hangzhou Tianlong's life.

Hangzhou Tianlong entered the hall and addressed the monks, saying, "All of you! Don't be waiting for me to come here so that you can come here, or for me to go back so that you can go back. Each of you already possesses the ocean of glorious treasure-nature and is fully endowed with virtuous merit and the pervasive illumination. Each of you partakes of it! Take care!"

❖

A monk asked, "How can one escape the three realms?" Tianlong said, "Where are you right this moment?"

CHANGSHA JINGCEN, "TIGER CEN"

CHANGSHA JINGCEN (d. 868) was a disciple of Nanquan Puyuan. He had the nickname "Tiger Cen." Although he is known to have lived in the city of Changsha at Lushan Temple, Jingcen roamed China expounding the Dharma according to the situations he encountered. He possessed an extremely pointed and aggressive style of instruction. Thus, after Jingcen literally climbed on top of Yangshan, he was widely likened to a tiger. The lamp records offer evidence of Jingcen's incisive lectures.

Zen master Changsha Jingcen entered the hall and addressed the monks, saying, "If I give you some religious teaching, then there will be grass growing in the hall ten feet deep! But this is something that can't be stopped. So I say to you that all worlds pervading the ten directions are the true monk's eye. All worlds pervading the ten directions are the true monk's complete body. Pervading all worlds in the ten directions is your own brilliant light. All worlds in the ten directions are within your own light. And throughout all worlds in the ten directions there is not a being that is not you. This is what I've taught you when I've said that all the buddhas, dharmas, and sentient beings of the three worlds are the great light of wisdom. But even before this light was propagated, what is the place where you existed? Before this light was propagated, before buddhas and before sentient beings, from where did the mountains, rivers, and the great earth come forth?"

A monk asked, "What is the true monk's eye?"

Changsha said, "So vast and wide that you can't leave it."

Changsha also said, "Those who become buddhas or ancestors can't leave it. The six realms of transmigration can't leave it."

The monk said, "I don't undertand what it is that they can't leave."

Changsha said, "In the day, see the sun. In the night, see the stars."

The monk said, "I don't understand."

Changsha said, "The lofty mountains are colored green upon green."

A monk asked, "Teachers of our order say to 'abide' by sitting in the *bodhi* seat. What is the seat?"

Changsha said, "Just now I'm sitting. Just now you're standing."

A monk asked, "What is the great way?"

Changsha said, "It doesn't exclude you."

The monk asked, "Who is the teacher of all buddhas?"

Changsha said, "For the incalculable eon, who has ever concealed this?"

A monk asked, "What was there before the buddhas?"

Changsha said, "Luzu entered the hall and spoke incoherently to the masters and disciples."

Changsha sent a monk to ask a question of Zen master Hui, who was a fellow student with Changsha under Nanquan.

The monk asked Zen master Hui, "What was it like after you saw Nanquan?"

Hui was silent.

The monk asked, "What was it like before you saw Nanquan?"

Hui said, "There couldn't be anything more."

The monk returned and told Changsha about this conversation.

Changsha then showed the monk a verse that said:

Atop a hundred-foot pole, an unmoving person,
Although he's gained entry, he hasn't reached the truth.
He must step forth from the top of the pole,
Then the world in ten directions is the complete body.

The monk then asked, "If one is at the very top of a hundred-foot pole, how does one step forward?"

Changsha said, "The Lang Province mountains. The Li Province rivers."

The monk said, "I don't understand."

Changsha said, "The four seas and five lakes are splendid within it."

Changsha and Yangshan were enjoying the moon.

Yangshan said, "Everyone is completely endowed with this, but they are unable to make use of it."

Changsha said, "I invite you to use it now."

Yangshan asked, "How would you use it?"

Changsha knocked Yangshan down with a shove to the chest, then stepped on him.

Yangshan said, "Whoa, just like a tiger!" (Changqing Huileng said, "Before they were one family. Afterwards they were not of one family." He also said, "Heresy is difficult to support.")

From this time forward Changsha was known to all as "The Tiger."

A monk asked, "Fundamentally, can people become buddhas or not?"

Changsha said, "Do you think that the emperor of the Great Tang still plows a field and harvests the rice?"

The monk said, "I still don't understand who it is who becomes a buddha."

Changsha said, "It's you that becomes a buddha."

The monk was silent.

Changsha said, "Do you understand?"

The monk said, "No."

Changsha said, "If someone trips on the ground and falls down, and then they use the ground to get up again—does the ground say anything?"

A monk asked, "'Form is emptiness; emptiness is form.' What does this mean?"
Changsha said, "Listen to this verse of mine:

"An obstruction is not a barrier,
A passage is not empty.
If people understand in this manner,
Mind and form are fundamentally the same."

Changsha also said:

"Buddha nature grandly manifests,
But passions obscure abiding nature.
When the selfless nature of beings is realized,
How does my face differ from Buddha's?"

⸻ ◆ ⸻

A monk asked, "What is my mind?"
Changsha said, "All worlds in the ten directions are your mind."
The monk said, "If so, then there's no particular place where my body is manifested."
Changsha said, "*It is* the place where your body is manifested."
The monk said, "*What* is the place where it manifests?"
Changsha said, "The great ocean, vast and deep."
The monk said, "I don't understand."
Changsha said, "Dragons and fish frolic freely, leaping and diving."

⸻ ◆ ⸻

Changsha eulogized his teacher Nanquan, saying, "Great and august Nanquan! His teaching shows the origin of the three worlds—an eternal diamond—radiating limitlessly. He manifested numberless buddhas. Now he's gone back."
Long before, upon his enlightenment under Nanquan, Changsha had composed the following verse:

Today I've returned to my old home's gate,
And Nanquan speaks intimately of the entire universe.
All things reveal the ancients' meaning.
The prodigal regrets unfilial acts.

To this verse Nanquan responded with another that said:

Today's great function is not discussed,
For Nanquan speaks not of the entire universe.
Returning home is the affair of descendants,
The ancients never left the gate.

ZHAOZHOU CONGSHEN

 ZHAOZHOU CONGSHEN (778–897) was a disciple of Nanquan. He came from ancient Caozhou (near the modern city of Heze in Shandong Province). Zhaozhou's first great awakening was at the age of eighteen. After receiving ordination on Mt. Song as a young man, he found guidance for several decades under Nanquan, until that teacher's death. At that time, while already in his fifties, Zhaozhou set out traveling to further cultivate his practice. During this period he met several illustrious teachers such as Huangbo, Jiashan, Yanguan, and others. Eventually, Zhaozhou was invited to settle and teach at the Kwan Yin Monastery located in Zhaozhou (now the Bailin Monastery in Zhaoxian City, Hebei Province).[90]

Zhaozhou's fame spread throughout China. Although he had thirteen Dharma heirs, his lineage soon died out.

Among the many stories and kōans concerning Zhaozhou, it is "Zhaozhou's Wu!" that is the most famous. This story is the first great kōan gate through which countless Zen students have passed.

A monk asked Zhaozhou, "Does a dog have buddha nature?"
Zhaozhou answered "Wu! [in Japanese, 'Mu!']"

Zhaozhou's arrival at Mt. Nanquan is recorded in the lamp records.

Upon their first meeting, Nanquan, who was lying down and resting, asked Zhaozhou, "Where have you come from?"
Zhaozhou said, "I've come from Ruixiang ['Omen Figure']."
Nanquan said, "Did you see the standing omen's figure?"
Zhaozhou said, "No, but I've seen a reclining Tathagata."

Nanquan got up and asked, "As a novice monk, do you have a teacher or not?"

Zhaozhou replied, "I have a teacher."

Nanquan said, "Who is your teacher?"

Zhaozhou stepped in front of Nanquan, bowed, and said, "In the freezing winter cold, a prostrate monk only asks for the master's blessings."

Nanquan approved Zhaozhou's answer and permitted him to enter the monk's hall.

———— ◆ ————

One day, Zhaozhou asked Nanquan, "What is the Way?"

Nanquan said, "Everyday mind is the Way."

Zhaozhou said, "Does it have a disposition?"

Nanquan said, "If it has the slightest intention, then it is crooked."

Zhaozhou said, "When a person has no disposition, then how can he know that this is the Way?"

Nanquan said, "The Way is not subject to knowledge, nor is it subject to no-knowledge. Knowledge is delusive. No-knowledge is nihilistic. When the uncontrived way is really attained, it is like great emptiness, vast and expansive. So how could there be baneful right and wrong?"

At these words Zhaozhou was awakened.

Thereafter Zhaozhou traveled to Mt. Song where he received ordination. He then returned to continue his practice under Nanquan.

———— ◆ ————

One day Zhaozhou asked Nanquan, "Where do people with knowledge go [when they die]?"

Nanquan said, "They go to be bull water buffaloes down at the Tans' and Yues' houses at the base of the mountain."

Zhaozhou said, "Thank you for your instruction."

Nanquan said, "Last night during the third hour the moon reached the window."

———— ◆ ————

Nanquan said, "People of this time must practice among different species."

Zhaozhou said, "Not to speak of 'different,' what do you mean by 'species'?"

Nanquang got down on all fours.

Zhaozhou shoved him over with his foot. Zhaozhou then went into the nirvana hall [the temple infirmary] and yelled, "Sorry! Sorry!"

Nanquan instructed his attendant to ask Zhaozhou, "What are you sorry about?"

Zhaozhou said, "I'm sorry I didn't kick him again."

Zhaozhou went to see Huangbo. When Huangbo saw him coming he closed the door to his room. Zhaozhou picked up a piece of flaming firewood from the stove, and walking into the Dharma hall, he yelled, "Fire! Fire!"

Huangbo threw open his door, and grabbing Zhaozhou he said, "Speak! Speak!"

Zhaozhou said, "After the thief has run off you've drawn your bow."

Zhaozhou also went to Baoshou Yanzhao's place. Baoshou saw him coming and sat on the meditation platform facing away from him. Zhaozhou laid out his meditation mat and bowed toward Baoshou. Baoshou then got down from the meditation platform. Zhaozhou went out.

Zhaozhou also went to Tianhuang Daowu's place. Just when Zhaozhou entered the hall, Daowu yelled, "Here comes an arrow from Nanquan!"

Zhaozhou said, "See the arrow!"

Daowu said, "It's already passed."

Zhaozhou said, "Bulls-eye!"

Zhaozhou entered the hall and addressed the monks, saying, "It's like a lustrous pearl in your hand. If a foreigner comes a foreigner reveals it. If a Chinese comes a Chinese reveals it.

"This old monk uses a blade of grass as a sixty-foot golden statue. I also use a sixty-foot golden statue as a blade of grass.

"Buddha is affliction. Affliction is Buddha."

A monk said, "I don't understand whose house is afflicted by Buddha."

Zhaozhou said, "All people are afflicted by Buddha."

The monk asked, "How can affliction be avoided?"

Zhaozhou said, "Why avoid it?"

One day Zhaozhou was sweeping.

A monk asked, "The master is a great worthy. Why are you sweeping?"

Zhaozhou said, "Dust comes in from outside."

The monk said, "It is a pure temple. Why, then, is there dust?"

Zhaozhou said, "There's some more."

One day Zhaozhou was walking with an official in a park. A rabbit saw them and, becoming alarmed, ran away.

The official asked Zhaozhou, "Master, you are a great worthy. When the rabbit saw you why did it run away?"

Zhaozhou said, "Because I'm good at killing."

---------- ♦ ----------

A monk asked, "Before the flower of awakening has come forth, how does one distinguish pure reality?"

Zhaozhou said, "It's blossomed!"

The monk asked, "Is it purity or is it reality?"

Zhaozhou said, "Purity is reality and reality is purity."

The monk asked, "What is the transcendent affair of people?"

Zhaozhou said, "I'm part of it. You're part of it."

The monk said, "What about before I was ordained?"

Zhaozhou pretended not to hear the monk. The monk remained silent.

Zhaozhou said, "Go! The rock flag has been blown in two by the wind!"

---------- ♦ ----------

Zhaozhou entered the hall and addressed the monks, saying, "A metal buddha does not withstand the furnace. A wooden buddha does not withstand the fire. A mud buddha does not withstand water. The genuine buddha sits within you. 'Bodhi' and 'nirvana,' 'true thusness' and 'buddha nature'—these things are just clothes stuck to the body and they are known as 'afflictions.' Where is the actual ground-truth revealed?

"Big mind is unborn. The myriad dharmas are flawless. Try sitting for twenty or thirty years, and if you still don't understand then cut off my head! The empty flowers of delusion and dreams—disciples work so hard to grab them!

"When nothing deviates from mind, then the myriad dharmas are but one thusness. Since it can't be attained from outside, what will you try to grasp? You're like goats—haphazardly picking up just anything and keeping it in your mouth!

"I heard Yaoshan say, 'People ask me to reveal *it*, but when I teach, it is like something taken from a dog's mouth.' What I teach is like something taken from a dog's mouth. Take what I say as dirty. Don't take what I say as clean. Don't be like a hound always looking for something to eat.

"Where is the Buddhadharma? Thousands of fellows are seeking Buddha, but if you go looking among them for a person of the Way you can't find one. If you're going to be a disciple of Buddha then don't let the mind's disease be so hard to cure.

"This nature existed before the appearance of the world. If the world ends, this will not end. From the time I saw my true self, there hasn't been anyone else. There's just the one in charge. So what is there to be sought elsewhere? At the moment you have this, don't turn your head or shuffle your brains! If you turn your head or shuffle your brains it will be lost!"

————— ◆ —————

A monk was traveling to Mt. Wutai. He asked an old woman, "Which way is the road to Mt. Wutai?"

The old woman said, "Just go straight ahead."

Then the old woman would say, "Another good monk goes on the way."

A monk reported this to Zhaozhou.

Zhaozhou said, "Wait, and I'll go check her out."

The next day Zhaozhou went to the old woman and asked her, "Which way is the road to Mt. Wutai?"

The old woman said, "Just go straight ahead."

As Zhaozhou was leaving she said, "Another good monk goes on the way."

Zhaozhou returned and reported this to the monk, saying, "I've checked out the old lady of Mt. Wutai for you."

————— ◆ —————

A monk asked Zhaozhou, "What is the essential meaning of the Buddha-dharma?" Zhouzhou said, "The cypress tree at the front of the courtyard."

············· ◆ ·············

Zen master Zhaozhou said, "Attaining the Way is not difficult. Just disdain choosing. As soon as words are present there is choosing—there is understanding. It's not to be found in understanding. Is understanding the thing you uphold and sustain?"

A monk asked, "Since it is not found in understanding, what is to be upheld and sustained?"

Zhaozhou said, "I don't know."

The monk said, "Since the master doesn't know what it is, how can you say it isn't within understanding?"

Zhaozhou said, "Ask and you have an answer. Then bow and withdraw."

············· ◆ ·············

A new monk came to the monastery. He said to Zhaozhou, "I've just arrived here. I ask the master to provide me instruction."

Zhaozhou said, "Have you eaten?"

The monk said, "Yes, I've eaten."

Zhaozhou said, "Go wash your bowl."

Upon hearing these words the monk was enlightened.

───────◆───────

A monk asked, "How old is the master?"

Zhaozhou said, "A long string of pearls without end."

The monk asked, "Whose Dharma did the master inherit?"

Zhaozhou said, "Congshen's."

The monk asked, "If suddenly someone from outside asked the master, 'What Dharma does Zhaozhou expound?' what would you say?"

Zhaozhou said, "The salt is expensive but the rice is cheap."

───────◆───────

Zhaozhou heard a novice monk call for permission to enter his quarters for *canqing*.[91]

Zhaozhou said to his attendant, "You go teach him."

The attendant went and gave the student instruction. Afterwards the novice thanked the attendant.

Zhaozhou said, "The novice has come in the door but the attendant is outside." ([Later,] Yunju Ci said, "What place is it that the novice entered and the attendant is outside? If you understand this, you can see Zhaozhou.")

───────◆───────

Zhaozhou asked a monk, "How many sutras do you read in one day?"

The monk said, "Sometimes seven or eight. Sometimes ten."

Zhaozhou said, "Oh, then you can't read scriptures."

The monk said, "Master, how many do you read in a day?"

Zhaozhou said, "In one day I read one word."

───────◆───────

Zhaozhou entered the hall and addressed the monks, saying, "When a true person speaks a heresy, all heresies become true. When a heretic speaks a truth, all truth becomes heresy."

───────◆───────

Zhaowang asked Zen master Zhaozhou, "At your venerable age, Master, how many teeth do you have left?"

Zhaozhou said, "Just one."

Zhaowang said, "Can you still eat things?"

Zhaozhou said, "Although there's only one, it's still chewing."

Zhaozhou then gave Zhaowang his whisk and said, "If you asked where this came from, I couldn't tell you even if I spent my whole life trying to do so."

⸻ ◆ ⸻

An official asked Zhaozhou, "Will the master go into hell or not?"
Zhaozhou said, "I entered hell long ago."
The official said, "Why do you enter hell?"
Zhaozhou said, "If I don't enter hell, who will teach you?"

⸻ ◆ ⸻

A monk asked, "Does the cypress tree in the garden have buddha nature or not?"
Zhaozhou said, "It has."
The monk asked, "When will it become a buddha?"
Zhaozhou said, "When the great void falls to earth."
The monk asked, "When will the great void fall to earth?"
Zhaozhou said, "When the cypress becomes a buddha."

⸻ ◆ ⸻

On the second day of the eleventh month in [the year 897], Zhaozhou lay down on his right side and passed away. He was 120 years old. He received the posthumous title "Great Teacher Truth's Limit."

YUNYAN TANSHENG

YUNYAN TANSHENG (780–841) was a disciple of Yaoshan Weiyan. Yunyan came from ancient Jianchang.[92] Although he studied for about twenty years under Baizhang Huaihai he did not attain enlightenment. After Baizhang passed away, Yunyan traveled to many other teachers before completely ripening under Yaoshan. Yunyan was a close friend of his fellow student Daowu Yuanzhi. The recorded exchanges between these two monks were widely known and quoted by later generations of Zen students. Yunyan later lived on Yunyan Mountain in Tanzhou (near modern Changsha). Among his Dharma heirs was Dongshan Liangjie, the founder of the Caodong (in Japanese, Sōtō) Zen school.

Yunyan Tansheng of Tanzhou came from Jianchang in Zhongling. His lay name was Wang. He left home at a young age to live at Shimen Mountain.[93] He studied under Baizhang Huaihai for twenty years but did not meet with the source. Later, he studied with Yaoshan.

Yaoshan asked him, "Where have you come from?"

Yunyan answered, "From Baizhang."

Yaoshan asked, "What did Baizhang say to his disciples?"

Yunyan said, "He often said, 'I have a saying which is, "The hundred tastes are complete."'"

Yaoshan said, "Something salty tastes salty. Something bland tastes bland. What is neither salty nor bland is a normal taste. What is meant by the phrase, 'One hundred tastes are complete'?"

Yunyan couldn't answer.

Yaoshan said, "What did Baizhang say about the life and death before our eyes?"

Yunyan said, "He said that there is no life and death before our eyes."

Yaoshan said, "How long were you at Baizhang's place?"

Yunyan said, "Twenty years."

Yaoshan said, "So you spent twenty years with Baizhang, but you still haven't rid yourself of rustic ways."

One day when Yunyan was serving as Yaoshan's attendant, Yaoshan asked him, "What else did Baizhang have to say?"

Yunyan said, "Once he said, 'Go beyond three phrases and enlightenment's gone. But within six phrases there's comprehension.'"

Yaoshan said, "Three thousand miles distant the joy can't be felt."

Then Yaoshan said, "What else did Baizhang say?"

Yunyan said, "Once Baizhang entered the hall to address the monks. Everyone stood. He then used his staff to drive everyone out. Then he yelled at the monks, and when they looked back at him he said, 'What is *it?*'"

Yaoshan said, "Why didn't you tell me this before. Thanks to you today I've finally seen elder brother Hai."

Upon hearing these words Yunyan attained enlightenment.

One day Yaoshan asked, "Besides living at Mt. Baizhang, where else have you been?"

Yunyan answered, "I was in Guangnan [Southern China]."

Yaoshan said, "I've heard that east of the city gate of Guangzhou there is a great rock that the local governor can't move, is that so?"

Yunyan said, "Not only the governor! Everyone in the country together can't move it!"

One day Yaoshan said, "I've heard that you can tame lions. Is that so?"
Yunyan said, "Yes."
Yaoshan said, "How many can you tame?"
Yunyan said, "Six."
Yaoshan said, "I can tame them too."
Yunyan asked, "How many does the master tame?"
Yaoshan said, "One."
Yunyan said, "One is six. Six is one."

Later, Yunyan was at Mt. Gui.
Guishan asked him, "I've often heard that when you were at Yaoshan you tamed lions. Is that so?"
Yunyan said, "Yes."
Guishan asked, "Were they always under control, or just sometimes?"
Yunyan said, "When I wanted them under control they were under control. When I wanted to let them loose, they ran loose."
Guishan said, "When they ran loose where were they?"
Yunyan said, "They're loose! They're loose!"

Yunyan was making tea.
Daowu asked him, "Who are you making tea for?"
Yunyan said, "There's someone who wants it."
Yunyan said, "Why don't you let him make it himself?"
Yunyan said, "Fortunately, I'm here to do it."

Once, when Yunyan was sweeping, Daowu said to him, "Too hurried!"
Yunyan said, "You should know that there is a something that is not hurried."
Daowu said, "In that case, is there a second moon?"
Yunyan held up the broom and said, "What moon is this?"
Daowu then went off. (Xuansha heard about this and said, "Exactly the second moon.")

After becoming an abbot, Yunyan addressed the monks, saying, "There is the son of a certain household. There is no question that he can't answer."

Dongshan came forward and asked, "How many classic books are there in his house?"

Yunyan said, "Not a single word."

Dongshan said, "Then how can he be so knowledgeable?"

Yunyan said, "Day and night he has never slept."

Dongshan said, "Can he be asked about a certain matter?"

Yunyan said, "What he answers is not spoken."

———— ◆ ————

Zen master Yunyan asked a monk, "Where have you come from?"

The monk said, "From Tianxiang ['heavenly figure']."

Yunyan said, "Did you see a buddha or not?"

The monk said, "I saw one."

Yunyan said, "Where did you see him?"

The monk said, "I saw him in the lower realm."

Yunyan said, "An ancient buddha! An ancient buddha!"

———— ◆ ————

During [the year 841] Yunyan became ill. After giving orders to have the bath readied he called the head of the monks and instructed him to prepare a banquet for the next day because a monk was leaving. On the evening of the twenty-seventh of the month he died. His cremated remains contained more than a thousand sacred relics that were placed in a stone stupa. Yunyan received the posthumous title "Great Teacher No Abode."

CHUANZI DECHENG

CHUANZI DECHENG (805–81), also known as the "Boatman" or "Boat Monk," was a disciple and Dharma heir of Yaoshan. His lay home was located in Suining (now a place in modern Sichuan Province). Decheng studied with Yaoshan for thirty years and received the mind seal. Later, he lived in relative seclusion at Huating, on the bank of the Wu River (in the area of modern Shanghai), where he used a small boat to ferry people across the river.

Zen master Chengzi Decheng of Huating in Xiuzhou possessed great integrity and unusual ability. At the time when he received Dharma transmission from

Yaoshan he intimately practiced the Way with Daowu and Yunyan. When he left Mt. Yao he said to them, "You two must each go into the world your separate ways and uphold the essence of our teacher's path. My own nature is undisciplined. I delight in nature and in doing as I please. I'm not fit [to be head of a monastery]. But remember where I reside. And if you come upon persons of great ability, send one of them to me. Let me teach him and I'll pass on to him everything I've learned in life. In this way I can repay the kindness of our late teacher."

Then Decheng departed and went to Huating in Xiuzhou. There he lived his life rowing a small boat, transporting travelers across the river. People there didn't know that he possessed far-reaching knowledge and ability. They called him the "Boat Monk."

Once at the boat landing at the side of the river an official asked him, "What do you do each day?"

Decheng held the boat oar straight up in the air and said, "Do you understand?"

The official said, "I don't understand."

Decheng said, "If you only row in the clear waves, it's hard to find the golden fish."

Decheng composed a verse that said:

Thirty years on the river bank,
Angling for the great function,
If you don't catch the golden fish, it's all in vain.
You may as well reel in and go back home.

Letting down the line ten thousand feet,
A breaking wave makes ten thousand ripples.
At night in still water, the cold fish won't bite.
An empty boat filled with moonlight returns.

Sailing the sea for thirty years,
The fish seen in clear water won't take the hook.
Breaking the fishing pole, growing bamboo,
Abandoning all schemes, one finds repose.

There's a great fish that can't be measured.
It embraces the astonishing and wondrous!
In wind and thunder transformed,
How can it be caught?

Others only seek gathering lotus flowers,
Their scent pervading the wind.
But as long as there are two shores and a lone red boat,
There's no escape from pollution, nor any attainment of emptiness.

If you asked, "Is this lone boat all there is in life?"
I'd say, "Descendants will each see the results."
Not depending on earth or heaven,
When the rain shawl is removed, nothing's left to pass on.

[Later,] Daowu went to Jingkou where he happened to see Jiashan Shanhui give a lecture. A monk attending the talk asked Jiashan, "What is the dharmakaya?"

Jiashan said, "The dharmakaya is formless."[94]

The monk asked, "What is the Dharma eye?"

Jiashan said, "The Dharma eye is without defect."

When he heard this, Daowu laughed loudly in spite of himself.

Jiashan got down off the lecture platform and said to Daowu, "Something I said in my answer to that monk was not correct and it caused you to laugh out loud. Please don't withhold your compassionate instruction about this!"

Daowu said, "You have gone into the world to teach, but have you not had a teacher?"

Jiashan said, "I've had none. May I ask you to clarify these matters?"

Daowu said, "I can't speak of it. I invite you to go see the Boat Monk at Huating."

Jiashan said, "Who is he?"

Daowu said, "Above him there's not a single roof tile, below him there's no ground to plant a hoe. If you want to see him you must change into your traveling clothes."

After the meeting was over, Jiashan packed his bag and set out for Huating.

When Decheng saw Jiashan coming he said, "Your Reverence! In what temple do you reside?"

Jiashan said, "I don't abide in a temple. Where I abide is not like..."

Decheng said, "It's not like? It's not like what?"

Jiashan said, "It's not like the Dharma that meets the eye."

Decheng said, "Where did you learn this teaching?"

Jiashan said, "Not in a place which the ears or eyes can perceive."

Decheng said, "A single phrase and you fall into the path of principle. Then you're like a donkey tethered to a post for countless eons."

Then Decheng said, "You've let down a thousand-foot line. You're fishing very deep, but your hook is still shy by three inches. Why don't you say something?"

As Jiashan was about to speak Decheng knocked him into the water with the oar. When Jiashan clambered back into the boat Decheng yelled at him, "Speak! Speak!"

Jiashan tried to speak but before he could do so Decheng struck him again. Suddenly Jiashan attained great enlightenment. He then nodded his head three times.

Then Chuanzi said, "Now you're the one with the pole and line. Just act by your own nature and don't defile the clear waves."

Jiashan asked, "What do you mean by 'throw off the line and cast down the pole'?"

Chuanzi said, "The fishing line hangs in the green water, drifting without intention."

Jiashan said, "There is no path whereby words may gain entry to the essence. The tongue speaks, but cannot speak it."

Chuanzi said, "When the hook disappears into the river waves, then the golden fish is encountered."

Jiashan then covered his ears.

Chuanzi said, "That's it! That's it!" He then enjoined Jiashan, saying, "Hereafter, conceal yourself in a place without any trace. If the place has any sign don't stay there. I stayed with Yaoshan for thirty years and what I learned there I've passed to you today. Now that you have it, stay away from crowded cities. Instead, plant your hoe deep in the mountains. Find one person or one-half a person who won't let it die."

Jiashan then bid Chuanzi good-bye. As he walked away he looked back at Chuanzi.

Suddenly Chuanzi yelled, "Your Reverence!"

Jiashan stopped and turned around.

Chuanzi held up the oar and said, "Do you say there's anything else?" He then tipped over the boat and disappeared into the water, never to be seen again.

Daowu Yuanzhi, "Zongzhi"

Daowu Yuanzhi (769–835) was a disciple of Yaoshan Weiyan. He came from ancient Yuzhang (now Nanchang City in Jiangxi Province). As a young man he is said to have studied and received ordination under Baizhang Niepan. Later he studied with Yaoshan and received the mind seal of the Qingyuan lineage. After traveling for many years to various Zen mountains, he resided and taught on Mt. Daowu (near modern-day Changsha in Hunan Province).

One day, Zen master Yaoshan asked his student Daowu, "Where have you been?"

Daowu said, "Walking on the mountain."

Yaoshan said, "Without leaving this room, quickly speak!"

Daowu said, "On the mountain the birds are white as snow. At the bottom of the brook the fish never stop swimming."

◆

Once when Daowu and Yunyan were with Yaoshan, Yaoshan said, "Saying that there is a place where wisdom does not reach violates the taboo. Anyone saying this will grow horns. Monk Zhi [Daowu], what do you say?"

Daowu then went out.

Yunyan then asked Yaoshan, "Why didn't elder brother answer you?"

Yaoshan said, "My back hurts today. Anyway, he knows why. Why don't you go ask him?"

Yunyan then went to Daowu and said, "Why didn't you answer the master today?"

Daowu said, "Go ask the master." ([Later,] A monk asked Zen master Yunju Daoying, "What is it that 'violates the taboo'?" Yunju said, "It is a most poisonous phrase." The monk asked, "What is a most poisonous phrase?" Yunju said, "With one strike it slays dragons and snakes.")

When Yunyan died, his disciples conveyed his farewell letter to Daowu. When Daowu opened and read the letter he said, "Yunyan didn't understand. I regret that at that time I didn't explain it to him. Even so, in the end he did not become Yaoshan's heir in vain." ([Later,] Zen master Xuanjue said, "When the ancients speak in this manner do you understand them or not? What do you say is the place that Yunyan didn't understand?")[95]

◆

Yaoshan entered the hall and addressed the monks, saying, "I have a single phrase that I have never said to anyone."

Daowu stood up and said, "I follow you."

A monk asked Yaoshan, "How is Yaoshan's one phrase spoken?"

Yaoshan said, "Without words."

Daowu said, "It's already spoken."

———— ◆ ————

One day, Daowu picked up his hat to go out.

Yunyan pointed to the hat and said, "What does this do?"

Daowu said, "It has a use."

Yunyan said, "If you suddenly encountered a violent storm, then what?"

Daowu said, "It would cover me."

Yunyan said, "Does the hat also have a cover?"

Daowu said, "Yes it does, but its cover never leaks."

———— ◆ ————

Guishan asked Yunyan, "With what does *bodhi* sit?"

Yunyan said, "It sits with nonaction."[96]

Yunyan then asked Guishan the same question.

Guishan said, "It sits with all empty dharmas."

Yunyan then asked Daowu, "What do you say?"

Daowu said, "Bodhi sits listening to it. Bodhi lies down listening to it. But as for the one who neither sits nor lies down—speak! Speak!"

Guishan got up and left.

———— ◆ ————

Guishan asked Daowu, "Where did you go?"

Daowu said, "To see a doctor."

Guishan said, "How many people are sick?"

Daowu said, "Some are sick. Some are not."

Guishan said, "Is one who is not sick the monk Zhi?"

Daowu said, "Being sick or not sick has nothing to do with *it*. Speak! Speak!"

Guishan said, "Being able to speak has nothing to do with *it*."

———— ◆ ————

In the ninth month of [the year 835], Daowu became ill. His condition turned grave. The monks came to inquire about his welfare.

Daowu said to them, "Do you understand the phrase, 'Having received, making restitution'?"

The monks were startled by these words. Ten days later, just before his death, Daowu said to the congregation, "I'll go to the west. I shouldn't go east."

Upon saying these words Daowu died. A few bones remained in his cremated remains. His stupa was named Daowu. Later it was struck by lightning and moved to the south side of Mt. Shishuang.

CUIWEI WUXUE

CUIWEI WUXUE (n.d.) was a disciple of Danxia Tianran. His life is obscure. The first meeting between Cuiwei and Danxia is recorded in the lamp records.

Cuiwei asked Danxia, "What is [the teaching of] all buddhas?"

Danxia exclaimed, "Fortunately, life is fundamentally wonderful. Why do you need to take up a cleaning cloth and broom?"

Wuxue retreated three steps.

Danxia said, "Wrong."

Wuxue again came forward.

Danxia said, "Wrong. Wrong."

Wuxue then lifted one foot into the air, spun in a circle and went out.

Danxia said, "Such an answer! It's turning one's back on all the buddhas."

Upon hearing these words, Wuxue attained great enlightenment.

Later, when Wuxue was abbot of a temple, Touzi Yiqing said to him, "I'm not clear about what resulted when the Second Ancestor first saw Bodhidharma."

Zen master Wuxue said, "Right now you can see me. What is the result?"

At that moment Touzi suddenly awakened to the profound mystery.

◆

One day Zen master Cuiwei Wuxue was walking in the Dharma hall. Touzi walked up in front of him, bowed to him and said, "The essential meaning of the First Ancestor coming from the west—how does the master demonstrate this to people?"

The master stopped walking and stood there.

Touzi said, "Please demonstrate it, Master."

Cuiwei said, "Do you want another ladle full of polluted water?"

Touzi then bowed in thanks.

Cuiwei said, "Don't make matters worse."

Touzi said, "It's the season when weeds grow everywhere."

When Cuiwei was making offerings to the sacred images a monk [Yunju Daoying] asked, "Zen master Danxia burned a wooden buddha. Why then, Master, do you make offerings to the wooden statues?"

Cuiwei said, "Because they won't burn. But if you want to make them an offering they'll let you do so."

The monk asked, "If you make an offering to the sacred figures will they come or not?"

Cuiwei said, "Aren't you able to eat every day?"

The monk didn't answer.

Cuiwei said, "There aren't many clever ones."

LONGTAN CHONGXIN

LONGTAN CHONGXIN (n.d.) was a disciple of Tianhuang Daowu. He came from ancient Zhugong (near modern Jiangling City in Hubei Province). His family members were cake sellers.

Daowu's home was near the entrance to Tianhuang Temple. Each day Chongxin would present ten small cakes as an offering to Daowu. Each time, Daowu would leave one cake, saying, "This is for the sake of your descendants."

One day, Chongxin said, "I take cakes everywhere, so why do you leave one for me? Does it have any special meaning?"

Daowu said, "You bring the cakes, so what harm is there to return one to you?"

At these words Chongxin grasped the deeper meaning. Because of this he left home.

Daowu said, "Previously you've been respectful to virtue and goodness and now you've placed your faith in what I say, so you'll be named 'Chongxin' ['Respect Faith']."

Thereafter Chongxin remained close to Daowu as his attendant.

One day, Chongxin asked Zen master Daowu, "Since I've come here, you've never taught me about essential mind."

Daowu said, "Since you came here, I've never stopped giving you instruction about your essential mind."

Chongxin said, "Where have you pointed it out?"

Daowu said, "When you bring tea to me, I receive it for you. When you bring food to me, I receive it for you. When you do prostrations before me, I bow my head. Where have I not given instruction about your essential mind?"

Chongxin bowed his head for a long time.

Daowu said, "Look at it directly. If you try to think about it you'll miss it."

Upon hearing these words Chongxin woke up.

Chongxin then asked Dongwu, "How does one uphold it?"

Daowu said, "Live in an unfettered manner, in accord with circumstances. Give yourself over to everyday mind, for there is nothing sacred to be realized outside of *this*."

Later, when Chongxin was abbot of Longtan Temple in Lizhou, a monk asked him, "Who is it who attains a jewel on his head [signifying bodhisattvahood]?"

Chongxin replied, "The one who does not delight in it."

The monk asked, "What place is the jewel found?"

Chongxin replied, "If there's such a place then tell me, where is it?"

One day a nun asked Zen master Longtan, "How can I become a monk?"

Longtan said, "How long have you been a nun?"

The nun said, "Will there be a time I can become a monk or not?"

Longtan said, "What are you right now?"

The nun said, "I have a nun's body. Don't you recognize this?"

Longtan asked, "Who knows you?"

Provincial Governor Li Ao asked Zen master Longtan, "What is the wisdom of true thusness?"

Longtan said, "I have no wisdom of true thusness."

The governor said, "I am fortunate to have met you, Master."

Longtan said, "You still speak outside the essential matter."

Deshan asked Zen master Longtan, "Long have I heard of Longtan. Up to now I haven't seen the marsh, nor has the dragon appeared."[97]

Longtan said, "You yourself have arrived at Dragon Marsh."

Eleventh Generation

LINJI YIXUAN   MUZHOU DAOMING   DASUI FAZHEN

LINGYUN ZHIQIN   JINGZHAO MIHU   YANGSHAN HUIJI

XIANGYAN ZHIXIAN   LIU TIEMO   JINHUA JUZHI   MOSHAN LIAORAN

YANYANG SHANZHAO   DONGSHAN LIANGJIE   JIASHAN SHANHUI

SHISHUANG QINGZHU   TOUZI DATONG   DESHAN XUANJIAN

LINJI YIXUAN "HUIZHAO"

LINJI YIXUAN (d. 866) was a disciple of Huangbo Xiyun. Linji is a preeminent figure in the history of Zen. He came from the city of Nanhua in ancient Caozhou (now the city of Dongming in Shandong Province). As the founder of the Linji school of Zen (in Japanese, *Rinzai*), his tradition remains, along with the Caodong school, as one of the two lineages that survive to the present day.

After taking the vows of a monk, Linji studied the sutras, the Vinaya, and the various doctrines that were carried on the currents of Buddhism in his era. Although he practiced under Guishan Lingyou, his enlightenment came about under Huangbo Xiyun, with the teacher Gao'an Dayu a key player in the drama.

The lamp records provide this account of Linji's enlightenment:

> From the beginning of his residence at Huangbo, Linji's performance of his duties was exemplary. At that time, Muzhou Daoming served as head monk.
>
> Muzhou asked Linji, "How long have you been practicing here?"
>
> Linji said, "Three years."
>
> Muzhou said, "Have you gone for an interview with the master or not?"
>
> Linji said, "I haven't done so. I don't know what to ask him."
>
> Muzhou said, "Why not ask him, 'What is the essential meaning of Buddhism?'"
>
> So Linji went to see Huangbo, but before he could finish his question Huangbo struck him.
>
> Linji went out, and Muzhou asked him, "What happened when you asked him?"
>
> Linji said, "Before I could get the words out he hit me. I don't understand."
>
> Muzhou said, "Go ask him again."
>
> So Linji asked Huangbo again, and Huangbo once again hit him. Linji asked

a third time, and Huangbo hit him again.

Linji revealed this to Muzhou, saying, "Before you urged me to ask about the Dharma, but all I got was a beating. Because of evil karmic hindrances I'm not able to comprehend the essential mystery. So, today I'm going to leave here."

Muzhou said, "If you're going to leave, you must say good-bye to the master."

Linji bowed and went off.

Muzhou then went to Huangbo and said, "That monk who asked you the questions—although he's young he's very extraordinary. If he comes to say good-bye to you please give him appropriate instruction. Later he'll become a great tree under which everyone on earth will find refreshing shade."

The next day when Linji came to say good-bye to Huangbo, Huangbo said, "You don't need to go somewhere else. Just go over to the Gao'an Monastery and practice with Dayu. He'll explain it to you."

When Linji reached Dayu, Dayu said, "Where have you come from?"

Linji said, "From Huangbo."

Dayu said, "What did Huangbo say?"

Linji said, "Three times I asked him about the essential doctrine and three times I got hit. I don't know if I made some error or not."

Dayu said, "Huangbo has old grandmotherly affection and endures all this difficulty for your sake—and here you are asking whether you've made some error or not!"

Upon hearing these words Linji was awakened.

Linji then said, "Actually, Huangbo's Dharma is not so great."

Dayu grabbed him and said, "Why you little bed-wetter! You just came and said you don't understand. But now you say there's not so much to Huangbo's teaching. What do you see? Speak! Speak!"

Linji then hit Dayu on his side three times.

Dayu let go of him, saying: "Your teacher is Huangbo. I've got nothing to do with it."

Linji then left Dayu and returned to Huangbo.

Huangbo saw him and said, "This fellow who's coming and going. How can he ever stop?"

Linji said, "Only through grandmotherly concern."

Linji then bowed and stood in front of Huangbo.

Huangbo said, "Who has gone and returned?"

Linji said, "Yesterday I received the master's compassionate instruction. Today I went and practiced at Dayu's."

Huangbo said, "What did Dayu say?"

Linji then recounted his meeting with Dayu.

Huangbo said, "That old fellow Dayu talks too much! Next time I see him I'll give him a painful swat!"

Linji said, "Why wait until later, here's a swat right now!"

Linji then hit Huangbo.

Huangbo yelled, "This crazy fellow has come here and grabbed the tiger's whiskers!"

Linji shouted.

Huangbo then yelled to his attendant, "Take this crazy man to the practice hall!"

◆

One day, Linji was sleeping in the monks' hall. Huangbo came in and, seeing Linji lying there, struck the floor with his staff. Linji woke up and lifted his head. Seeing Huangbo standing there, he then put his head down and went back to sleep. Huangbo struck the floor again and walked to the upper section of the hall. Huangbo then saw the head monk, who was sitting in meditation.

Huangbo said, "There's someone down below who is sitting in meditation. What do you imagine you're doing?"

The head monk said, "What's going on with this old fellow?" (Guishan recounted this story to Yangshan, saying, "Just like old Huangbo! What was his meaning?" Yangshan said, "Two bettors, one race.")

◆

Huangbo entered the kitchen and asked the cook, "What are you doing?"

The cook said, "Selecting rice for the monks' meal."

Huangbo said, "How much do they eat in one meal?"

The cook said, "Two and a half stone [one hundred fifty kilos]."

Huangbo said, "Isn't that too much?"

The cook said, "I'm afraid it's not enough!"

Huangbo hit him.

The cook related this event to Linji. Linji said, "I'll check out the old fellow for you."

Linji then went and stood in attendance for Huangbo.

Huangbo brought up his conversation with the cook. Linji said, "The cook doesn't understand. Please, Master, say a turning phrase on his behalf."

Huangbo said, "You ask it."

Linji said, "Isn't that too much?"

Huangbo said, "Tomorrow, have another meal."

Linji said, "Why say 'tomorrow'? Have a meal right now!" And so saying he hit Huangbo.

Huangbo yelled, "This crazy man has come in here and grabbed the tiger's whiskers again!"

Linji shouted and went out.

(Guishan brought up this case to Yangshan, asking, "What was the idea behind these two worthies?" Yangshan said, "What do you think, Master?" Guishan said, "When raising a child you learn a father's compassion." Yangshan said "No, it's not like that." Guishan said, "What do you say?" Yangshan said, "It's like enticing a thief to destroy the house.")

◆

Linji went to visit Bodhidharma's stupa. The caretaker there said, "Will you first bow to the Buddha, or will you first bow to the First Ancestor?"

Linji said, "I don't bow to either one."

The caretaker said, "How did the Buddha and First Ancestor offend you?"

Linji shook his sleeves and left.

◆

Linji said, "There's a type of student who goes to Mt. Wutai to seek out Manjushri. That student has already made a mistake! There's no Manjushri at Mt. Wutai. Do you want to know Manjushri? It's just what is in front of your eyes! From first to last it's not anything else. Don't doubt it anywhere you go! It's the living Manjushri!"

◆

When Linji was about to die he sat upright and said, "After I'm gone, my *Treasury of the True Dharma Eye* cannot be destroyed."

Linji's disciple, Sansheng, said, "How could we dare destroy the Master's *Treasury of the True Dharma Eye*?"

Linji said, "In the future if someone asks about my teaching, what will you say to them?"

Sansheng shouted.

Linji said, "Who would have thought that my *Treasury of the True Dharma Eye* would be destroyed by this blind ass!"

Upon saying these words Linji passed away, sitting upright.

Muzhou Daoming, "Chen Zunsu"

Muzhou Daoming (780–877) was a disciple of Huangbo Xiyun. He lived and taught at Kaiyuan Temple in ancient Muzhou.[98] Muzhou's surname was Chen. He was widely known in China by the name "Honored Elder Chen." The *Wudeng Huiyuan* records that as a youth he went to a temple to offer incense to Buddha, and upon seeing the monks, he felt as though he had known them from some ancient time. He then returned home and received permission from his parents to become a monk. He looked unusual, with foreboding eyes and seven pockmarks on his face. As a young man Muzhou first studied the Vinaya and was well acquainted with Buddhist scriptures. Later, when he traveled, he met with Huangbo and eventually became his Dharma heir. Muzhou also played a key role in the story of Linji's enlightenment. He later taught the great Zen master Yunmen Wenyan.

Muzhou possessed a severe teaching style. None but the most confident students dared to address him. It is said he could tell the disposition of a student by the student's footsteps as he approached his room. When the student came near, Muzhou would often slam the door shut and yell, "Nobody's here!" If the master would see a monk talking in the meditation hall he'd call the head monk and say, "That monk's a lumber carrier!"

At one time, during the chaos of the Huang Chao uprising, Muzhou took up residence in his old home and supported his mother by fixing sandals. A legend says that he placed a pair of sandals on the city gate to advertise his service. Huang Chao and his forces entered the city, and Huang Chao himself tried to take the sandals off of the gate, but they magically could not be picked up. This shocked the rebel leader, and he is reported to have said, "A holy person lives in this city!" The frightened bandit leader and his forces then fled the city in fear.

One day, Zen master Muzhou said to his congregation, "Has any one of you gained an entrance? If you haven't gained an entrance then that's what you must do. If you gain an entrance then you won't show ingratitude toward me."

A monk bowed and said, "I don't dare have ingratitude toward you."

Muzhou said, "You've already shown ingratitude."

❖

Muzhou said, "Since I've been abbot, I've never seen someone without an issue come before me. Why can't one of you come forward?"

A monk then came forward. Muzhou said, "The temple director isn't here. So take yourself out the front gate of the monastery and get twenty hits with the staff."

The monk said, "What did I do wrong?"

Muzhou said, "Your head's already in a *cangue* and now you've put on manacles."[99]

⋄

Muzhou asked a monk, "Where do you come from?"

The monk said, "From Liuyang."

Muzhou said, "What does the teacher there say when a student asks him about the great meaning of the Buddhadharma?"

The monk said, "He says, 'Traveling everywhere without a path.'"

Muzhou said, "Does that teacher really say that or not?"

The monk said, "He really does say that."

Muzhou took his staff and struck the monk, saying, "This fool just repeats words!"

⋄

One day Muzhou was standing on a corridor path in the monastery.

A monk came up to him and asked, "Where is Abbot Muzhou's room?"

Muzhou took off a sandal and hit himself on top of the head.

The monk walked off.

Muzhou yelled, "Worthy!"

The monk turned his head.

Muzhou pointed and said, "It's that way!"

⋄

The head monk came to Muzhou for an interview.

Muzhou said, "Can you expound on the consciousness-only doctrine?"[100]

The monk said, "I dare not."

Muzhou said, "In the morning, traveling to the Western Paradise.[101] In the evening, returning to the land of Tang. Do you understand?"

The head monk said, "I don't understand."

Muzhou said, "Oh! Oh! Not upholding five precepts!"[102]

⋄

A "purple robed" worthy came to visit Muzhou.

When he bowed, Muzhou grabbed the string that hung from his hat and said, "What is this called?"

The monk said, "It's called a facing heaven hat."

Muzhou said, "Oh, in that case I won't pull it off."

Muzhou also said, "What doctrine do you expound?"

The monk said, "The consciousness-only doctrine."

Muzhou said, "What do you say of it?"

The monk said, "The three worlds are only mind. The myriad dharmas are only consciousness."

Muzhou pointed to the door screen and said, "What's that?"

The monk said, "A form dharma."

Muzhou said, "In front of the screen you received the purple robe and expounded scripture to the emperor. Why can't you uphold the five precepts?"

The monk couldn't answer.

A newly arrived monk bowed to Muzhou.

Muzhou yelled at him, "Why have you stolen the fruit that has been here so long?"

The monk said, "Master, I've just arrived here. How can you speak of stealing fruit?"

Muzhou said, "I see the stolen goods!"

When Muzhou was near death, he summoned the monks and said, "My karma is exhausted. I'm dying."

He then sat in a cross-legged position and passed away. The monks cremated his body with sandalwood. His ashes fell like rain. They then stored his sacred relics and placed a statue of his likeness in the temple. The master was ninety-eight years old and had been a monk for seventy-six years.

DASUI FAZHEN, "SHENZHAO"

DASUI FAZHEN (878–963) was a disciple of Changqing Da'an. He came from ancient Zizhou (now the city of Santai in Sichuan Province). He is recorded to have experienced great enlightenment while still quite young. After becoming a monk at Huiyi Temple, he traveled extensively and studied with the teachers Daowu Yuanzhi, Yunyan Tansheng, and Dongshan Liangjie, among others. Some accounts describe him as a diligent student and heir of the Guiyang Zen lineage, although both the *Transmission of the Lamp* and the *Book of Serenity* describe him as a student of Changqing Da'an, making Guishan his Dharma uncle. Eventually returning to his native Sichuan, he first lived at Mt. Shankou's Longhuai Temple. Later he dwelled for more than ten years in a large hollow tree at the site of an old temple behind Mt. Dasui.

Guishan asked Dasui Fazhen, "You've been practicing here with me for some time. Why haven't you asked any questions?"

Dasui said, "What would you have me ask?"

Guishan said, "Why don't you ask, 'What is Buddha?'"

Dasui abruptly covered Guishan's mouth with his hand.

Guishan exclaimed, "You've truly attained the marrow!"

❖

Zen master Dasui entered the hall and addressed the monks, saying, "Self-nature is originally pure and replete with virtue, but due to purity and pollution there is differentiation. Thus, the enlightenment of the saints has been realized entirely through purity, while the delusions of common people are engendered by pollution, and are always pulling them down into the cycle of birth and death.

"But the essence of purity and pollution is undifferentiated. Thus the *Maha-prajnaparamita Sutra* says, 'Not two, thus no separation.'"

❖

A monk asked Zen master Dasui, "When the aeonic fire engulfs everything, is *this* annihilated or not?"

Dasui said, "Annihilated."

The monk said, "Then it is annihilated along with everything else?"

Dasui said, "It is annihilated along with everything else."

The monk refused to accept this answer. He later went to Touzi Datong and relayed to him his conversation with Dasui.

Touzi lit incense and bowed to the figure of the Buddha, saying, "The ancient buddha of West River has appeared."[103]

Then Touzi said to the monk, "You should go back there quickly and atone for your mistake."

The monk went back to see Dasui, but Dasui had already died. The monk then went back to see Touzi, but Touzi had also passed away.

❖

A monk asked Dasui, "What is the sign of a great man?"

Dasui said, "He doesn't have a placard on his stomach."

Dasui asked a monk, "Where are you going?"

The monk said, "I'm going to live alone on West Mountain."

Dasui asked, "If I call out to the top of East Mountain for you, will you come or not?"

The monk said, "Of course not."

Dasui said, "You haven't attained 'living alone' yet."

A monk asked, "When the great matter of life and death arrives, then what?"

Dasui said, "If there's tea, drink tea. If there's food, eat food."

The monk said, "Who receives this support?"

Dasui said, "Just pick up your bowl."

Next to Dasui's cottage there was a tortoise.

A monk asked, "Most beings grow bones inside their skin. Why does this being grow skin inside its bones?"

Dasui took off his grass sandal and put it on the tortoise's back.

The monk didn't know what to say.

A monk asked, "What is the essential Dharma of all the buddhas?"

Dasui held up his whisk and said, "Do you understand?"

The monk said, "No."

Dasui said, "A whisk."

Dasui held up his staff and said, "Where did it arise from?"

Someone said, "From causation."

Dasui said, "How wretched! How bitter!"

Dasui asked, "Where did that monk go?"

Someone said, "He went to Mt. Emei to venerate Samantabhadra."

Dasui held up his whisk and said, "Manjushri and Samantabhadra are always right here."

A monk drew a circle in the air and then made the motion of throwing it behind him. He then bowed. Dasui called for his attendant to serve tea to the monk.

When a large number of people were assembled to hear Dasui, he contorted his mouth into a pained position and said, "Is there anyone here who can cure my mouth?"

The monks competed with one another to offer medicine, and when lay people heard about this matter, many of them also sent potions. But Dasui refused them all. Seven days later he slapped himself and caused his mouth to assume a normal appearance.

Dasui then said, "These two lips have been drumming against each other all this time—up until now no one has cured them!"

He then sat in an upright position and passed away.

LINGYUN ZHIQIN

LINGYUN ZHIQIN (n.d.) was a disciple of Guishan Lingyou. He came from the ancient city of Changxi in Ben Province (now the city of Xiapu on the coast of Fujian Province). He gained enlightenment when he saw a peach tree in bloom. He then composed a verse that gave evidence of his awakening. The lamp records offer this account.

When Lingyun saw the peach blossoms, he composed a verse:

For thirty years I've sought the swordsman.
Many times the leaves have fallen, the branches bare.
After seeing the peach blossoms,
Never doubting again.

Guishan read Lingyun's verse and questioned him. He then confirmed Lingyun's enlightenment, saying, "Those who arrive due to conditions never fall away. From now on uphold and sustain it."

Zen master Lingyun entered the hall and addressed the monks, saying, "Among you there are persons with various strengths and weaknesses, but you should all observe the vegetation of the four seasons, the leaves falling and the flowers blooming—events which have gone on for an incalculable eon. The gods, human kind, all the realms of existence—earth, water, fire, and wind—all of these things come to completion and pass away in the cycle of existence. But when all of cause and effect is exhausted and the nether realms are finished, still throughout the universe not a single hair will have been created or taken away. There remains only a fundamental numinous consciousness that is eternal.

"No matter where it is that those of high ability permanently abide with their good companions of the Way, and make this truth evident by renouncing the world, that place is where Dharma is revealed. Those of middling and low ability who remain ignorant, unable to realize illumination, they remain submerged in the three realms and in transmigration through life and death.

"Shakyamuni Buddha provided a teaching to evidence this truth for gods and humanity, revealing the path of wisdom. Can you understand it?"

A monk asked, "How can one escape from birth, old age, sickness, and death?"

Lingyun said, "The green mountain is fundamentally unmoving, but the floating clouds pass back and forth."

A monk asked, "At the time the emperor emerges, then what?"

Lingyun said, "Outside there's a luminous springtime. Don't ask about Changan City."

A monk asked, "How can one gain an audience with the emperor?"

Lingyun said, "The blind crane dives into the clear pond. Fish scatter from its feet."

A monk asked, "What is the great meaning of our school?"

Lingyun said, "The donkey's matters are unfinished, yet the horse's affairs arrive."

The monk said, "I don't understand."

Lingyun said, "Spectacles happening every night, but the essential spirit seldom met."

Jingzhao Mihu, "Mi the Seventh"

The monk Jingzhao Mihu (n.d.) was a Dharma heir of Guishan. He taught in the ancient Chinese capital city of Jingzhao [another name for ancient Changan]. Mihu means "Mi [the] Foreigner." The *Book of Serenity* describes him as having a wonderful beard. The *Transmission of the Lamp* provides some accounts of his life and teachings.

> When Mihu resided at Jingzhao, an old worthy asked him, "Nowadays if people see a piece of broken well rope in the light of the moon they say it's a snake. I'd like to know what you would call it if you saw a buddha?"
>
> Mihu said, "If there's a buddha to be seen, it's not other than all beings."
>
> The old monk said, "A thousand years of peach pits."

◆

> Mihu had a monk ask Yangshan Huiji, "During these times is there authentic enlightenment or not?"
>
> Yangshan said, "It's not that enlightenment is lacking, but how does one avoid falling into what's secondary?"
>
> The monk went back to Mihu and related what Yangshan said. Mihu deeply approved.

◆

> Mihu sent a monk to ask Dongshan, "What do you have to say about that?"
>
> Dongshan said, "You have to turn around and ask him, then you can find out."
>
> Mihu also agreed with this.

Yangshan Huiji

Yangshan Huiji (807–83) was the main disciple of Guishan Lingyou. Yangshan came from ancient Shaozhou (now the city of Shaoguan in Guangdong Province). His parents refused him permission to leave home and become a monk, so Yangshan demonstrated his resolve to them by cutting off two of his fingers, vowing that he would seek the true Dharma to repay his filial obligations. Accounts vary about where he first entered the clergy. It is likely that he first studied under Zen master Bu Yutong, the abbot of He'an Temple in Guangzhou.

After Yangshan received tonsure, but before receiving full ordination, he traveled north to visit the famous temples that existed in the area of modern Hunan and Jiangxi provinces.

After traveling for some time, Yangshan resided and studied under the teacher Danyuan Yingzhen, the famous disciple of National Teacher Nanyang Huizhong. There he had his first great insight.

Yangshan then traveled to study under Guishan Lingyou, under whom he attained enlightenment, and remained to become his foremost disciple. Teacher and student had the closest spiritual affinity. Their names were later combined to form the name of the Guiyang school of Zen. Eventually moving to Mt. Yang (in modern Jiangxi Province), Yangshan drew students from throughout the realm.

The Guiyang school of Zen employed sacred symbols to convey Buddhist truths. According to tradition, the Sixth Ancestor himself was the source of these symbols. The symbols were passed to National Teacher Nanyang, and in turn to Danyuan, who gave the symbols in a secret manuscript to Yangshan.

Danyuan greatly esteemed Yangshan, and said to him, "Previously the National Teacher Huizhong received the transmission of a total of ninety-seven symbolic circles from the Sixth Ancestor. He in turn passed these to me, saying, 'Thirty years after I've died, a novice monk will come from the South who will greatly revive this teaching. When that time comes, pass the teaching on to him and don't let it end.' Today I transmit them to you. You must uphold and preserve them."

When he had finished speaking he passed the secret text to Yangshan. After receiving and examining the text, Yangshan burned it.

One day Danyuan said to Yangshan, "The symbols that I gave you are extremely rare, esoteric, and precious."

Yangshan said, "After I examined them I burned them."

Danyuan said, "This Dharma gate of ours can't be understood by most people. Only the Buddha, the ancestors, and all the holy ones can fully understand it. How could you burn it?"

Yangshan said, "After examining it, I fully comprehended its meaning. Then there was no use keeping the text."

Danyuan said, "Even so, when transmitting this to disciples, people of future times won't believe it."

Yangshan said, "If you would like another copy that won't be a problem. I'll make another copy and give it to you. Then it won't be lost."

Danyuan said, "Please do."

The story of Yangshan's meeting with Guishan and his subsequent great enlightenment is recounted in the *Wudeng Huiyuan*.

Later, Yangshan went to practice under Guishan.
Guishan asked Yangshan, "As a novice monk do you have a host or not?"
Yangshan said, "I have one."
Guishan said, "Who is it?"
Yangshan walked from west to east and then stood there erect.
Guishan realized that Yangshan was extraordinary.

———— ❖ ————

Yangshan asked Guishan, "What is the true abode of Buddha?"
Guishan said, "Think of the unfathomable mystery and return your thoughts to the inexhaustible numinous light. When thoughts are exhausted you've arrived at the source, where true nature is revealed as eternally abiding. In that place there is no difference between affairs and principle, and the true Buddha is manifested."
Upon hearing these words Yangshan experienced great enlightenment.

———— ❖ ————

Zen master Yangshan entered the hall and addressed the monks, saying: "Each and every one of you, turn the light inward! Don't try to remember what I'm saying! For a beginningless eon you have faced away from the light and been shrouded in darkness. The roots of delusion are deep. They're difficult to cut off and uproot. So [the Buddha] established expedient means to grab your attention. These are like showing yellow leaves to a crying child, who imagines they're gold and thus stops crying. You act as though you're in a shop where someone sells a hundred goods made from gold and jade, but you're trying to weigh each item. So you say that Shitou has a real gold shop? Well in my shop there's a wide range of goods! If someone comes looking for mouse turds then I give him some. If someone comes looking for real gold then I give it to him."
A monk asked, "I don't want mouse turds. May I have the master's real gold?"
Yangshan said, "If you try to bite down on the head of a flying arrow you can try until the year of the ass but you won't succeed!"
The monk couldn't answer.
Yangshan said, "If you want to exchange something we can make a deal. If you don't want to exchange anything then we can't.

"If I truly speak of Zen, then there won't be a single companion at your side. How can this be if there's five or seven hundred in the assembly? If I talk about this and that, and you strain your neck trying to pick something up, then it will be like fooling a little child with an empty hand. There's nothing authentic about it. Today I'm clarifying what is holy, which is not a matter of collecting and calming the mind. Instead you must practice to realize the true sea of self-nature. Of what use is there for 'three clarifications' or 'six understandings'? What I speak of is the ultimate sacred matter. If right now you want to know mind and arrive at the root, then arrive at the root. Don't worry about the tips of the branches. If you do this, then hereafter you will possess it yourself. But if you don't attain the root, and just use your emotions to seek *it*, then you will never succeed. You'll never see what Master Guishan spoke of—the place where ideas of mundane and sacred are exhausted, where matter and principle are united, and the true eternal body of the Tathagata is manifested."

------------------ ◆ ------------------

A man named Liu Shiyu asked Yangshan, "May I hear the principle of attaining mind?"

Yangshan said, "If you want to attain mind, then there's no mind which can be attained. It is this unattainable mind which is known as truth."

------------------ ◆ ------------------

A monk came to practice under Yangshan. He asked, "Does the master recognize written characters?"

Yangshan said, "I recognize some."

The monk then drew a circle in the air and acted as though he presented it to Yangshan.

Yangshan acted as if to use his sleeves to erase it.

The monk then made another circle in the air and presented it to Yangshan.

Yangshan received the circle with both hands and then threw it behind him.

The monk then stared at Yangshan. Yangshan looked down.

The monk then walked in a circle around Yangshan. Yangshan hit the monk with his staff.

The monk then went out.

The following story illustrates the arcane and mystical tendencies of the Guiyang school of Zen. The school's use of symbolism gave rise to apocryphal stories.

Once, when Yangshan was sitting in the hall, a monk came in and bowed. Yangshan didn't look at him.

The monk said, "Does the master recognize [written] characters?"

Yangshan said, "I recognize some."

The monk walked in a circle to his right. Then he asked, "What character is this?"

Yangshan then answered by drawing the character for "ten" (十) on the ground.

The monk walked in a circle to his left. Then he asked, "What character is this?"

Yangshan then altered the "ten" character to become the mystical Buddhist swastika. (卐)

The monk then drew a circle and offered it to Yangshan, striking the pose of an *asura* holding the sun and moon.[104] Then he said, "What character is this?"

Yangshan answered by drawing a circle around the swastika. (卐)

The monk acted as if to throw the symbol away and then stood upright.

Yangshan said, "Just so! Just so! This is the realization that is protected by all buddhas. You are thus. I am also thus. Uphold and sustain it well!"

The monk then bowed and flew out of the hall into the sky.

———— ◆ ————

A monk asked Yangshan, "What is the difference between heaven and hell?"

Yangshan drew a line on the ground.

———— ◆ ————

A monk named Siyi asked Yangshan, "The sudden enlightenment of the Zen school—what is the meaning of entering this Dharma gate?"

Yangshan said, "The meaning is extremely difficult to understand. In our ancestral school, those of superior ability and wisdom hear this teaching but once and they have a thousand awakenings—complete understanding. People of this type are hard to find. As to those of lesser ability and inferior wisdom, if they don't calmly practice meditation and quiet their thoughts, they will certainly flounder in ignorance when they hear this teaching."

Siyi asked, "Besides this teaching, is there another place of entry into the Way or not?"

Yangshan said, "There is."

Siyi asked, "What is it?"

Yangshan said, "What place are you from?"

Siyi said, "From You Province."

Yangshan said, "Do you still think of that place?"

Siyi said, "I often think of it."

Yangshan said, "That which thinks is the mind. That which is thought of is the environment. In the environment are buildings, towers, forests, gardens, people, horses, and other things. If you stop your thoughts, are there still so many categories of things or not?"

Siyi said, "When I reach here, I don't see any existing."

Yangshan said, "What you have realized is still within mind. It brings about the stage of belief. It is not the stage of person."

Siyi said, "Aside from this, is there any greater meaning or not?"

Yangshan said, "There is greater meaning! If there weren't then it would have no value."

Siyi said, "After reaching this stage of understanding, what should a person do?"

Yangshan said, "What you have realized up to now is just the first mystery. Now you must sit until you penetrate *it*. Later you will see for yourself."

Siyi then bowed in gratitude.

Yangshan acted according to conditions to benefit beings and became a great example of the Zen school. When near death, he returned to Dongping Temple. There, a great many disciples were at his side to attend to him.

Yangshan took a brush and wrote a verse for the monks to read:

Countless disciples,
I look across you all, and you gaze back,
Two mouths, one without a tongue,
This is my teaching.

At exactly noon, Yangshan sat on the dais and bade farewell to the congregation. He then recited another verse:

Completing seventy-seven years,
Today it ends.
When the orb of the sun is just at noon,
The two hands fold the legs.

Upon saying these words, Yangshan used his hands to fold his legs into a cross-legged posture and then passed away. In the second year after Yangshan's death, Zen master Nanta Guangyong transferred Yangshan's remains back to

Mt. Yang. He placed them in a stupa that was built beneath the clouds and peaks. Yangshan received the posthumous name "Great Teacher Penetrating Wisdom." The stupa was named "Wondrous Light."

XIANGYAN ZHIXIAN

XIANGYAN ZHIXIAN (d. 898) was a disciple of Guishan. He came from ancient Qingzhou (the modern city of Yidu in Shandong Province). Extremely intelligent and quick witted, Xiangyan first studied under Baizhang, but was unable to penetrate the heart of Zen. After Baizhang died, Xiangyan studied under Guishan. Despite his cleverness, he was unsuccessful at realizing his teacher's meaning. Years later, his mind far removed from his earlier confused attempts to attain what he thought to be enlightenment, Xiangyan realized the great way. The following passage is from the *Transmission of the Lamp*.

One day, Guishan said to Xiangyan, "I'm not asking you about what's recorded in or what can be learned from the scriptures! You must say something from the time before you were born and before you could distinguish objects. I want to record what you say."

Xiangyan was confused and unable to answer. He sat in deep thought for a some time and then mumbled a few words to explain his understanding. But Guishan wouldn't accept this.

Xiangyan said, "Then would the master please explain it?"

Guishan said, "What I might say would merely be my own understanding. How could it benefit your own view?"

Xiangyan returned to the monks' hall and searched through the books he had collected, but he couldn't find a single phrase that could be used to answer Guishan's question.

Xiangyan then sighed and said, "A picture of a cake can't satisfy hunger."

He then burned all his books and said, "During this lifetime I won't study the essential doctrine. I'll just become a common mendicant monk, and I won't apply my mind to this any more."

Xiangyan tearfully left Guishan. He then went traveling and eventually resided at Nanyang, the site of the grave of National Teacher Nanyang Huizhong.

One day as Xiangyan was scything grass, a small piece of tile was knocked through the air and struck a stalk of bamboo. Upon hearing the sound of the tile hitting the bamboo, Xiangyan instantly experienced vast enlightenment.

Xiangyan then bathed and lit incense. Bowing in the direction of Guishan, he said, "The master's great compassion exceeds that of one's parents! Back then if you had explained it, then how could this have come to pass?"

Xiangyan then wrote a verse:

One strike and all knowledge is forgotten.
No more the mere pretense of practice.
Transformed to uphold the ancient path,
Not sunk in idle devices.

Far and wide, not a trace is left.
The great purpose lies beyond sound and form.
In every direction the realized Way,
Beyond all speech, the ultimate principle.[105]

Xiangyan then dispatched a monk to take the verse to Guishan and recite it.

Upon hearing it, Guishan said to Yangshan, "This disciple has penetrated!"

Yangshan said, "This is a good representation of mind function. But wait and I'll personally go and check out Xiangyan's realization."

Later Yangshan met with Xiangyan and said, "Master Guishan has praised the great matter of your awakening. What do you say as evidence for it?"

Xiangyan then recited his previous verse.

Yangshan said, "This verse could be composed from the things you've studied earlier. If you've had a genuine enlightenment, then say something else to prove it."

Xiangyan then composed a verse that said:

Last year's poverty was not real poverty.
This year's poverty is finally genuine poverty.
In last year's poverty there was still ground where I could plant my hoe,
In this year's poverty, not even the hoe remains.

Yangshan said, "I grant that you have realized the Zen of the Tathagatas. But as for the Zen of the Ancestors, you haven't seen it even in your dreams."

Xiangyan then composed another verse that said:

I have a function.
It's seen in the twinkling of an eye.
If other's don't see it,
They still can't call me a novice.

When Yangshan heard this verse, he reported to Guishan, "It's wonderful! Xiangyan has realized the Zen of the Ancestors!"

———— ✦ ————

When Xiangyan assumed a position as abbot, Guishan sent him a message along with a staff.

When Xiangyan received them he exclaimed, "Blue heavens! Blue heavens!"

A monk asked, "Why is the master acting this way?"

Xiangyan said, "Because of an evil moon and flourishing weeds."

———— ✦ ————

Zen master Xiangyan entered the hall and addressed the monks, saying, "The Way is attained by means of enlightenment and is not found in words. It is mysterious and majestic, and without the slightest breach. Don't belabor your mind! Just turn the light inward. Those disciples using total effort every day to realize enlightenment are just backward and confused."

———— ✦ ————

A monk asked, "What is Xiangyan's great situation?"

Xiangyan said, "Don't fertilize the flowers and trees."

———— ✦ ————

A monk asked, "What is a '*sindhava*'?"[106]

Xiangyan struck the meditation platform and said, "Come here!"

———— ✦ ————

Xiangyan entered the hall and addressed the monks, saying, "Talking about this, you could compare it to a person who has climbed a tree and is grasping a branch, supported only by his teeth. His feet are hanging freely, as are his hands. Suddenly someone down on the ground yells out to him, 'What is the meaning of the First Ancestor coming from the west?' To not answer isn't acceptable, but if he does so he'll fall, and so lose his life. At this very moment what can he do?"

At that time a monk named Tiger Head Zhao came forth from the congregation and addressed Xiangyan, saying, "Leaving aside the question of the tree top, I ask the master to comment about before climbing the tree."

Xiangyan then laughed, "Ha, ha."

◆

Zen master Xiangyan had a verse that said:

The chick pecks from within, the hen from without.
The chick breaks free through the shell.
When hen and chick are both gone,
The function has not gone astray.
Singing the same song,
The mystical voice goes on alone.

To all of his disciples, Xiangyan provided his teachings in a clear and direct manner. He left more than two hundred verses such as this one that were composed to meet the situations he encountered. These unmetered verses were popular throughout the country.

Xiangyan received the posthumous name "Zen Master Harmonious Light."

LIU TIEMO, "IRON GRINDER LIU"

LIU TIEMO (n.d.) was a disciple of Guishan Lingyou. Little is known of the details of her life. After receiving the Dharma seal from Guishan, Liu lived a few miles away from him and would periodically come to visit. She taught Zen in a style described as "precipitously awesome and dangerous." Her ability to test the true mettle of Zen adepts brought her the name "Iron Grinder."

Aside from her prominent appearances in cases sixty of the *Book of Serenity* and twenty-four of the *Blue Cliff Record*, there are few other stories of the Iron Grinder in classical records. She is mentioned in an episode of Dharma combat with the truculent Zen master Zihu, and despite her own reputation for ferocity, was not spared one of his characteristic beatings. The following passage is taken from the *Guzunsu Yulu (The Record of the Venerable Ancients).*[107]

The leader of a congregation, named "Iron Grinder Liu," came to visit Zen master Zihu.

Zihu said, "I've heard of 'Iron Grinder Liu.' They say you're not easy to contend with. Is that so?"

Iron Grinder said, "Where did you hear that?"

Zihu said, "It's conveyed from left and right."[108]

Iron Grinder said, "Don't fall down, Master."

Zihu drove her out of the room with blows.

Zen master Fojian [Taiping Huiqin] selected this episode for comment, saying, "Zihu's stick had eyes. He had authority to take the staff in his hands. Beneath Iron Grinder's skin was blood. She let Zihu wield the stick, but though she appeared soft, she had steel-like strength.

"But look at what was said! The enlightened words were 'It's conveyed from left and right.' The motive arose from this. Zihu did not fall down. His body was upright, his appearance unbending."

Jinhua Juzhi

JINHUA JUZHI (n.d.) was a disciple of Hangzhou Tianlong. He lived and taught in ancient Wuzhou (in modern Zhejiang Province, south of the city of Hangzhou). Details of his life are sketchy. A few facts are provided in the lamp records.

When Jinhua first became the priest of a small temple, a Buddhist nun named Shiji visited him. Wearing her hat and grasping her staff, she walked around him three times and said, "If you can speak, I'll take off my hat."

Three times she did this, but Hangzhou did not reply. She then began to leave.

Hangzhou said, "It's getting late. Why don't you stay here."

"Say the right word and I'll stay."

Again Hangzhou did not reply.

After the nun left, he sighed and said, "Though I inhabit the form of a man, I don't have a man's spirit. It would be better if I left the temple and went traveling, seeking knowledge."

That night a mountain spirit appeared and advised him that he must not leave, for a great bodhisattva would appear in the flesh to teach him the Dharma. Ten days later Master Tianlong came to the temple. Jinhua received him and bowed. Then he told him what had happened previously.

Tianlong simply held up one finger. Jinhua thereupon attained great enlightenment. From that time forward students came from everywhere, but Jinhua merely raised one finger and offered no other teaching.

There was a boy living at Jinhua's temple who, each time he was asked by someone about some matter, held up one finger.

Someone told Jinhua, "Master, the boy also understands the Buddhadharma. Anytime someone asks him something he holds up his finger just like the master."

One day Jinhua concealed a knife in his sleeve and asked the boy, "I heard you understand the essential doctrine. Is that so?"

The boy said, "Yes."

Jinhua then asked him, "What is Buddha?"

The boy then held up one finger. Jinhua grabbed the boy's finger and cut it off with a knife. The boy screamed and ran for the door.

As the boy ran away Jinhua yelled at him. When the boy turned his head Jinhua said, "What is Buddha?"

The boy held up his hand but his finger was gone and there was nothing there. The boy instantly was awakened.

When Jinhua was about to die, he said to the monks, "I attained Tianlong's one-fingered Zen. In my entire life I have not exhausted it." When he finished saying this he passed away. (Changqing said on behalf of the congregation, "Sweets don't satisfy people's hunger." Xuansha said, "If at that time I'd seen it, I would have twisted off the finger." Xuanjue said, "What do you think Xuansha's meaning was when he spoke in this manner?" Yunju Ci said, "If Xuansha speaks like this, do you agree or not agree? If you agree, why would you say 'twist off his finger'? If you don't agree, where was Juzhi's mistake?" The first Caoshan (Benji) said, "The position Juzhi carried was crude. What is recognized is one function—one condition. It's all clapping the hands." Xuansha also said, "Do you say Juzhi was enlightened or not? If he was enlightened, how can it be said that the position he carried was crude? If he was not enlightened, then he also said his use of one-fingered Zen was never exhausted. What do you say about Caoshan's meaning?")

MOSHAN LIAORAN

MOSHAN LIAORAN (n.d.) was a disciple of Gao'an Dayu. Although little is recorded of her life and teachings, she is the primary remaining example of a prominent female teacher among the early records of the Zen school. She is known from a dialogue with a monk named Xian of Guanxi that is found in the lamp records. Guanxi Xian first studied with Linji Yixuan, but left that teacher and set off traveling, eventually coming to Moshan's temple in ancient Ruizhou, the area of modern Gao'an City in Jiangxi Province. Moshan is recognized by the male-dominated Zen tradition as a true Zen master. Guanxi Xian became her student and studied under her for three years. Later, he equated her with Linji, saying:

> "I received half a ladle at Father Linji's place and half a ladle at Mother Moshan's. Since I took that drink, I've never been thirsty."

◆

Zen master Moshan Liaoran of Ruizhou was a student of Gao'an Dayu. Once, the monk Guanxi Xian arrived at Mt. Mo and said, "If there's someone here who's worthy, I'll stay here. If not, I'll overturn the meditation platform!"

He then entered the hall.

Moshan sent her attendant to query the visitor, saying, "Your Reverence, are you here sightseeing, or have you come seeking the Buddhadharma?"

Guanxi Xian said, "I seek the Dharma."

So Moshan sat upon the Dharma seat [in the audience room] and Xian entered for an interview.

Moshan said, "Your Reverence, where have you come from today?"

Guanxi said, "From the intersection on the main road."

Moshan said, "Why don't you remove your sun hat?"

Guanxi didn't answer for some time. ([Later,] Shushan said, "The battle begins here.") Finally, he [removed his hat, and] bowed, saying, "What about Mt. Mo? [Moshan]."

Moshan said, "The peak isn't revealed."

Guanxi said, "Who is the master of Mt. Mo?"

Moshan said, "Without the form of man or woman."

Guanxi shouted, then said, "Why can't it transform itself?"

Moshan said, "It's not a god or a demon. So how could it become something else?"

Guanxi then submitted to become Moshan's student. He worked as head gardener for three years.

◆

A poor and thin monk came to study with Moshan.

Moshan said, "How thin you are!"

The monk said, "Even so, I'm still a lion cub!"[109]

Moshan said, "Since you are a lion cub, why do you let Manjushri ride upon you?"

The monk didn't answer. Then he asked, "What is the mind of the ancient buddhas?"

Moshan said, "The world is collapsing!"

The monk said, "Why is the world collapsing?

Moshan said, "It's not my body."

A Song dynasty writer penned a verse in praise of Moshan that is recorded in a classic Zen text named the *Guzunsu Yulu*.

Mt. Mo does not reveal its pure summit,
But through all time the pinnacle is before the eyes.
It's said it has no male or female form,
But do distinguish the lotus amidst the flames.
Without form, without mind, without intention,
Becoming male or female just accords with conditions,
These times are replete with monks and lay practitioners,
Each one shines with flawless incandescence.

YANYANG SHANZHAO

YANYANG SHANZHAO (n.d.) was one of the few students of Zhaozhou Congshen who went on to become recognized Zen teachers. Few details about his life remain. He lived and taught in Xinxing, located in ancient Hongzhou.

When Yanyang first met Zhaozhou, he asked, "When not even a single thing can be picked up, what then?"

Zhaozhou said, "Put it down."

Yanyang said, "Since not a single thing can be taken up, how can it be put down?"

Zhaozhou said, "If you can't put it down, then carry it away."

Upon hearing these words Yanyang experienced great enlightenment.

———— ❖ ————

After Yanyang assumed the abbacy of a temple, a monk asked him, "What is Buddha?"

Yanyang said, "A clump of dirt."
The monk asked, "What is Dharma?"
Yanyang said, "The ground is moving."
The monk asked, "What is Sangha?"
Yanyang said, "Eating porridge and rice."

A monk asked, "What is Xinxing's water?"[110]
Yanyang said, "It's in the river before your eyes."

A monk asked, "What is 'meeting a thing as it manifests'?"
Yanyang said, "Give me a meditation bench."

Yanyang kept a snake and a tiger that would eat from his hand.

DONGSHAN LIANGJIE

DONGSHAN LIANGJIE (807–69) was a disciple of Yunyan Tansheng. He is recognized to have founded the Caodong school of Zen. This school, along with the Linji school, remains today as one of the two existing Zen schools that began in China during the Tang dynasty (618–905), the "golden age" of Zen. Dongshan came from ancient Huiji (in modern Zhejiang Province). A story relates how, as a youth, he read the *Heart Sutra* and came upon the words "No eye, no ear, no nose, no tongue, no body…" and asked his teacher, "I have eyes, ears, a nose, and so on. So why does the sutra say there is none?" The teacher was reportedly dumbfounded at the insight revealed by Dongshan's question, and replied, "I can't be your teacher." He then sent the young prodigy to study under Zen master Limo at Mt. Wuxie.

At the age of twenty-one, Dongshan took the monk's vows on famous Mt. Song. In the tradition of the Zen school he then went traveling to visit the great adepts of his time.

Dongshan first went to see Zen master Nanquan Puyuan. At that time the congregation was working to prepare a feast for the following day in honor of Nanquan's late master, Mazu.

Nanquan asked the congregation, "Tomorrow we will have Mazu's feast, but will Mazu come or not?"

The monks were unable to answer. Dongshan then stepped forward and said, "If he has a companion, he'll come."

When Nanquan heard this, he approved and said, "Though this child is young, he's a gem worthy of polishing."

Dongshan said, "Master, don't crush something good into something bad."

Next, Dongshan studied with Guishan. One day he said, "I've heard that National Teacher Huizhong taught that inanimate beings expound Dharma. I don't understand this clearly."

Guishan said, "Do you remember what he said or not?"

Dongshan said, "I remember."

Guishan said, "Please repeat it."

Dongshan said, "A monk asked the National Teacher, 'What is the mind of the ancient buddhas?'

"The National Teacher said, 'A wall tile.'

"The monk said, 'A wall tile? Isn't a wall tile inanimate?'

"The National Teacher said, 'Yes.'

"The monk asked, 'And it can expound the Dharma?'

"The National Teacher said, 'It expounds it brilliantly, without letup.'

"The monk said, 'Why can't I hear it?'

"The National Teacher said, 'You yourself may not hear it. But that doesn't mean others can't hear it.'

"The monk said, 'Who are the people who can hear it?'

"The National Teacher said, 'All the holy ones can hear it.'

"The monk said, 'Can the master hear it or not?'

"The National Teacher said, 'I cannot hear it. If I could hear it I would be the equal of the saints. Then you could not hear me expound the Dharma.'

"The monk said, 'All beings can't understand that sort of speech.'

"The National Teacher said, 'I expound Dharma for the sake of beings, not for the sake of the saints.'

"The monk said, 'After beings hear it, then what?'

"The National Teacher said, 'Then they're not sentient beings.'

"The monk asked, 'What scripture teaches about inanimate [things] expounding Dharma?'

"The National Teacher said, 'Obviously, this is not found in the scriptures, nor is it something that some noble one has said. But haven't you heard the words of the *Flower Garland Sutra* that say, "The chiliocosm, sentient beings, and the three realms all proclaim it"?'" When Dongshan finished speaking, Guishan said, "I have this teaching. But one seldom encounters a person who understands it."

Dongshan said, "I'm not clear about it. I ask you for instruction about this."

Guishan lifted his whisk upright into the air and said, "Do you understand?"

Dongshan said, "I don't understand. Please explain it to me, Master."

Guishan said, "The mouth which my parents gave to the world is utterly unable to explain this to you."

Dongshan said, "Is there anyone else of your generation whom you respect and who can explain it?"

Guishan said, "Go to Liling in You County, where there are stone houses strung together.[111] There, find a man of the Way named Yunyan. If you can search the grass and face the wind [bear his teaching methods], then you'll certainly hold him in esteem."

Dongshan said, "Who is this person?"

Guishan said, "He once asked me, 'When a student greatly admires and respects a teacher, what should he do?'

"I said, 'He must stop all the leaks.'

"He said, 'And he should also not go against his teacher's teaching, right?'

"I said, 'First of all you can't say that I'm at this spot!'"

So Dongshan said good-bye to Guishan and proceeded on to Yunyan. He related to Yunyan the story about the National Teacher and asked, "Who can hear inanimate things expound Dharma?"

Yunyan said, "What is inanimate can hear it."

Dongshan said, "Can the master hear it or not?"

Yunyan said, "If I could hear it, then you could not hear me expound Dharma."

Dongshan said, "Why couldn't I hear you?"

Yunyan held up his whisk and said, "Can you still hear me or not?"

Dongshan said, "I can't hear you."

Yunyan said, "When I expound Dharma you can't hear me. So how could you hear it when inanimate things proclaim it?"

Dongshan said, "What scripture teaches about inanimate things expounding Dharma?"

Yunyan said, "Haven't you seen that in the *Amitabha Sutra* it says, 'The lakes and rivers, the birds, the forests; they all chant Buddha; they all chant Dharma'?"

Upon hearing this Dongshan experienced a great insight. He then wrote a verse:

How incredible!
How incredible!
Inanimate things proclaiming Dharma is inconceivable.
It can't be known if the ears try to hear it,
But when the eyes hear it, then it may be known.

Dongshan asked Yunyan, "Are there other practices I haven't completed?"

Yunyan said, "What were you doing before you came here?"

Dongshan said, "I wasn't practicing the Noble Truths."

Yunyan said, "Were you joyous in this nonpractice?"

Dongshan said, "It was not without joy. It's like sweeping excrement into a pile and then picking up a precious jewel from within it."

Dongshan asked Yunyan, "When I want to see *it* face to face, what should I do?"

Yunyan said, "Ask someone who's done it."

Dongshan said, "That's what I'm doing."

Yunyan said, "What can I say to you?"

As Dongshan prepared to leave Yunyan, Yunyan said, "Where are you going?"

Dongshan said, "Although I'm leaving the master, I don't know where I'll end up."

Yunyan said, "You're not going to Hunan?"

Dongshan said, "No, I'm not."

Yunyan said, "Are you returning home?"

Dongshan said, "No."

Yunyan said, "Sooner or later you'll return."

Dongshan said, "When the master has an abode, then I'll return."

Yunyan said, "If you leave, it will be difficult to see one another again."

Dongshan said, "It will be difficult to not see one another."

Just when Dongshan was about to depart, he said, "If in the future someone happens to ask whether I can describe the master's truth or not, how should I answer them?"

After a long pause, Yunyan said, "Just this is it."

Dongshan sighed.

Then Yunyan said, "Worthy Liang, now that you have taken on this great affair, you must consider it carefully."

Dongshan continued to experience doubt. Later as he crossed a stream he saw his reflection in the water and was awakened to Yunyan's meaning. He then composed this verse:

Avoid seeking elsewhere, for that's far from the self.
Now I travel alone, everywhere I meet it.
Now it's exactly me, now I'm not it.
It must thus be understood to merge with thusness.

Years later, Dongshan was making offerings to Yunyan's image when a monk asked, "Yunyan said, 'Just this is it,' did he not?"

Dongshan said, "Yes."

The monk asked, "What was his meaning?"

Dongshan said, "Back then I almost misunderstood my teacher's meaning."

The monk asked, "I'd like to know if Yunyan really knew this or not."

Dongshan said, "If he didn't know, how could he speak in this manner? And if he did know, why was he willing to speak this way?" (Later Changqing said, "If he knew, why did he speak this way?" Changqing also said, "A child then knew a father's compassion.")

----◆----

Dongshan hosted a feast of commemoration on the anniversary of Yunyan's death.

A monk asked, "When you were at Yunyan's place, what teaching did he give you?"

Dongshan said, "Although I was there, I didn't receive any teaching."

The monk asked, "But you are holding a commemorative feast for the late teacher. Doesn't that show you approve his teaching?"

Dongshan said, "Half approve. Half not approve."

The monk said, "Why don't you completely approve of it?"

Dongshan said, "If I completely approved, then I would be disloyal to my late teacher."

----◆----

A monk asked, "When the cold season comes, where can one go to avoid it?"

Dongshan said, "Why not go where there is no cold?"

The monk said, "What is the place where there's no cold?"

Dongshan said, "When it's cold, the cold kills you. When it's hot, the heat kills you."

Zen master Dongshan entered the hall and addressed the monks saying, "Are there any among you who haven't repaid the four benefits and three existences?"[112]

The congregation was silent.

Dongshan said, "If you don't understand this, how can you transcend the tribulations of karmic existence? The mind must not alight upon objects. The feet must walk where there is no place to do so. To finally realize this, you must expend effort and not pass your days idly."

Dongshan asked a monk, "Where have you been?"

The monk said, "Walking on the mountain."

Dongshan said, "Did you reach the peak?"

The monk said, "I reached it."

Dongshan said, "Were there people there?"

The monk said, "There weren't any people."

Dongshan said, "In that case you didn't reach the peak."

The monk said, "If I haven't been to the peak, how would I know there are no people?"

Dongshan said, "Why didn't you stay there?"

The monk said, "I would stay there, but there's someone in India who would disapprove."

Dongshan said, "Formerly I doubted this fellow."

The abbot of a temple was ill. Whenever he'd see a monk he'd yell, "Save me! Save me!" The monks of the temple couldn't say anything useful to deal with the situation. Dongshan went to pay him a visit.

The abbot said again, "Save me!"

Dongshan said, "What appearance should I save?"

The abbot said, "Aren't you a descendant of Yaoshan, and a Dharma heir of Yunyan?"

Dongshan said, "I dare not say so."

The abbot clapped his hands and said, "Everyone has brought you here."

He then passed away.

Dongshan and Spiritual Uncle Mi were crossing a stream.
Dongshan said, "What's it like crossing the stream?"
Uncle Mi said, "It doesn't leak to the feet."
Dongshan said, "So old and venerable, and yet you still speak in such a manner!"
Uncle Mi said, "What do you say?"
Dongshan said, "The feet aren't wet."

Dongshan became ill. He instructed a novice monk to go and speak to [Dongshan's Dharma heir] Zen master Yunju Daoying.

Dongshan told the novice, "If he asks whether I'm resting comfortably, you are to tell him that the lineage of Yunyan is ending. When you say this you must stand far away from him because I'm afraid he's going to hit you."

The novice monk did as Dongshan instructed him and went and spoke to Yunju. Before he could finish speaking Yunju hit him. The novice monk said nothing further.

A monk asked, "When the master is not well, is there still someone who is well or not?"

Dongshan said, "There is."

The monk asked, "Can the one who's not ill still see the master or not?"

Dongshan said, "I can still see him."

The monk asked, "What does the master see?"

Dongshan said, "When I observe him, I don't see any illness."

Dongshan then said to the monks, "When you leave the skin bag you inhabit, where will you go and see me again?"

The monks didn't answer. Dongshan then recited a verse:

Students as numerous as sands in the Ganges but none are awakened.
They err by searching for the path in another person's mouth.
If you wish to forget form and not leave any traces,
Wholeheartedly strive to walk in emptiness.

Dongshan then had his attendants help him shave his head, bathe, and get dressed. He then had the bell rung to summon the monks so that he could bid them farewell. He appeared to have passed away and the monks began wailing piteously without letup.

Suddenly Dongshan opened his eyes and said to them, "Homeless monks aren't attached to things. That is their authentic practice. Why lament an arduous life and pitiful death?"

Dongshan then instructed the temple director to organize a "delusion banquet." The monks' adoration for Dongshan was unending.

Seven days later the food was prepared. Dongshan had a final meal with the congregation.

He then said, "Don't make a big deal about it. When I pass away, don't go carrying on about it."

Dongshan then returned to his room, and, sitting upright, passed away. It was the third month in [the year 869]. Sixty-three years of age, he'd been an ordained monk for forty-two years. Dongshan received the posthumous name "Enlightened Source." His stupa was named "Wisdom Awakening."

JIASHAN SHANHUI

JIASHAN SHANHUI (805–81) was a disciple of Chuanzi Decheng (the Boat Monk). After taking the monk's vows at age twenty, he proceeded to study the sutras. He later met Zen master Daowu Yuanzhi, who recommended that he go see Chuanzi Decheng. Although Jiashan's understanding of Buddhism was already extensive, he did not attain complete awakening until his meeting with Decheng in the famous incident at Huating. Thereafter, he was recognized as Chuanzi Decheng's Dharma heir. Jiashan Shanhui was the first Zen master known to closely link Zen with drinking tea. He described their intimacy as "Zen, tea, one taste."

Zen master Jiashan Shanhui was from Guangzhou. His surname was Liao. He left home at a young age and was ordained as a priest. He studied the sutras and commentaries, and thoroughly practiced the three great studies [that is, the precepts, meditation, and wisdom]. Later, when he went out into the world [to preach], he lived at Helin in Run Province. At the urging of Daowu he went to see the Boat Monk, Chuanzi Decheng, from whom he completely received the teaching, without the slightest gap. Honoring his teacher's instructions, he forsook the world and lived in seclusion in the mountains. Large numbers of students came to study with him and their thatched huts were scattered [unorganized]. From morning until night they studied with the master. In the year 870 the assembly moved to Mt. Jia, where they built a temple.

One day, Jiashan entered the hall and addressed the monks, saying, "Since the times of the ancestors there have been those who misunderstand what has been passed down. Right up to now they have used the words of the buddhas and ancestors and made them models for study. If people do this then they'll go crazy and have no wisdom at all. The buddhas and ancestors have instructed you that the dharmaless root is the Way. The Way is without even a single Dharma. There is no buddha that you can become. There is no way that can be attained. Nor is there any Dharma that can be grasped or let go of. Therefore the ancients said, 'Before the eyes there is no Dharma, but the meaning is before the eyes.' Those who want to study the buddhas and ancestors haven't opened their eyes. Why do they want to submit to something else and not attain their own freedom? Basically it's because they are confused about life and death. They realize they don't have a bit of freedom, so they go thousands of miles to seek out some great teacher. Those people must attain the true eye, not spend their time grasping and discarding spurious views. But are there any here among you of definite attainment who can really hold forth about existence and nonexistence? If there's someone who's definite about this then I invite you to speak out.

"When persons of high ability hear these words they are clear about what's being said. Those of middle or low ability continue rushing around. Why don't you just directly face life and death? Don't tell me you still want the buddhas and ancestors to live and die in your place! People who understand will laugh at you.

"If you still don't get it, then listen to this verse:

"*Belaboring life and death,*
Just seeking Buddha's quarter,
Confused about the truth before your eyes,
Poking a fire to find a cool spot."

A monk asked, "There has always been meaning attributed to the teachings of the buddhas and ancestors. Why does the master say there isn't any?"
Jiashan said, "Don't eat for three years and you won't see anyone hungry."
The monk said, "If no one is hungry, why can't I gain awakening?"
Jiashan said, "Because awakening has confused you."
Jiashan then recited this verse to make his point:

"Clear and luminous, no Dharma of awakening,
Awakening confuses people.
In paradise with two feet and eyes,
Nothing false, and nothing true."

———— ◆ ————

Jiashan entered the hall and addressed the monks, saying, "I've been living on this mountain for twenty years, and the whole time I've never spoken a word about the essential teaching of Zen."

A monk asked, "Is the master saying that you've been here for twenty years and you've never spoken about the central matter of Zen?"

Jiashan said, "Yes."

One of the monks then overturned the meditation platform.

Jiashan stopped speaking and went out.

The next day, all the monks were called to assemble. The master dug a hole and had his assistant call out the monk who had overturned the platform the day before.

Addressing the monk, Jiashan said, "For twenty years I've been speaking meaninglessly. So today I invite you to kill me and bury me in this hole. Do it! Do it! If you can't kill me then kill yourself and bury yourself in this hole!"

The monk went to the monks' hall and packed his bag. He then quietly stole away.

·············· ◆ ··············

On the seventh day of the eleventh month in [the year 881], Jiashan called together his principal monks and said, "I've talked extensively for many years. As to the Buddhadharma, each of you should know for yourself. Now I'm just an empty form. My time is up and I must go. Take care of the teaching as if I were still here. Don't be like people of the world and be grief stricken after I'm gone."

Upon saying these words, Jiashan suddenly passed away. His remains were kept in a stupa built on the mountain. He received the posthumous name "Great Teacher Transmitting Clarity."

SHISHUANG QINGZHU

SHISHUANG QINGZHU (807–88) was a disciple of Yaoshan Weiyan. He came from the city of Xingan near ancient Luling. He was ordained by Zen master Xishan Shaolong on Mt. Tai at the age of twenty-three, and then proceeded to study the Vinaya. Finding this path to be too slow, he traveled to Mt. Gui, where he studied with Guishan Lingyou and worked preparing food in the kitchen.

In a famous exchange between Guishan and Shishuang, Guishan chided him for overlooking a grain of rice that had accidentally dropped on the floor.

Shishuang went to Mt. Gui, where he served as a rice cook. Once when he was preparing the rice, Guishan said to him, "Don't lose anything offered by our patrons."

Shishuang said, "I'm not losing anything."

Guishan reached down and picked up a single grain of rice which had fallen to the ground and said, "You said you haven't lost anything, but what's this?"

Shishuang didn't answer.

Guishan said, "Don't lightly regard this one grain, a hundred thousand grains are born from this one."

Shishuang said, "A hundred thousand grains are born from this one, but from what place is this one grain born?"

Guishan laughed, "Ha, ha," and went back to his room.

That evening Guishan entered the hall and addressed the monks, saying, "Everyone! There's an insect in the rice. You should all go and see it!"

When Shishuang met Daowu, he said, "What is the transcendent wisdom that meets the eye?"

Daowu called to an attendant and he responded. Daowu said to him "Add some clean water to the pitcher."

After a long pause, Daowu said to Shishuang, "What did you just come and ask me?"

Shishuang started to raise his previous question when Daowu got up and left the room. Shishuang then had a great realization.

When Daowu was about to die, he said, "There's something in my mind. An old trouble. Who can get rid of it for me?"

Shishuang said, "All things in your mind are unreal. Get rid of good and bad."
Daowu said, "Worthy! Worthy!"

Later, Shishuang hid from the world. He lived in obscurity in Liuyang as a potter's assistant. In the morning he would go to work and in the evening he would return home. No one knew him [to be an adept]. Dongshan Liangjie sent a monk to find him.

Shishuang asked him, "What does Dongshan say to provide instruction to his disciples?"

The monk said, "At the end of the summer practice period he said to the monks, 'The fall has begun and the summer has ended. If you brethren go traveling, you must go to the place where there isn't a blade of grass for ten thousand miles.'

"After a long pause, Dongshan said, 'How can one go to a place where a single blade of grass isn't found for ten thousand miles?'"

Shishuang said, "Did anyone respond or not?"

The monk said, "No."

Shishuang said, "Why didn't someone say, 'Going out the door, there's the grass'?"

The monk went back and relayed what Shishuang said to Dongshan.

Dongshan said, "This is the talk of wonderful knowledge appropriate for [an abbot of] fifteen hundred people."

Zen master Shishuang entered the hall and addressed the monks, saying, "All of you each has what is fundamental. There's no point searching for it. It's not to be found in right or wrong, nor in anything you can talk about. The entire source of the teaching of a lifetime, capable of setting people's lives to order, all ·comes down to this very moment, directly to the fact that the Dharma body has no body. This is the ultimate teaching of our school.

"We monks have no set path. If we have partiality then we've strayed. We just impartially sit in the mud. Delusive speech, sight, and hearing all come from the mind's intentions."

"Cease. Stop. Have one thought for ten thousand years. Be a cold, ashen, decayed tree. A strip of white silk without words upon it."

A monk asked, "What is the meaning of the First Ancestor's coming from the west?"

Shishuang said, "A single slab of stone in the empty void."

The monk bowed.

Shishuang said, "Do you understand?"

The monk said, "No."

Shishuang said, "It's good you don't understand. If you understood I'd hit you on your head."

Shishuang was in his abbot's room and a monk just outside the room's window said, "Master, why is it that you're so near yet I can't see your face?"

Shishuang said, "The entire world is not concealed."

Later, a monk related this story to Zen master Xuefeng Yicun and asked, "'The entire world isn't concealed.' What does this mean?"

Xuefeng said, "There's no place that isn't Shishuang."

When Shishuang heard of this he said, "What kind of blasphemy is that old fellow blathering?"

When Xuefeng heard about Shishuang's reaction, he said, "My mistake." ([Later,] Zen master Dong Chanji commented, "Was it that Xuefeng understood Shishuang or not? If he understood, then why was he talking blasphemy? If he didn't understand, what was it that he didn't understand? Of course, the Dharma doesn't differ. So why is their teaching different, and why is there a difference in their explanations?" Then Dong Chanji said, "First study the phrase, 'The entire world is not concealed,' and then you can begin to understand. Don't speak nonsense.")

The master was abbot at Mt. Shishuang for twenty years. There were some in the congregation who would constantly sit upright and never lie down, erect like tree stumps. Everywhere they were known as the "Dead Tree Congregation." Emperor Tang Xi Zong heard of Shishuang's reputation and praised him, offering him the honored purple robe. The master resolutely declined it. In the year 888, the master became ill and died. His ashes were interred at the northwest corner of the monastery. He received the posthumous name "Great Teacher Universal Understanding."

Touzi Datong

Touzi Datong (819–914) was a disciple of Cuiwei Wuxue. He came from ancient Shuzhou (in the southern part of modern Anwei Province). As a young man he left home to study under a Zen master named Bao Tangman. He first studied meditation techniques of the *Anapana Sutra*.[113] Some time later he read the *Flower Garland Sutra* and proceeded to study under Cuiwei Wuxue. After his enlightenment under Cuiwei, he roamed throughout China, eventually returning to his old home and settling on Mt. Touzi. There he built a thatched hut and remained obscure for more than thirty years. Touzi's eminence as a Zen adept could not be concealed, and the great Zhaozhou came looking for him.

One day Zhaozhou came to Dongcheng County [near Mt. Touzi]. Touzi left the mountain. They met each other on the road.

Zhaozhou asked him, "Aren't you the host of Mt. Touzi?"

Touzi said [like a beggar], "Tea, salt, a coin, please help me!"

Zhaozhou then proceeded to Touzi's hut on the mountain and sat down inside. Later Touzi returned to the hut carrying a jug of oil.

Zhaozhou said, "Long have I heard of Touzi, but since coming here all I've seen is an old-timer selling oil."

Touzi said, "You've only seen an old-timer selling oil. But you haven't recognized Touzi."

Zhaozhou said, "What is Touzi?"

Touzi lifted up the jug of oil and yelled, "Oil! Oil!"

Zhaozhou asked, "What do you say about the one who undergoes the great death, and thus attains life?"

Touzi said, "He can't make the journey at night. He must arrive in the daylight."

Zhaozhou said, "I've long committed thievery, but you're worse than me."

———— ❖ ————

Zen master Touzi Datong entered the hall and addressed the monks, saying, "All of you come here searching for some new words and phrases, collecting brilliant things which you intend to stick in your own mouth and repeat. But this old monk's energy is failing and my lips and tongue are blundering. I don't have any idle talk to give you.

"If you ask me then I will answer you directly. But there is no mystery that can be compared to you, yourself. I won't teach you some method to collect wisdom. I will never say that above or below there's a Buddha, a Dharma, something ordinary or something sacred, or that you will find it by sitting with your legs crossed. You all manifest a thousand things. It is the understandings that arise from your own life that you must carry into the future, reaping what you sow. I have nothing to give you here, neither overtly nor by inference. I can only speak to all of you in this manner. If you have doubts then question me."

A monk asked, "When it is not received overtly or by inference, then what?"

Touzi said, "Are you trying to collect wisdom?"

Touzi then left the hall.

❖

A monk asked, "In the entire store of scriptural teachings, is there any one particularly important matter or not?"

Touzi said, "Demonstrate the teaching of all the scriptures!"

❖

A monk asked, "What about when the golden manacles are not open?"

Touzi said, "They are open."

❖

A monk asked, "All buddhas and dharmas come forth from this sutra. What is this sutra?"

Touzi said, "It is due to this name that you esteem and sustain."

❖

A monk asked, "Does the dragon bellow from within the withered tree?"

Touzi said, "I say that inside the skull the lion roars."

❖

A monk asked, "One Dharma universally freshens all beings. What Dharma is this?"

Touzi said, "The falling rain."

❖

A monk asked, "All sounds are the sound of Buddha, are they not?"

Touzi said, "Yes."

The monk said, "Does the master not make farting sounds on the commode?"

Touzi struck the monk.

❖

A monk asked, "Refined and vulgar speech both have the same meaning, right?"

Touzi said, "Yes."

The monk said, "In that case may I call the master an ass?"

Touzi struck the monk.

A monk asked, "What is the final word?"

Touzi said, "The word you didn't understand at the beginning."

A monk asked, "Who is the master's teacher?"

Touzi said, "If you look from in front of him you can't see his head. If you look from behind him you can't see his back."

A monk asked, "Manjushri had seven buddhas as disciples. Did Manjushri have a teacher?"

Touzi said, "When you speak in this manner, it's as if you're belittling yourself and praising others."

A monk asked, "The lion is the king of beasts. Why is it devoured by the six senses?"[114]

Touzi said, "Don't build yourself up. Don't believe in self and other."

Zen master Touzi Datong resided on Mt. Touzi for more than thirty years, provoking and advancing Dharma in all directions. Those who came for his instruction often overflowed the hall. The master spoke in an unimposing manner, answering all questions, aiding each person's development, and expressing great meaning with few words. What is recorded now is but a small portion of what the master said.

The Huang Chao bandit uprising broke out during the Zhong He era [around the year 883]. At that time every place experienced disaster and chaos.

Once, a crazed bandit brandished a knife at the master and said, "What are you doing living here?"

Touzi calmly continued to espouse Dharma. When Touzi finished speaking the bandit bowed and took off his own clothes to leave as an offering.

On the sixth day of the fourth month in [the year 914] the master became slightly ill. The monks called for a doctor.

Touzi said to the congregation, "The four great activities of life ebb and flow unceasingly. You mustn't be concerned. I can take care of myself." After saying these words the master sat in a cross-legged position and passed away. He received the posthumous name "Great Teacher Compassionate Succor."

DESHAN XUANJIAN

DESHAN XUANJIAN (819–914) was a disciple of Longtan Chongxin. He came from ancient Jian Province (in the north of modern Sichuan Province). As a youth he thoroughly studied the rules of the Vinaya and was an authority on the *Diamond Sutra*. He thus earned the nickname, "Diamond Zhou."

Deshan said to his fellow practitioners, "It's like a feather falling into the ocean. The ocean's nature is unchanged. It's like throwing a seed against a sharp blade, the blade is not dulled by it. Whether one studies or not, it is only one-self that knows."

Later, when Deshan heard that the Southern school of Zen was flourishing, he railed against it, saying, "Those who leave home may study the great meaning of Buddhism for a thousand kalpas and spend a further ten thousand kalpas performing detailed Buddhist practice, yet they still won't become a buddha. How dare those southern devils say that just by pointing at the human mind one can see self-nature and attain buddhahood? I'll go drag them from their caves and exterminate their ilk, and thus repay the kindness of Buddha!"

With copies of the Qinglong commentaries on his back, Deshan set out from Min.[115] As he traveled on the road in Liyang he came upon an old woman selling dim sum. Stopping to rest, Deshan bought a small meal.

The old woman pointed at his bundle and asked, "What are those books?"

Deshan said, "They're the Qinglong commentaries."

The old woman said, "What sutra do they expound on?"

Deshan said, *"The Diamond Sutra."*

Then the old woman said, "I have a question for you. If you answer it right then I'll donate the dumpling to you. If you can't answer then you must go elsewhere. In the *Diamond Sutra* it says, 'The bygone mind can't be attained. The present mind can't be attained. The future mind can't be attained.' I want to know, monk, what mind are you revealing right now?"[116]

Deshan was speechless.

Deshan then went to see Longtan. Arriving in the Dharma hall, he said, "Long have I heard of Long Tan [in Chinese, "Dragon Marsh"]. But arriving here, I've seen no marsh, nor is there any dragon to be seen."

Longtan said, "Now you have seen Dragon Marsh."

Deshan said nothing, but remained there.

One evening as Deshan visited Longtan in his room, Longtan said, "It's getting late. You should go now."

Deshan said good-bye and started to go out. He then turned and said, "It's dark outside."

Longtan lit a paper candle and gave it to Deshan. Just as Deshan reached to take it, Longtan blew it out. At that moment Deshan experienced great enlightenment. He then bowed deeply.

Longtan said, "What have you seen?"

Deshan said, "From this day forward, I'll never again doubt the words of the of the old monk under heaven [Buddha]."

The next day, Longtan entered the hall and addressed the monks, saying, "Among you there's a fellow whose teeth are like a sword tree and whose mouth is like a bowl of blood. Striking him with the stick will not turn his head. Someday he will go to a solitary peak and establish what I've said there!"

Deshan then placed his commentaries in a pile in front of the Dharma hall. Lifting a candle he said, "All the mysterious doctrines are but a speck of dust in a vast void. All the great affairs of the world are but a drop of water cast into a boundless chasm."

Deshan then set fire to the books.

Deshan paid his respects to Longtan and proceeded to Mt. Gui [Zen master Guishan Lingyou's monastery]. There, Deshan went directly to the Dharma hall where, his traveling garment tucked under his arm, he entered the hall and walked first from the west side to the east side, then from east to west.

He then faced the abbot [Guishan] and said, "Is it here? Is it here?"

Guishan then sat down in meditation and did not pay special attention to Deshan.

Deshan said, "No! No!"

Deshan then walked out of the hall to the gate of the monastery. At the gate he stopped and said, "Although it's this way, still I shouldn't be so crude."

Deshan then went back to see Guishan with proper decorum.

Stepping through the door of the hall, Deshan raised a sitting cushion and said, "Master!"

Guishan began to pick up his whisk when Deshan suddenly shouted, shook his sleeves, and went out.

That evening Guishan said to the head monk, "Is that fellow who came today still here or not?"

The head monk said, "When he went out of the Dharma hall he put on his sandals and left."

Guishan said, "Later on this disciple will go and build a grass hut on a solitary mountain peak where he'll revile the buddhas and curse the ancestors."

———— ◆ ————

Zen master Deshan Xuanjian entered the hall and addressed the monks, saying, "If you have no affairs of the self, then you have no delusive craving. That which is obtained through delusive craving is not obtained. If you have no affairs in your mind, nor mind in your affairs, then you are unoccupied yet animated, empty, and wondrous. But if you allow yourself to stray from this upright state, all words will deceive you. Why is this?

"When bound by the slightest thought, you have entered the hell realms. A single glimpse of your impulsive life and you'll be bound tightly for ten thousand kalpas. The words 'sacred' and 'ordinary' are just empty talk. 'Superior' and 'inferior' appearances are just hallucinations. If you're constantly striving for these things will you not become exhausted? If you become belabored in this manner it will be a disaster. The result cannot be good."

———— ◆ ————

A monk asked Deshan, "What is bodhi?"
Deshan struck him and said, "Get out! Don't defecate here!"
The monk asked, "What is Buddha?"
Deshan said, "An old mendicant in India."

———— ◆ ————

Xuefeng Yicun asked Zen master Deshan, "Can I understand the great teaching of the ancients or not?"

Deshan struck Xuefeng and said, "What?"

Xuefeng said, "I don't understand."

The next day Xuefeng again came for instruction.

Deshan said, "My teaching has neither words nor phrases. It is actually without a Dharma that may be given to others."

At these words Xuefeng experienced enlightenment.

When Yantou heard about this, he said, "Old Deshan's backbone was as hard as iron. It couldn't be bent. Even so, within his Dharma gate there are quite a few students."

Deshan said to the monks, "If you speak, you get thirty blows. If you don't speak, you get thirty blows."

When Linji Yixuan heard this, he said to Luopu, "Go there and ask him, 'If I speak why do I still get thirty blows?' When he hits you, grab the staff and give it a shove. Then see what he does."

As instructed by Linji, Luopu went and questioned Deshan. Deshan struck him. Luopu grabbed the staff and gave it a shove. Deshan went back to his room.

Luopu returned and related these events to Linji, who said, "Formerly I had doubts about that fellow. Despite what happened, did you see Deshan or not?"

Luopu hesitated, not knowing what to say. Linji struck him. (Yantou said, "Old Deshan usually just relied on a white staff. If the Buddha came he hit him. If an ancestor came he hit him. Nevertheless he had many students.")

Deshan said to the monks, "As soon as you ask, you have erred. If you don't ask you're also wrong."

A monk came forward and bowed. Deshan struck him.

The monk said, "I just bowed. Why did you hit me?"

Deshan said, "What use would it be to wait until you opened your mouth?"

Deshan entered the hall and addressed the monks, saying, "I don't hold to some view about the ancestors. Here, there are no ancestors and no buddhas. Bodhidharma is an old stinking foreigner. Shakyamuni is a dried piece of excrement. Manjushri and Samantabhadra are dung carriers. What is known as 'realizing the mystery' is nothing but breaking through to grab an ordinary person's life. 'Bodhi' and 'nirvana' are a donkey's tethering post. The twelve divisions of scriptural canon are devils' texts; just paper for wiping infected skin boils. The four fruitions and the three virtuous states, original mind and the ten stages, these are just graveyard-guarding ghosts.[117] They'll never save you."

A monk came to see Deshan. Walking up to him, he posed as if to strike him.

Deshan said, "Why didn't you bow? You should get a blow from this mountain monk's staff!"

The monk shook his sleeves and started to walk out.

Deshan said, "Even if I grant you that. It's still just one-half."

The monk turned around and shouted.

Deshan struck him and said, "I have to hit you for it to happen."

The monk said, "In every direction there are clear-eyed people."

Deshan said, "In all nature there is the eye."

The monk opened his eyes wide and said, "Cat!"

Then the monk went out.

Deshan said, "In three thousand years the Yellow River runs clear but once."

———— ◆ ————

A monk asked, "Is there much difference between sacred and ordinary?"

Deshan shouted.

———— ◆ ————

Because Deshan had become ill, a monk asked, "Is there someone who is not ill?"

Deshan said, "Yes."

The monk asked, "What about the one who is not ill?"

Deshan yelled, "Aagh! Aagh!"

———— ◆ ————

Deshan gave a final admonishment to his congregation, saying, "Groping after what is empty and chasing echoes will only fatigue your mind and spirit. Beyond awakening from a dream and then going beyond this awakening, what matters remain?"

After saying this, Deshan peacefully sat and passed away. The date was the third day of the twelfth lunar month in [the year 865]. He received the posthumous name "Zen Master Behold Self-Nature."

Twelfth Generation

XINGHUA CUNJIANG   BAOSHOU YANZHAO   SANSHENG HUIRAN

TONGFENG ANZHU   XITA GUANGMU   NANTA GUANGYONG

YUNJU DAOYING   QINSHAN WENSUI   LONGYA JUDUN

YUEZHOU QIANFENG   CAOSHAN BENJI   QINGLIN SHIQIAN

SHUSHAN KUANGREN   LUOPU YUANAN   JIUFENG DAOQIAN

DAGUANG JUHUI   XUEFENG YICUN   YANTOU QUANHUO   GUIFENG ZONGMI

XINGHUA CUNJIANG

XINGHUA CUNJIANG (830–88) was a disciple and Dharma heir of Linji Yixuan. He lived and taught in ancient Weizhou (near the Yellow River, upstream from the modern city of Jinan in Shandong Province). The Linji lineage continued from Linji directly through Xinghua and his Dharma heirs down to the present day.

Xinghua often said, "When I was on pilgrimage in the South, I once suffered blows from the staff, but it never brought out a person who understands Buddhadharma."

Sansheng asked him, "What do you see that you can talk like that?"

Xinghua shouted.

Sansheng said, "You're beginning to get it."

Later, Dajue heard about this.[118]

He said, "How was this blown into Dajue's doorway?"

Later, Xinghua served as the head monk at Dajue's monastery. One day Dajue called to him and said, "I've heard that you said that when you were on pilgrimage in the South you once suffered blows from the staff, but it never revealed someone who understood Buddhadharma. By what principle could you speak like this?"

Xinghua shouted.

Dajue struck him.

Xinghua shouted again.

Dajue again struck him.

Then Xinghua said, "When I was at elder brother Sansheng's place, we learned a phrase about 'guest' and 'host.' Elder brother Sansheng turned everything topsy-turvy. I want you to provide me a blissful method of entering the Way."

Dajue said, "You blind fool! This gibberish you've said is sorely lacking! Take off your robe and I'll give you a painful whack!"

Upon hearing these words Xinghua grasped the meaning of his late master Linji's having suffered a beating at Huangbo's place.

Later Xinghua went into the buddha hall, and presenting a stick of incense to the Buddha, he said, "This stick of incense is for elder brother Sansheng, although Sansheng was too aloof from me. This is also for elder brother Dajue, although he was also removed. Neither can be compared to the honor I give to my late teacher, Linji."

◆

Master Xinghua asked a monk, "Where are you coming from?"
The monk said, "From a precipitous Zen place."
Xinghua said, "Did you bring the shout of a precipitous Zen place?"
The monk said, "I didn't bring it."
Xinghua said, "Then you haven't come from there."
The monk shouted. Xinghua hit him.

◆

Xinghua said to the monks, "I'm always hearing shouts in the corridor as well as in back of the hall. I tell you all that you mustn't blindly shout wild shouts. Even if you shout so loud that it takes my breath away and stops me cold, when my breath comes back I'll tell you, 'Still not it!' Why? I haven't been passing out precious gems in vermilion wrappings to all of you! What's all the shouting about?"

◆

The late Tang dynasty emperor Zhuang Zong honored master Xinghua with the gift of a riding horse. While the master was riding the horse it was startled and the master fell off, injuring his foot. The emperor sent some special medicine to the master to help heal his foot.

Xinghua gave instructions to the monastery director, saying, "Make me a walking stick."

The monastery director made the stick and brought it to Xinghua. The master took the stick and proceeded to circle the hall, and as he did so he asked the monks, "Do you recognize me?"

The monks answered, "How could we not recognize you?"

The Master said, "Dharma Master Foot! He can speak but he can't walk."

Xinghua then went into the hall and instructed the attendant to ring the bell and assemble the monks.

Xinghua then addressed the monks, saying, "Do you recognize me?"

The monks didn't know what to say.

Xinghua then threw down the staff and passed away solemnly in an upright position.

BAOSHOU YANZHAO

BAOSHOU YANZHAO (830–88) was a disciple of Linji Yixuan. He lived and taught at Baoshou Monastery in ancient Zhenzhou (near the modern city of Shijia-zhuang).

A monk asked Baoshou Zhao, "When all realms come forward and over-whelm you, then what?"

Baoshou answered, "Don't control it."

The monk bowed.

Baoshou then said, "Don't move. If you move it will break you in two at the waist."

-------------------- ◆ --------------------

When Baoshou was interviewing a monk in the abbot's room, he responded to a question by saying, "The hundred thousand saints are not outside of this room."

The monk said, "That sounds like the ancients saying that the innumerable worlds are like the bubbles in an ocean wave. I don't understand where the hundred thousand saints are revealed in this room."

Baoshou said, "They're manifested right here."

The monk said, "Who can demonstrate this?"

Baoshou threw down his whisk.

The monk walked from the west side of the room to the east side, and then stood there.

Baoshou hit him.

The monk said, "Without practicing Zen for a long time, how can someone realize its ultimate teaching?"

Baoshou said, "Thirty years from now, these words will be well known."

Zhaozhou came to visit the monastery. In the meditation hall Baoshou sat down facing away from him. Zhaozhou spread out his sitting cushion and bowed. Baoshou got up and went into the abbot's quarters. Zhaozhou picked up his meditation cushion and went out.

Baoshou asked a monk, "Where did you come from?"
The monk said, "From West Mountain."
Baoshou asked, "Did you see the monkey?"
The monk said, "I saw it."
Baoshou said, "How clever was it?"
The monk said, "I saw that I'm not the least bit clever."
Baoshou hit him.

A well-known person named Hu Dingjiao ["Door-nail Hu"] came to visit Baoshou.
Baoshou said, "Aren't you Hu Dingjiao?"
Hu said politely, "I dare not say so."
Baoshou said, "Let's see if you can nail down emptiness!"
Hu said, "Please explain it to me."
Baoshou then hit him.
Hu said, "The master is right to hit me."
Baoshou said, "In the future, a lot of teachers are going to hit you."
Later, Hu visited Zhaozhou and told him of his dialogue with Baoshou.
Zhaozhou said, "What did you do to make him hit you?"
Hu said, "I don't know what my error was."
Zhaozhou said, "It was just this split seam that Master Baoshou couldn't tolerate!"
At these words Hu had an insight.
Zhaozhou said, "Just nail up this seam."

A monk asked, "When there's not a single cloud for ten thousand miles, then what?"
Baoshou said, "The clear sky also gets the staff!"
The monk said, "I don't understand why the clear sky has an error."
Baoshou hit him.

The monk Xiyuan Siming came to study with Zen master Baoshou.

Xiyuan asked him, "When the 'illusion city' is knocked down, then what?"

Baoshou said, "Don't kill people by chopping them in two."

Xiyuan said, "Chop."

Baoshou hit him.

Xiyuan continued saying, "Chop! Chop!" and Baoshou struck him each time he spoke.

Baoshou then went back to his abbot's quarters and said, "That monk who just arrived! I beat him until he was red. What a blasphemy."

SANSHENG HUIRAN

SANSHENG HUIRAN (n.d.) was a prominent disciple of Linji Yixuan. He compiled his teacher's words in *The Record of Linji*. After Linji's death, Sansheng traveled to encounter Yangshan, Xiangyan, Deshan, Daowu, and other well-known Zen teachers. Each of them in turn sharpened Sansheng's abilities. Eventually Sansheng settled in Zhenzhou (now the city of Zhengding in Hebei Province) and taught at the Sansheng Monastery, where he derived his mountain name.

When Sansheng arrived at Mt. Yang, Yangshan asked him, "What's your name."

Sansheng said, "Huiji."

Yangshan said, "Huiji is my name."

Sansheng said, "My name is Huiran."

Yangshan laughed loudly.

When Sansheng met Xiangyan, Xiangyan asked, "Where are you from?"

Sansheng said, "From Linji."

Xiangyan said, "Did you bring Linji's shout?"

Sansheng suddenly picked up a cushion and struck Xiangyan in the mouth with it.

When Sansheng arrived at Mt. De, he started to arrange his sitting [meditation] items when Deshan said, "Don't put out your meal apron. There's no rice here."

Sansheng said, "Although it's here, it can't be shown."

Deshan took his staff and made to strike Sansheng. Sansheng grabbed it and pushed Deshan onto the meditation platform. Deshan laughed loudly.

Sansheng shouted and went out.

———— ◆ ————

A monk asked, "Why did the First Ancestor come from the west?"

Sansheng said, "Spoiled meat draws flies." ([Later,] Xinghua Cunjiang said, "An injury on the back of a donkey is full of green flies.")

The following two passages are recorded about Sansheng in the *Transmission of the Lamp*.

When Sansheng was at Xuefeng's, he heard Xuefeng give a teaching that "all persons without exception have an ancient mirror. This monkey has an ancient mirror."

Sansheng stepped forth and said, "For endless kalpas it has been nameless. Why does the master propose it to be an ancient mirror?"

Xuefeng said, "It's because of defective existence."

Sansheng said, "As for me, I don't see where you came up with this."

Xuefeng said, "My mistake! I have many duties as abbot."

———— ◆ ————

Sansheng watched as Baoshou entered the lecture hall. When Baoshou passed by, Sansheng shoved another monk out in front of him. Baoshou hit the monk.

Sansheng said, "If the elder treats people in this manner, then he's blind, even though the eyes of everyone in Zhenzhou City are here."

Tongfeng Anzhu

Tongfeng Anzhu (n.d.) was a student of Linji. Like many other disciples of that master, his origins are obscure. During the era of Linji's life, the persecution of Buddhists caused the loss of many contemporary records. The *Transmission of the Lamp* provides a few dialogues involving Tongfeng.

A monk asked Tongfeng, "Master, if you suddenly encountered a huge tiger here, what would you do?"

The master made a roaring noise. The monk acted as though he were scared. The master laughed out loud.

The monk said, "You old thief."

Tongfeng said, "How can you fight this old monk?"

A monk came to the front of Tongfeng's hut, then started to leave.

Tongfeng called out, "Your Reverence! Your Reverence!"

The monk turned his head and then shouted.

Tongfeng didn't speak.

The monk said, "So the old fellow is dead."

Tongfeng then hit him. The monk didn't speak.

The master laughed, "Ha, ha, ha!"

A monk entered the hut and grabbed Tongfeng.

Tongfeng yelled, "Murder! Murder!"

The monk let loose of him, saying: "What's the use of shouting?"

The master said, "Who are you?"

The monk shouted.

The master hit him.

The monk went out and turned his head as he went away, saying: "Just wait. Just wait."

Tongfeng laughed out loud.

XITA GUANGMU

XITA GUANGMU (n.d.) was a student of Yangshan Huiji. He succeeded his teacher and taught on Mt. Yang. Little is recorded about his life. The *Transmission of the Lamp* offers the following brief accounts of his teachings.

A monk asked, "What is upright listening?"
Xita said, "It doesn't enter through your ear."
The monk said, "How can that be?"
Xita said, "Do you hear it?"

———— ◆ ————

A monk asked, "Is the meaning of the ancestors the same as the meaning of the scriptural teaching or not?"
Xita said, "Putting aside 'same' or 'different,' can you say what it is that goes in and out of the mouth of a water pitcher?"

———— ◆ ————

A monk asked, "What's the essential meaning of Zen?"
Xita replied, "You don't have buddha nature."
The monk said, "What is sudden enlightenment?"
Xita drew a circle on the ground for the monk to see.
The monk asked, "What is gradual enlightenment?"
Xita poked the middle of the empty space three times with his hand.

NANTA GUANGYONG

NANTA GUANGYONG (850–938) was a disciple of Yangshan Huiji. He came from ancient Fengcheng City (still called Fengcheng and located in modern Jiangxi Province). According to legend, as his mother nursed the infant Nanta, the room filled with a spiritual light, scaring some nearby horses. As a youth he was handsome and clever, mastering the Confucian classics at the age of thirteen. In his late teens, he studied the *Vimalakirti Sutra* at Kaiyuan Temple. Subsequently, Nanta went to Shiting Temple in Hongzhou where Yangshan served as abbot. There he took up residence as a novice monk. At nineteen, he underwent ordination and then went to study under the great teacher Linji Yixuan.

Linji later directed him back to Yangshan, and he went on to become Yang-shan's attendant, student, and eventual Dharma heir.

When Nanta returned to Yangshan, Yangshan said, "Why have you come?"

Nanta said, "To pay respects to the master."

Yangshan said, "Do you still see me?"

Nanta said, "Yes."

Yangshan said, "Do I look like a donkey?"

Nanta said, "When I observe the master, you don't look like a buddha."

Yangshan said, "If I don't look like a buddha, then what do I look like?"

Nanta said, "If I must compare you to something, then how do you differ from a donkey?"

Yangshan cried out excitedly, "He's forgotten both ordinary and sacred! The passions are exhausted and the body is revealed. For twenty years I've tested them in this way and no one has gotten it. Now this disciple has done it!"

Yangshan would always point to Nanta and say to people, "This disciple is a living buddha."

———— ◆ ————

A monk asked Zen master Nanta, "Manjushri was the teacher of seven buddhas. Did Manjushri have a teacher or not?"

Nanta said, "Manjushri was subject to conditions, and therefore had a teacher."

The monk said, "Who was Manjushri's teacher?"

Nanta held up his whisk.

The monk said, "Is that all?"

Nanta put down the whisk and clasped his hands.

———— ◆ ————

A monk asked, "What is a sentence of mystic function?"

Nanta said, "The water comes and the ditch fills up."

———— ◆ ————

A monk asked, "Where does the real Buddha reside?"

Nanta said, "It doesn't appear in words, nor anywhere else, either."

YUNJU DAOYING

 YUNJU DAOYING (d. 902) was a disciple and Dharma heir of Dongshan Liangjie. He came from ancient Youzhou (located in modern Hubei Province). At the age of twenty-five he took the monk's vows at Yanshou Temple in Fanyang (now in Zhuo County, Hebei Province). It is recorded that as a young man he was versed in the Vinaya. Later he made his way to Mt. Nan where he studied under Zen master Cuiwei Wuxue. Hearing of Dongshan's reputation, he proceeded to Mt. Dong to study with him. Dongshan later allowed him to lead other monks of the temple. After leaving Dongshan, he first lived at "Three Peak Hermitage," and later established Jenru ("True Thusness") Temple on Mt. Yunju (northwest of modern Nanchang City in Jiangxi Province). He taught at this site for more than thirty years, and his congregation's size reached up to fifteen hundred people.

Dongshan asked Yunju, "Where have you come from?"

Yunju said, "From Cuiwei."

Dongshan said, "What teaching does Cuiwei convey to his disciples?"

Yunju said, "Once, when Cuiwei was making offerings to the sacred images, I asked him, 'If you make offerings to the arhats, will they come or not?'

"Cuiwei said, 'Aren't you able to eat every day?'"

Dongshan said, "Did he really say that or not?"

Yunju said, "Yes."

Dongshan said, "Don't dismiss it when a great man appears!"

Then Dongshan asked Yunju, "What is your name?"

Yunju said, "Daoying."

Dongshan said, "Look up and then say it."

Yunju said, "If I look up, then there's nothing named 'Daoying.'"

Dongshan said, "You talk just like I did when I spoke with Daowu."

◆

Yunju asked Dongshan, "What was the First Ancestor's intention?"

Dongshan answered, "Behind him was a reed hat."

◆

Dongshan asked Yunju, "If suddenly a monk asked, 'Your Reverence?' How would you answer?"

Yunju said, "My fault."

————— ◆ —————

Once, Dongshan said to Yunju, "I heard that a monk named 'Great Thought' was reborn in the Kingdom of Wei and became the king. Is this true or not?"

"If his name was 'Great Thought,' then even the Buddha couldn't do it."

Dongshan agreed.

————— ◆ —————

One day Dongshan asked, "Where are you going?"

Yunju said, "Tramping on the mountain."

Dongshan said, "How can the mountain endure?"

Yunju said, "How can it not endure?"

Dongshan said, "If you go on like this, then you'll eventually teach the whole country."

Yunju said, "No, I won't."

Dongshan said, "If you go on like this, then your disciples will gain a way of entrance."

Yunju said, "No such way."

Dongshan said, "No such way? I challenge you to show me."

Yunju said, "If there's such a path, then I'll leave you immediately to go on it."

Dongshan said, "In the future, a thousand or ten thousand people won't be able to grab this disciple."

————— ◆ —————

Yunju was crossing a river with Dongshan.

Dongshan said, "How deep is it?"

Yunju said, "It's not wet."

Dongshan said, "You rustic!"

Yunju said, "What would you say, Master?"

Dongshan said, "Not dry."

————— ◆ —————

Zen master Nanquan once asked a monk, "What sutra are you reading?"

The monk said, "*The Rebirth of Maitreya Sutra*."

Nanquan said, "When will Maitreya be reborn?"

The monk said, "Now he's in Tushita Heaven. He'll be reborn in the future."

Nanquan said, "Up above there's no Maitreya. Down below there's no Maitreya."

Yunju said to Dongshan, "Up above there's no Maitreya. Down below there's no Maitreya. I don't understand to whom this name applies."

When Yunju asked Dongshan this question, Dongshan shook the meditation platform.

Then Dongshan said, "Worthy Ying! When I was at Yunyan's I once asked him something and he shook the stove. Today, when you asked me this question, my entire body broke out in a sweat!"

———— ❖ ————

Yunju built a cottage on nearby Sanfeng peak. For ten days thereafter he didn't return to the monk's hall.

Dongshan asked him, "Why haven't you come to meals lately?"

Yunju said, "Every day a heavenly spirit brings me food."

Dongshan said, "I say you're a person. Why do you still have such an understanding? Come see me tonight!"

That evening when Yunju came to see Dongshan, Dongshan called out to him, "Hermit Ying!"

Yunju answered, "Yes?"

Dongshan said, "Not thinking of good and not thinking of evil, what is *it*?"

Yunju went back to his cottage and sat in Zen meditation. Because of this the god couldn't find him, and after three days did not come again.

———— ❖ ————

Yunju entered the hall and addressed the monks. He quoted an ancient teacher, saying, "'Hell is not a great misery. The greatest misery is to wear these clothes but not understand the great matter.' You here who have embarked on this undertaking, you've gone only nine-tenths of the way. If you show a little more spirit, then you monks won't spend your whole life on pilgrimage and you won't forsake our order. An ancient said, 'If you take on the responsibility of this affair, you must stand on top of the hightest peak, and you must walk on the bottom of the deepest ocean, then you'll have a disciple's resolution.'"

———— ❖ ————

A monk asked Zen master Yunju Daoying, "What is the one Dharma?"

Yunju said, "What are the ten thousand dharmas?"

The monk said, "I don't understand how to comprehend this."

Yunju said, "The one Dharma is your own mind. The ten thousand dharmas are your fundamental nature. Are they one thing or two?"

The monk bowed.

Yunju showed the monk a poem that said:

The single Dharma is the essence of all dharmas.
The myriad dharmas penetrate the one Dharma.
"Mind-only" and "nature-only,"
Don't say they're different or the same.

———— ◆ ————

A monk asked, "What is the place of the transcendent path?"
Yunju said, "Below Heaven, great peace."

Upon his death, Yunju received the posthumous title "Zen Master Vast Awakening."

QINSHAN WENSUI

QINSHAN WENSUI (n.d.) was a disciple of Dongshan Liangjie. He came from ancient Fuzhou. As a young man he entered a Zen monastery in Hangzhou headed by a teacher named Zishan Huanzhong. Later he studied with his friends Yantou and Xuefeng under the famous teacher Deshan Xuanjian. Deshan's strict methods were too severe for Qinshan, and he left to study under Dongshan Liangjie. Under Dongshan's instruction Qinshan realized the Buddhadharma and went on to become a well-known teacher.

Qinshan asked Deshan, "Tianhuang spoke thus, and Longtan spoke thus. How does the master speak?"
Deshan said "Why don't you check out Tianhuang and Longtan and see?"
Qinshan started to speak when suddenly Deshan hit him.
Qinshan went back to the Long Life Hall and said, "Right is right, but hitting me is going too far."
Yantou said, "If you speak like this, you'll never see Deshan."

············ ◆ ············

Qinshan studied under Dongshan and attained realization. He became Dongshan's Dharma heir. At the age of twenty-seven, Qinshan traveled to Mt. Qin. There, in front of the entire congregation, he realized great enlightenment. He then told the congregation about his initial meeting with Dongshan.

"Dongshan asked me, 'Where have you come from?'"

"I said, 'From Mt. Dazi ["Great Compassion"].'"

"Dongshan said, 'Did you see Great Compassion?'"

"I said, 'I saw it.'"

"Dongshan said, 'Did you see it before form? Or did you see it after form?'"

"I said, 'I saw it neither before nor after form.'"

"Dongshan was silent."

Qinshan then [said to the congregation at Mt. Qin], "I left the master too soon. I had not yet fully realized Dongshan's meaning."

———— ◆ ————

A monk asked, "All of the buddhas and all of the Buddhadharmas come forth from this sutra. What is this sutra?"

Qinshan said, "Forever turning."

———— ◆ ————

A monk asked, "What is the style of the master's house?"

Qinshan said, "A silver embroidered fragrant sachet. When the wind blows the entire road is filled with fragrance."

———— ◆ ————

Once, Qinshan, Yantou, and Xuefeng were sitting together and Dongshan brought some tea. Qinshan closed his eyes.

Dongshan said, "Where have you gone?"

Qinshan said, "I've entered samadhi."

Dongshan said, "Samadhi has no gate, so how have you entered it?"

———— ◆ ————

Qinshan went into the bathhouse. A monk there was turning the water wheel.

Qinshan said, "Luckily, I've already turned the wheel. So why are you doing that?"

The monk got off the wheel and said, "What if you hadn't turned it?"

Qinshan said, "If not, then what good would Qinshan's eye be for anyone?"

The monk said, "What is the master's eye?"

Qinshan pointed at his own eye brows.

The monk said, "How can the master act like this?"

Qinshan said, "It's what I do. It's not what you do! It's not what you do!"

The monk was silent.

Qinshan said, "If you enter battle without valor, you'll lose morale at the first engagement."

After a long pause, Qinshan asked the monk, "Do you understand?"

The monk said, "I don't understand."

Qinshan said, "Qinshan will only do half of it for you."

The following passages are taken from the *Transmission of the Lamp*.

Qinshan, along with Yantou Quanhuo and Xuefeng Yicun, were once passing through Jiangxi, where they stopped at a teahouse.

Qinshan said, "Anyone who can't turn with penetrating spirit doesn't get tea."

Yantou said, "In that case I certainly won't get tea."

Xuefeng said, "The same with me."

Qinshan said, "You two fellows don't recognize the words right here."

Yantou said, "The words where?"

Qinshan said, "Although the crow inside the bag is alive, it's like it was dead."

Yantou said, "Retreat! Retreat!"

Qinshan said, "Elder brother Huo is dismissed. What will Duke Cun do?"

Xuefeng used his hand to draw a circle.

Qinshan said, "No gaining, no asking."

Yantou laughed and said, "Too far."

Qinshan said, "Some mouths don't get any, but there are many who are drinking tea."

Yantou and Xuefeng were silent.

While speaking to some monks, Qinshan raised his fist straight up and said, "I open my fist and the five fingers are separated. And if I now close my fist then there is nothing that surpasses it. Now tell me, does Qinshan have penetrating talk or not?"

The monk came forward and raised his fist.

Qinshan said, "If that's it, then it's just a mouthless fellow."

A monk said, "I'm not familiar with how the master receives people."

"If I receive people, then each and every one of you go!"

A monk said to Qinshan, "It's something special about meeting with you, Master, that causes one to vomit up the doctrinal wind of our school."

Qinshan said, "If you come in some special way, I'll have to vomit."

The monk said, "Please do."

Qinshan hit him.

The monk was silent.

Qinshan said, "Trying to catch a rabbit by waiting for it to run into a stump. You're wasting your mind."

LONGYA JUDUN, "ZHENGKONG"

LONGYA JUDUN (835–923) was a disciple of Dongshan Liangjie. He came from ancient Fuzhou (now in modern Jiangxi Province). At the age of fourteen he left home to live at Mantian Temple in Jizhou. Later he received ordination on Mt. Song. Longya traveled far and wide, meeting and studying with many famous teachers such as Cuiwei Wuxue and Deshan Xuanjian. Eventually he came to study with Dongshan, under whom he realized great enlightenment. After a period of study with Dongshan, Longya continued traveling and engaged still more teachers, including Linji Yixuan, to deepen his understanding. Finally, he took up the abbacy of Miaoji Temple on Mt. Longya (near modern Changsha City), where a large congregation gathered from throughout the country. The following account of Longya's initial encounters with the great Zen adepts is taken from the *Transmission of the Lamp*.

When Longya met with Cuiwei he said, "Your student has been here for more than a month. Every day the master enters the hall to speak but we have not received any instruction about even one Dharma."

Cuiwei said, "So what?" (A monk asked Dongshan this same question. Dongshan said, "Are you accusing me of something?" [Later,] Fayan said, "The ancestors are here!" Zen master Dongshan also said, "Were these three worthies intimate with *it* or not? If so, where? If not, where is the eye?")

So Longya went to study under Deshan. He asked, "From afar I've heard of Deshan's 'one phrase' Buddhadharma, but up to now I haven't heard the master say one phrase about the Buddhadharma. Why is this?"

Deshan said, "So what?"

Longya couldn't accept this, and so he went to study with Dongshan. Longya asked Dongshan the same question.

Dongshan said, "Are you accusing me of something?"

Longya then relayed the words spoken by Deshan. Suddenly awakening to their meaning on his own, he thereupon settled on Mt. Dong and sought instruction from Dongshan along with the other monks.

One day Longya asked, "What is the essential meaning of Zen?"

Dongshan said, "Wait until Dong Creek flows uphill. Then I'll tell you."

Longya suddenly awoke to the deepest meaning of Dongshan's words.

After becoming abbot of Miaoji Temple, Longya's fame spread widely and he had many students. One day he entered the hall and addressed the monks, saying, "You who study must pass through the buddhas and ancestors before you'll understand. Zen master Xinfeng said, 'The buddhas and ancestors are like deceptive thieves. If you gain some understanding, but are unable to penetrate beyond them, then they have deceived you.'"

A monk asked, "Do the buddhas and ancestors have deceptive minds or not?"

Longya said, "You're asking whether rivers and lakes have obstructive minds or not. Although rivers and lakes don't have obstructive minds, yet sometimes there are people who can't get across them, and they become like obstacles for people. So one can't say they don't obstruct people. Although the buddhas and ancestors don't have deceptive intent, sometimes people can't penetrate their meaning, and so they in effect become deceptive. Thus, one can't say they don't deceive people. When one penetrates the buddhas' and ancestors' deception, then one goes beyond the buddhas and ancestors and, for the first time, experiences their meaning. Then that person is the same as all the ancients. If one has not penetrated this understanding, but only studies the buddhas and ancestors, then in incalculable eons there will not be an instance of realization."

The monk then asked, "How can one avoid being deceived by the buddhas and ancestors?"

Longya said, "You must awaken on your own."

Yuezhou Qianfeng

Yuezhou Qianfeng (n.d.) was a disciple of Dongshan Liangjie. Little is record-ed about his life. He taught in Yuezhou (a place southeast of modern Hangzhou in northern Jiangxi Province).

Qianfeng entered the hall and said, "The dharmakaya has three types of ill-ness and two types of light, and you must penetrate them one by one before you can return to your home and sit solidly. You must know that there is a yet more pivotal realization."

Yunmen stepped forward and asked, "Why does one who is in the hut not know of affairs outside the hut?"

Qianfeng laughed loudly, "Ha, ha, ha."

Yunmen said, "This is still a place of doubt for this student."

Qianfeng said, "Where is your mind moving?"

Yunmen said, "I want the master to speak directly."

Qianfeng said, "Then you must do as I said before you can sit solidly."

Yunmen said, "Okay."

———— ◆ ————

Yuezhou entered the hall and addressed the monks, saying, "If you put forth the first principle, then there is no need for the second principle. Let go of the first principle and you will fall into the second principle."

Yunmen came forward from the congregation and said, "Yesterday a person came from Mt. Tiantai. Now he's gone on to Mt. Jing."

Yuezhou said, "Tomorrow the chief cook does not need to do *puqing*."[119]

Yuezhou then got down from the seat.

———— ◆ ————

Qianfeng asked a monk, "Where did you come from?"

The monk said, "From Mt. Tiantai."

Qianfeng said, "I've heard that the stone bridge there has two sections, is that so or not?"

The monk said, "Where did the master learn this news?"

Qianfeng said, "From someone called 'the former guest of Hua Peak [a peak on Mt. Tiantai].'

Formerly he was a 'Flat Field Village Person.'"

············ ◆ ············

A monk asked Qianfeng, "How does one escape the Three Realms?"

The master said, "Call the temple director and have him chase this monk out of here!"

························· ◆ ·························

Qianfeng asked the monks, "The six tendencies of the turning wheel of transmigration have what eye?"

The monks didn't answer.

························· ◆ ·························

A monk asked, "What is the talk that is beyond the buddhas and ancestors?"

Qianfeng said, "I ask you."

The monk said, "Master, please don't ask me."

Qianfeng said, "If I ask you, it doesn't make any difference. So I ask you, what is the talk that is beyond the buddhas and ancestors?"

························· ◆ ·························

A monk asked, "There are temples in the ten directions and there is a single road to the gate of nirvana. Where does this road begin?"

Qianfeng raised his staff and drew a circle in the air, saying, "Right here." ([Later,] a monk asked Yunmen to explain this. Yunmen picked up a fan and said, "This fan leaps into heaven and blocks the nostrils of the heavenly king. Strike the fish in the Eastern Sea but once, and the rain falls in a downpour! Do you understand?")

CAOSHAN BENJI

CAOSHAN BENJI (840–901) was a foremost disciple of Dongshan. He was so closely associated with his teacher that their names were used together to form the name of their Zen school, Caodong. Caoshan came from ancient Quanzhou (a place still called Quanzhou in modern Fujian Province). When a youth, he studied Confucianism. Leaving home at the age of nineteen, Caoshan entered Lingshi Monastery in Fuzhou. When he received ordination at the age of twenty-five, Zen Buddhism was flourishing in Tang dynasty China. Later, after becoming Dongshan's Dharma heir, Caoshan started a new temple in Fuzhou and named it Cao Shan (Mt. Cao), after the Sixth Ancestor, whose mountain name was derived from Cao Xi (Cao Creek). Thereafter, Caoshan lived and taught at Mt. Heyu, and is said to have changed the name of that place to Cao Shan as well.

Caoshan used Dongshan's "five ranks" as a method of instruction, leading to its wide use in Zen monasteries. This helped differentiate Caodong Zen as a unique Zen school.

Caoshan's fame spread widely after he wrote a commentary in praise of verses composed by the famous poet Hanshan. These selections are taken from the *Transmission of the Lamp*.

> Upon meeting Caoshan, Dongshan said, "What is your name?"
> Caoshan said, "Benji."
> Dongshan said, "What is your transcendent name?"
> Caoshan said, "I can't tell you."
> Dongshan said, "Why not?"
> Caoshan said, "There I'm not named Benji."
> Dongshan then realized that this disciple was a great Dharma vessel.
> After starting study under Dongshan at this time, Caoshan remained for many years and realized the secret seal of Dongshan's teachings.
> Later, when Caoshan left Dongshan, Dongshan said, "Where are you going?"
> Caoshan said, "I'm not going to a different place."
> Dongshan asked, "You're not going to a different place but there is still 'going'?"
> Caoshan said, "I'm going, but not to a different place."

———— ◆ ————

> A monk asked, "Who is it that is not a companion to the myriad dharmas?"
> Caoshan said, "Tell me, where is it that many people in Hongzhou are going?"

·········· ◆ ··········

> A monk asked Caoshan, "Can the eyebrows and the eyes distinguish each other or not?"
> Caoshan said, "They can't distinguish each other."
> The monk said "Why not?"
> Caoshan said, "Because they're in the same place."
> The monk said, "If that's so one couldn't tell them apart."
> Caoshan said, "Eyebrows, after all, are not eyes."
> The monk asked, "What are eyes?"
> Caoshan said, "[Eyes are] what is upright."
> The monk said, "What are eyebrows?"
> Caoshan said, "I'm not sure."
> The monk said, "Why is the master not sure?"

Caoshan said, "If one lacks doubt, one is upright."

The monk said, "What truth is there in form?"

Caoshan said, "Form is truth."

The monk said, "How would you demonstrate this?"

Caoshan picked up his tea cup saucer.

The monk asked, "How can illusion be truth?"

Caoshan said, "Illusion is fundamentally truth." ([Later,] Fayan commented, "Illusion is fundamentally not truth.")

The monk asked, "When illusion is faced, what is revealed?"

Caoshan said, "Illusion is revealed." (Fayan said, "Illusion is not faced.")

The monk said, "In that case, then from start to finish one can't escape illusion."

Caoshan said, "But if you pursue illusive forms you can't attain them."

A monk asked, "Who is the person who is here forever?"

Caoshan said, "Just when you encounter Caoshan, he is instantly revealed."

The monk asked, "Who is the one who is never here?"

Caoshan said, "Hard to find."

The monk Qingrui said to Caoshan, "I am alone and destitute. Master, please give me some assistance."

Caoshan said, "Worthy Rui, come here!"

Qingrui came forward.

Caoshan said "You already drank three cups of Quan Province 'Hundred Houses' wine, yet you still say your lips are not wet."

Yunmen asked, "The unchanging person has come. Will the master receive him or not?"

Caoshan said, "On Mt. Cao there's no spare time for that."

A monk asked, "An ancient said, 'Everyone has brothers in the dust.' Can you demonstrate this to me?"

Caoshan said, "Give me your hand."

Caoshan then pointed at the monk's fingers and counted, "One, two, three, four, five. That's enough."

A monk asked, "What was Luzu trying to show when he faced the wall?"
Caoshan covered his ears with his hands.

Caoshan asked Venerable Qiang, "The true body of Buddha is like vast empti-
ness. When a thing appears there, it is like the moon reflected in water. How
would you express this teaching?"
Qiang said, "It's like a donkey looking into a well."
Caoshan said, "You've said a lot, but you've only gotten eighty percent of it."
Qiang said, "What would you say, Master?"
Caoshan said, "It's like the well looking at the donkey."

A monk asked, "From old times there's a saying, 'Until a person has fallen
down, the earth can't help him arise.' What is 'fallen down'?"
Caoshan said, "It's allowing."
The monk asked, "What is 'arise'?"
Caoshan said, "It's 'arise.'"

A monk asked, "There's a teaching which has the words, 'The great ocean
does not harbor dead corpses.' What is the ocean?"
Caoshan said, "It includes everything."
The monk said, "Why doesn't it include corpses?"
Caoshan said, "Those who have ceased breathing are not manifested."
The monk said, "Since it includes everything, why are those who've stopped
breathing not manifested?"
Caoshan said, "The myriad things don't have this ability. The cessation of
breath has moral power."

In the summer of [the year 901], Caoshan asked a monk, "What month and
day is this?"
The monk said, "It's the fifteenth day of the sixth month."
Caoshan said, "Caoshan has traveled his entire life. Everywhere it is observed
that a summer has ninety days."
The next day during the hour of the dragon [7–9 A.M.] Caoshan died. He was
sixty-two years old and had been a priest for thirty-one years. He was cremated

on the west side of the mountain. He received the posthumous name "Zen Master Evidence of the Source." His stupa was named "Blessed Perfection."

QINGLIN SHIQIAN

QINGLIN SHIQIAN (n.d.) was a disciple of Dongshan Liangjie. His origins are obscure. An account of his life from the time he met his teacher is given in the *Wudeng Huiyuan*:

> When Qinglin first met Dongshan, Dongshan asked him, "Where did you come from?"
> Qinglin said, "Wuling."
> Dongshan said, "How does the Dharma teaching in Wuling compare with here?"
> Qinglin said, "In a foreign land, bamboo sprouts are picked in winter."
> Dongshan said, "Provide this man fragrant rice cooked in a separate pot."
> Qinglin then shook his sleeves and went out.
> Dongshan said, "Someday this one will trample everyone on earth to death."

———— ◆ ————

> Once when Qinglin was planting pine trees on Mt. Dong, an old man asked him for a poem. Qinglin composed and recited this verse:

> *More than three feet long,*
> *The thick green grass,*
> *I don't know what generation*
> *Will see this pine's old age.*

> The monk showed the poem to Dongshan, who said, "Here is the third leader of Mt. Dong."

———— ◆ ————

> Qinglin prepared to leave Mt. Dong.
> Dongshan asked, "Where are you going?"
> Qinglin said, "The golden wheel is not concealed; in every realm the red dust is cut off."
> Dongshan said, "The great good is entrusted to you."

Qinglin thanked Dongshan and began to leave. Dongshan accompanied him to the gate and said, "In a phrase, how would you describe what you're doing?"

Qinglin replied, "Step by step walking on red dust—a shadowless, pervasive body."

Dongshan was silent for a long while.

Qinglin said, "Why doesn't the master speak more quickly?"

Dongshan said, "What makes you in such a hurry?"

Qinglin said, "I'm sorry."

He then bade Dongshan farewell.

◆

Qinglin went to Qingcun Mountain in Shannanfu and lived in a hut. After ten years he suddenly recalled something Dongshan had told him, and said, "I should try to benefit the many benighted beings. Why limit it to a few?"

He then went to Suizhou where he was invited to become the abbot at Green Forest Monastery. Later he moved back to Mt. Dong.

◆

The monastery rules at Mt. Dong required a newly arrived monk to first make three trips hauling firewood before entering the hall.

Once, a monk was unwilling to do this and asked Qinglin, "Not asking about inside three trips, I ask what about outside three trips?"

Qinglin said, "Iron Wheel Emperor issues a decree at the center of the universe."

The monk was silent.

Qinglin then drove him away with blows.

◆

A monk asked, "For a long time I've been miserably ill, and I took poisonous medicine. Please cure me."

Qinglin said, "Gold! Poke it into your brain! Pour the rich liquor on the top of your head."

The monk said, "Thank you for this cure."

Qinglin then hit the monk.

◆

Zen master Qinglin Shiqian entered the hall and addressed the monks, saying, "The gate of the ancestors is obscure and mysterious. Through exhaustive merit they have transmitted it. Without careful investigation it is most difficult to realize. You must practice apart from mind, intention, or consciousness. If you leave the path of studying 'sacred' and 'mundane,' then you are upholding it. If you do not practice thus, then you can't be considered my disciples."

A monk asked Qinglin, "What is the Way?"

Qinglin said, "Turn your head and look at that distant mountain ravine."

The monk then asked, "What is a person who has realized the Way?"

Qinglin said, "Embracing the ice and snow, head and eyebrows held high."

A monk asked, "The path diverges and twists. What about sudden enlightenment?"

Qinglin said, "You face away from the black jewel beneath your feet toward a sky filled to the moon with anxiety."

A monk asked Zen master Qinglin Shiqian, "When a student tries to go there directly, what then?"

Qinglin said, "There is a deadly snake in the road. I urge you to not confront it."

The monk said, "If the student confronts it, then what?"

Qinglin said, "He loses his innermost self."

The monk said, "What if he doesn't confront it?"

Qinglin said, "There's no place to retreat."

The monk said, "Just at such a time, what then?"

Qinglin said, "Gone!"

The monk said, "Gone where?"

Qinglin said, "Everyplace you look the grass is deep!"

The monk said, "You must also watch out, teacher!"

Qinglin clapped his hands and said, "Here's another poisonous one!"

Qinglin entered the hall and said, "The essential teaching of the ancestors is proceeding right now. The Dharma is apparent. What other matter is there?"

A monk asked, "*The Treasury of the True Dharma Eye* has been passed down from ancestor to ancestor. Is there anyone to whom the master can pass it?"

Qinglin said, "There is ground where the numinous sprouts grow. Great awakening has no teacher."

SHUSHAN KUANGREN

SHUSHAN KUANGREN (n.d.) is regarded as a disciple and Dharma heir of Dong-shan Liangjie, but his search for enlightenment took him to many teachers. He came from ancient Jizhou (the site of the modern city of Ji'an in Jiangxi Province). Shushan eventually lived and taught at a Mt. Shu. He was very short in physical stature, and thus earned the nickname "the dwarf teacher."

Shushan first studied with a teacher named Yuanzheng in Jizhou.

One day he told his teacher, "I'm traveling east to the capital city of Luoyang."

He studied in Luoyang for less than a year. Then one day he suddenly said, "Seeking brings only darkness and talking isn't as good as silence. Forget oneself and help others. The false can't compare to the true."

He then went to study under Dongshan Liangjie.

He asked Dongshan, "In words not yet heard, please, Master, provide me instruction."

Dongshan said, "I don't say people can't realize it."

Shushan said, "Can it be obtained through practice or not?"

Dongshan said, "Are you realizing it now through practice?"

Shushan said, "Not realizing it through practice should not be avoided."

——— ◆ ———

On one occasion Dongshan entered the hall and said, "I want you to understand this matter. You must be like a dead tree that blossoms flowers. Then you will merge with it."

Shushan asked, "What about when every place is corrupted?"

Dongshan said, "Your Reverence! You're talking about practicing a practice. Fortunately there is a realm of nonpracticing practice. Why don't you ask about that?"

Shushan said, "Practicing a nonpracticing practice? Can there be such a person?"

Dongshan said, "Many people will laugh at you for asking such a question."

Shushan said, "In that case, my thinking has gone astray."

Dongshan said, "Astray is not astray, nor not astray."

Shushan said, "What is 'astray'?"

Dongshan said, "If you say, 'such a person,' then you still don't understand."

Shushan said, "What is 'not astray'?"

Dongshan said, "A place of no differentiation."

❖

Dongshan asked Shushan, "In the empty eon there is no person. Who is it who resides there?"

Shushan said, "I don't know."

Dongshan said, "Does that person have a thinking mind or not?"

Shushan said, "Why don't you ask him?"

Dongshan said, "I'm asking him right now."

Shushan said, "What is this mind?"

Dongshan didn't answer.

Although Shushan Kuangren is credited as being a disciple of Dongshan Liangjie, he studied under a succession of teachers before realizing enlightenment. The following account, which appears in the *Wudeng Huiyuan*, relates that after Dongshan died, Shushan traveled to visit Guishan. Since Guishan Lingyou died prior to Dongshan, the text must here be referring to Guishan Da'an, the Dharma brother of Lingyou who assumed the abbacy at Mt. Gui after Lingyou's death. The *Wudeng Huiyuan* goes on to say that Shushan later left Guishan and traveled to study with Dagui An of Fuzhou. The name "Dagui An" is another name for Guishan Da'an, from whom Shushan had just departed. No other reference to Dagui An of Fuzhou exists in the *Wudeng Huiyuan* or other major Zen texts, and thus some confusion exists about this account of Shushan's life.

After Dongshan died and the mourning period for the monks had passed, Shushan went to Mt. Gui in Tanzhou. There, he heard Guishan [Da'an] address the monks, saying, "Worthies who are on a pilgrimage, you must sleep in sound and form. You must sit and you must lie down in sound and form."

Shushan came forward and said, "What is a phrase that does not fall into sound and form?"

Guishan raised his whisk into the air.

Shushan said, "This is a phrase that falls into sound and form."

Guishan then lowered the whisk and went back to his quarters.

Shushan felt no affinity with Guishan, and so he told Xiangyan of his intention to leave.

Xiangyan asked him, "Why don't you stay here a little longer?"

Shushan said, "The teacher and I do not have affinity."

Xiangyan said, "Why so? Will you tell me about it?"

Shushan then described the foregoing incident.

Xiangyan said, "I have a saying."

Shushan said, "What is it?"

Xiangyan said, "When words emanate there is no sound. Before form there are no things."

Shushan said, "Fundamentally, there is a person here."

Shushan then said to Xiangyan, "Hereafter, if you find a place to serve as abbot, I'll come to see you there."

He then said goodbye to Xiangyan.

Guishan later said to Xiangyan, "Is the short worthy who asked about sound and form here?"

Xiangyan said, "He's gone away."

Guishan said, "Did he tell you about what he asked me?"

Xiangyan said, "Yes, and I gave him an answer concerning it."

Guishan asked, "What did he say?"

Xiangyan said, "He deeply approved my answer."

Guishan said, "I think that short disciple has some tall points. He just arrived here. In the future if he finds a place to abide, then on that mountain there won't be firewood to burn or water to drink."

Shushan heard that the teacher Guishan An of Fuzhou said to his congregation, "There are phrases that are not phrases. They are like a creeping plant that relies on a tree for support."

Shushan then went into the mountains of Fuzhou to see Dagui An. When he arrived, Dagui was doing masonry work on a wall.

Shushan asked him, "I've heard that the master has said, 'There is a phrase that is not a phrase. It's like a creeping plant that relies on a tree for support.' Have you said this or not?"

Dagui said, "Yes."

Shushan then asked, "If suddenly the tree falls down and the creeper withers, to where do the words return?"

Dagui put down the masonry board and laughed out loud. Then he walked back to his abbot's quarters.

Shushan followed him, saying, "I've sold my shirt and walked three thousand li to come here, just to ask you this question. How can the master treat me like this?"

Dagui then yelled to his attendant, saying, "Give two hundred cash to this monk!"

Then Dagui said to Shushan, "In the future, a one-eyed dragon's instruction will help you break through."

The next day, when Dagui addressed the monks in the hall, Shushan stepped forward and asked, "The principle of the dharmakaya is deep and profound. It is a realm beyond good and evil. What is an affair that is beyond the dharmakaya?"

Dagui lifted his whisk into the air.

Shushan said, "This is an affair of the dharmakaya."

Dagui then asked Shushan, "What is an affair beyond the dharmakaya?"

Shushan grabbed the whisk, broke it in two, threw it on the ground, and then retreated into the congregation.

Dagui said, "Dragons and snakes are easy to tell apart. I'm hard to fool."

Later, Shushan heard about a teacher named Mingzhao Qian who was teaching in Wuzhou. He had only one eye. Shushan went straight there and paid his respects to Mingzhao.

Mingzhao said to him, "Where have you come from?"

Shushan said, "From Minzhong [Fuzhou]."

Mingzhao then asked, "Did you go see Dagui An there?"

Shushan said, "Yes."

Mingzhao said, "What did he say?"

Shushan then told Mingzhao what Dagui said.

Mingzhao said, "It may be said that from beginning to end, Dagui was correct. But you haven't encountered his words."

Shushan did not yet understand, and he asked Mingzhao, "If suddenly the tree collapses and the creeper withers, to where do the words return?"

Mingzhao said, "You've made Dagui laugh again!"

When Shushan heard these words, he experienced great enlightenment.

Shushan then said, "Before, Dagui's laughter contained a knife." He then faced in the direction of Dagui's monastery and bowed in belated gratitude.

———————— ◆ ————————

Shushan went to see Jiashan. Once when Jiashan was addressing the monks, Shushan asked, "I've heard that the master has said, 'Before the eyes there are no dharmas. The meaning is before the eyes.' What about a dharma that is not before the eyes?"

Jiashan said, "Shining streams of moonlight, unreflected by the clear pond."

Shushan made as if to overturn the meditation platform.

Jiashan said, "Your Reverence! What are you doing?"

Shushan said, "Dharmas not before the eyes cannot be attained!"

Jiashan said, "Everyone! Look! Here is a military commander!"

--------------- ❖ ---------------

When Shushan was about to die, he composed the following verse:

My way lies outside the blue emptiness.
White clouds have no place to drift.
In the world is a rootless tree,
Yellow leaves sent back by the wind.

Luopu Yuanan

Luopu Yuanan (834–98) was a disciple of Jiashan Shanhui. He came from ancient Linyou (now located in modern Jiangxi Province). Ordained at the age of twenty, he was well versed in Buddhist scriptures and doctrine. He studied under Linji Yixuan and served as his attendant. Later he practiced under Jiashan Shanhui for many years, becoming his Dharma heir. After leaving Jiashan, he first lived at Lizhou (now Li County in Hunan Province) on Mt. Luopu, where he gained his mountain name. He then lived at Suxi (in modern Hunan Province).

Luopu was known as a skilled expounder of Dharma, and students came from throughout China to study under him.

Linji once praised Luopu before the congregation, saying, "Here is an arrow of the Linji school. Who dares to withstand its point?" Linji bestowed Dharma transmission upon Luopu, giving him the Dharma name Yizu ["Already Complete"].

When Luopu was acting as Linji's attendant, a scriptural master came to meet with Linji.

Linji asked the scriptural master, "If there is a person who understands the three vehicles and twelve divisions of scripture, and there is another person who does not understand the three vehicles and twelve divisions of scripture, then do you say these two people are the same or different?"

The scriptural master said, "What they understand is the same. What they don't understand is different."

Luopu interjected, saying, "How can you say such a thing? Talking about 'same' and 'different'!"

Linji looked at Luopu and said, "What are you doing?"

Luopu then shouted.

Linji sent away the scriptural master, then asked Luopu, "Do you think it's appropriate to shout at me?"

Luopu said, "Yes."

Linji then hit him.

Some time later, when Luopu prepared to leave Linji, Linji asked him, "Where are you going?"

Luopu said, "I'm going south."

Linji took his staff and drew a circle in the air. Then he said, "Pass through this and then go."

Luopu shouted.

Linji hit him.

Luopu bowed and then left.

The next day, Linji entered the hall and said, "Beneath the gate of Linji is a red-tailed carp. Shaking its head and wagging its tail, it goes south. I don't know in whose pickled vegetable pot it will drown."

Luopu traveled for a year, and then came to Mt. Jia, where he built a hut and stayed. He remained there a year without visiting Zen master Jiashan's monastery [on the same mountain]. Jiashan wrote a letter and instructed a monk to take it to Luopu. Luopu received the letter, then went back and sat down without reading it. He then extended his hand to the monk [as if to say, "Do you have something else?"].

When the monk didn't answer, Luopu hit him and said, "Go back and tell your teacher about this."

The monk recounted to Jiashan what had happened.

Jiashan said, "If he opens the letter, then he'll come here within three days. If he doesn't open it, then no one can save him."

Three days later, Luopu came. Upon coming before Jiashan, he didn't bow, but just folded his hands and stood there.

Jiashan said, "A chicken is roosting in a phoenix's nest. They aren't the same species. Go away!"

Luopu said, "I've come from afar to seek your teaching style. I ask you to receive me."

Jiashan said, "Before me there is no you. I am not over here."

Luopu shouted.

Jiashan said, "Stop! Stop! Don't be crude. The moon, though eclipsed by clouds, remains the same. But every valley and peak is different. It's not that you can't cut off the tongues of everyone on earth. But can you make a tongueless man talk?"

Luopu was lost in thought.

Jiashan hit him.

Luopu then acquiesced to Jiashan.

◆

Luopu asked Jiashan, "How does one realize the place that isn't reached by buddhas and demons?"

Jiashan said, "A candle illuminates a thousand miles of forms. Inside my room I'm confused."

Luopu also asked, "How is it when the morning sun has risen and the night moon is not visible?"

Jiashan said, "In the dragon's mouth is a pearl, but the swarming fish don't notice it."

◆

When Jiashan was about to die, he said, "The Shitou branch! Look! Look! The last teacher passes away."

Luopu said, "Not so."

Jiashan said, "Why?"

Luopu said, "His house has a green mountain."

Jiashan said, "If indeed that's so, then my teaching won't collapse."

Jiashan then passed away.

◆

Luopu went to Cenyang where he encountered an old friend. They talked about hiding out [during the Wuchang era suppression of Buddhism], and his friend asked, "Where did you flee during the persecution?"

Luopu said, "I just remained in the middle of the market."

His friend said, "Why didn't you go where there weren't any people?"

Luopu said, "What problems are there where there are no people?"

His friend asked, "How did you escape by being in the market?"

Luopu said, "Although I remained in the middle of the market, no one knew me."

His friend was perplexed. He also asked, "The teachings of all buddhas, the transmission of all the ancestors, when these were not concealed, then what happened?"

Luopu said, "Before an old rustic's door, there is no talk of the affairs of the royal court."

His friend asked, "What do you mean by this?"

Luopu said, "If one doesn't encounter others, after all, nothing is revealed."

His friend said, "When someone who's not from the royal court arrives and you meet him, can you speak with him or not?"

Luopu said, "The immeasurable function! It's seen in arduous circumstances."

A monk asked Zen master Luopu, "What if I want to return to my country home?"

Luopu said, "The houses are demolished and the people are dead. To where would you return?"

The monk said, "In that case I won't go back."

Luopu said, "The sun melts the snow at the front of the courtyard, but who will sweep the dust that has drifted into the room?"

Luopu then recited the following verse:

"If your resolve is to return home,
Then board the boat that ferries o'er the five lakes.
Raise the boat pole; stars and moon are hidden.
Stop the oar; the sun is alone.
Slip the moorage and leave the baneful shore.
Hoist the sail and set off on the true way."

On the first day of the twelfth lunar month, Luopu said to the monks, "If I don't die tomorrow then it will be soon after. Today I have one question to ask you all. If you say *this* is it, then you are putting a head on top of your head. If you say *this* isn't it, then you're seeking life by cutting off your head."

The head monk said, "The green mountain does not lift its feet. Don't carry a lamp in broad daylight."

Luopu said, "Why talk in such a way at a time like this?"

At that time a monk named Yancong spoke to Luopu, saying, "Apart from these two roads, I ask the master to not ask."

Luopu said, "That's not it. Speak again."

Yancong said, "I can't say it entirely."

Luopu said, "I don't care if you can say it entirely or not."

Yancong said, "I answered you undeferentially."

Luopu then was quiet. That evening he had his attendant summon Yancong, and then said to him, "Your answer today had meaning. You are in accordance with understanding my late teacher's meaning. He taught, 'What is in front of the eyes is not the Dharma. Consciousness is in front of the eyes. It is not Dharma that is in front of the eyes. *It* is not what *meets* the ear and eyes.'"

Then Luopu said, "Now tell me, what phrase is the 'guest,' and what phrase is the 'host.' If you can tell them apart, then I'll give you the robe and bowl of succession."

Yancong said, "I don't understand."

Luopu said, "You can understand."

Yancong said, "I really can't do it!"

Luopu shouted and said, "How awful!" ([Later,] Xuanjue commented on this, saying, "If monk Cong says he doesn't understand, then Luopu is afraid that the bowl and robe will be stuck to him.")

The next day during the noon session, a different monk asked the master about the previous day's conversation.

Luopu said, "The boat of compassion is not rowed across pure waves. In a narrow strait the disciple futilely put out a wooden goose."[120] The master then passed away.

Jiufeng Daoqian

Jiufeng Daoqian (d. 923) was a disciple of Shishuang Qingzhu. He came from ancient Fuzhou. Until Shishuang's death, Jiufeng served as his student and personal attendant. At the invitation of the other monks Jiufeng then assumed the vacant abbacy of the monastery. Later he moved to Jiufeng ("Nine Peaks") in Ruizhou (near modern Gao'an in Jiangxi Province), where he acquired his mountain name. During his later years he lived first at Shimen, where he had many students, and finally at Letan.

Jiufeng served as Shishuang's attendant. When Shishuang passed away, the congregation invited the head monk to become abbot.

Jiufeng said to the congregation, "First, he must show that he understood our late master's great meaning, then he can become abbot."

The head monk said, "What teaching do you mean?"

Jiufeng said, "Our late teacher said, 'Desist! Become barren autumn ground! Have one thought for ten thousand years. Be a cold dead tree. Be an ancient incense dish. Be a blank strip of white silk.' Not asking about the rest, what is a 'strip of white silk'?"

The head monk said, "This teaching illuminates a matter of form."

Jiufeng said, "Fundamentally, you don't comprehend our late teacher's meaning."

The monk said, "You don't approve of my answer? Then light a stick of incense, and if I don't go before it is burned up, then you can say I don't understand our late master's meaning."[121]

A stick of incense was then lit, but before it burned down, the head monk died.

Shishuang patted the head monk's body on the back and said, "Dying while sitting or passing away while standing isn't it. You didn't see our late master's meaning even in your dreams."

After he became abbot, a monk asked, "On what path are those who do not adhere to the nine paths [that cut off defilement]?"

Jiufeng said, "The path of beasts."

The monk said, "Then what path is it that beasts travel?"

Jiufeng said, "Not the nine paths."

The monk said "On that path there are many transmigrations before one becomes a person."

Jiufeng said, "You should understand that there are those without a common life."

The monks said, "What life is it that isn't common?"

Jiufeng said, "Immortality with the breath ceasing. Have you all gained an understanding of life? You should want to know about it. A flowing spring is life. Profound solitude is the body. The thousand surging waves are Manjushri's condition. The revolving empty firmament is Samantabhadra's bed. Or next time I explain it, I may borrow a phrase and say it's pointing at the moon. When you meet daily affairs it's talking about the moon. When from the gate of our ancestors you meet daily affairs it's as if you're employing the banner of truth in each moment. Or it's the transcendent virtue that comes before the ordered creation of myriad names in all realms. Brothers, what body and speech bind you? It's right here. I'm not deceiving you an inch. Examine my words and you'll see. I don't deceive your ears. Test my words. I don't deceive your eyes. Sort it out and see it clearly. Thus, what precedes the sound of words can't be avoided. What follows words can't be stored away. All of heaven and earth come forth from your own body. So where would you go to gain peace for the eyes, the ears, the nose, and the tongue? If you try to realize it by delving beneath the root of meaning, then through an endless future you will never have a bit of rest. The unending future meets us without rest. Therefore the ancients said, 'Trying to use your mind to study the great mystery, you seem to face the west, but you're traveling east.'"

Daguang Juhui

Daguang Juhui (836–903) was a disciple of Shishuang Qingzhu. He came from the ancient capital of Luoyang. Daguang was an eminent "dead tree" in Shishuang's "dead tree hall," so named because Shishuang's disciples constantly sat in meditation (resembling tree stumps). Daguang is described in the records as "wearing a hemp robe and grass sandals, forgetting his body for the sake of the Dharma."

One day, Shishuang decided that the time was ripe to test Daguang's understanding, and so asked him, "Each year the country brings forth persons who achieve a degree [by passing the imperial exams]. Do those persons still pay homage at the imperial court or not?"

Daguang said, "There is someone who doesn't ask for entry."

Shishuang said, "Who told you that?"

Daguang said, "He doesn't have a name."

Shishuang said, "If not today, is there some other time?"

Daguang said, "He doesn't even say there is a 'today.'"

In these types of dialogues, Daguang never faltered. After he lived in the temple for more than twenty years, a congregation invited him to assume the abbacy of a temple.

———— ◆ ————

A monk asked Daguang, "People like Bodhidharma become ancestors, right?" Daguang said, "No."

The monk said, "If Bodhidharma isn't our ancestor, then why did he come from the west?"

Daguang said, "So that you won't worship ancestors."

The monk asked, "After you stop worshipping ancestors, then what?"

Daguang said, "Then you know they aren't your ancestors."

XUEFENG YICUN

XUEFENG YICUN (822–908) was a disciple of Deshan Xuanjian. He came from the city of Nanan in ancient Quanzhou (a place in modern Fujian Province). It's recorded that as a toddler Xuefeng refused to eat nonvegetarian food. One day, while being carried on his mother's back, a funeral spectacle of flags and flowers appeared. This caused a profound change in the child's countenance. At the age of twelve he left home to live at Yujian Temple in Putian City. Later he traveled widely, eventually coming to Baocha Temple in ancient Youzhou (modern Beijing), where he was ordained. Later, he went on to Wuling (near the modern city of Changde in Hunan Province), where he studied under the great teacher Deshan, eventually becoming his Dharma heir. However, Xuefeng's most profound realization occurred with his Dharma brother, Yantou, while they were traveling and staying at a mountain inn during a snowstorm. In the year 865, Xuefeng moved to Snow Peak on Elephant Bone Mountain in Fuzhou, where he established the Guangfu Monastery and obtained his mountain name. The monastery flourished, the congregation's size reaching up to 1500 monks.

True to the spirit of Zen, Xuefeng's teaching did not rely on words or ideas. Instead, he emphasized self-realization and experience. The Yunmen and Fayan Zen schools, two of the traditionally recognized five houses of Zen, evolved from Xuefeng's students.

Xuefeng served as a rice cook at Dong Shan.

One day as he was straining the rice, Dongshan asked him, "Do you strain the rice out from the sand, or do you strain the sand out from the rice?"

Xuefeng said "Sand and rice are both strained out at once."

Dongshan said, "In that case, what will the monks eat?"

Xuefeng then tipped over the rice pot.

Dongshan said, "Go! Your affinity accords with Deshan!"

◆

When Xuefeng left Dongshan, Dongshan asked him, "Where are you going?"

Xuefeng said, "I'm returning to Lingzhong [Fuzhou]."

Dongshan said, "When you left Lingzhong to come here, what road did you take?"

Xuefeng said, "I took the road through the Flying Ape Mountains."

Dongshan said, "And what road are you taking to go back there?"

Xuefeng said, "I'm returning through the Flying Ape Mountains as well."

Dongshan said, "There's someone who doesn't take the road through Flying Ape Mountains. Do you know him?"

Xuefeng said, "I don't know him."

Dongshan said, "Why don't you know him?"

Xuefeng said, "Because he doesn't have a face."

Dongshan said, "If you don't know him, how do you know he doesn't have a face?"

Xuefeng was silent.

——————— ◆ ———————

When Xuefeng was traveling with Yantou on Tortoise Mountain in Li Province, they were temporarily stuck in an inn during a snowstorm. Each day, Yantou spent the entire day sleeping. Xuefeng spent each day sitting in Zen meditation.

One day, Xuefeng called out, "Elder Brother! Elder Brother! Get up."

Yantou said, "What is it?"

Xuefeng said, "Don't be idle. Monks on pilgrimage have profound knowledge as their companion. This companion must accompany us at all times. But here today, all you are doing is sleeping."

Yantou yelled back, "Just eat your fill and sleep! Sitting there in meditation all the time is like being some clay figure in a villager's hut. In the future you'll just spook the men and women of the village."

Xuefeng pointed to his own chest and said, "I feel unease here. I don't dare cheat myself [by not practicing diligently]."

Yantou said, "I always say that some day you'll build a cottage on a lonely mountain peak and expound a great teaching. Yet you still talk like this!"

Xuefeng said, "I'm truly anxious."

Yantou said, "If that's really so, then reveal your understanding, and where it is correct I'll confirm it for you. Where it's incorrect I'll root it out."

Xuefeng said, "When I first went to Yanguan's place, I heard him expound on emptiness and form. At that time I found an entrance."

Yantou said, "For the next thirty years, don't speak of this matter again."

Xuefeng said, "And then I saw Dongshan's poem that said, 'Avoid seeking elsewhere, for that's far from the Self, now I travel alone, everywhere I meet it, now it's exactly me, now I'm not it.'"

Yantou said, "If that's so, you'll never save yourself."

Xuefeng then said, "Later I asked Deshan, 'Can a student understand the essence of the ancient teachings?' He struck me and said, 'What did you say?' At that moment it was like the bottom falling out of a bucket of water."

Yantou said, "Haven't you heard it said that 'what comes in through the front gate isn't the family jewels'?"

Xuefeng said, "Then, in the future, what should I do?"

Yantou said, "In the future, if you want to expound a great teaching, then it must flow forth from your own breast. In the future your teaching and mine will cover heaven and earth."

When Xuefeng heard this he experienced unsurpassed enlightenment. He then bowed and said, "Elder Brother, at last today on Tortoise Mountain I've attained the Way!"

———— ◆ ————

After Xuefeng assumed the abbacy at Snow Peak, a monk asked him, "When the Master was at Deshan's place, what was it you attained that allowed you to stop looking further?"

Xuefeng said, "I went with empty hands and returned with empty hands."

———— ◆ ————

A monk asked Xuefeng, "Is the teaching of the ancestors the same as the scriptural teaching or not?"

Xuefeng said, "The thunder sounds and the earth shakes. Inside the room nothing is heard."

Xuefeng also said, "Why do you go on pilgrimage?"

··············· ◆ ···············

One day, Xuefeng went into the monks' hall and started a fire. Then he closed and locked the front and back doors and yelled "Fire! Fire!"

Xuansha took a piece of firewood and threw it in through the window. Xuefeng then opened the door.

———— ◆ ————

Xuefeng asked a monk, "Where have you come from?"

The monk said, "From Zen master Fuchuan's place."[122]

Xuefeng said, "You haven't crossed the sea of life and death yet. So why have you overturned the boat?"

The monk was speechless. He later returned and told Zen master Fuchuan about this.

Fuchuan said, "Why didn't you say, 'It is not subject to life and death.'?"

The monk returned to Xuefeng and repeated this phrase.

Xuefeng said, "This isn't something you said yourself."

The monk said, "Zen master Fuchuan said this."

Xuefeng said, "I send twenty blows to Fuchuan and give twenty blows to myself as well for interfering in your own affairs."

———— ◆ ————

A monk asked, "What is it if my fundamentally correct eye sometimes goes astray because of my teacher?"

Xuefeng said, "You haven't really met Bodhidharma."

The monk said, "Where is my eye?"

Xuefeng said, "You won't get it from your teacher."

———— ◆ ————

A monk asked Xuefeng, "All the ancient masters each said they all penetrated the meaning of the phrase, 'In the threefold body of Buddha there is one which does not falter.' What is the meaning of this?"

Xuefeng said, "This fellow has climbed Mt. Dong nine times."

When the monk started to ask another question Xuefeng said, "Drag this monk out of here!"

———— ◆ ————

A monk asked, "What is it when one is solitary and independent?"

Xuefeng said, "Still sick."

———— ◆ ————

A monk asked, "When one pivots, then what?"

Xuefeng said, "The Boat Monk fell in the river."

———— ◆ ————

A monk asked, "What are the words passed down by the ancients?"

Xuefeng lay down.

After a long time he got up and said, "What was your question?"

The monk asked again.

Xuefeng said, "An empty birth, a fellow drowned in the waves."

———— ◆ ————

A monk asked, "The ancients said that if you meet Bodhidharma on the road, speak to him without words. I'd like to know how one speaks this way?"

Xuefeng said, "Drink some tea."

Zen master Xuefeng entered the hall and addressed the monks, saying "South Mountain has a turtle-nosed snake. All of you here must take a good look at it."

Changqing came forward and said, "Today in the hall there are many who are losing their bodies and lives."

Yunmen then threw a staff onto the ground in front of Xuefeng and affected a pose of being frightened.

A monk told Xuansha about this and Xuansha said, "Granted that Changqing understands, still I don't agree."

The monk said, "What do you say, Master?"

Xuansha said, "Why do you need South Mountain?"

❖

Xuefeng asked a monk, "Where are you from?"

The monk said, "From Shenguang ['spirit light']."

Xuefeng asked, "During the day it's called daylight. At night it's called firelight. What is it that's called spirit light?

The monk didn't answer.

Speaking for the monk, Xuefeng said, "Daylight. Firelight."

❖

Xuefeng's Dharma seat never had less than fifteen hundred monks living there. In the third month of [the year 908] Xuefeng became ill. The governor of Fuzhou sent a doctor to cure him, but Xuefeng said, "I'm not ill. There's no need for medicine." Xuefeng then composed a poem to convey the Dharma. On the second day of the fifth month, he went for a walk in the fields in the morning. In the evening he returned and bathed. He passed away during the night.

After Xuefeng's death, the emperor Tang Xi Zong bestowed upon him the posthumous title "Great Teacher True Awakening."

YANTOU QUANHUO

YANTOU QUANHUO (828–887) was a disciple of Deshan Xuanjian. He came from ancient Quanzhou. He received the precepts at Baoshou Temple in the city of Changan. As a young man he studied the Vinaya and Buddhist sutras. He traveled widely with his friends Xuefeng Yicun and Qinshan Wensui. Finally, Yantou studied under Deshan, becoming his Dharma heir. Eventually, Yantou settled at Yantou Monastery in Ezhou. There, a large congregation of monks gathered to study with him.

Yantou, Xuefeng, and Qinshan went traveling to visit Linji, but they arrived just after Linji had died. They then went to Mt. Yang.

Yantou entered the door, picked up a sitting cushion, and said to Zen master Yangshan, "Master."

Before Yangshan could raise his whisk into the air, Yantou said, "Don't hinder an adept!"

Yantou then went to study with Deshan. There, Yantou took a meditation cushion into the hall and stared at Deshan.

Deshan said, "What are you doing?"

Yantou shouted.

Deshan said, "What is my error?"

Yantou said, "Two types of kōans."

Yantou then went out.

Deshan said, "This fellow seems to be on a special pilgrimage."

The next day, during a question-and-answer period, Deshan asked Yantou, "Did you just arrive here yesterday?"

Yantou said, "Yes."

Deshan said, "Where have you studied to have come here with an empty head?"

Yantou said, "For my entire life I won't deceive myself."

Deshan said, "In that case, you won't betray me."

◆

One day, when Yantou was studying with Deshan, Yantou stood in the doorway and said to Deshan, "Sacred or mundane?"

Deshan shouted.

Yantou bowed.

A monk told Dongshan about this.

Dongshan said, "If it wasn't Yantou, then the meaning couldn't be grasped."

Yantou said, "Old Dongshan doesn't know right from wrong. He's made a big error. At that time I lifted up with one hand and pushed down with one hand."

———— ✦ ————

Xuefeng was working at Mt. De as a rice cook. One day the meal was late. Deshan appeared carrying his bowl to the hall. When Xuefeng stepped outside to hang a rice cloth to dry, he spotted Deshan and said, "The bell hasn't been rung and the drum hasn't sounded. Where are you going with your bowl?"

Deshan then went back to the abbot's room.

Xuefeng told Yantou about this incident.

Yantou said, "Old Deshan doesn't know the final word."

When Deshan heard about this, he had his attendant summon Yantou.

Deshan then said to Yantou, "Don't you agree with me?"

Yantou then told Deshan what he meant by his comments. Deshan then stopped questioning Yantou.

The next day, Deshan went into the hall and addressed the monks. What he said was quite unlike his normal talk. Afterward, Yantou went to the front of the monks' hall, clapped his hands, laughed out loud and exclaimed, "I'm happy that the old fellow who's the head of the hall knows the last word after all!"

———— ✦ ————

One day, Yantou was talking with Xuefeng and Qinshan. Xuefeng suddenly pointed at a basin of water.

Qinshan said, "When the water is clear the moon comes out."

Xuefeng said, "When the water is clear the moon does not come out."

Yantou kicked over the basin and walked away.

———— ✦ ————

One day, Yantou and Xuefeng were leaving the mountain.

Deshan asked, "Where are you going?"

Yantou said, "We're going down off the mountain for awhile."

Deshan said, "What are you going to do later?"

Yantou said, "Not forget."

Deshan said, "Why do you speak thus?"

Yantou said, "Isn't it said that only a person whose wisdom exceeds his teacher's is worthy to transmit the teaching, and one only equal to his teacher has but half of his teacher's virtue?"

Deshan said, "Just so. Just so. Sustain and uphold the great matter."

The two monks bowed and left Deshan.

Once a monk asked, "Without a teacher, is there still a place for the body to manifest or not?"

Yantou said, "Before the sound, an old ragged thief."

The monk said, "When he grandly arrives, then what?"

Yantou said, "Pokes out the eye."

A monk asked, "What is the meaning of the ancestor's coming from the west?"

Yantou said, "When you move Mt. Lu to this place, I'll tell you."

Once, Jiashan sent a monk to Shishuang's temple. The monk then stood straddling the gate and said, "I don't understand!"

Shishuang said, "Your Reverence, there's no need."

The monk then said, "In that case, I'll say farewell."

The monk then went to Yantou's temple.

Acting as before, he said, "I don't understand."

Yantou gave out a great roar.

The monk said, "In that case, I'll say farewell."

Yantou said, "Although he's young, he's capable."

The monk went back and reported to Jiashan.

Jiashan entered the hall and said to the monks, "Will the monk who yesterday came back from Shishuang's and Yantou's places please come forward and tell the story as he did before?"

The monk came forward and told his story.

Jiashan said, "Does anyone in the congregation understand this?"

The assembly was silent.

Jiashan said, "If no one will speak, then I'm not afraid to risk losing my eyebrows by doing so!"[123]

Then Jiashan said, "Although Shishuang has the knife that kills, he doesn't have the sword that gives life. Yantou has the knife that kills as well as the sword that gives life!"

During the chaos at the end of the Tang dynasty, bandits were to be found everywhere. The congregation all left the temple to hide in the forest. Yantou alone stayed at the temple, where he sat in meditation. One day, the head of the bandits came to the temple. Enraged because there was no booty there, he brandished his knife and stabbed Yantou. Yantou remained composed, then let out a resounding scream and died. The sound was heard for ten miles around. It was the eighth day of the fourth month of [the year 887]. His disciples cremated the master's remains and recovered forty-nine relics. They then constructed his stupa. He received the posthumous name "Zen Master Clear Severity."

GUIFENG ZONGMI

GUIFENG ZONGMI (780–841) is remembered as the disciple of the Sichuan school Zen master Suizhou Daoyuan. However, Zen history also regards him to belong to the Heze Zen school of Heze Shenhui. He is widely respected as the leading Buddhist scholar of the late eighth and early ninth centuries. He possessed an intimate understanding of various Buddhist schools and doctrines, and made important contributions to the advancement of Buddhism in China. He was also the fifth ancestor of the Buddhist Huayan school, which based its teachings on the Huayan ("Flower Garland") Sutra.

Guifeng came from ancient Guozhou (now the city of Xichong in Sichuan Province). In the year 807, when Guifeng was already twenty-seven, he happened to pass through Suizhou during a trip to the capital city of Luoyang. There he listened to a lecture by Zen master Daoyuan that profoundly affected him, leading him to enter that teacher's congregation and receive ordination. Later, at Daoyuan's urging, he went to study under Daoyuan's teacher Nanyin, another master of the Sichuan Zen school. During the next decade, Guifeng studied under other teachers, including a Huayan master named Chengyuan.

Guifeng then spent several years practicing on Mt. Zhongnan near the western capital, Changan. During this period he completed a famous commentary on the *Perfect Enlightenment Sutra* and other works. Later he moved to Gui Peak, to the south of his former residence, where he devoted himself to teaching, Zen meditation, and the chanting of sutras. Guifeng's reputation as a Zen master spread widely during this time. In the year 828, the emperor invited him to the capital and bestowed on him the honorific purple robe. During Guifeng's extended stay in the capital he received several famous statesmen and poets as his students, including Peixiu, a high official who later composed a famous treatise known as the *Chuanxin Fayao [Essential Dharma on the Transmission of Mind]*. Later, Guifeng returned to his mountain retreat.

Guifeng's writings included commentaries on several Buddhist scriptures, including the *Huayan*, the *Perfect Enlightenment*, and the *Diamond* sutras. He also wrote a treatise on the *Ullambala Sutra*, an apocryphal work that is the basis for the Hungry Ghosts Festival observed in East Asia. In that treatise, Guifeng discussed Chinese ancestor worship and filial behavior from a Buddhist perspective.

During Guifeng's era, Zen Buddhism suffered disputes between its various schools. The main arguments centered on the well-known division between "Northern" and "Southern" Zen. Guifeng compiled a collection of teachings from all the Zen schools into one text known as *The Complete Compilation of the Sources of Zen*. This collection may have been Chinese Zen's earliest historical survey. The text was broadly read, and helped to cement the religion into the foundation of Chinese culture as a unified movement. The body of the text is now lost, although its introduction still exists. Guifeng also compiled extensive genealogies and lineage charts of the various Zen schools.

Guifeng disdained the sectarianism between Zen schools of his age. He claimed to regard the division between the Northern "gradualist" and Southern "sudden" viewpoints as fundamentally artificial. He was impatient with the extreme teaching methods that he felt resulted from overemphasis on "sudden" teaching methods. He thus especially criticized the Hongzhou School of Mazu and its descendants, disdaining some teachers' repudiation of established Buddhist practices.[124]

What follows is an excerpt from the introduction to *The Complete Compilation of the Sources of Zen*.

Chan is an Indian word. It comes from the complete word *chan na* [in Sanskrit, *dhyana*]. Here, we say that this word means "the practice of mind" or "quiet contemplation." These meanings can all be put under the title of "meditation." The source of Zen is the true enlightened nature of all beings, which is also called "buddha nature," or "mind-ground." Enlightenment is called "wisdom." Practice is called "meditation." "Chan" is the unity of these two terms.

This nature is the fundamental source of Zen. The ancients called it "Zen's source," or "chan na," or "The practice of principle." This fundamental source is the Zen principle. When one forgets the passions and meets this principle, then that is Zen practice, which is what the ancients called the "practice of principle." Of course, now authors from the various Zen schools all write much about the Zen principle, but very little about Zen practice. For this reason I have entitled this book, "*The Sources of Zen.*"

In these times there are people who have seen that true nature is Zen, but they have not attained the practice of principle, and moreover they don't understand the meaning of these Chinese and Indian sounds.

There is a Zen body that is not separate from true nature. Yet living beings are confused about the truth and are caught up in the world. This is known as "distraction." When the world is left behind and one unites with truth, this is "Zen meditation."

If we speak directly about "fundamental nature," then there is no "truth" and no "delusion," no "leaving behind" and no "uniting with," no "meditation" and no "dissipation." So what is it that we call "Zen"?

Moreover, this true nature is not only the source of the Zen gate. It is also the source of the ten thousand things of the world. Thus, it is also called Dharma nature. It is also the source of the delusion and enlightenment of living beings, and is thus called [in the *Surangama Sutra*] the "Tathagatas' Storehouse Consciousness."[125] It is also the source of the ten thousand virtues of the buddhas, and thus it is called "buddha nature." It is also the source of the ten thousand practices of a bodhisattva, and thus is known as the "mind-ground." [In the *Brahma-Net Sutra*] it says, "It is the fundamental source of all buddhas; it is the foundation of the path of practicing bodhisattvas; and it is the source of all beings and all buddhas." These ten thousand practices do not go beyond the six *paramitas.*[126] Zen meditation is only one of the six paramitas. It is the fifth one. Yet, it can be said that anyone who witnesses true nature is practicing Zen. Moreover, the practice of Zen meditation is most sublime and mysterious, and it fosters an imperturbable wisdom upon its practitioner's nature. All of the sublime functions, the ten thousand practices, and the ten thousand virtues that lead to the pervasive spiritual light come forth from Zen meditation.

For this reason, persons of the three vehicles [Buddhists] who wish to follow the sacred path must all practice Zen. Aside from this there is no other entrance gate. Aside from this there is no other path, including the paths of calling out Buddha's name to gain birth in the Western Paradise, practicing the sixteen precepts, attaining samadhi by chanting Buddha's name, practicing the *pratyupanna samadhi*, and so on.[127]

True nature has no pollution or purity, nor is there a difference between sacred and mundane. Zen schools that hold to ideas of "shallow" and "deep," various "stages" of practice, and so on, or who claim to have some mystical "strategy," or who practice while taking pleasure in what is above and despising what is down below, are practicing heretical Zen. If someone believes in karma and practices with the idea of good and bad, then that is the Zen of ordinary people. Practicing for the sake of the partial truth of self-enlightenment is the way of Hinayana Zen. Practicing for the enlightenment of the self and all beings is the way of Mahayana Zen. (Within these four types of Zen, each has its own different type of form and emptiness.) If you instantly realize that your mind is fundamentally pure, that from the beginning there are no defilements, and that you are fully endowed with an imperturbable wisdom, then you know that this mind is buddha mind, without any difference.

Practicing in this manner is the Zen of the highest vehicle, and it is known as the pure Zen of the Tathagatas, the Zen of one practice and three samadhis, or the samadhi of true thusness.

Guifeng died in the year 841 while visiting Xingfuta Monastery to perform ordination ceremonies. His body was returned to Gui Peak for cremation and his remains were interred there. He received the posthumous name "Meditation Wisdom."

Thirteenth Generation

NANYUAN HUIYONG   XIYUAN SIMING   ZIFU RUBAO

BAJIAO HUIQING   TONGAN DAOPI   HUGUO SHOUCHENG

YUNMEN WENYAN   CUIYAN LINGCAN   JINGQING DAOFU

TAIYUAN FU   XUANSHA SHIBEI   BAOFU CONGZHAN

CHANGQING HUILENG   LUOSHAN DAOXIAN   RUIYAN SHIYAN

NANYUAN HUIYONG, "BAOYING"

NANYUAN HUIYONG (860–930) was a disciple of Xinghua Cunjiang. He came from ancient Hebei. Nanyuan was extremely strict and uncompromising in his approach to teaching Zen. He lived and taught at the "South Hall" (in Chinese, *Nanyuan*) of the Baoying Zen Monastery at Ruzhou. Nanyuan is the most important teacher of the third generation of the Linji school, and is a direct link in the lineage that stretches down to modern times.

Nanyuan entered the hall and said to the assembled monks, "On top of a lump of red flesh, a shear precipice of 8,000 feet."

A monk asked, "'On top of a lump of red flesh, a shear precipice of eight thousand feet.' Isn't this what you said?"

Nanyuan said, "It is."

The monk then lifted and turned over the meditation bench.

Nanyuan exclaimed, "This blind ass has run riot!"

The monk started to speak.

Nanyuan hit him.

Nanyuan asked a monk, "Where have you come from?"

The monk said, "From Longwater."

Nanyuan asked him, "Did it flow east or west?"

The monk said, "Neither way."

Nanyuan then asked, "What did it do?"

The monk bowed and began to leave.

Nanyuan hit him.

A monk came for instruction. Nanyuan raised his whisk.
The monk said, "Today a failure."
Nanyuan put down the whisk.
The monk said, "Still a failure."
Nanyuan hit him.

Nanyuan asked a monk, "Where did you come from?"
The monk said, "From Xiangzhou."
Nanyuan said, "What did you come here for?"
The monk said, "I came especially to pay respects to the master."
Nanyuan said, "You've come here just when old Baoying isn't here."
The monk shouted.
Nanyuan said, "I said Baoying isn't here. What good will it do to shout any-more?"
The monk shouted again.
Nanyuan hit him.
The monk bowed.
Nanyuan said, "Actually, you have struck me, so I hit you back. You want this to be widely known. Blind fellow! Go to the hall!"

A monk asked, "What is a seamless monument?"
Nanyuan said, "Eight seams and nine cracks."
The monk asked, "What is the person inside the monument?"
Nanyuan said, "Hair uncombed. Face unwashed."

Nanyuan asked a monk, "What is your name?"
The monk said, "Pucan ['Practice Everywhere']."
Nanyuan said, "What would you do if you encountered a turd?"
The monk bowed.
Nanyuan hit him.

A monk asked Nanyuan, "When the sacred and the mundane abide in the same place, then what?"
Nanyuan said, "Two cats. One of them is fierce."

XIYUAN SIMING

XIYUAN SIMING (n.d.) was a disciple of Baoshou Yanzhao. He lived and taught in Ruzhou. Little is recorded about Xiyuan in the main lamp records.

A monk asked Xiyuan, "What is a Zen monastery?"
Xiyuan said, "A forest of thorns."
The monk then asked, "What is a person who lives there?"
Xiyuan replied, "A badger. A weasel."

———— ❖ ————

A monk asked, "What is something that is unchangeable?"
Xiyuan said, "A rock for pounding fabrics."

·········· ❖ ··········

A monk asked, "What is Linji's shout?"
Xiyuan said, "A thirty-thousand-pound crossbow is not used on a mouse."
The monk said, "Where is the master's compassion?"
Xiyuan hit him.

·········· ❖ ··········

The monk Tianping Congyi came and stayed at Xiyuan's place for ten days.
Congyi often said, "Don't say that someone who understands the Buddha-dharma seeks someone who can talk about it."
Xiyuan heard this but said nothing.
Later, when Congyi went into the Dharma hall to speak, Xiyuan called out to him.
Congyi lifted his head.
Xiyuan said, "Wrong."
Congyi came forward two or three steps.
Xiyuan said, "Wrong!"
Congyi walked to Xiyuan.
Xiyuan said, "These two mistakes just now, were they committed by you or by me?"
Congyi said, "They were committed by Congyi."
Xiyuan said, "Wrong! Wrong!"
Xiyuan then said, "Stay here during the summer period, monk, and I'll discuss these two mistakes with you."
Congyi wouldn't agree to this. He then left the monastery.

Later, when Congyi became the abbot on Mt. Tianping, he would always refer to this incident by saying, "When I was on pilgrimage an evil wind blew me to Ru Province. There, an old worthy named Xiyuan tested me. I made two mistakes, and he wanted me to remain there for the summer to discuss them. I wouldn't say that I erred at that time. When I set out to travel south I understood the mistake." ([Later,] Shoushan said, "If Congyi had such an understanding, then he didn't see Xiyuan even in his dreams. Why is this? Discuss it.")

ZIFU RUBAO

ZIFU RUBAO (n.d.) was a disciple of Xita Guangmu in the Guiyang lineage. Zifu taught at Zifu Temple in Jizhou. Little is recorded about Zifu's background.

A monk asked, "What is the phrase that is in accordance with the great function?"
Zifu was silent.

⸻ ◆ ⸻

A monk asked, "What is the essential mystery?"
Zifu said, "Close the door for me."

⸻ ◆ ⸻

A monk asked, "Luzu faced the wall. What was the meaning?"
Zifu said, "He never got involved."

⸻ ◆ ⸻

A monk asked, "What is the true transcendent eye?"
Zifu beat his chest and said, "Blue heavens! Blue heavens!"
The monk asked, "What problem is there with my question?"
Zifu said, "Misery."

⸻ ◆ ⸻

A monk asked, "What is the ultimate condition of a patch-robed monk?"
Zifu said, "Don't go beyond *this*."

⸻ ◆ ⸻

A monk asked, "Please, Master, speak of what is before a monk's question."
Zifu exclaimed, "Ai!"

A monk asked, "What is the upright receipt of a single mote of dust?"
Zifu appeared to enter a deep samadhi.
The monk asked, "What is the arising samadhi of all dust?"
Zifu said, "Of whom are you asking this question?"

A monk asked, "What is the style of the master's house?"
Zifu said, "After the rice, three cups of tea."

One day, Zifu held up a meditation cushion and said, "All buddhas, bodhisattvas, and saints who have attained the Way come forth from this."

Then Zifu threw it down, opened his robe at his chest and said, "What do you say?"

The monks were speechless.

A monk asked, "Since I've arrived here, the summer practice period has nearly passed and I haven't received instruction from you. I want you to support my efforts."

Zifu gave the monk a push and said, "Since I became abbot here, I've never blinded a monk's eye!"

Once, the master sat for a long time in silence, then he looked back and forth at the monks and said, "Understand?"
The monks answered, "We don't understand."
Zifu said, "If you don't understand then I've deceived you."

One day Zifu placed a meditation cushion on his head and said, "When you are like this, then it's difficult for us to speak to each other."
The monks were silent.
Zifu then sat on the cushion and said, "This is better."

Bajiao Huiqing

Bajiao Huiqing (n.d.) was a disciple of Nanta Guangyong. He came from Korea. At the age of twenty-eight, he arrived at Mt. Yang in Yuanzhou (now Yichun City in Jiangxi Province) and began studying with Nanta. One day Nanta said to the assembled monks, "All of you, if you are brave, come out from the womb and roar like a lion!"

At these words, Bajiao gained enlightenment.

Bajiao held up his staff and said to the monks, "If you have a staff, I give you a staff. If you don't have a staff, then I take it away from you."

Then, using his staff for support, he got down and left the hall.

———— ◆ ————

A monk asked Bajiao, "What is banana juice?" [Bajiao translates as "banana."]

Bajiao said, "Winter warm, summer cool."

———— ◆ ————

A monk asked, "What is the blown feather sword?"

Bajiao said, "Come forward three steps."

The monk said, "What for?"

Bajiao said, "Go back three steps."

———— ◆ ————

A monk asked, "What phrase does the master have for people?"

Bajiao said, "I'm just afraid you won't ask."

———— ◆ ————

Bajiao entered the hall and addressed the monks, saying, "Do you understand? Those who know are few. Take care."

———— ◆ ————

A monk asked, "What is it when one has a question but doesn't speak?"

Bajiao said, "Without going out of the monastery, you take a thousand-mile journey."

———— ◆ ————

A monk asked, "What is the self?"

Bajiao said, "Facing south and seeing the Big Dipper."

Bajiao addressed the monks, saying, "It's like a person who's traveling who suddenly encounters a ten-thousand-fathom-deep hole, and moreover, behind him a wild fire is pursuing him. On both sides are forests of thistles. The only way forward is into the hole, and going back means getting burned by the fire. Thistles obstruct both sides. How can a person get out of such a situation? If someone can get out of this, then he is in accord with the transcendent path. If he can't escape then he's lost!"

A monk said, "I wish to see if the master can speak of the Way."

Bajiao said, "I thought it was a merchant on a great ship, but after all it was just a peddler from Dangzhou."

A monk asked, "Without asking about principles or points of discussion, I invite the master to point directly at the original face."

Bajiao sat upright, silently.

The monk asked, "Isn't it that when a thief comes you must beat him, when a guest comes you must greet him? So what do you do when a thief and guest both arrive?"

Bajiao said, "In the room there are a pair of worn-out grass sandals."

The monk said, "If the sandals are worn out, do they have any use or not?"

Bajiao said, "If you use them, then wherever you go—before you unlucky, behind you misfortune."

A monk asked, "What is the meaning of 'concealing the body in the Big Dipper'?"

Bajiao said, "Nine, nine, eight, ten, one."

Then Bajiao said, "Do you understand?"

The monk said, "I don't understand."

Bajiao said, "One, two, three, four, five."

A monk asked, "What is a phrase that penetrates the dharmakaya?"

Bajiao said, "The first principle cannot be queried. The second principle does not cease."

The monk said, "I don't understand."

Bajiao said, "Get past the third principle, then I'll show you."

Tongan Daopi

Tongan Daopi (n.d.) was a disciple of Yunju Daoying. Little is recorded of his life. He is known to have been the abbot of the Tongan Monastery on Mt. Fengchi in Hongzhou, near modern Nanchang City. He is remembered for preserving the Caodong Zen lineage and passing the Dharma seal of Dongshan on to his student Tongan Guanzhi.

A monk asked Zen master Tongan Daopi, "What is a seamless monument?"

Tongan said, "Om! Om!"

The monk asked, "Who is the person inside the monument?"

Tongan said, "Many people are visiting here today from Jianchang."

＊

A monk asked, "What if one understands everything with one look and then leaves?"

Daopi said, "Fine. So why have you come back here?"

＊

A monk asked, "What is the master's family style?"[128]

Daopi said, "The golden hen gathers her chicks into the Milky Way. The pregnant jade rabbit scurries into the crape myrtle bushes."

The monk asked, "If suddenly a guest arrives, how do you treat him?"

Daopi said, "At early dawn a monkey picked the golden fruit. At late dusk a phoenix carried away the jade flower."

＊

A monk asked, "Can inanimate things expound Dharma?"

Daopi said, "The jade dog roams at night, never knowing the daylight."

＊

A monk asked, "If on the road one meets a person of the Way, how could one respond to that person with neither words nor silence?"

Daopi said, "With kicks and punches."

———— ❖ ————

A monk asked, "'Explaining by using scripture is a sin against the buddhas of the three realms. Deviating a single word from scripture is devils' talk.' What does this mean?"

Tongan recited a verse that said:

The solitary peak is high and grand,
Not a single layer of mist.
The crescent moon crosses the void,
The white clouds come forth.

———— ❖ ————

A monk asked, "What is Tongan's arrow?"

Daopi said, "Look behind you."

The monk asked, "What's back there?"

Daopi said, "It's gone past already."

———— ❖ ————

A monk asked, "How can one avoid harming the imperial way?"

Daopi said, "Eat gruel. Eat rice."

The monk said, "If one doesn't do so, is the imperial way not harmed?"

Daopi said, "You've slid off to the left!"

———— ❖ ————

Once, when Daopi was reading a sutra he saw a monk coming for instruction. Daopi lifted his arm and covered his head with his sleeve. The monk came up to him and affected a sympathetic demeanor.

Daopi pulled his sleeve from his head, picked up the sutra, and said, "Do you understand?"

The monk then covered his own head with his sleeve.

Daopi said, "Blue heavens! Blue heavens!"

Huguo Shoucheng, "Jingguo"

Huguo Shoucheng (n.d.) was a disciple of Shushan Kuangren. Little is recorded about Huguo's life. He is known mainly by his appearance in case twenty-eight of the *Book of Serenity*. He taught at Huguo Monastery on Mt. Suicheng in ancient Suizhou (north of modern Wuhan City). The *Wudeng Huiyuan* provides a glimpse of this teacher's style.

Huguo entered the hall and addressed the monks, saying, "All the great masters in every quarter, in all circumstances, have ascended the lecture platform for the sake of people. And whenever anyone has asked them the meaning of Bodhidharma's coming from the west, not one of them has directly spoken the answer."

A monk then said, "I ask the master to answer this question."

Huguo said, "A Hebei ass brays. A Henan dog barks."

The monk asked, "What is Buddha?"

Huguo uttered in disgust, "You ass!"

◆

A monk asked, "If someone for whom the great vast earth is but one eye comes forth, then what?"

Huguo said, "A low-class fellow."

◆

A monk asked, "Who is it that walks in the place where all the buddhas can't go?"

Huguo said, "Blockhead!"

◆

A monk asked, "Why did Bodhidharma come from the west?"

Huguo said, "When one person says it, it's a rumor. When a thousand say it, it's a fact."

◆

A monk asked, "When a white crane sits in the pine tree, what is it?"

Huguo said, "An embarrassment on the ground."

◆

A monk asked, "During the era of the Hui Chang suppression, where were the good guardian deities?"

Huguo said, "An embarrassment in front of the temple gate."[129]

◆

A monk asked, "What is it when dripping water turns into ice?"

Huguo said, "An embarrassment when the sun comes out."

Yunmen Wenyan

Yunmen Wenyan (864–949) was a disciple of both Muzhou Daoming and Xuefeng Yicun. Although he first attained realization under Muzhou, he is generally recognized as a Dharma heir of Xuefeng. He came from ancient Jiaxing (located midway between the modern cities of Shanghai and Hangzhou). As a young man, he first entered monastic life under a Vinaya master named Zhicheng. After serving as that teacher's attendant for many years, Yunmen exhausted the teachings of the Vinaya and set off to study elsewhere. Eventually, he studied with Muzhou Daoming.

The *Wudeng Huiyuan* provides an account of Yunmen's enlightenment under Zen master Muzhou.

> When Muzhou heard Yunmen coming he closed the door to his room. Yunmen knocked on the door.
>
> Muzhou said, "Who is it?"
>
> Yunmen said, "It's me."
>
> Muzhou said, "What do you want?"
>
> Yunmen said, "I'm not clear about my life. I'd like the master to give me some instruction."
>
> Muzhou then opened the door and, taking a look at Yunmen, closed it again.
>
> Yunmen knocked on the door in this manner three days in a row. On the third day when Muzhou opened the door, Yunmen stuck his foot in the doorway.
>
> Muzhou grabbed Yunmen and yelled, "Speak! Speak!"
>
> When Yunmen began to speak, Muzhou gave him a shove and said, "Too late!"
>
> Muzhou then slammed the door, catching and breaking Yunmen's foot. At that moment, Yunmen experienced enlightenment.

Muzhou directed Yunmen to go see Xuefeng. When Yunmen arrived at a village at the foot of Mt. Xue, he encountered a monk.

Yunmen asked him, "Are you going back up the mountain today?"

The monk said, "Yes."

Yunmen said, "Please take a question to ask the abbot. But you mustn't tell him it's from someone else."

The monk said, "Okay."

Yunmen said, "When you go to the temple, wait until the moment when all the monks have assembled and the abbot has ascended the Dharma seat. Then step forward, grasp your hands, and say, 'There's an iron cangue on this old fellow's head. Why not remove it?'"

The monk did as Yunmen instructed him.

When Xuefeng saw the monk act this way, he got down from the seat, grabbed the monk and said, "Speak! Speak!"

The monk couldn't answer.

Xuefeng pushed him away and said, "It wasn't your own speech."

The monk said, "It was mine."

Xuefeng called to his attendant, "Bring a rope and a stick" [to bind and beat the monk].

The monk said, "It wasn't my question. It was from a monk in the village."

Xuefeng said, "Everyone! Go to the village and welcome the worthy who will have five hundred disciples."

The next day Yunmen came up to the monastery.

When Xuefeng saw him he said, "How is it that you've reached this place?"

Yunmen then bowed his head. In this manner did the affinity [between Xuefeng and Yunmen] come about.

On the day when Yunmen first entered the hall as abbot, the governor of Guangzhou attended in person and said to the master, "Your disciple asks for your valued teaching."

Yunmen said, "There is nothing special to say. It is better if I don't speak and thereby deceive you all. I'm sorry that I've already played the part of a wily old fox for all of you. If a man of clear vision were to suddenly see me now, I'd be the object of laughter. But if I can't avoid it, then I'll just ask you all, from the beginning, what's the big deal? What are you lacking? I don't have anything to say. There's nothing to be seen. You have to break through to *this* on your own. And don't ask silly questions. In my mind there's just a dark fog. Tomorrow morning and the day after there are a lot of affairs going on here. If your disposition is to tarry here and not return to your usual lives, to look here and there at the gates and gardens built by the ancients, what point is there in all this? Do you want to understand? That's just due to your own quagmire of delusion accumulated for endless eons. You hear someone expound on something and it puts a doubt in your mind, so you ask about Buddha and you ask about the ancestors, looking high and low, searching for a solution, getting caught up in things. This scheming mind is wide of the mark. It's always caught up in words and phrases. Isn't what you require the non-intentioned mind? Don't be mistaken about this. There's nothing more to say. Take care!"

Yunmen entered the hall to address the monks, saying, "Why are you all aimlessly coming here looking for something? I only know how to eat and shit. What use is there in explaining anything else?

"You've taken pilgrimages everywhere, studying Zen and inquiring about Tao. But I ask you, what have you all learned in those places? Let's see it and check it out! In the midst of all this what's the master of your own house attained? You've trailed around behind some old fellows, grabbing something they have already chewed on and spit out, and then calling it your own. Then you say, 'I understand Zen!' or 'I understand Tao!' Even if you can recite the whole Buddhist canon, what will you do with it?

"The ancients didn't know when enough was enough. They saw you scurrying around, and when they said 'bodhi' and 'nirvana' they covered you up and staked you down. Then when they saw you didn't understand they said 'no bodhi' and 'no nirvana.' It should have been made clear from the start that this just goes around and around! Now you just keep looking for commentaries and explanations!

"You who act like this destroy our school. You've been going on like this endlessly, and where has it brought you to today?

"Back when I was making pilgrimages there was a group of people who gave me explanations. They were well intentioned. But one day I saw through what they were saying. They are a bunch of laughingstocks. If I live a few more years I'll break the legs of those people who destroy our school! Nowadays there're plenty of things to get mixed up with. Why don't you go do them? What piece of dried shit are you looking for here?"

Yunmen then got down from the seat and drove the monks from the hall with his staff.[130]

Yunmen is remembered for his terse "one-word barriers."

A monk asked, "What is Zen?"
Yunmen said, "Yes."
The monk said, "What is Tao?"
Yunmen said, "Attain."

———— ◆ ————

A monk asked, "If one's parents won't allow it then one can't leave home. How can one leave home?"
Yunmen said, "Shallow."
The monk said, "I don't understand."
Yunmen said, "Deep."

———— ◆ ————

Yunmen said to the congregation, "Every day you come and go, asking endless questions. If you were crossing a river how would you do so?"
A longtime resident of the monastery responded, "Step."
Yunmen was highly pleased with this answer.

———— ◆ ————

Yunmen said, "A true person of the Way can speak fire without burning his mouth. He can speak all day without moving his lips and teeth or uttering a word. The entire day he just wears his clothes and eats his food, but never comes in contact with a single grain of rice or thread of cloth.
"When we speak in this fashion it is just the manner of our school. It must be set forth like this to be realized. But if you meet a true patch-robed monk of our school and try to reveal the essence through words, it will be a waste of time and effort. Even if you get some great understanding by means of a single word you are still just dozing."

———— ◆ ————

A monk asked, "What is the meaning of 'All dharmas are the Buddha-dharma'?"
Yunmen said, "Country grannies crowd the road."
The monk said, "I don't understand."
Yunmen said, "Not only you. Many others don't understand."

———— ◆ ————

A monk asked, "How should one act during every hour of the day such that the ancestors are not betrayed?"

Yunmen said, "Give up your effort."

The monk said, "How should I give up my effort?"

Yunmen said, "Give up the words you just uttered."

———— ◆ ————

Zen master Yunmen once took his staff and struck a pillar in the hall, saying, "Are the three vehicles and twelve divisions of scripture talking?"

He then answered himself, saying, "No, they're not talking."

Then he shouted, "Bah! A wild fox spirit!"

A monk asked, "What does the master mean?"

Yunmen said, "Mr. Zhang drinks the wine and Mr. Li gets drunk."

Yunmen's influence as a teacher is demonstrated by the many stories transmitted about him in the classic Zen texts. The first Song dynasty emperor, Tai Zu, posthumously honored Yunmen with a name that is nearly a eulogy: "Zen Master Great Compassionate Cloud Delivering Truth Vast Clarity."

CUIYAN LINGCAN, "YONGMING"

CUIYAN LINGCAN (n.d.) was a disciple of Xuefeng Yicun. He came from ancient Anji (southwest of Xuzhou in modern Zhejiang Province). He lived and taught at Mt. Cuiyan in Mingzhou. One of the foremost students of Xuefeng, he attracted a large congregation of students from throughout China.

A monk said, "Without words, I ask the master to speak."

Cuiyan said, "Go in shame to the tea hall!"

———— ◆ ————

A monk asked, "What is the meaning of the National Teacher's three calls to his attendant?"

Cuiyan said, "What point is there in looking up to or down at other people?"

Cuiyan is most often remembered for this exchange with his fellow students when he was the head monk in Xuefeng's congregation.

At the end of the summer practice period Cuiyan addressed the other monks, saying: "Throughout the summer I've been speaking to you about everything under the sun. Now I ask, do I still have eyebrows?"

(Bajiao said, "The thief's heart is empty." Changqing said, "They've grown!" Yunmen said, "Barrier." Cuiyan Zhi said, "Expending complete effort for others, tragedy goes out of one's own house.")

⸻ ◆ ⸻

A monk asked, "There are words and phrases everywhere and all of it is polluted. What is the higher truth?"

Cuiyan said, "There are words and phrases everywhere and all of it is polluted."

The monk said, "What is a place where there are none?"

Cuiyan said, "The assembly is laughing at you."

⸻ ◆ ⸻

A monk said, "A speck of dust turns into cinnabar, and with one touch iron turns to gold. A single phrase becomes vast wisdom, and a commoner a saint. I have come here to ask the master for a touch."

Cuiyan said, "I won't touch you."

The monk said, "Why not?"

Cuiyan said, "I'm afraid you'll fall into discriminating between mundane and sacred."

⸻ ◆ ⸻

A monk asked, "What is the most profound teaching you offer?"

Cuiyan called to his attendant, "Come and boil some tea!"

⸻ ◆ ⸻

A monk asked, "When the ancients grasped the handle and raised their whisk into the air, what did this mean?"

Cuiyan said, "A heretical teaching is hard to support."

⸻ ◆ ⸻

A monk asked, "Without resorting to the sacred or mundane, how do you reveal the great function?"

Cuiyan said, "Don't tell people that I'm clever."

A monk asked, "When all of the words and phrases of the mysterious function are exhausted but the central matter of our school's great vehicle is not understood, then what?"

Cuiyan said, "Bow."

The monk said, "I don't understand."

Cuiyan said, "You've left home to go on a pilgrimage but you still don't know how to bow?"

During his final years Cuiyan was invited to reside and teach in the Longce Temple in Hangzhou. There he passed away.

JINGQING DAOFU, "XUN DE"

JINGQING DAOFU (868–937) was a disciple of Xuefeng Yicun. He came from ancient Yongjia (in the district of the modern city of Wenzhou in Zhejiang Province). According to the *Transmission of the Lamp*, at the age of six he refused to eat meat or strong foods. When his parents forced him to eat dried fish he would immediately vomit it up. As a youngster he entered the Kaiyuan Temple, where he received ordination. He later traveled to Fujian where he met Xuefeng Yicun on Elephant Bone Mountain. The following exchange occurred during their first encounter.

Xuefeng asked, "Where are you from?"

Jingqing said, "From Wenzhou."

Xuefeng said, "In that case you're from the same village as the Overnight Guest."

Jingqing said, "But from where does the Overnight Guest come?"

Xuefeng said, "You deserve a blow from the staff, but I'll let it pass."

One day Jingqing asked, "Didn't the virtuous of old use mind to transmit mind?"

Xuefeng said, "Nor did they establish written or spoken words."

Jingqing said, "Then without using written or spoken words, how would the master transmit the teaching?"

Xuefeng sat silently.

Jingqing bowed in thanks.

Xuefeng asked, "Would you like to ask me something else?"

Jingqing said, "Rather that the master should ask me."

Xuefeng said, "If this is so, is there anything else to discuss?"

Jingqing said, "In just this way the master attains it."

Xuefeng said, "And how about you?"

Jingqing said, "Betraying and killing others!"

Xuefeng said to the congregation, "So majestic! So subtle!"

Jingqing came forward and said, "What is it that's majestic and subtle?"

Xuefeng said, "What?"

Jingqing retreated and stood there.

Xuefeng said, "This matter is in this way esteemed, in this way subtle."

Jingqing said, "In the years since I came here, I've never heard the master give instruction in this manner."

Xuefeng said, "Although I have not done so, what is now revealed has never been lacking. Is there any difficulty?"

Jingqing said, "None at all! This is what the master has not taught, but what has always been present."

Xuefeng said, "And it makes me speak thus."

From this, Jingqing found an entrance, and moreover gained prominence in the congregation. At that time he was called "Little Patch-robed Fu."

One day during the work session, Xuefeng said, "Zen master Guishan said, 'Seeing form is seeing mind.' Is there any error or not?"

Jingqing said, "What about the ancient teachers?"

Xuefeng said, "Although that's true, I still want you all to discuss it."

Jingqing said, "In that case, it can't be compared to my hoeing the ground."

Once, Jingqing went traveling and then returned to practice with Xuefeng.

Xuefeng asked him, "From where have you come?"

Jingqing said, "From beyond the mountains."

Xuefeng said, "Where did you see Bodhidharma?"

Jingqing said, "Could he be anyplace else?"

Xuefeng said, "I don't believe you!"

Jingqing said, "The master shouldn't tarnish me so!"

Xuefeng was silent.

When Jingqing visited Caoshan Benji, Caoshan asked, "Where have you come from?"

Jingqing said, "Yesterday I left Clearwater."

Caoshan said, "When did you arrive at Clearwater?"

Jingqing said, "I arrived when you arrived there, Master."

Caoshan said, "When do you say I arrived?"

Jingqing said, "Just now when I arrived here I remembered."

Caoshan said, "Just so. Just so."

After leaving Xuefeng, Jingqing resided in Yuezhou [now the city of Zhaoxing in Zhejiang Province]. There, a large number of monks assembled to study with him.

A monk asked Jingqing, "I'm breaking out. I ask the master to break in."[131]

Jingqing said, "Will you live or not?"

The monk said, "If not, then I'll suffer others' laughter."

Jingqing said, "A fellow in the grass."

A monk said to Zen master Jingqing Daofu, "This student has not yet arrived at the source. I ask for the master's expedient guidance."

Jingqing said, "What source is that?"

The monk said, "*The* source."

Jingqing said, "If it's *that* source, how could you get any expedient guidance?"

The monk bowed in thanks and went away.

Jingqing's attendant said, "Just now did the master give that monk support or not?"

Jingqing said, "No."

The attendant said, "Then you didn't answer his question?"

Jingqing said, "No."

The attendant said, "I don't understand the master's meaning."

Jingqing said, "One drop is just black ink. Two drops and a dragon is created." [132]

Zen master Jingqing Daofu entered the hall and addressed the monks, saying, "If you have not already realized the great matter that is before us today, then listen carefully to what I say and see if it hits the mark. If it hits the mark, then why does your understanding of it have some special quality? It is only because it has been a long time since you have left your homes, and you have traveled for many years. During this whole time you have merely experienced the conditions and dust of the world. This is called 'turning your back on enlightenment and facing the dust,' or 'forsaking your father and running away.'

"Today I urge you all to not give up, nor turn away. Wouldn't it be disappointing if you children of the great worthies did not exert yourself in this manner? Throughout the day, look everywhere for the 'official road.' But don't come ask me to give you the 'official road.'"

Jingqing entered the hall. When the monks had assembled, he threw down his staff and said, "If anyone moves he gets twenty strokes with the staff. If anyone doesn't move he gets twenty strokes with the staff!"

A monk then came forward, picked up the staff, put it on his head and went out.

Jingqing said, "Today, I, Jingqing, am defeated."

The following passages are taken from the *Transmission of the Lamp*.

Jingqing asked a monk, "What's that noise outside the door?"

The monk said, "The sound of raindrops."

Jingqing said, "All beings have it backwards. They don't see their own body and chase after objects."

Jingqing asked a monk, "What's that sound outside?"

The monk said, "The sound of a snake eating a toad."

Jingqing said, "When you acknowledge the suffering of beings, then there are more suffering beings."

A monk came to study under Jingqing.

Jingqing asked him, "Where have you come from?"

The monk said, "From Buddha Country."

Jingqing asked, "What did Buddha use to make his country?"

The monk said, "Wonderful purity and grandeur are the country."

Jingqing said, "And what does the country take to be Buddha?"

The monk said, "Pure enduring truth is taken as Buddha."

Jingqing said, "You have come from wonderful purity. You have come from grandeur."

--------------- ◆ ---------------

At the request of the local ruler of the region known as Wuyue, Jingqing took up residence to teach at Longce Temple. According to the *Transmission of the Lamp*, after that time Zen flourished in the region.

In [the year 937], at the age of seventy-four, Jingqing passed away. A vast number of mourners accompanied his body to its resting place on Great Compassion Mountain.

Taiyuan Fu

Taiyuan Fu (868–937), before becoming a student of Xuefeng, lectured on the *Mahaparinirvana Sutra*. Once, when he lectured at the Guangxiao Temple in Yangzhou, a group of Zen monks listened to his talk. When Taiyuan relayed the sutra's teaching about the dharmakaya, the monks suddenly broke out laughing, causing Taiyuan great concern. Later, Taiyuan asked the monks for guidance about what error he may have committed. The monks advised him to sit in meditation and let go of all notions of good and bad. Following the monks' instructions, Taiyuan sat earnestly, and near the end of an all-night session of meditation he suddenly gained enlightenment upon hearing the sound of a hammer striking a gong. Thereafter, he traveled to many Zen monasteries and his reputation as a Zen adept spread throughout the country. In the course of his travels he climbed famous Mt. Jing in Zhejiang Province.

One day, in front of the Buddha hall [on Mt. Jing], a monk asked Taiyuan Fu, "Have you been to Mt. Wutai or not?"

Taiyuan said, "I've been there."

The monk asked, "Did you see Manjushri?"

Taiyuan said, "I saw him."

The monk asked, "Where did you see him?"

Taiyuan said, "I saw him in front of the Buddha hall on Mt. Jing."

Later, this same monk traveled to Snow Peak in Fuzhou. There, he told Xuefeng about his conversation with Taiyuan.

Xuefeng said, "Why didn't you tell him to come here?"

When Taiyuan heard of this, he packed his luggage and set off to Snow Peak.

When Taiyuan arrived at Snow Peak, the monks were having a special leisure day, and enjoying an offering of sugarcane they had received.

Changqing asked Taiyuan, "From where have you come?"

Taiyuan said, "From beyond the mountains."

Changqing said, "It's a difficult journey. What did you carry with you?"

Taiyuan said, "Sugarcane. Sugarcane."

The next day at the monastery, when Xuefeng heard about this, he summoned the monks to the hall.

When Taiyuan entered the hall, he looked up at Xuefeng, then looked down at the monks.

The following day, Taiyuan went to Xuefeng, bowed, and said, "Yesterday I acted unfilial toward you."

Xuefeng said, "I understand this matter, so forget about it."

———— ⬥ ————

One evening, as the monks assembled for an evening meeting, Xuefeng was lying down in the middle of the hall.

Taiyuan said, "In all of Wuzhou, only this old master is prominent."

Xuefeng then got up and went out.

———— ⬥ ————

Xuefeng asked Taiyuan, "I understand that Linji has three phrases. Is that so?"

Taiyuan said, "Yes."

Xuefeng said, "What's the first one?"

Taiyuan looked up and stared directly at Xuefeng.

Xuefeng said, "That's the second phrase. What's the first?"

Taiyuan clasped his hands and left.

After this incident Xuefeng held Taiyuan in high esteem. Taiyuan received Dharma transmission and had a special affinity with Xuefeng. He remained with Xuefeng for a long period and served as the bath attendant.

———— ⬥ ————

One day the monk Xuansha Shibei came to Elephant Bone Mountain and inquired after the master Xuefeng.

Xuefeng said to him, "There's a rat here. It's over in the bath house."

Xuansha said, "I'll go check him out."

When Xuansha saw Taiyuan at the bathhouse, he said, "Now I see your eminence."

Taiyuan said, "You've seen me before."

Xuansha said, "In what eon did we see each other?"

Taiyuan said, "Are you asleep?"

Xuansha then went into the abbot's room and reported this to Xuefeng, saying, "I checked him out."

Xuefeng said, "What did you find out?"

Xuansha relayed the conversation he had with Taiyuan.

Xuefeng said, "You've revealed a thief!"

One day, the monk Baofu Congzhan was cutting a melon when Taiyuan Fu came up to him.

Baofu said, "If you say the right thing I'll give you a piece of melon to eat."

Taiyuan said, "Give me one."

Baofu gave him a piece of melon.

Taiyuan took it and went away.

Because Taiyuan Fu never assumed the abbacy of a temple, he was known throughout the world as "Eminent [instead of 'Master'] Taiyuan Fu."

Late in life Taiyuan went back to Weiyang, where the household of an official named Chen Shangshu supported him.

One day Taiyuan said to Shangshu, "Tomorrow, to repay your kindness, I will recite a passage from the *Mahaparinirvana Sutra*."

The next day Shangshu presented food and tea to Taiyuan Fu. Taiyuan then ascended the Dharma seat to speak. For a long while he said nothing. Then, with the wave of a small scepter, he said, "Thus I have heard."

Taiyuan then called Chen Shangshu's name.

Shangshu said, "Yes?"

Taiyuan said, "The Buddha in the single moment."

Upon saying these words, Taiyuan passed away.

XUANSHA SHIBEI

XUANSHA SHIBEI (835–908) was a disciple of Xuefeng Yicun. He came from ancient Fuzhou. As a young man he lived as a fisherman on the Nantai River. At the rather late age of thirty he left lay life to enter a temple on Lotus Mountain. Later he was ordained by the Vinaya master Lingxun at Kaiyuan Temple in Yuzhang (near modern Nanchang). He carried on an ascetic practice, wearing only a patched robe and straw sandals. He often fasted instead of taking the evening meal, and was regarded as unusual by the other monks. He was called "Ascetic Bei." His relationship with Xuefeng was like that of a younger brother. As his close disciple, Xuansha worked with Xuefeng to build his teacher's practice center. He is said to have awakened one day upon reading the words of the *Surangama Sutra*.

After leaving Xuefeng he first lived at the Puying Monastery. Later he moved to Xuansha Mountain in Fuzhou, where he remained for the next thirty years. The governor of Min honored him, presenting him with the purple robe and the title "Great Teacher of the One Doctrine."[133]

> One day, Xuefeng asked Xuansha, "What is Ascetic Bei?"
>
> Xuansha said, "I dare not deceive people."
>
> Another day, Xuefeng called out to Xuansha, saying, "Why doesn't Ascetic Bei go off to practice at other places?"
>
> Xuansha said, "Bodhidharma didn't come from the west. The Second Ancestor didn't go to India."
>
> Xuefeng approved this answer.

> One day, Xuefeng entered the hall and addressed the monks, saying, "If you want to understand this matter, it's like looking into an ancient mirror. If a foreigner comes, a foreigner is revealed. If a Han comes, a Han is revealed."[134]
>
> Xuansha said, "If the clear mirror suddenly comes forth, then what?"
>
> Xuefeng said, "The foreigner and Han are both hidden."
>
> Xuansha said, "The master's feet still don't touch the ground."

> After Xuansha became the abbot at Mt. Xuan Sha, he entered the hall and addressed the monks, saying, "Buddha's way is vast and serene. There is no path on which to travel there. There is no gate of liberation. There are no thoughts about a 'person of the Way.' There are no 'three worlds.' Therefore one cannot

'transcend' or 'fall into.' Setting something up runs counter to the truth. Negation is a formation. Movement gives rise to the root of birth and death. Stillness is the province of falling into delusion. When movement and stillness are extinguished, one falls into empty negation. When movement and stillness are both accepted, buddha nature is concealed. With respect to worldly affairs or states of mind, you should be like a cold dead tree. Then you will realize the great function and not forfeit its grace. All forms will be illuminated as if in a mirror. Brightness or obscurity will not confuse you. The bird will fly into emptiness, it will not be apart from empty form. Then in the ten directions there will be no form and in the three worlds there will be no traces."

The following passages are from *The Record of Zen Master Xuansha Shibei.*

One day Xuansha entered the hall but remained silent. The monks grew tired of waiting for him to expound the Dharma, and after a time all of them got up to leave the hall. Xuansha called out, "See, they're all the same! Not a single one with wisdom! You see my two lips here and you cluster around seeking to get meaning out of some words. When I really bring it forth, none of you know it. Look! So hard! So difficult!"

◆

Once Xuansha said, "All of you practitioners of Zen, you've traveled here from every quarter on foot, asking me to help you practice Zen and study Tao. You've taken this place to be special, and when you get here you ask every sort of question. Since this is what you've done, then you should check this place out thoroughly! Haven't I been completely forthcoming with you? I extinguish what you know. Then what is there left? If nothing is left, then of what use is your knowledge? Since you've come here I now ask you, do any of you have the eye of wisdom or not? If so, then let us see it now. Can we see it? If not, then I call you all blind and deaf. Is that it? Are you willing to speak up in this manner? Virtuous Zennists do not willingly submit. Are you authentic monks? The top of your head is exposed to all buddhas in the ten directions. You don't dare show the slightest error!"

◆

Xuansha gave instruction to the congregation, saying: "The great masters everywhere speak extensively of reaching and benefiting beings. If they encountered three persons with different disabilities, how would they reach them? For a blind person, if they wielded the staff or raised their whisk then the person would not see it. For a deaf person, if they spoke of samadhi, then he would not hear it. For a mute person, if they called on them to speak, he could not do so. So what would they do to reach them? If these types cannot be reached, then the Buddhadharma has no effect."

———— ◆ ————

Zen master Xuansha said to the monks, "All of you are seeing great peril. You see tigers, knives, and swords threatening your life, and you're experiencing unlimited terror. What's it like? It is like the world is painting itself with images from hell, making tigers, knives, and swords, all right there in front of you, and you feel terrified. But if you are now having such experiences then it's a terror that arises from your own personal illusions, and not something that someone else is creating for you. Do you want to understand these illusions and confused feelings? If so, then know that you have the diamond-eye. If you know this, then you realize that all the things of the world don't truly exist. So where could tigers, wolves, knives, and swords threaten you? If Shakyamuni had dealt with this like you're doing he'd never have made it.

"This is why I say to you that the eye of a true practitioner envelops the entire world. It encompasses the whole universe. Not a single strand of hair leaks out. So where would there be a single thing left for you to see or to realize? This transcendence! This miraculous state! Why don't you investigate it?"

———— ◆ ————

Xuansha said, "It's as if all of you are sitting on the bottom of a great ocean, completely submerged, and you're still holding your hand out to people and begging for water. Do you understand? If you want to realize wisdom and bodhisattvahood you can do so if you have great wisdom ability. With great wisdom ability you can do it right now. But if your basic ability is somewhat lacking, then you have to be diligent and press on, day and night forgetting about food and sleep, enduring as if both your parents had died, being in just such anxiety. Give over your entire life, and with the help of other people, truly endeavoring for the truth, you'll certainly reach enlightenment."

———— ◆ ————

A monk asked, "Why can't I speak?"
Xuansha said, "Close your mouth. Now can you speak?"

———— ◆ ————

A monk asked, "What is it? And why is it so hard to realize?"

Xuansha said, "Because it's too close." ([Later,] Fayan said, "It couldn't be closer. Actually it's the monk himself.")

A monk said, "I've just arrived here and I beg the master to point out a gate whereby I may enter."

Xuansha said, "Do you hear the sound of the water in Yan Creek?"

The monk said, "I hear it."

Xuansha said, "That's the place of your entry."

BAOFU CONGZHAN

BAOFU CONGZHAN (d. 928) was a disciple of Xuefeng Yicun. Baofu came from ancient Fuzhou. According to the *Transmission of the Lamp*, at the age of fifteen he became a student of Xuefeng. Ordained at the age of eighteen at Dazhong Temple in his native city, he traveled to other areas in China before returning to become Xuefeng's attendant.

One day Xuefeng suddenly called him, saying, "Do you understand?"

Baofu wanted to approach Xuefeng, but Xuefeng pushed him away with his staff. Baofu thereupon understood.

Baofu often inquired of his Dharma brother, Changqing Huileng, concerning ancient and current expedient methods of teaching.

Several ancient lamp records, as well as case 95 of the *Blue Cliff Record*, provide this exchange between Changqing and Baofu.

One day Changqing said, "I'd say that an *arhat* has three poisons, but the *Tathagata* does not have two ways of speaking.[135] I don't say that the Tathagata doesn't speak, just that he doesn't have two ways of speaking."

Baofu said, "What is the speech of the Tathagata?"

Changqing said, "The deaf struggle to hear it."

Baofu said, "Master Qing has spoken of the secondary!"

Changqing asked, "In that case, what is the speech of the Tathagata?"

Baofu said, "Go drink tea!" (Yunju Ci said, "Where is the place that Changqing speaks of the secondary?")

Baofu brought up for consideration Panshan's statement, "When all illuminated realms are gone, what is it that remains?" and Dongshan's statement, "When all illuminated realms are undiminished, what else is there?"

Baofu then said, "According to what was expounded by these two worthies, there is something left over that isn't annihilated."

He then asked Changqing, "What would you say now to exterminate it?"

Changqing was silent for a long time.

Baofu said, "You're seeking speaking strategies in a mountain spirit's cave."

Changqing asked, "Then what would you say?"

Baofu said, "Both hands on the plough, water above the knees."

During the [year 918], Magistrate Wang of Zhangzhou honored the master's great reputation by building and supporting the Baofu Zen Monastery and inviting the master to become the abbot and teach there. On the day when the temple opened, Magistrate Wang knelt on his knees and begged the master to speak to the assembly. He even personally supported the master to help him ascend the dais.

The master said, "Why are you making all this into a joke? Still, since you've asked three times, I can't avoid it."

The master then addressed the crowd, "Worthies! Do you understand? If you understand then you're no different from the ancient buddhas."

A monk came forward. Just as he began to speak the master said, "You can't soar into the clear sky yet! You must wait until rain drenches your head!"

Baofu said, "This affair is like striking flint to make fire. Whether you reach *it* or not, you can't avoid losing your body and life."

A monk asked, "I don't understand whether people who can reach *it* still lose their lives or not."

Baofu said, "Leaving aside what I just said, can you reach it or not?"

The monk said, "If I can't, I won't avoid the derisive laughter of the congregation."

Once when Zen master Baofu saw a monk he struck a nearby pillar with his staff. He then struck the monk on the head. The monk refrained from expressing pain.

Baofu said, "Why didn't that hurt?" (Xuanjue said on behalf of the monk, "A wretched teacher.")

A monk asked, "During the twelve hours of the day how should one be watchful?"

Baofu said, "Be watchful like you are now."

The monk said, "Why can't I see something?"

Baofu said, "Quit poking your eyes and calling the spots you see flowers!"

A monk asked, "What do you say about finding meaning in speech?"

Baofu said, "What speech is that?"

The monk looked down and didn't answer.

Baofu said, "The sword of function is like lightning. Thinking about it is futile!"

Baofu saw a monk counting money. He held out his hand and said, "I beg you for a string of cash!"

The monk said, "How is it that the master could have fallen to such straits?"

Baofu said, "I've fallen to these straits."

The monk said, "If it's really so, then take a string of cash."

Baofu said, "How have you fallen to such straits?"

Baofu asked a monk, "Where have you come from?"

The monk said, "From Kwan Yin."

Baofu said, "Did you see Kwan Yin?"

The monk said, "I saw her."

Baofu said, "Did you see her right side or her left side?"

The monk said, "When I saw her, I didn't pass her on the right or left."

A monk asked, "If one wants to reach the road of no life and death, one must first see the original source. What is the original source?"

Baofu was silent for a long while. Then he said to his attendant, "What was it that that monk just asked me?"

The monk repeated his question.

Baofu yelled, "I'm not deaf!"

---- ◆ ----

A monk said, "I've just arrived at the monastery. I ask the master to reveal to me the complete entrance." Baofu said, "If I were to show you the complete entrance, then I would just bow to you."

---- ◆ ----

The master lived at Baofu Temple only one year, and during that time not less than seven hundred students gathered there. The benefits they received were too numerous to record. The governor of Fuzhou deeply respected him, memorializing the emperor for him to receive the purple robe. In the third year of the Tian Cheng era [928] the master showed signs of a slight illness. The monks entered his quarters to inquire about him.

Baofu said to them, "We've known each other these many years, what artistry could possibly help me?"

The monks said, "There are such arts." Hearing this did not dispel Baofu's objections.

He also said to the monks, "During these last ten days my strength has failed. Don't worry about it. It's just that my time has come."

A monk asked, "If your time has come, then will the master go or will the master stay?"

Baofu said, "Speak! Speak!"

The monk said, "If it is thus, then I dare not speak hastily."

Baofu said, "I've been robbed of my money."

When he finished speaking, the master crossed his legs and passed away.

CHANGQING HUILENG

CHANGQING HUILENG (854–932) was a disciple of Xuefeng Yicun. He came from ancient Yanzhou (southwest of the modern city of Haining in Zhejiang Province). He entered Tongxuan ("Penetrate Mystery") Temple in Suzhou at the age of thirteen. Subsequently, he studied under various Zen teachers. In about the year 879 he went to Fujian Province, where he studied under Xiyuan Siming. He then studied under Lingyun Zhiqin, where he experienced difficulty and doubt about his practice. Finally he traveled to Fuzhou, where only after arduous meditation under Xuefeng did he gain enlightenment (tradition holds that he wore out seven meditation cushions). Xuefeng provided Changqing with "the medicine a horse doctor uses to bring a dead horse alive again." He instructed Changqing to practice meditation in the hall as if he were a "dead tree stump." Changqing followed this practice for two and a half years, until late one night, after others had gone to bed, he rolled up a bamboo screen and his eye fell upon the light of a lantern. At that moment he woke up. The next day he composed the following verse to attest to his understanding:

> I was so far off, so far off,
> Then all the earth was revealed when I rolled up a screen.
> If anyone asks me to explain our school,
> I'll raise the whisk and slap his mouth.

[After Changqing presented this verse to his teacher Xuefeng] Xuefeng presented it to [the senior monk] Xuansha Shibei and said, "This disciple has penetrated the Way."

Xuansha said, "I don't approve. This verse could have been composed with [mundane] conscious understanding. We have to test him further before we can confirm him."

That evening, when the monks assembled for a question-and-answer session, Xuefeng said to Changqing, "Ascetic Bei [Xuansha] doesn't approve your understanding. If you have been genuinely enlightened, please present your understanding now to the assembly."

Changqing then recited another verse, saying:

> "Amidst the myriad realms the solitary body is revealed.
> Only persons self-allowing are intimate with it.
> Before, I wrongly searched amongst the paths,
> But today I see, and it's like ice in fire."

Xuefeng then looked at Xuansha and said, "I don't accept this. It still could be composed with conscious understanding."

Changqing then asked Xuefeng, "Please, Master, demonstrate what has been passed down by all the ancestors."

Xuefeng remained silent.

Changqing then bowed and walked out of the hall.

Xuefeng smiled.

When Changqing went into Xuefeng's quarters for an interview, Xuefeng asked him, "What is it?"

Changqing said, "The weather is clear. It's a good day for *puqing*."

Xuansha said, "Your answer is not apart from the great mystery." [And thus Changqing's enlightenment was confirmed.]

Changqing remained with Xuefeng for twenty-nine years, becoming his Dharma heir. Subsequently he lived at Zhaoqing Temple in Quanzhou, as well as Changqing Monastery in Fuzhou, where he remained for twenty years.

When Changqing was at the Western Hall, he asked the senior priest Shen, "Elephant Bone Mountain is close by, have you been there or not?"

Shen said, "I haven't been there."

Changqing asked "Why not?"

Shen said, "I have affairs to attend to."

Changqing said, "What are the affairs of a senior priest?"

Shen held up the corner of his priest's robe.

Changqing said "You're just doing this and nothing else?"

Shen said, "What do you see?"

Changqing said, "A good beginning and a poor finish."

———— ❖ ————

Changqing stayed with Xuefeng for twenty-nine years. Then [in the year 908], the governor of Fuzhou, Wang Yanbin, invited Changqing to become abbot of the Changqing Monastery.

During the opening ceremonies for the monastery, Wang Yanbin urgently implored Master Changqing, "Please expound the Dharma."

Changqing said, "Do you hear it?"

Wang then bowed.

Changqing said, "Although it is thus, I'm afraid there are people who won't accept this."

———— ❖ ————

Zen master Changqing Huileng entered the hall to address the monks. After a long silence he said, "Don't say that it will be any better tonight."

He then got down and left the hall.

———— ❖ ————

Changqing addressed the monks, saying, "If I truly expound the vehicle of our school, then I should simply close the door to the Dharma hall. Therefore I'll just say that in the inexhaustible Dharma there are no persons."

In the year 932, Changqing passed away. Wang Yanbin built his stupa.

Upon his death, Changqing received the posthumous title "Great Teacher Beyond Realization."

LUOSHAN DAOXIAN

LUOSHAN DAOXIAN (n.d.) was a student and Dharma heir of Yantou Quanhuo. He came from ancient Changxi (now the modern city of Xiapu in Fujian Province). Upon leaving home to join the Buddhist orders, he is said to have first lived at Gui Shan ("Tortoise Mountain").[136] After receiving ordination, Luoshan traveled widely and met various teachers.

Once, when Luoshan studied under Shishuang, he asked, "When one is unable to find a place where one can go or remain, then what?"

Shishuang said, "Give it up completely."

Luoshan didn't penetrate this answer and later he continued his travels. Then he met Yantou and asked him the same question.

Yantou said, "Going or abiding in some other place, of what use is it?"

Upon hearing these words Luoshan woke up.

The governor of Fuzhou tasted the flavor of Luoshan's Dharma. He invited him to become the abbot of Mt. Luoshan, naming him Zen Master Fabao ["Precious Dharma"].

On the day when he opened the hall Luoshan entered and took his seat on the lecture platform. He arranged his robes carefully, and then he said to the assembled monks, "Take care!"

For some time, the monks remained, not leaving.

After a long while Luoshan said, "Those who don't know come forward."

A monk came forward and bowed.

Luoshan said reprovingly, "It's terrible."

When the monk began to ask his question, Luoshan shouted and left the hall.

A monk asked, "When someone gets the point, how does he know it?"
Luoshan said, "Luoshan lifted his scepter."
The monk said, "Please, Master, show your compassion."
Luoshan said, "Wide of the mark."

A monk asked, "With complete submission, I ask the master to accept me as a student."
Luoshan said, "Do you understand?"
The monk said, "I don't understand."
Luoshan said, "The arrow has passed."

A monk came to study with Luoshan.
Luoshan asked him, "What's your name?"
The monk said, "Mingjiao ['Bright Teaching']."
Luoshan said, "So can you teach or not?"
The monk said, "A little."
Luoshan raised up a fist and said, "If you can climb spirit mountain, what do you call this?"
The monk said, "Fist teaching."
Luoshan laughed and said, "So if I do this you call it the fist teaching."
He then extended his feet and said, "What teaching is this?"
The monk was silent.
Luoshan said, "Don't you call it the 'foot teaching'?"

A monk asked, "What is the meaning of 'On a hundred blades of grass is the complete meaning of the ancestors'?"
Luoshan said, "A thorn pierces your eye."

A monk asked, "Just when in front of you is a ten-thousand-foot cliff and behind you are tigers, wolves, and lions, then what?"
Luoshan said, "Be there."

A monk asked, "Who is the boss of the three realms?"

Luoshan said, "Have you eaten?"

---------◆---------

When Luoshan was near death, he entered the hall and sat before the assembled monks. After some time he held out his left hand. The head monk misunderstood Luoshan's meaning, and had the monks on the east side of the hall move back. Luoshan then held out his right hand. The head monk had the monks on the west side move back.

Luoshan then said, "If one want's to repay Buddha's compassion, the best way is to propagate the great teaching. Go back! Go back! Take care."

Luoshan then smiled and passed away.

Ruiyan Shiyan

RUIYAN SHIYAN (n.d.) came from what is now Fujian Province. During his early years Ruiyan studied under Jiashan Shanhui. Later, Ruiyan studied under one of the most colorful and dynamic teachers of the era, Yantou Quanhuo. The initial meeting between Ruiyan and Yantou is recorded in case seventy-five of the *Book of Serenity* and other classical references.

Upon meeting Yantou, Ruiyan asked, "What is the fundamental constant principle?"

Yantou said, "Moving."

Ruiyan said, "And if moving, then what?"

Yantou said, "Then it's not the fundamental constant principle."

Ruiyan sank deep in thought for a long while.

Yantou said, "If you agree, then you've not shed the root of samsaric existence. If you don't agree then you're forever sunk in life and death."

Upon hearing these words Ruiyan experienced deep awakening. He then bowed to Yantou. Thereafter, whenever Yantou questioned Ruiyan to test his understanding, Ruiyan never erred.

Later, Ruiyan went back to see Jiashan.

Jiashan asked, "Where have you come from?"

Ruiyan said, "From Wolong ['Reclining Dragon']."

Jiashan said, "When you came, had the dragon arisen or not?"

Ruiyan stared at Jiashan.

Jiashan said, "When the wound is cauterized a scar is left there."

Ruiyan said, "Why is the master still embittered in this manner?"

Jiashan let it rest.

Ruiyan then said to Jiashan, "Acting in this manner is easy. Not acting in this manner is hard. Acting this way over and over again is being alert. Not acting in this way over and over again is residing in the empty world. Acting or not acting, please, Master, speak!"

Jiashan said, "I deceived you."

Ruiyan said, "This old monk, what time is this?"

Ruiyan then went out.

(Later, a monk told Yantou about this. Yantou said, "How difficult! My branch came from acting in this way.")

Ruiyan went to live at Ruiyan Monastery in Taizhou where he sat on a large rock. Each day he would call out, "Master!"

Then he himself would answer, "What?"

"Stay alert!"

"Yes!"

"And in the future don't be deceived by anyone!"

"Yes, yes!"

A monk asked, "When a crown appears on the head and flowery clouds at the feet, what is it?"

Ruiyan said, "A fool in manacles."

The monk said, "When there's no crown above nor flowery clouds underfoot, then what?"

Ruiyan said, "Still in manacles."

The monk said, "Then, after all is said and done, what is it?"

Ruiyan said, "Being tired after the banquet."

A monk asked, "What is Buddha?"

Ruiyan said, "A stone ox."

The monk asked, "What is Dharma?"

Ruiyan said, "The child of a stone ox."

The monk said, "Then they're not the same?"

Ruiyan said, "Don't combine them."

The monk said, "Why can't you combine them?"

Ruiyan said, "They're in no way equivalent. How could you combine them?"

---- ❖ ----

A monk asked, "How can one speak without falling into stages [of spiritual development]?"

Ruiyan said, "They aren't arranged."

The monk said, "Why aren't they arranged?"

Ruiyan said, "Because originally there are no stages."

The monk said, "I don't know where one should abide."

Ruiyan said, "Don't sit in the universal light hall."

The monk said, "Is it concealed or not?"

Ruiyan said, "In what are known as the three realms, where can one not return to the court?"

---- ❖ ----

Once, an old woman from the village came to pay her respects to the master.

Ruiyan said to her, "Quick, go back and save the lives of thousands of beings."

The woman hurried back to her house. There she found that her daughter-in-law had brought in snails from the fields. The old woman released them at the shore of a lake. Strange occurrences related to Master Ruiyan are too numerous to record here.

Upon his death, Ruiyan's stupa was built on the mountain where he taught. He received the posthumous title "Zen Master Empty Illumination."

Fourteenth Generation

FENGXUE YANZHAO   XINGYANG QINGRANG

TONGAN GUANZHI   XIANGLIN CHENGYUAN

FENGXIAN DAOSHEN   BALING HAOJIAN

DESHAN YUANMING   DONGSHAN SHOUCHU

LUOHAN GUICHEN   WANG YANBIN   MINGZHAO DEQIAN

FENGXUE YANZHAO

FENGXUE YANZHAO (896–973) was a disciple of Nanyuan Huiyong. He transmitted the Linji Zen lineage to future generations. Fengxue came from ancient Yuzhou. He studied Confucianism as a youth and failed on his first attempt to pass the state civil exams. In disappointment, he left home and entered the Kaiyuan Monastery, where he received ordination under the Vinaya master Zhigong. He delved into the *Lotus Sutra* and practiced the *zhiguan* style of self-cultivation used in the Tiantai school. Fengxue traveled to broaden his understanding and studies. At the age of twenty-five, he studied with Zen master Jingqing Daofu. Still unsuccessful at uncovering the root of Zen, he continued his travels, and eventually studied under the rigorous Zen master Nanyuan Huiyong. He remained with Nanyuan for six years, finally awakening to the Way and becoming his teacher's Dharma heir.

In 931, Fengxue traveled to Ruzhou, where he began teaching at the already old and dilapidated Fengxue Temple. There he derived his mountain name. News of Fengxue's ability spread, and before long Zen students gathered around him. The temple's poor physical condition was beyond repair, however, and in the year 951 Fengxue and his students moved to the newly built Guanghui Temple. Fengxue remained there as abbot for twenty-two years.

Upon first meeting Nanyuan, Fengxue did not bow. Nanyuan said, "Entering the gate, one must distinguish who is the host."

Fengxue said, "To start with, I invite the master to do so."

Nanyuan slapped his own knee with his left hand.

Fengxue shouted.

Nanyuan slapped his knee with his right hand.

Fengxue shouted again.

Nanyuan said, "Leaving aside slapping the left hand, what about slapping the right hand?"

Fengxue said, "Blind."

Nanyuan picked up his staff.

Fengxue said, "Don't blindly strike people or I'll grab that staff and beat you. Don't say I didn't warn you."

Nanyuan threw down the staff and said, "Today I've been fooled by a yellow-faced child from Zhe who's come to the gate."

Fengxue said, "It's as though the master, unable to hold up his begging bowl, pretends to not be hungry."

Nanyuan said, "Have you been here before?"

Fengxue said, "How can you say that?"

Nanyuan said, "I'm just kindly asking."

Fengxue said, "I won't let it pass."

Fengxue then went out and into the hall. Then he turned around, came back, and bowed to Nanyuan.

Nanyuan said, "Who did you see before you came here?"

Fengxue said, "I spent the summer with your attendant Kuo at Huayan Temple in Xiangzhou."

Nanyuan said, "You truly saw an adept."

———— ◆ ————

Nanyuan asked Fengxue, "What's your opinion about the 'staff of the South' [Linji Zen]?"

Fengxue said, "I say it's quite unusual."

Fengxue then asked Nanyuan, "What does the master say about the staff in this place?"

Nanyuan picked up his staff and said, "Those unable to endure the staff will not see Linji as their teacher."

At these words Fengxue deeply realized the great meaning of the Linji house.

·············· ◆ ··············

Once, when he addressed the monks, Fengxue cited an ancient who said, "I have an arrow. I have sharpened it for many ages. When I shoot it flies through the ten directions. No one can see where it falls to earth."

Then Fengxue said, "But as for me, I don't go along with this. I have an arrow that has never been sharpened. It doesn't shoot through the ten directions. But still, no one can see it."

A monk then asked, "What is the master's arrow?"

Fengxue pretended to shoot the monk with a bow and arrow.

The monk bowed.

Fengxue yelled, "Drag this dead fellow out of here!"

———— ❖ ————

Fengxue said to the monks, "Establish one mote of dust and the nation flourishes. The villagers knit their brows in anxiety. Not establishing one mote of dust and the nation is lost. Then the hundred households live in peace. When you understand this, then there is nothing more, and everything is your teacher. If this in not understood, then your teacher is a priest. This teacher and priest can together enlighten the entire world, or blind the entire world. Do you want to know who the priest is?"

Fengxue then slapped his right side and said, "He's right here."

Then Fengxue said, "Do you want to know the teacher?"

Fengxue then slapped his left side and said, "He's right here."

❖

A monk asked, "The ancient song has no tune. How can one be in harmony with it?"

Baoshou said, "The wooden cock crows at night. The matted dog barks in the daylight."

❖

In the hall, Fengxue quoted a poem by Hanshan to the monks:

"The Brahmin transmigrates through life and death,
His soul always suffering decay and old age.
Even reading a hundred imperial books,
He can't avoid beatings and chains.
But uttering Namufo even once,[137]
And all together attain the Buddha Way."

XINGYANG QINGRANG

XINGYANG QINGRANG (n.d.) was a disciple of Bajiao Huiqing. He lived and taught on Mt. Xingyang in ancient Ezhou (the modern Mt. Jing in Hubei Province). Although little is recorded about this teacher, he is notable as one of the last masters of the Guiyang school of Zen. Subsequently, the Guiyang school passed out of existence, although it was partially absorbed by the Linji tradition. The *Transmission of the Lamp* provides an example of Xingyang's teachings.

A monk asked Xingyang Qingrang, "How was it in the time before the appearance of the Buddhadharma, when the Buddha of Supreme Wisdom and Penetration sat in meditation for ten kalpas before becoming a buddha?"[138]

Xingyang said, "Your question truly hits the mark."

The monk said, "Since he sat in the seat of meditation, why didn't he attain the buddha way?"

Xingyang said, "Because he had not become a buddha."

TONGAN GUANZHI

TONGAN GUANZHI was a student of Tongan Daopi. There is no record of his life before becoming a monk, and little about his life as a teacher. The lamp records offer an obscure account of his life and teachings.

When Zen master Tongan Daopi was about to die, he entered the hall and addressed the monks, saying, "The disciples before the stupa are adept, but what about the affair before the five old peaks?"

He asked this question three times, but none of the monks responded.

Finally, Tongan Guanzhi stood up and said, "Beyond the window screen, the chiliocosm is arrayed in the clear night. Everywhere, a song of great peace."

Daopi said, "You should all be like this foolish ass!"

⸺⸺⸺ ◆ ⸺⸺⸺

A monk asked, "How do you sing of the place where duality can't reach?"

Tongan said, "There is no place where this can be encountered. But within the mystic principle it is never lost."

A monk asked, "Everywhere are words and phrases, but they are all exhausted in the present moment. I come before the master to request that you point directly at *it*."

Tongan said, "If it is not revealed before the eyes, there's no confusion after the words."

⋯⋯⋯ ◆ ⋯⋯⋯

A monk asked, "What is the transcendent matter?"

Tongan said, "Pivoting but not changing position. Any special sign is bad."

XIANGLIN CHENGYUAN

XIANGLIN CHENGYUAN (908–987) was a disciple of Yunmen Wenyan. He came from the city of Mianzhu in Hanzhou (a location in Sichuan Province). As a youth, he entered Zhenxiang Monastery in Chengdu City. There, at the age of sixteen, he took his vows.

The *Wudeng Huiyuan* provides this story about the young monk:

One day, while hoeing in the field with the other monks, Xianglin heard a monk yell, "Look! The Su house is on fire!"[139]

Xianglin, not seeing anything, said, "Where's the fire?"

The monk said, "Don't you see it?"

Xianglin said, "No, I don't."

The monk then said, "This blind fellow!"

For some time all the monks said that Xianglin suffered a failing.

⋯⋯⋯⋯ ◆ ⋯⋯⋯⋯

Xianglin later traveled widely, eventually becoming the disciple and Dharma heir of the great teacher Yunmen. After serving Yunmen for several years he returned to Chengdu to assume the abbacy of the Tianwang Monastery. In the year 964, he moved to the Xianglin Monastery on Mt. Chingcheng. There, he preached the Dharma in the style of the Yunmen school for more than twenty years.

⋯⋯⋯⋯ ◆ ⋯⋯⋯⋯

A monk asked Master Xianglin Chengyuan, "Why does sweet-tasting cream turn into poison?"[140]

Xianglin said, "Paper from Daojiang is expensive."

———— ✦ ————

A monk asked, "How is it that when one observes form, one thus observes mind?"

Xianglin said, "Just when it comes, where does it return to?"

———— ✦ ————

A monk asked, "What is it when mind and environment are both gone?"

Xianglin said, "Eyes open, sitting asleep."

———— ✦ ————

A monk asked, "What is the meaning of the phrase, 'concealing the body in the Big Dipper'?"

Xianglin said, "The moon like a curved bow. A light rain and big wind."

———— ✦ ————

A monk asked, "What is the mind of all buddhas?"

Xianglin said, "Clarity. From beginning to end, clarity."

A monk asked, "How can I understand this?"

Xianglin said, "Don't be deceived by others."

———— ✦ ————

A monk asked, "What is the master's special medicine?"

Xianglin said, "It's not other than a common taste."

The monk said, "How about those that eat it?"

Xianglin said, "Why not taste it and see?"

———— ✦ ————

A monk asked, "What is a monk's affair?"

Xianglin said, "In the twelfth month, fire engulfs the mountain."

———— ✦ ————

A monk asked, "What is the monk's true eye?"

Xianglin said, "No separation."

———— ✦ ————

Xianglin entered the hall and addressed the monks, saying, "All of you who've been carrying your pack and bowl and have come here on pilgrimage, do you see self-nature yet or not? If you've seen it, then come forward to speak. We'll check you out and see! If you haven't seen it, then you've been cheated on your journey. So I ask all of you—you've been practicing for some time now, mindfully sweeping the ground and boiling tea, hiking in the mountains and enjoying the rivers, and you've got it nailed down, right? What do you call self-nature?

"All of you say, 'From beginning to end there is no change and no deviation, no high and no low, no good and no bad, no birth and no death.' But do you actually know this place? Do you know what this actually is?

"If right here you know the place, then it's the realized Dharma gate of all the buddhas. It is awakening to the Way and seeing self-nature, from start to finish without doubt or design. And if you go off traveling no one will question you. Then the words you're spitting out will have some actual basis in understanding.

"If a person were to buy a rice field, then he must get the original title to the property. If he can't get the original title then the whole situation is uncertain. Then, if there's any official inquiry about it, the person won't be able to hold onto it. If a person can't get the original title document then someone else will take the property away from him.

"All of you here who are practicing Zen and studying the Way, you're also like this! Who here has managed to get the original title? Bring it out and let's see it! What is this thing you're calling the original title? Let everyone see it! If you're clever, then when you hear me speak in this manner you'll know what to do. If you don't know what to do then even if you go somewhere and learn a thousand strategies and memorize solutions until your mouth overflows like a river, it still won't avail you anything. You'll still be as far from yourself as the sky is from the earth. Go look right underneath your bowl and your clothes, at your very body. And if you see something, then come up here and speak and we'll examine it. I'll confirm what you say. If you can't find anything then you're just passing your time like everyone else."

———— ◆ ————

When Zen master Xianglin Chengyuan was about to die, he bade farewell to an official named Song Gongdang, saying, "I'm going on a pilgrimage."

But [a different official] said, "That monk is crazy. Where's he going on a pilgrimage when he's eighty years old?"

But Song Gongdang replied, "When a venerable master goes on a pilgrimage, he goes or abides freely."

Xianglin Chengyuan addressed the congregation, saying, "For forty years I've hammered out a single piece."

When he finished speaking these words he passed away. His stupa was built near the monastery.

Fengxian Daoshen

Fengxian Daoshen (n.d.) was a student of Yunmen Wenyan. Little is known of his life. He taught at Baoning Temple in what is now Nanjing City during the latter half of the tenth century. During the years 943 to 984 the temple was named "Fengxian."

This period of time coincided with the final years of the life of Zen master Fayan Wenyi, the founder of the Fayan school of Zen. Fayan lived and taught at nearby Qingliang Temple.

The governor of Jiangnan invited Zen master Daoshen to assume the abbacy of Fengxian Temple and to preside at its dedication ceremonies.

As Daoshen ascended the seat, the temple director struck the gavel and said, "Assembled worthies! Behold the first principle!"

Daoshen said, "Actually I know nothing whatsoever. My ignorance is deadly!"

A monk came forward and asked, "What is the first principle?"

Daoshen said, "I just spoke of it."

The monk said, "How should it be understood?"

Daoshen said, "Quick, bow three times."

Then Daoshen said, "Everyone! Tell me! Now who is demonstrating his ignorance?"

Zen master Fengxian and a monk named Ming were among an assembly at Fayan Wenyi's congregation, and they heard a monk ask Fayan the question, "What is form?"

Fayan lifted his whisk into the air.

Then Fayan said, "Cockscomb."

Then Fayan said, "A sweaty robe pressed to your skin."

Fengxian and Ming went forward and asked to address Fayan.

They asked him, "We have just heard the master express form in three ways. Is this not so?"

Fayan said, "Yes."

Fengxian said, "The hawk has flown past Korea."

He then retreated into the congregation.

At that time a certain person named Li Wang was in the assembly. He did not like Fengxian's statement.

Li Wang said to Fayan, "Tomorrow, I will invite these two to come here for tea and we can discuss this again."

The next day after tea, Li Wang was prepared with an embroidered box and some "sword speech."

He addressed Fengxian and Ming, saying, "If you two worthies can ask the appropriate question, then I'll present you with the embroidered box. If you can't, you get the 'sword speech.'"

Fayan then ascended the Dharma seat.

Fengxian again came forward from the congregation and addressed Fayan, saying, "Today I would like to pose another question. Will you permit this, Master?"

Fayan said, "Yes."

Fengxian then said, "The hawk has flown past Korea."

Fengxian then picked up the box and went out. In a few moments the congregation dispersed.

At that time a monk named Fadeng was acting as temple director. He rang the bell to call the monks for a meeting in front of the monks' hall. Fengxian, Ming, and the monks assembled there.

Fadeng then said, "I understand that you two worthies resided for a long while at Yunmen's place. What special teaching do you have? Tell us a thing or two and we'll discuss it."

Fengxian said, "An ancient said that 'when the white egret lands in the field it's like a thousand snowflakes, and when the oriole alights on a tree a branch blooms.' How would the director discuss this?"

The temple director was hesitant. Fengxian hit a sitting cushion and retreated into the crowd.

◆

Once, Fengxian and Ming traveled together to the Huai River. They saw a man pull in a fishing net. Some fish were leaping out of the net and escaping. Fengxian said, "Brother Ming! What a sight! It's just like what a monk does!"

Ming said, "You're right. But it would be better if they didn't get caught in the net in the first place."

Fengxian said, "Brother Ming, your realization is still lacking."

During the middle of the following night, Ming attained enlightenment.

BALING HAOJIAN

BALING HAOJIAN (n.d.) was a disciple of Yunmen Wenyan. The record of Baling's life is sketchy. He taught at Xinkai Temple in ancient Baling City in Yuezhou (now the city of Yueyang in Hunan Province).

At their first meeting, Yunmen asked Baling, "Master Xuefeng said, 'Open the gate and Bodhidharma comes.' I ask you, what does this mean?"

Baling said, "Blocking the master's nostrils."

Yunmen said, "The Spirit King of the earth unleashes his evil! A demon leaps from Mt. Sumeru up to Brahma Heaven and pinches the nostrils of the Heavenly Emperor! Why have you concealed your body in Japan?"

Baling said, "Better that the master not deceive people."

Yunmen said, "Pinching this old monk's nostrils, how will you do it?"

Baling was silent.

Yunmen said, "Now I know you're just studying the flow of words."

❖

When Baling took up residence as a teacher, he did not create a document of succession for his students. He only used three turning phrases as the way to attain the essence of the Yunmen school.

A monk asked, "What is Tao?"

Baling said, "A clear-sighted person falls in a well."

❖

A monk asked, "What is the 'blown feather sword'?"

Baling said, "Coral branches hold up the moon."

❖

A monk asked, "What is old-lady Zen?"

Baling said, "Fresh snow in a silver bowl."

❖

Yunmen said, "In the future, on my remembrance day, just restate these three turning phrases, then you will have repaid my benevolence." Later, when Yunmen's memorial occurred, it was in accordance with his instructions.

❖

A monk asked, "The meaning of the ancestors and the meaning of the scriptural teachings, are they the same or different?"

Baling said, "The cold fowl flies up in the tree. The cold duck dives into the water."

The monk asked, "I don't doubt the three vehicles and the twelve divisions. What is the main affair of our school?"

Baling said, "It's not an affair of patch-robed monks."

The monk asked, "What is the affair of patch-robed monks?"

Baling said, "While eating, seeing the white waves. Losing the hands and forearms."

Baling asked a monk, "Did you come to walk on the mountain? Or did you come for the Buddhadharma?"

The monk said, "In the vast, peaceful world, what Buddhadharma can be spoken?"

Baling said, "A good Zen guest, without affairs."

The monk said, "There have always been affairs."

Baling said, "Didn't you spend the summer here last year?"

The monk said, "No."

Baling said, "In that case, you've come here before but we didn't meet."

When Baling was leaving the mountain, he gave his whisk to a monk. The monk said, "Originally there is only purity. Of what use is a whisk?"

Baling said, "Once you have known purity, nothing can be forgotten."

DESHAN YUANMING, "YUANMI"

DESHAN YUANMING (908–87) was a disciple of Yunmen. Almost nothing is recorded of this teacher's personal life in the ancient texts. He taught at Mt. De, located south of the modern city of Changde in Hunan Province. In case 46 of the *Book of Serenity*, Wansong provides a brief introduction to this teacher, saying that of all of Yunmen's students, it was Deshan who developed the largest group of followers.

Deshan Yuanmi entered the hall to address the monks and said, "Sometimes people understand the affairs which are in front of the monk's quarters. But what about the affairs behind the Buddha hall?"

One day, Deshan Yuanmi said to the assembly, "I have three phrases to reveal to you all. One phrase is 'containing heaven and earth.' One phrase is 'cutting off the myriad streams.' One phrase is 'following wave upon wave.' How do you explain them? If you can do so, then you gained some understanding. If not, you must make haste for the capital city of Changan!"

A monk asked, "What is the phrase which penetrates the dharmakaya?"
Yuanmi said, "A three-foot staff stirs the Yellow River."

A monk asked, "What is it before the hundred flowers bloom?"
Yuanmi said, "The Yellow River's turbid flow."
The monk asked, "What about after they bloom?"
Yuanmi said, "The top of the flag pole points toward the sky."

A monk asked, "How was it before Buddha appeared in the world?"
Yuanmi said, "The river filled with wooden boats."
The monk asked, "What about afterward?"
Yuanmi said, "Stepping here, lifting there."

Zen master Deshan Yuanmi entered the hall and addressed the monks, saying, "You must study living phrases. Do not study dead phrases. Enlightenment that is realized through living phrases is never lost. 'A single mote of dust—a buddha world'; 'a single leaf—a Shakyamuni.' These are dead phrases. 'With a raised eyebrow and the twinkling of an eye'; 'lifting a single finger and establishing Buddha.' These are also dead phrases. 'The mountains, rivers, and great earth'; 'never again making errors'; these are also dead phrases."
A monk then asked, "What are living phrases?"
Yuanmi answered, "A Persian looks up to see it!"
The monk said, "If it is as you say, then we won't make a mistake."
Yuanmi hit the monk.

Deshan Yuanmi entered the hall and said, "Whenever anyone came calling, Master Juzhi just held up one finger. When it was cold, all of heaven was cold; when it was hot, all of heaven was hot."

A monk asked, "What is the style of the master's house?"

Yuanmi said, "The clouds rise on South Mountain. The rain falls on North Mountain."

A monk asked, "Before the ram gets its horns, what is it?"

Yuanmi said, "A rat-shit dog."

The monk asked, "What about after it gets its horns?"

Yuanmi said, "A rat-shit dog."

A monk asked, "How was it before Niutou met the Fourth Ancestor?"

Yuanmi said, "In the fall, yellow leaves fall."

A monk asked, "How was it after he met him?"

Yuanmi said, "In the spring, the grass is itself green."

DONGSHAN SHOUCHU

DONGSHAN SHOUCHU (910–90) was a disciple of Yunmen. He taught in ancient Xiangzhou.

Upon their first meeting, Yunmen asked Dongshan Shouchu, "Where did you come from?"

Shouchu replied, "From Chadu."

Yunmen said, "Where did you spend the summer?"

Shouchu said, "At Baoci Temple in Hunan."

Yunmen then asked, "When did you leave there?"

Shouchu said, "The twenty-fifth day of the eighth month."

Yunmen said, "I spare you three blows with the staff."

The next day Shouchu inquired to Yunmen about the previous day's conversation.

"Yesterday the master said he would spare me three blows of the staff. I don't know what mistake I committed."

Yunmen said, "Rice bag![141] Will you go on like this throughout Jiangxi and Hunan?"[142]

At these words, Shouchu experienced great enlightenment.

Shouchu then said, "From this time forward, I forsake any abode, I'll store not a grain of rice, nor plant even a stalk of vegetable. Receiving what comes from the ten directions, I'll use it to pull out nails and draw out wedges.[143] Taking off the greasy hat and smelly shirt, I'll spread the teaching freely. Is it not joyous to be a monk unconcerned with the world's affairs!"

Yunmen said, "Your body's as big as a palm tree, your mouth is wide like a tiger's!"

Shouchu then bowed.

⸺ ◈ ⸺

After taking up residence as a teacher, Shouchu addressed the monks, saying: "Language doesn't help matters. Speech does not bring forth the truth. Those burdened by language are lost. Those held up by words are deluded. Do you understand? You patch-robed monks should be clear about it. If you come here you must start using the Dharma eye. It's just like I say, but I've erred about one thing. What error is there in the words I've spoken?"

⸺ ◈ ⸺

A monk asked, "What is it when one takes the distant journey?"

Shouchu said, "If the weather is clear you can't go. Wait until the rain soaks your head."

⸺ ◈ ⸺

A monk asked, "What did all the ancient holy ones do?"

Shouchu said, "Enter the mud. Enter the water."

⸺ ◈ ⸺

A monk asked, "What is Buddha?"

Shouchu said, "Three pounds of hemp."

⸺ ◈ ⸺

A monk asked, "What is a seamless monument?"

Shouchu said, "A stone lion at the intersection."

A monk asked, "What is Buddha?"

Shouchu said, "The crystal-clear truth."

A monk asked, "What is the meaning of the phrase, 'The ten thousand conditions cease'?"

Shouchu said, "Inside the pot, the stone person sells date-fruit balls."

A monk asked, "What is Shouchu's sword?"

Shouchu said, "Why?"

The person said, "This student wants to know."

Shouchu said, "Wrong!"

LUOHAN GUICHEN, "DIZANG"

LUOHAN GUICHEN (867–928) was a disciple of Xuansha Shibei. He came from ancient Changshan (located in what is now Zhejiang Province). Classical records say that from early childhood he could speak very well and would not eat meat. He was ordained at Wansui Temple, located in his home province, under a teacher named Wuxiang. At first he closely followed the teachings of the Vinaya, but later declared that just guarding against breaking the vows and adhering to the precepts did not equal true renunciation. He then set off to explore the teachings of the Zen school.

Dizang first studied with Xuefeng Yicun, but was unsuccessful at penetrating the Way. It was Xuefeng's disciple, Xuansha, who is said to have brought Dizang to full awakening. The lamp records indicate that when the following exchange between teacher and student occurred, all of Dizang's doubts were erased.

Xuansha questioned Dizang, saying, "In the three realms there is only mind. How do you understand this?"

Dizang pointed to a chair and said, "What does the master call that?"

Xuansha said, "A chair."

Dizang said, "Then the master can't say that in the three worlds there is only mind."

Xuansha said, "I say that it is made from bamboo and wood. What do you say it's made from?"

Dizang said, "I also say it's made from bamboo and wood."

Xuansha said, "I've searched across the great earth for a person who understands the Buddhadharma, but I haven't found one."

Xuansha passed on certain esoteric teachings, known as the *Samaya*, that Dizang promoted throughout his life. Although Dizang did not aspire to a leading position in the Buddhist community, his reputation as an adept nevertheless spread widely. The magistrate of Zhangzhou [now the city of Zhangpu in Fujian Province] established the Dizang ["Earth Store"] Monastery and invited Dizang to become the abbot there.

Dizang entered the hall and addressed the monks, saying, "If you want to come face-to-face with the essential mystery of our order—here it is! There's no other special thing. If it is something else, then bring it forth and let's see it. If you can't show it, then forget about it. You can't just recite a couple of words and then say that they are the vehicle of our school. How could that be? What two words are they? They are known as the 'essential vehicle.' They are the 'teaching vehicle.' Just when you say 'essential vehicle,' that is the essential vehicle. Speaking the words 'teaching vehicle' is itself the teaching vehicle. Worthy practitioners of Zen, our school's essential vehicle, the Buddhadharma, comes from and is realized through nothing other than the names and words from your own mouths! It is just what you say and do. You come here and use words like 'tranquillity,' 'reality,' 'perfection,' or 'constancy.' Worthy practitioners! What is this that you call 'tranquil' or 'real'? What is it that's 'perfect' or 'constant'? Those of you here on a pilgrimage, you must test the principle of what I'm saying. Let's be open about it. You've stored up a bunch of sounds, forms, names, and words inside your minds. You prattle that 'I can do this,' or 'I'm good at figuring out that,' but actually what can you do? What can you figure out? All that you're remembering and holding on to is just sounds and forms. If it weren't all sounds and forms, names and words, then how would you remember them or figure them out?

"The wind blows and the pine makes a sound. A frog or a duck makes a sound. Why don't you go and listen to those things and figure them out? If everywhere there are meaningful sounds and forms, then how much meaning can be ascribed to this old monk? There's no doubt about it. Sounds and forms assault us every moment. Do you directly face them or not? If you face them directly then your diamond-solid concept of self will melt away. How can this be? Because these sounds penetrate your ears and these forms pierce your eyes, you are overwhelmed by conditions. You are killed by delusion. There's not enough room inside of you for all of these sounds and forms. If you don't face them directly then how will you manage all of these sounds and forms? Do you understand? Face them or not face them. See for yourself!"

After a pause, Dizang continued, "'Perfection.' 'Constancy.' 'Tranquillity.' 'Reality.' Who talks like this? Normal people in the village don't talk like this. Its just some old sages that talk this way and a few of their wicked disciples that spread it around. So now, you don't know good from bad, and you are absorbed in 'perfection' and 'reality.' Some say I don't possess the mysterious excellence of our order's style. Shakyamuni didn't have a tongue! Not like you disciples here who are always pointing at your own chests. To speak about killing, stealing, and lewdness is to speak of grave crimes, but they are light by comparison. It's unending, this vilification of nirvana, this blinding the eyes of beings, this falling in the Avici Hell[144] and swallowing hot iron balls without relief.

"Therefore the ancients said, 'When the transgression is transformed into the host, it no longer offends.' Take care!"

A monk asked, "What is Luohan's single phrase?"
Luohan said, "If I tell you it will turn into two phrases."

A monk asked, "What is Luohan's house style?"
Luohan said, "I can't tell you."
The monk said, "Why not?"
Luohan said, "Because it's my house style."

Zen master Luohan saw a monk approach. He held up his whisk and said, "Do you understand?"
The monk said, "Thank you for your compassionate instruction, Master."
Luohan said, "You see me raise the whisk and you say I'm instructing you. When you see the mountains and rivers each day, do they not instruct you?"
Another time Luohan saw a monk approaching and held up his whisk. The monk shouted in praise and bowed.
Luohan said, "When you saw me raise the whisk you bowed and shouted.

Why is it that when someone holds up a broom you don't shout in praise?"

———— ❖ ————

Luohan asked a monk, "From where do you come?"
The monk said, "From Zouzhou."
Luohan said, "What did you bring with you?"
The monk said, "I didn't bring anything with me."
Luohan said, "Why are you deceiving people?"
The monk remained silent.
Luohan then asked, "Doesn't Zouzhou produce parakeets?"
The monk said, "Those are produced in Longzhou."
Luohan said, "About the same."

———— ❖ ————

Once, Luohan traveled to the provincial capital with Baofu and Changqing.
They saw some discarded peonies by the road.
Baofu said, "What a wonderful bunch of flowers."
Changqing said, "I've never seen such flowers."
Luohan said, "Too bad. It's a bunch of flowers."
([Later,] Xuanjue said, "Was the speech of these three old Zen masters intimate or not? If Luohan spoke like this, to where had he fallen?")

———— ❖ ————

Upon his death, Dizang received the posthumous title "Zen Master True Response."[145]

WANG YANBIN

WANG YANBIN (n.d.) was the governor of ancient Quanzhou and a lay disciple of Changqing Huileng.

Once, lay official Wang Yanbin entered the Buddha hall at Zhaoqing Temple. He pointed to an offering bowl and asked the temple attendant, "Whose bowl is this?"
The attendant said, "It's the Medicine Buddha's bowl."[146]
Layman Wang said, "I've heard that it is the 'Great Dragon's' bowl."

The attendant said, "Wait until a great dragon comes here, then it will be a great dragon bowl."

Layman Wang said, "What would you do if a dragon suddenly arrived here riding the wind and waves?"

The attendant said, "I wouldn't pay attention to anything else."

Layman Wang said, "What you said misses the mark." ([Later,] Xuansha commented, "Even if you expended your effort to the utmost, how could you go anywhere?" Baofu Zhan said, "Zen master Baizhang, like an inverted bowl, firmly supported taking refuge in Buddha, Dharma, and Sangha." Yunmen said, "His sun shone brightly in the sky. He didn't want to let down his teacher.")

——— ◆ ———

Zen master Changqing said to the layman Wang, "Xuefeng once raised his whisk to give instruction to a monk. The monk then walked out. If I saw such behavior, I'd call him back and give him a painful blow."

Layman Wang said, "From what mind would such behavior arise?"

Changqing said, "If he were more amenable, I'd let him go."

············· ◆ ·············

Layman Wang once visited Zhaoqing Temple during tea time. Head monk Lang and Mingzhao tried to pick up the teapot from the stove, but it fell between them and spilled.

Layman Wang said, "What's under the stove?"

Lang said, "The Oven God."

Wang said, "If it's the Oven God, why did the tea get spilled?"

Lang said, "Manage it for a thousand days and lose it in a morning."

Wang shook out his sleeves and went out.

Mingzhao said, "Head Monk Lang eats Zhaoqing Temple rice, but still enjoys snacks outside."

Lang said, "What do you mean?"

Mingzhao said, "No one gets it that easily."

············· ◆ ·············

One day, Wang Yanbin entered the temple. He saw that the door to the abbot's quarters was closed.

He asked attendant Yan, "Does anyone dare to say that the abbot is here or not?"

Attendant Yan said, "Does anyone dare to say that the abbot isn't here or not?"

Mingzhao Deqian

Mingzhao Deqian (n.d.) was a disciple of Luoshan Daoxian. He taught in ancient Wuzhou (now the city of Jinhua in Zhejiang Province). In the *Wudeng Huiyuan* it is recorded that Mingzhao's quick and incisive Zen style led his contemporaries to fear his formidable skills in Dharma combat. Mingzhao taught at Wuzhou for forty years.

Mingzhao pointed to a painting on the wall and asked a monk, "What god is that?"

The monk said, "The benevolent god who protects the Dharma."

Mingzhao said, "Where did he go during the Hui Chang persecution?"

The monk didn't answer.

Mingzhao told the monk to ask attendant Yan. Yan said, "In what kalpa did you encounter this problem?"

The monk related this to Mingzhao. Mingzhao said, "Be lenient with attendant Yan. Later he'll reside over a congregation of a thousand, so of what use is it?"

The monk bowed and then asked Mingzhao the question again.

Mingzhao said, "He went everywhere!"

\+

Mingzhao went to Tan Chang's place.

Tan said, "People study the phrase 'One person present must arrive. A half-person present also must arrive.'"

Mingzhao then asked, "Not asking about 'one person being present,' what is a 'half-person being present'?"

Tan didn't answer. Later Tan instructed Xiaoshi to ask Mingzhao about this.

Mingzhao said, "If you want to know what a half-person being present is— it's just a fellow making mud balls."

\+

Qing Balu raised a question to Mingzhao concerning the story of Yangshan sticking a hoe in the ground. He said, "Did the ancient's meaning lie in his clasping his hands or was it in his sticking the hoe in the ground?"

Mingzhao called, "Qing!"

Qing responded, "Yes?"

Mingzhao said, "Are you still dreaming about Yangshan?"

Qing said, "I don't want the master to give an explanation of this. I just want to talk about it."

Mingzhao said, "If you only want to talk then there are fifteen hundred teachers in front of the hall."

◆

Mingzhao went to Shuangyan Monastery. On one occasion the abbot there invited Mingzhao to drink tea. Yan said, "I'll present you with a question. If you answer it successfully, then I'll give up my position as abbot and hand it over to you. If you don't answer successfully, then I won't give it up."

He then quoted a verse from the *Diamond Sutra*, "'All of the buddhas and all of their *anuttara-samyaksambodhi* dharmas come forth from this scripture.' Who is it who speaks this scripture?"

Mingzhao said, "The one who speaks it does not speak, and thereby it is revealed. But what about you, Master, who do you say recites this scripture?"

Yan did not answer.

Mingzhao then said, "All the sages and saints each hold a difference from the Dharma of nonaction, and thus they take nonaction as the highest principle. From where does the difference arise? As for the difference, is it an error or not? If it is an error, then all of the sages and saints have each erred. If it is not an error, then what is it that is a difference?"

Yan again did not speak.

Mingzhao said, "Yee! It's what Xuefeng said."

◆

When Mingzhao was at Zhizhu Temple in Wuzhou, he often did not get his ration of pure water. The temple attendant asked him, "Your Reverence, you don't know tainted from pure. Why don't you get your pure water?"

Mingzhao jumped off the meditation bench, picked up the pure water pitcher and said, "Is this tainted or pure?"

The attendant didn't answer.

Mingzhao then broke the pitcher.

◆

When Mingzhao was near death, he went into the hall to say farewell to the monks and give them final instructions.

A monk asked, "Master, where will you be one hundred years from now?"

Mingzhao lifted one foot and said, "Look beneath my foot."

In the middle of the night he said to his attendant, "Formerly, at the assembly on Vulture Peak, the Tathagata Shakyamuni lifted both feet and they emitted a hundred rays of brilliant light."[147]

Mingzhao then lifted his feet and said, "How many do I have?"

The attendant said, "In former times, Shakyamuni. Tonight, the master."

Mingzhao then pointed at the attendant's eyebrows and said, "You're not forsaking me?"

Mingzhao then recited a verse:

"A flashing blade exposes the monastery's complete majesty.
All of you, protect it well.
Within the fire, an iron ox gives birth to a calf.
At this juncture, who will compile my teaching?"

After reciting this verse, Mingzhao sat in a cross-legged position and passed away. His stupa was built at the temple.

Fifteenth Generation

SHOUSHAN XINGNIAN   LIANGSHAN YUANGUAN

ZHIMEN GUANGZUO   LIANHUA FENGXIAN

WENSHU YINGZHEN   FAYAN WENYI

QINGXI HONGJIN   LONGJI SHAOXIU

SHOUSHAN XINGNIAN

SHOUSHAN XINGNIAN (926–93) was a disciple of Fengxue Yanzhao. He came from ancient Laizhou (now in Ye County in Shandong Province). Shoushan is remembered for having concealed and carried on the Linji lineage during the turbulent end of the Tang dynasty. As a young man, he left home to live at Nanchan Temple, where he took the monk's vows. Later, as he roamed China, Shoushan daily chanted the *Lotus Sutra* and thus gained the nickname "Nian-fahua ['Chanting Lotus Sutra']." The *Wudeng Huiyuan* provides an account of the circumstances of the transmission from Fengxue to Shoushan.

One day when Shoushan was in attendance, Fengxue said tearfully, "Tragically, the way of Linji will perish with me."

Shoushan asked, "Among the monks is there no one who can carry on?"

Fengxue said, "There are many clever ones, but few who see self-nature."

Shoushan said, "Is there no one in particular?"

Fengxue said, "Although I've watched for a long while, still I'm afraid that as for this path, I can't pass it to anyone."

Shoushan said, "It should be possible. Please tell me more about it."

Later Fengxue entered the hall. With the blue lotus eye of the World-Honored One he gazed across the assembled monks. Then he said, "The time has come for you to speak out. If you say nothing you will have buried the ancients. But what will you say?"

Shoushan shook his sleeves and went out.

Fengxue then threw down his staff and returned to his room. His attendant followed him and asked, "Why can't Nianfahua face you?"

Fengxue said, "Nianfahua understands."

The next day, Shoushan and a monk named Zhen Yuantou were talking with Fengxue.

Fengxue asked Zhen, "What is it that the World-Honored One didn't say?"

Zhen said, "The dove coos in the treetop."

Fengxue said, "Why say these silly verses? Why don't you grasp and embody the words?"

Then Fengxue asked Shoushan, "How about you?"

Shoushan said, "In deportment, uphold the ancient road, not letting the silent function fall."

Then Fengxue said to Zhen, "Why can't you see what Nianfahua has said?"

Fengxue thus passed on the Dharma seal to Shoushan. During the chaotic fall of the Tang dynasty, Shoushan "covered his tracks and concealed his light," coming forth again with the teaching only when conditions were appropriate. Then Shoushan began teaching in Ruzhou on the mountain from which he gained his name. He later served as abbot at the Guangjiao Monastery on Bao'an Mountain (located in modern Hebei Province).

Shoushan held up a bamboo comb before the assembly and said, "If you say it's a bamboo comb then you're grasping. If you don't call it a bamboo comb you're turning away. So what do you say?"

------- ◆ -------

A monk asked Zen master Shoushan Xingnian, "Can a single tree blossom or not?"

Shoushan said, "It's long been in blossom."

The monk said, "Can it bear fruit or not?"

Shoushan said, "It suffered a frost last night!"

------- ◆ -------

A monk said, "I'd like to know if you can explain Linji's shout and Deshan's stick."

Shoushan said, "You try it."

The monk shouted.

Shoushan said, "Blind!"

The monk shouted again.

Shoushan said, "What's this blind fellow shouting for?"

The monk bowed.

Shoushan hit him.

A monk asked, "What is the mind of the ancient buddhas?"

Shoushan said, "Three pounds of Zhen Province hemp."

A monk asked, "I have long been submerged in delusion. I ask the master to receive me as a student."

Shoushan said, "I don't have time for that."

The monk said, "How can the master act in this manner?"

Shoushan said, "If you want to practice, then practice. If you want to sit, then sit."

A monk asked, "What is a bodhisattva before she becomes a buddha?"

Shoushan said, "All beings."

The monk said, "How about after she becomes a buddha?"

Shoushan said, "All beings. All beings."

A monk asked, "What is Shoushan?"

Shoushan said, "East Mountain is high. West Mountain is low."

The monk asked, "What about the person inside the mountain?"

Shoushan said, "Fortunately for you my staff isn't in my hand."

A monk asked, "A single phrase from Caoxi was heard by everyone on earth. I'd like to know if the master has a phrase that everyone can hear?"

Shoushan said, "They don't go outside the gate."

The monk said, "Why don't they go outside the gate?"

Shoushan said, "Because they are given to everyone on earth."

Near death, Shoushan entered the hall to bid farewell to the monks. He then recited this verse.

"The Silver World, the Golden Body,
Impassioned or passionless, together one Truth,
When brightness and darkness are exhausted, neither shines forth.
The sun past its apex reveals the whole body."

After reciting this verse, the master sat peacefully and then passed away. A stupa was built to house his sacred relics.

Liangshan Yuanguan

Liangshan Yuanguan (n.d.) was a disciple of the Caodong lineage master, Tongan Guanzhi.

A monk asked Zen master Liangshan Yuanguan, "What is the style of the master's house?"

Liangshan said, "The current in Yiyang River is swift, and the fish move slowly. The pine trees on White Deer Mountain are tall, and the birds nest there with difficulty."

◆

A monk asked, "What is the self?"

Liangshan said, "The emperor of the universe. The general who commands the strategic pass."

The monk then asked, "When this state is realized, then what?"

Liangshan said, "The bright moon in the sky. Sitting silently in one's room."

◆

Zen master Liangshan would recite this verse:

"The song of Liangshan,
Even the skilled find it hard to sing.
These ten years I've searched for someone to sing it,
But 'til now I've found no one."

◆

Zen master Liangshan said to the monks, "If you let down your line into the four seas you'll only catch ferocious dragons. But if you demonstrate true ability, you'll seek to know your own self."

ZHIMEN GUANGZUO

ZHIMEN GUANGZUO (d. 1031) was a disciple of Xianglin Chengyuan. His home was in Zhejiang Province. He traveled to Yizhou (near modern Chengdu City) where he studied under Xianglin Chengyuan. After receiving the mind-seal from Xianglin he first taught at Shuangchuan in Suizhou. Later, he moved to Zhimen Temple, from which he derived his mountain name.

A monk asked Zen master Zhimen, "What is Buddha?"

Zhimen said, "When the straw sandals are worn out, continue barefoot."

The monk asked, "What is the affair that is beyond Buddha?"

Zhimen said, "The tip of the staff upholds the sun and moon."

⸰

A monk asked, "What is the meaning of the First Ancestor's coming from the west?"

Zhimen said, "The eyes can't see the nose."

The person then asked, "What is it when one understands in this manner?"

Zhimen said, "Smelling your nose."

⸰

Zhimen entered the hall and addressed the monks, saying, "If there is one Dharma, then Vairochana becomes a commoner. If the ten thousand dharmas are lacking, then Samantabhadra loses his realm. Just when it is like this, Manjushri has nowhere to show his head, and if he can't show his head, then the golden-haired lion is cut in two. If you enjoy a bowl of food, don't eat the spicy meat cakes."

⸰

A monk asked, "What is the pure dharmakaya?"

Zhimen said, "The entire eye is dust."

⸰

A monk asked, "What is it before the ancient mirror is polished?"

Zhimen said, "It's just a piece of copper."

The monk then asked, "What about after it is polished?"

Zhimen said, "Then you can take it."

⸰

A monk asked, "What is perceived by the pupil of the diamond-eye?"

Zhimen said, "A handful of sand."

The monk then asked, "Why is it like that?"

Zhimen said, "It's not a noble realm."

◆

Zen master Zhimen entered the hall and addressed the monks, saying, "All of you put your staffs over your shoulder and go traveling, leaving one monastery and traveling to the next. How many different types of monasteries do you say there are? It's either a sandalwood monastery surrounded by sandalwood, or it's a thistle monastery surrounded by thistles. Or it could be a thistle monastery surrounded by sandalwood, or a sandalwood monastery surrounded by thistles. Of these four types of monasteries, in which type is each of you willing to spend your life? If you don't find a place to pass your life securely then you're just wearing out your sandals for no reason, and eventually the day will come when the King of Hell will take away all of your sandal money!"

LIANHUA FENGXIAN, "HERMIT OF LOTUS FLOWER PEAK"

LIANHUA FENGXIAN (n.d.) was a disciple of Fengxian Daoshen in the Yunmen Zen school. He lived on Lotus Flower Peak in the vicinity of Mt. Tiantai in Zhejiang Province.

A monk asked Lianhua Fengxian, "What is the call of the mud ox of the snowy peaks?"

Lianhua said, "Listen."

The monk said, "What is the cry of Yunmen's wooden horse?"

Lianhua said, "Sound."

◆

When Lianhua was about to die, he held up his staff and asked the assembly, "When the ancients reached *this*, why didn't they agree to remain here?"

The monks didn't answer.

Lianhua said, "Because by this path no power is attained."

Then, Lianhua said, "After all, what is it?"

He then placed the staff on his shoulder and said, "Just place your staff over your shoulder and pay no mind to people. Enter directly into the thousand, the ten thousand peaks."

When he finished saying these words, he passed away.

WENSHU YINGZHEN

WENSHU YINGZHEN (n.d.) was a student of Deshan Yuanming in the Yunmen Zen school. He lived and taught in ancient Dingzhou (the area of modern Changde City in Hunan Province).

Zen master Wenshu Yingzhen entered the hall and addressed the monks, saying, "A straight hook catches fierce dragons. A crooked hook catches shrimp, frogs, and worms. Are there any dragons here?"

After a long pause, Wenshu said, "There's no merit in belaboring it."

◆

A monk asked Zen Master Wenshu, "Before the jeweled sword comes out of the sheath, what then?"

Wenshu said, "Where is it?"

The monk asked, "What about after it comes out?"

Wenshu said, "The arms are long but the sleeves are short."

◆

A monk asked, "When the ancients clapped their hands, what did this mean?"

Wenshu said, "If the house has no young gentlemen, it won't produce any princes."

FAYAN WENYI, "QINGLIANG"

 FAYAN WENYI (885–958) was a disciple of Dizang. He came from ancient Yuhang (near the city of Hangzhou). At the age of seven, he entered a monastery headed by a Zen master named Quanwei. Well educated and erudite as a young man, Fayan studied the Confucian classics. He received ordination at the age of twenty at Kaiyuan Temple in Yuezhou (now the city of Shaoxing in Zhejiang Province). He then proceeded to Maoshan, a seaport in Ye County of Zhejiang Province, where he studied under the Vinaya master Xijiao. Later, Fayan studied Zen under Changqing Huileng. While on a pilgrimage with some other monks, Fayan and his friends were sidetracked by a snowstorm and forced to stay at the Dizang Monastery. Luohan Guichen served as abbot there. The *Transmission of the Lamp* provides the following account of their exchange:

> Guichen asked, "Where are you going?"
> Fayan replied, "On an ongoing pilgrimage."
> Guichen said, "Why do you go on a pilgrimage?"
> Fayan replied, "I don't know."
> Guichen said, "Not knowing is most intimate."
> At these words Fayan instantly experienced enlightenment.

The record of Zen master Fayan Wenyi provides a different account of his encounter with Dizang and his subsequent awakening:

> When the snow was gone, the three monks bade farewell and started to depart. Dizang accompanied them to the gate and asked, "I've heard you say several times that 'the three realms are only mind and the myriad dharmas are only consciousness.'"
> Dizang then pointed to a rock lying on the ground by the gate and said, "So do you say that this rock is inside or outside of mind?"
> Fayan said, "Inside."
> Dizang said, "How can a pilgrim carry such a rock in his mind while on pilgrimage?"
> Dumbfounded, Fayan couldn't answer. He put his luggage down at Dizang's

feet and asked him to clarify the truth. Each day for the next month or so Fayan spoke about the Way with Dizang and demonstrated his understanding.

Dizang would always say, "The Buddhadharma isn't like that."

Finally, Fayan said, "I've run out of words and ideas."

Dizang said, "If you want to talk about Buddhadharma, everything you see embodies it."

At these words Fayan experienced great enlightenment.

Penetrating the great affair under Zen master Luohan Guichen, Fayan became his Dharma heir. He went on to establish one of the five traditionally recognized schools of Zen. The Fayan school style is popularly traced to Dizang's teacher, Xuansha. However, Fayan successfully spread the school's influence, and its teachings became synonymous with his name.

Fayan first taught at Chongshou Monastery in Linchuan. Later he resided at the Qingliang Monastery in Jinling, where his students are said to have numbered up to one thousand. During Fayan's lifetime the regent of the Southern Song dynasty honored him with the title, "Great Teacher Peaceful Wisdom." The school he established incorporated elements from the Huayan school of Buddhism, including the principle "in all things manifested."

The great Zen adepts used everyday events and discourses as leavening for realization. Fayan was no exception. His recorded talks and actions demonstrate numerous examples of turning a pivotal phrase.

Fayan traveled to Linchuan, where the provincial governor invited him to become abbot of Chongshou Monastery. On dedication day, Fayan remained sitting in the tea hall and did not leave it.

A monk said to him, "Monks from everywhere are now crowded around the master's Dharma seat waiting for you to speak."

Fayan said, "In that case, the monks are practicing with a genuine worthy!"

After a while, Fayan ascended the Dharma seat.

A monk said, "The assembly has gathered. We ask the master to expound the Dharma."

Fayan said, "You've all been standing here too long!"

Then he said, "Since all of you have assembled here, I can't say nothing at all. So I'll give you all an expedient that was offered by one of the ancients. Take care!"

Fayan then left the Dharma seat.

———— ◆ ————

Once, when a monk was visiting Fayan, he pointed to a blind. Two monks went to roll it up. Fayan said, "One gain, one loss."

◆

A monk asked, "What was the style of the ancient buddhas?"
Fayan said, "Where can it not be completely seen?"

◆

Fayan directed a monk to get soil for the lotus plant basin. When the monk came with the soil, Fayan said, "Did you get the soil from the east side or the west side of the bridge?"
The monk said, "From the east side."
Fayan said, "It's real. It's illusory."

◆

Fayan asked the monk Jiao, "Did you come by boat or by land?"
Jiao replied, "By boat."
Fayan said, "Where is the boat?"
Jiao said, "The boat is in the river."
Jiao then left. Fayan turned to a monk standing to one side and asked, "Did that monk who was just here have the eye or not?"

◆

Fayan asked a monk where he came from.
The monk said, "From Libai Dasheng ['worship the great holy one'] in Sizhou."
Fayan said, "Did the 'great holy' come out of his stupa this year or not?"
The monk said, "He came out."
Fayan then asked a monk standing to one side, "Do you say he went to Sizhou or not?"

◆

A monk asked, "If someone is seeking an understanding of Buddha, what's the best path to doing so?"
Fayan said, "It doesn't pass here."

◆

A monk asked, "What is the thing toward which an advanced student should pay particular attention?"

Fayan said, "If the student has anything whatsoever which is particular then he can't be called advanced."

————— ✦ —————

A monk asked, "What is a true patch of earth?"
Fayan said, "Not a single patch of earth is true."

————— ✦ —————

A monk asked, "What is the ultimate teaching of all buddhas?"
Fayan said, "You have it too."

————— ✦ —————

When Fayan became abbot of Qingliang Temple, he addressed the monks, saying, "Students of Zen need only act according to conditions to realize the Way. When it's cold, they're cold. When it's hot, they're hot. If you must understand the meaning of buddha nature then just pay attention to what's going on. There is no shortage of old and new expedients. Haven't you heard about Shitou? Upon reading the *Zhao Lun* he exclaimed, 'Understanding that all things are the self. This is what all the ancient holy ones realized!' Shitou also said, 'The holy ones did not have a self. Nor was there anything that was not their selves.' Shitou composed the *Cantongjie*. The first phrase in that text says, 'The mind of the great sage of India.' There's no need to go beyond this phrase. Within it is what is always put forth as the teaching of our school. All of you should understand that the myriad beings are your own self, and that across the great earth there isn't a single dharma that can be observed. Shitou also admonishes, 'Don't pass your days and nights in vain.' What I have just said may be realized if you seize the opportunity before you. If you miss the opportunity, then that is 'passing your days and nights in vain.' If you spend your time trying to understand form in the middle of nonform, just going on in this way, you are missing your opportunity. So, do we therefore say that we should realize nonform in the midst of form? Is that right? If your understanding is like this, then you're nowhere near it. You're just going along with the illness of two-headed madness. Of what use is it? All of you, just do what is appropriate to the moment! Take care!"

————— ✦ —————

A monk asked, "What is the first principle?"
Fayan said, "When I speak to you, that is the second principle."

There is a story that in former times a Zen monk lived alone in a cottage. Above his door he wrote the word "mind." Above his window he wrote the word "mind," and on his wall he wrote the word, "mind."

Zen master Fayan said, "Above his door he should have written, 'door.' Above his window he should have written 'window,' and on his wall he should have written the word 'wall.'"

A monk asked, "What is the second moon?"

Fayan said, "The phenomena of the universe."

The monk asked, "What is the first moon?"

Fayan said, "The universe of phenomena."

Once, when sand filled in and obstructed a new spring that was being dug at the temple, Zen master Fayan said, "The mouth of the spring is obstructed by sand. When the Dharma eye is obstructed, what is it that obscures it?"

The monks were unable to answer.

Fayan said, "It's obstructed by the eye."

Fayan had sixty-three Dharma heirs. Though the influence of his school was widespread during and for a period after his life, the lineage died out after five generations.

After his death, Fayan received the posthumous title "Great Zen Master Dharma Eye."

QINGXI HONGJIN, "JINSHAN"

QINGXI HONGJIN (d. 954) was the disciple of and head monk and attendant for Luohan Guichen. He first met his teacher when, with his friends Fayan and Xiushan, he sought shelter from a snowstorm at Dizang Temple. The initial story about Jinshan in the *Wudeng Huiyuan* does not follow the usual practice of describing the circumstances of his enlightenment. Instead, it contrasts Jinshan's understanding with that of his friend Xiushan, and it is Xiushan who comes to a realization.

Jinshan served as head monk at Dizang Monastery. One day, Dizang entered the hall. Two monks came forward and bowed.

Dizang said, "Both wrong."

The two monks were speechless.

After leaving the hall they asked Xiushan [Longji Shaoxiu] about this matter.

Xiushan said, "You yourself are grand and majestic. Is it not a mistake to bow and inquire of others?"

When Jinshan heard this he did not agree with it.

Xiushan then asked him, "What do you think?"

Jinshan said, "If you are in the midst of darkness, how can you help others?"

Xiushan angrily went to the abbot's room and sought the opinion of Dizang.

Dizang pointed down the pathway and said, "The cook should go into the kitchen."

At these words, Xiushan realized his error.

Little biographical information is recorded about Jinshan. He appears in case 70 of the *Book of Serenity*, which is entitled "Jinshan Asks about the Nature of Life." The same story also appears in the *Wudeng Huiyuan*, although the text is somewhat different. The following translation is from the latter volume.

Jinshan asked Xiushan, "Clearly understanding that the nature of life is unborn, why is there a stream of birth and death?"

Xiushan said, "These bamboo shoots will later become bamboo, so if you try to use them now for strapping, will they work properly?"

Jinshan said, "In the future you will be self-enlightened."

Xiushan said, "I am just what you see. So what do you mean?"

Jinshan pointed and said, "This is the superintendent's room. That is the head cook's room."

Xiushan then bowed.

———— ❖ ————

After Jinshan took up residence as a teacher, a monk asked, "Everyone blindly gropes for form, each espousing some erroneous view. If you suddenly encountered a clear-eyed person, then what?"

Jinshan said, "You go ask this to the ten directions."

———— ❖ ————

Once, when Jinshan went for a walk, a large group of monks followed him. He said to them, "What were the words and phrases of the ancients? Everyone discuss it."

A monk of the congregation named Congyi started to ask a question. Jinshan said, "This hairless ass!" Congyi was suddenly enlightened.

LONGJI SHAOXIU, "XIUSHAN"

LONGJI SHAOXIU (d. 954) was a disciple of Dizang and a Dharma brother of Fayan Wenyi. He is remembered by the name Xiushan. According to the *Transmission of the Lamp*, Xiushan's spiritual attainment was comparable with that of Fayan, and these two friends set off together from Dizang's temple on a pilgrimage:

> Talking as they traveled, Fayan suddenly asked Xiushan a question, saying: "The ancients said that the single body is revealed in the ten thousand forms. Did they thus dispel the ten thousand forms or not?"
>
> Xiushan said, "They didn't dispel them."
>
> Fayan said, "What do you say dispels or doesn't dispel them?"
>
> Xiushan was confused, and returned to see Dizang.
>
> Dizang asked him, "You haven't been gone long, why have you come back?"
>
> Xiushan said, "There's an unresolved matter, so I'm not willing to go traveling to mountains and rivers until it's resolved."
>
> Dizang said, "It's not bad that you travel to difficult mountains and rivers."
>
> But Xiushan didn't understand Dizang's meaning, so he asked, "The single body is revealed in the ten thousand forms. What does this mean?"
>
> Dizang said, "Do you say the ancients dispelled the ten thousand forms or not?"
>
> Xiushan said, "They didn't dispel them."
>
> Dizang said, "It's two."
>
> For a time Xiushan was lost in thought, and then he said, "I don't know whether the ancients dispelled the ten thousand forms or not."
>
> Dizang said, "What is it you call the ten thousand forms?"
>
> Xiushan thereupon attained enlightenment.

Xiushan entered the hall and addressed the monks, saying, "Ordinary people possess it completely but they don't know it. The saints possess it completely but don't understand it. If the saint understands it, then he or she is an ordinary person. If ordinary people understand it, then they are saints. In these forms of speech there is one principle and two meanings. If a person can distinguish this principle, then he will have no hindrance to finding an entrance to the essential doctrine. If he can't distinguish it, then he can't say he has no doubt. Take care!"

Zen master Xiushan asked a monk, "Where have you come from?"
The monk said, "From Cuiyan."
Xiushan said, "What does Cuiyan say to provide instruction to his disciples?"
The monk said, "He often says, 'Going out—meeting Maitreya Buddha.[148] Going in—seeing Shakyamuni.'"
Shaoxiu said, "How can he talk like that?"
The monk said, "What do you say, Master?"
Xiushan said, "Going out—who do you meet? Going in—who do you see?"
At these words the monk had an insight.

A monk asked, "How can one get out of the three realms?"
Xiushan said, "When the three realms become one, then you escape them."
The monk said, "If not the three realms, what is it?"
Xiushan said, "Where is a place that isn't of the three realms?"

Xiushan addressed the monks, saying, "Rolling up the screen removes the barrier. Closing the door creates an obstruction. It is just this opening or closing that people have not understood from ancient times to the present. What is to be understood is itself an obstruction, but if one doesn't understand then one's function is unrealized."

Sixteenth Generation

FENYANG SHANZHAO   SHEXIAN GUIXING

DAYANG JINGXUAN   JIUFENG QIN   XUEDOU CHONGXIAN

BAO'EN XUANZE   GUIZONG CEZHEN   BAOCI XINGYAN

CHONGSHOU QIZHOU   TIANTAI DESHAO

TIANPING CONGYI

FENYANG SHANZHAO, "WUDE"

FENYANG SHANZHAO (947–1024) was a disciple and Dharma heir of Shoushan Xingnian. He came from ancient Taiyuan (now a place in modern Shanxi Province). Both of Fenyang's parents died before he reached the age of fourteen, so at this young age, he entered upon the homeless life of a monk. Extremely intelligent and well versed in the Confucian and other classics, Fenyang embodied the keen intelligence and wisdom that imbued the greatest masters of ancient times. He traveled widely and reportedly gained instruction from seventy-one teachers. In Ruzhou, Fenyang studied under Shoushan Xingnian, who confirmed his great awakening and passed to him the mind-seal of the Linji school. After Shoushan died, Fenyang was invited to live and teach at the Taizi Zen Temple, a subtemple of the Taiping ("Great Peace") Monastery in Fenzhou (now the city of Fenyang in Shanxi Province). He remained there for the next thirty years, forcefully expounding a brilliant Dharma. Fenyang's familiarity with the teaching styles of many masters was turned to great use. His teachings drew widely from the different schools. As one example, he is known as the first Linji master to use the Caodong school system of "five ranks."

Fenyang is particularly remembered for his literary achievements and the direct use of Zen stories as a part of Zen training. The development of "literary Zen," including the formal collection and incorporation into practice of kōans, is traced to Fenyang. This emphasis on the use of kōans gave rise to their widespread collection into songgu texts, books of kōans with amended verses. Later, others amended commentaries to the songgu texts and yet another literary form, known as niansong, was the result. Well-known examples of these books, such as the *Blue Cliff Record* and the *Gateless Gate*, became widely incorporated into Zen practice.

The development of "literary Zen" was a new and significant development for Zen practice and culture. It has already been shown that, although Zen purportedly shunned using literature of any sort to transmit its essential teaching, the use of certain scriptures is nevertheless closely associated with Zen's historical development. As noted earlier, Bodhidharma and Daman Hongren employed the *Lankavatara* and *Diamond* sutras respectively as teaching devices. Later, students recorded their teachers' lectures and compiled these lectures into books. But Fenyang went beyond what existed and created a new corpus of literature unique in style and content to the Zen tradition. The songgu literary style that developed from his efforts flourished in the Zen monastic system and spilled into the greater current of Chinese conventional literature.

The songgu genre of literature took as its basis the dialogues between Zen masters and students of earlier times. Presenting an introduction to each of these "public cases," songgu writers then appended their own laudatory verses to the core stories. The writers did not try to directly explain what the public cases meant. After all, the essential meaning was still considered to be beyond words. Instead, their verses contained allegories and subtle inferences to evoke an intuitive or abstract appreciation and realization.

Other writers amended songgu texts with their own commentaries. The resulting niansong texts would often accumulate the unique comments of different enlightened teachers over a long period of time.

Although Fenyang Shanzhao was himself of the Linji lineage, the stories used in his songgu were of no particular school or current of Zen history. Stories from all of the Zen schools were used in his works. Similarly, the later niansong texts, the *Blue Cliff Record* and the *Book of Serenity*, although associated with the Linji and Caodong Zen schools respectively, contained a large number of stories about Yunmen Wenyan and others of different Zen schools.

The public cases that songgu praised were not always concerned with famous figures in Zen history. Some stories took as their basis traditional scriptural passages, an indication of the influence that sutras continued to exert upon Zen practitioners.

Fenyang's contribution to the development of Zen literature, and thus to the preservation of the Zen tradition, can hardly be overstated. His verses were widely read and quoted during his own lifetime.

Fenyang studied under fifty-seven teachers. At last he came to Shoushan.

Fenyang asked Shoushan, "What was the meaning of Baizhang rolling up his sitting mat?"

Shoushan said, "When the dragon robe sleeve is shaken open the entire body is revealed."

Fenyang said, "What does that mean?"

Shoushan said, "It's like a king that goes out walking. There are no fox tracks."

At these words Fenyang was enlightened. He prostrated himself to Shoushan, then arose and said, "The moon of empty worlds reflected in ten thousand ancient pools, sought twice, thrice, is finally found."

◆

Fenyang traveled through the regions of Hunan and Hubei. Everywhere he went the local officials invited him to assume the abbacy of well-known temples. In all, he received eight invitations, but he did not accept any of them. When Shoushan Xingnian died, the Buddhist clergy and lay officials of his district in Fenzhou dispatched the monk Qicong as an envoy to invite Fenyang to assume the vacant abbacy.[149]

[When Qicong arrived] Fenyang was sleeping with the door to his room closed. Qicong pushed it open, walked in, and said, "Because of the great matter of Buddhadharma, you should abandon trifling matters. Zen master Fengxue feared that spurious talk would exterminate the Linji school. Fortunately, he discovered our late master. But now he also has left the world. You have the ability to carry on the great Dharma of the Tathagatas. There's no time for lazily napping."

Fenyang jumped up and grabbed Qicong's hand, saying, "Only you could make such a speech. I'll pack my things immediately. I'm going with you."

◆

After Fenyang assumed the abbacy at Fenzhou, he said to the monks, "Beneath Fenyang's gate a West River lion crouches.[150] If anyone comes near he chomps them to death. Is there any expedient to help people enter Fenyang's gate and personally see the person of Fenyang? Anyone who sees the person of Fengyang can become the teacher of the buddhas and ancestors. Those who can't see the person of Fenyang are dead right where they stand. Right now, is there anyone who can enter? Hurry up and go in so that you can avoid a wasted life! If you're not an adept of the dragon gate then you'll get a mark on your forehead![151] Who here is an adept of the Dragon Gate? You're all getting a mark!"

Fenyang then raised his staff and said, "Go back! Go back!"

◆

A monk asked, "What is the source of the great way?"

Fenyang said, "Digging in the earth to find the blue sky."

The monk asked, "What is attained by doing this?"

Fenyang said, "Not knowing the deep mystery."

———— ❖ ————

A monk asked, "What is it when guest meets guest?"

Fenyang said, "Put your palms together in front of the hut and ask the World-Honored One."

The monk asked, "What is it when guest meets host?"

Fenyang said, "The other is not a companion."

The monk asked, "What about when host meets guest?"

Fenyang said, "The clouds are arrayed above the sea. Draw the sword and disturb the dragon's gate."

The monk then asked, "What is it when host meets host?"

Fenyang said, "Three heads and six arms terrify heaven and earth. Furiously the emperor's bell is struck."

The following passages appear in *The Record of Fenyang Wude*.

A monk asked, "What is the Way?"

Fenyang said, "Emptiness is unobstructed. You can roam everywhere."

The monk said, "I deeply thank the master for this instruction."

Fenyang said, "What do you proclaim as the Way?"

The monk was silent.

Fenyang said, "You can ride the tiger, but you can't get off."

———— ❖ ————

A monk asked, "When Zen master Qingyuan Xingsi was asked about the great meaning of our school, why did he answer, 'What is the price of rice in Luling?'"

Fenyang said, "When that home-leaver in pursuit of the Way asked about the great meaning of our school, and Qingyuan answered about the price of rice in Luling, mind and environment were, in one instant, both annihilated."

———— ❖ ————

A monk asked, "What should be done if the mind-ground is troubled?"

Fenyang said, "Who is troubling you?"

The monk said, "How can one deal with this?"

Fenyang said, "What you do, you receive."

A monk asked, "What is the essential flavor of the Buddhadharma?"

Fenyang said, "Exactly where one's body and life are liberated."

A monk asked, "Is the essential teaching of the ancestors the same as the general teachings of Buddhism?"

Fenyang said, "The cold pine on the high peak stands noble and straight. The winding brook in the gully moves lazily."

Fenyang said, "Zen teachers everywhere, because of the demands placed upon them, constantly talk about this or that without let up. So all of you think this is what you should be doing, and you confusedly gather in groups, go sleepless, and say that you are 'pursuing practice.' Where do you think you're going in order to practice? An ancient said, 'Anyone who makes external effort is a fool.' You should listen to what I'm saying. You won't be around long! Take care!"

A monk asked, "When the lamp is not clear, then what?"

Fenyang said, "Extinguish it!"

The monk said, "After it is extinguished, then what?"

Fenyang said, "It's clear."

The monk said, "What if one can't see that it's burning brightly?"

Fenyang said, "It burns constantly, without interruption. It has been clear from the infinite past down to the present."

Fenyang addressed the monks, saying, "The sound of the bell. The chirp of the sparrow. Through these things the true source can be met. Seeking it someplace else is a deluded waste of effort. If you grasp some belief then it will be like a brisk wind extinguishing a flame. Not believing will be like a ditch in a flat plain.

"Affairs press upon us without end, rising forms and painted patterns. Therefore Lingshan spoke of the moon. The Sixth Ancestor pointed to the moon. Where is this moon? Point it out for me. Tell me directly and don't go looking for it up in the sky!"

A monk asked, "What is it when a student is not yet enlightened?"

Fenyang said, "No one is enlightened."

The monk asked, "How about after he is enlightened?"

Fenyang said, "There's no fooling a clear-headed one."

◆

Duke Li of Longdehou Township was an old friend of the master. Because Xu Chengtian Temple became vacant there, Li wanted to invite the master to come there and expound the Dharma. An emissary from the Duke came to Fenyang three times, but each time Fenyang refused to leave the mountain. The emissary was threatened with severe punishment by Duke Li, so he came to the mountain yet another time and said, "I must insist that the master accompany me. Otherwise I'll be put to death!"

Fenyang laughed and said, "I haven't left the mountain because I've been quite sick. But, if I must do so, then must we go together? Should I go first or should you go first?"

The emissary said, "It only matters that you agree to go. It doesn't matter who goes first."

Fenyang then ordered that a banquet be prepared.

Taking up his traveling bag, he said, "I'll go first."

Upon saying these words he passed away. His disciples cremated the master, retrieved his relics, and built a stupa to house them.

SHEXIAN GUIXING

SHEXIAN GUIXING (n.d.) was a disciple of Shoushan Xingnian. He came from ancient Jizhou (located southwest of Shijiazhuang in Hebei Province). As a novice monk he lived in Baoshou Monastery. After taking ordination he traveled widely, finally studying under Shoushan. Later, he lived and taught at Guangjiao Monastery in Ruzhou.

One day Shoushan held up a bamboo comb and asked, "If you call it a bamboo comb you commit an offense. If you don't call it a bamboo comb then you've turned away from what you see. What do you call it?"

Shexian grabbed the comb out of Shoushan's hand, threw it to the floor and said, "What is it?"

Shoushan said, "Blind."

At these words Shexian suddenly experienced unsurpassed awakening.

When Shexian began teaching, a monk asked him, "All the ancestors have one after the other passed on the ancestral seal. Whose heritage have you now attained?"

Shexian said, "At the center of the realm, an emperor. Beyond the frontier, a general."

A monk asked, "What is 'within the dust, a single revealed body'?"

Shexian said, "In the cold north, a thousand people's flags. South of the river, ten-thousand-ton ships."

The monk said, "In that case, it isn't the dust."

Shexian said, "If you study the flow of words, a single page has ten thousand lines."

Shexian entered the hall and addressed the monks, saying, "The blood and marrow of the teachers of our school; what is mundane and holy; Longshu and Maming [names of famous Buddhists of earlier times]; heaven and hell; the scalding cauldron and furnace embers [tortures of hell]; the ox-headed jailers [demons in hell]; the myriad phenomena of the universe; heavenly bodies; all things of the earth, animate and inanimate…" Shexian drew a circle in the air with his hand and then continued, "…all of them enter this essential teaching. Within this teaching people can be killed and they can be given life. Those who die endure the killing knife. Those who live must attain the life-giving phrase. What are the killing knife and the life-giving phrase? Can you answer me? Come out of the congregation and we'll test you. If you can't speak, then you've betrayed your life! Take care!"

A monk asked, "I'm confused about my self. How should I examine it?"

Shexian said, "In the bustling market, beat the silent hammer."

A monk asked, "Vimalakirti's room did not use the sun or moon for light. What does the master's room use for light?"

Shexian said, "Eyebrows separate the 'eight' words."

The monk said, "I don't understand your meaning."

Shexian said, "Your ears hang down to your shoulders."

A monk asked, "What is the work that goes beyond the teacher?"
Shexian said, "Look how long my eyebrows have gotten!"

---◆---

A monk asked, "What is the pure dharmakaya?"
Shexian said, "Toilet paper by the latrine."
The monk asked, "What is wisdom?"
Shexian said, "Breaking furniture."

---◆---

A monk asked, "What is the meaning of Zhaozhou's cypress tree in the garden?"
Shexian said, "I won't refuse to tell you, but will you believe me or not?"
The monk said, "How could I not believe the master's weighty words?"
Shexian said, "Can you hear the water dripping from the eaves?"
The monk was suddenly enlightened. He unconsciously exclaimed, "Oh."
Shexian said, "What principle have you observed?"
The monk then composed a verse:

"Water drips from the eaves,
So clearly,
Splitting open the Universe,
Here the mind is extinguished."

The verse pleased Shexian.

DAYANG JINGXUAN, "JINGYAN"

DAYANG JINGXUAN (943–1027) was a disciple of Liangshan Yuanguan, and a transmitter of the Caodong Zen lineage. He came from ancient Jiangxia (now the city of Wuchang in Hubei Province). He left lay life to enter Chongxiao Temple in Jinling. There he studied under Zen master Zhitong. At the age of nineteen, after ordination, he left Jinling and traveled widely throughout the country. He first studied under Zen master Yuanjiao Liaoyi. Unsuccessful with that teacher, he continued his travels and eventually met and studied under Liangshan. He remained with Liangshan for a long period, realizing enlightenment and becoming his Dharma heir. When Liangshan died, Dayang traveled to Mt. Dayang in Yingzhou (now the city of Jingshan in Hubei Province), where he assumed his mountain name. There he met and studied with Zen master Huijian. When Huijian died, Dayang assumed the abbacy of the temple. During the period 1008–16 Dayang changed his name from "Jingxuan" to "Jingyan."[152]

During Dayang's life, the Caodong school of Zen experienced serious decline. At the age of eighty, Dayang despaired that the Caodong Zen line had no worthy heirs and would cease to exist when he died. He then took the highly unusual step of enlisting the assistance of the eminent Linji lineage teacher Fushan Fayuan, entrusting to him the Dharma transmission of the Caodong school.[153] Dayang then passed away, and the essential teachings of Caodong remained with Fushan, who was a famous master of Linji Zen. After many years, Fushan encountered Touzi Yiqing, an exceptional young monk and worthy "Dharma vessel." To him, Fushan transmitted the heritage that he previously inherited from Dayang Jingxuan.

Dayang's first encounter with Liangshan is recorded in the *Wudeng Huiyuan*.

Upon first meeting Liangshan, Dayang asked, "What is the formless place of realization?"

Liangshan pointed to a painting of Kwan Yin and said, "This was painted by Wu Chu."

Dayang was about to speak when Liangshan cut him off, saying, "Does this have form? Where is the form?"

At these words, Dayang awakened. He then bowed.

Liangshan said, "Why don't you say something?"

Dayang said, "It's true I don't speak, and I fear putting it to brush and paper."

Liangshan laughed and said, "Engrave the words on a stone memorial!"

Dayang then offered the following verse:

"Formerly my means of studying the Way were confused,
Seeking understanding among myriad streams and countless mountains.
But immediate clarity is not found by sorting through the past.
Directly speaking "no mind" engendered more delusion.
Then, a teacher revealed my situation upon leaving Qin,
Illuminating the time before my parents' birth.
And now, everything realized, what has been attained?
The night frees crow and cock to fly with the snow."

Liangshan said, "Here the Dongshan line is entrusted."
In time, Jingxuan's reputation spread widely.

A monk asked Dayang, "What is a phrase that penetrates the dharmakaya?"
Dayang said, "Red dust rises from the bottom of the sea. Rivers flow sideways at Mt. Sumeru's summit."

A monk asked Dayang, "What is Dayang's state of being?"
Dayang said, "A gaunt crane and an old ape call across the valley in harmony. A slender pine and the cold bamboo are enveloped in blue mist."
The monk said, "What about the person in that state?"
Dayang said, "What are you doing? What are you doing?"
The monk asked, "What is the master's family style?"
Dayang said, "A full pitcher that can't be emptied. Across the great earth, no one hungry."

A monk asked, "What is a phrase that embodies infinite clarity?"
Dayang said, "When the finger points at emptiness, heaven and earth revolve. On the returning path, a stone horse emerges from a gauze basket."

A monk asked, "What is a person who has 'completely arrived'?"
Dayang said, "Throughout vast emptiness no such thing exists."
The monk said, "What is the pure dharmakaya?"
Dayang said, "A white ox spits up white silk. A black horse rides a crow."

Zen master Dayang entered the hall and addressed the monks, saying, "A ten-thousand-foot-high peak and a precipitous path to the top, beset with swords, knives, and ice! Who can walk this path? The phrase of the wondrous vehicle cannot be found on the path of words. As to the unsurpassed Dharma gate, even Vimalakirti remained close-lipped. For this reason, Bodhidharma came from the west, sat facing a wall for nine years, and thus allowed us to learn of it. Oh, look how I'm carrying on today! Take care!"

After his death, Dayang received the posthumous title "Great Teacher Bright Peace."

JIUFENG QIN

JIUFENG QIN (n.d.) was a disciple of Zhimen Guangzuo. He lived and taught in ancient Ruizhou (the area of Gao'an City in modern Jiangxi Province).

A monk said to Zen master Jiufeng Qin, "I ask the master to reveal an expedient method to enter the Way."

Jiufeng said, "The Buddha does not fight against people's wishes."

The monk said, "Thank you, Master, for this expedient."

Jiufeng said, "You still earn blows from the staff!"

———— ◆ ————

Zen master Jiufeng entered the hall and addressed the monks, saying, "No matter if you talk until you're blue in the face, or say 'Hey!' a thousand times, or shout ten thousand times. Why is it that the temple pillar still won't acknowledge you?"

After a long pause, Jiufeng said, "Delicious food doesn't satisfy the hungry."

He then got down from the Dharma seat.

XUEDOU CHONGXIAN, "MINGJUE"

XUEDOU CHONGXIAN (980–1052) was a disciple of Zhimen Guangzuo. Xuedou came from Suining (near the modern city of Tongnan in Sichuan Province). Born into a prominent and wealthy family, the young man possessed extraordinary skills as a scholar. Determined to leave secular life and enter the Buddhist priesthood, he entered the Pu'an Monastery in Yizhou (near modern Chengdu City), where he studied the Buddhist scriptures under a teacher named Renxian.

Xuedou was recognized as an adept in both Buddhist and non-Buddhist disciplines. After receiving ordination he traveled to ancient Fuzhou (near the modern city of Tianmen in Hubei Province), where he studied under Zhimen Guangzuo. After five years Xuedou received Zhimen's seal as an heir of the Yunmen lineage. Xuedou later lived at the Lingyin Temple in Hangzhou and Cuifeng Temple in Suzhou before finally taking up residence on Mt. Xuedou (near modern Ningbo City in Zhejiang Province).

Xuedou compiled the hundred kōans that are the core of the *Blue Cliff Record,* the well-known Zen text later annotated by Zen master Yuanwu Keqin.

Xuedou's grand style of teaching rejuvenated the Yunmen lineage. The prominent Zen master Tianyi Yihuai was among his eighty-four disciples.

When he began studying with Zhimen, Xuedou put forth the question, "Before a single thought arises, can what is said be wrong?"

Zhimen summoned Xuedou to come forward. Xuedou did so. Zhimen suddenly struck Xuedou in the mouth with his whisk. Xuedou began to speak but Zhimen hit him again. Xuedou suddenly experienced enlightenment. He first assumed the abbacy at Cuiyan. He later moved to Xuedou.

───── ✦ ─────

Upon first entering the hall as abbot, but before ascending the seat, Xuedou looked out over the assembly and said, "If I'm to speak about coming face-to-face with the fundamental principle, then there's no need to ascend the Dharma seat."

He then used his hand to draw a picture in the air and said, "All of you follow this old mountain monk's hand and see! Here are innumerable buddha lands appearing before you all at once. All of you look carefully. If you are on the river bank and still don't know, don't avoid moving mud and carrying water." He then ascended the seat.

───── ✦ ─────

The head monk struck the gavel. A monk came forward to speak. Xuedou told him to stop and go back, and then said, *The Treasury of the True Dharma Eye* of the tathagatas is manifested before us today. In its illumination even a piece of tile is radiant. When it is obscured, even pure gold loses its luster. In my hand is the scepter of authority. It will now kill and give life. If you are an accomplished adept in the practice of our school, then come forward and gain authentication!"

The monk came forward and said, "Far from the ancestral seat at Cuifeng, now expounding at Xuedou, do you still not know if it's one or if it's two?"

Xuedou said, "A horse cannot beat the wind for a thousand miles."

The monk said, "In that case, the clouds disperse and the clear moon is above the households."

Xuedou said, "A dragon-headed, snake-tailed fellow."[154]

A monk came forward, bowed, and then rose to ask, "Master, please respond."

Xuedou then hit him.

The monk said, "Can't you offer an expedient method?"

Xuedou said, "Don't make the same mistake again."

Another monk came forward, bowed, and then said, "Master, please respond."

Xuedou said, "Two important cases."

The monk said, "Master, please don't respond."

Xuedou then hit him.

A monk asked, "What is 'blowing feather sword'?"

Xuedou said, "Arduous!"

The monk said, "Will you allow me to use it?"

Xuedou said, "Ssshhh! If you're going to ask questions before the entire assembly, you should have attained being a true person. If you don't have instantaneous vision, then there's no use in asking questions. Thus it is said that, 'It's like a great bonfire. If you walk too close to it the portals of your face will be burned away.' Or it's like the great Taia Jeweled Sword. Whoever encounters it loses his body and life.[155] When you take the Taia sword in your hand, the ancestral hall becomes cold, and in every direction for ten thousand miles all mental activity must cease. Don't wait until you see the glimmer of the sword! Look! Look!"

Xuedou then got down from the seat and left the hall.

A monk came forward and bowed.

Xuedou said, "Monks of the congregation! Remember this monk's *huatou*!"

Xuedou then left the hall.

A monk asked, "An ancient said, 'Conceal the body in the Big Dipper.' What does this mean?"

Xuedou said, "Hearing it a thousand times is not as good as seeing it once."

Xuedou addressed the monks, saying, "If there is a Dharma-treasure swordsman present, then I invite you to demonstrate this to the congregation."

A monk then came forward to ask a question. Before he could speak, Xuedou said, "Where are you going?"

Xuedou then left the hall.

Xuedou addressed the monks, saying, "Even if you experience the earth shaking and the sky raining flowers, how can that compare to going back to the monk's hall and building a fire in the stove?"

The master then left the hall.

Xuedou addressed the monks, saying, "So vast that nothing is outside of it. So small that nothing is inside of it. Both open and closed; both diverse and unified. Due to the barbarian having cut off form, many students of the Zen world have turned around. For endless eons the gully has been dammed up and people have not understood."

Xuedou then struck his staff on the ground and said, "Go back to the monks' hall."

Upon his death, Xuedou received the posthumous title "Great Teacher Clear Awakening."

BAO'EN XUANZE

BAO'EN XUANZE (n.d.) was a student of Fayan Wenyi. Bao'en came from Weinan City in Huazhou (now in the northwest portion of Hua County, Henan Province). He first studied under a Zen teacher named Qingfeng.[156] He then continued his practice under Fayan Wenyi.

Upon meeting Qingfeng, Bao'en asked, "What is the student's own self?"
Qingfeng said, "It's the boy of fire coming to seek fire."[157]
Later, Bao'en met Fayan.
Fayan asked, "Where'd you come from?"
Bao'en said, "From Qingfeng."

Fayan said, "What words did Qingfeng have to say?"

Bao'en related the above exchange.

Fayan said, "How do you understand it?"

Bao'en said, "The child is of the fire, and still he seeks fire. It's like the self looking for the self."

Fayan said, "How can it be understood like this?"

Bao'en said, "My understanding is just thus. How do you see it, Master?"

Fayan said, "Ask me and I'll tell you."

Bao'en said, "What is the student's own self?"

Fayan said, "It's the boy of fire seeking fire."

At these words Bao'en was enlightened.

A monk asked, "What is the place of the saints?"

Bao'en said, "You must understand yourself."

The monk asked, "What is the master's hidden wondrous mystery?"

Bao'en said, "Wait until you realize awakening. Then you'll understand."

When Bao'en [while acting as head monk] spoke at the opening of the temple at Jinling, he said, "Li Wang, [a local official] as well as Fayan are here."

A monk asked, "The dragon sighs and the fog rises. The tiger growls and the wind comes up. This student knows that these are unworldly events. Why can't I understand them?"

Bao'en said, "You understand them!"

The monk raised his head and looked at Bao'en, then he looked at Fayan, and then he slipped back into the crowd of the congregation without bowing. Fayan and Li Wang appeared shocked. Fayan returned to the abbot's room and instructed the attendant to call for the monk to come there.

Fayan said to the monk, "Because of your question, the head monk acknowledged that you have the wisdom eye, so why did you retreat without bowing?"

Three days later the monk manifested light and died.

Bao'en addressed the congregation, saying, "All of you monks fully possess an eternal perfect moon. Each of you possesses a priceless jewel. Because the moon is obscured by fog its luster does not shine forth. Your wisdom is concealed within delusion, and although it is the truth, you haven't realized it. There's nothing more to say. You've been standing too long for nothing!"

A monk asked, "What is the meaning of 'no movement'?"

Bao'en said, "The river rapids heave and crash. The sun and moon swirl in orbit."

Guizong Cezhen

Guizong Cezhen (n.d.) was a disciple of Fayan Wenyi. He came from Caozhou. Few other details about Guizong's life are available in the classical records.

Guizong's initial encounter with Zen master Fayan Wenyi is classically cited as an example of the Fayan school's teaching on inherent enlightenment. When a student comprehends this teaching, it is said to be like "two arrowhead points striking each other in midflight, where words and meaning unite in function."[158]

Guizong's first Dharma name was "Huichao" ["Surpassing Wisdom"].

Upon first meeting Fayan, he asked, "Surpassing Wisdom inquires of the master, what is Buddha?"

Fayan said, "You are Surpassing Wisdom."

At these words Guizong entered enlightenment.

When Guizong assumed the position of abbot, he addressed the monks, saying, "Zen Worthies! If you want to hear and witness the wisdom of enlightenment, there is only one way to do so. But if you realize it in this manner, is it witnessing and hearing the wisdom of enlightenment or is it *not* witnessing and hearing enlightenment? Do you understand? I'll explain it to you when you are enlightened. You've been standing too long! Take care!"

A monk asked Zen master Guizong, "What is Buddha?"

Guizong said, "When I tell you it becomes something else."

A monk asked, "What is Guizong's realm?"

Guizong said, "It's 'what do you see?'"

The monk then asked, "Who is the person in the middle of this realm?"

Guizong said, "Go!"

A monk asked, "The king has commanded that you expound Dharma without resorting to what can be seen or heard. Master, quickly speak!"

Guizong said, "Casual conversation."

The monk said, "What is the master's meaning?"

Guizong said, "Talking gibberish again."

———— ❖ ————

A monk said, "In the scriptures there is the passage, 'When this deep mind pays honor to the ten thousand worlds, this is known as "repaying Buddha's compassion."' I don't ask you about 'ten thousand worlds,' but tell me, what is 'repaying Buddha's compassion'?"

Guizong said, "If you are thus, that is 'repaying Buddha's compassion.'"

············· ❖ ·············

A monk asked, "Inanimate objects expound the Dharma and the great earth hears it. But when the lion roars, then what?"

Guizong said, "Do you hear it?"

The monk said, "In that case it's the same as inanimate objects."

Guizong said, "You understand it well!"

———— ❖ ————

A monk asked, "The ancients held that the essential teaching does not depart from sights and sounds. I'd like to know what the master holds as the essential teaching?"

Guizong said, "This is a very good question."

The monk said, "Do you regard the essential teaching as 'conditional causation'?"

Guizong said, "Don't talk gibberish."

BAOCI XINGYAN

BAOCI XINGYAN (n.d.) was a disciple of Fayan Wenyi. Xingyan came from Quanzhou. He assumed the abbacy of Baoci Monastery in Jiangnan (modern Nanjing).

Xingyan entered the hall and addressed the monks, saying, "Everywhere there are monks on pilgrimage who practice good and perform the observances. When they reach a monastery, they put down their water jug and bowl. You can just call what they are doing, 'following the bodhisattva way.' Why come here to hear some pointless talk? As for 'true thusness' and 'nirvana'—there's no good time to speak of them.

"Still, the ancients had a way of talking about it. They said it's like spying a treasure in the sand. Clearing away the rocks and pebbles the pure gold itself shines forth. This is called 'abiding in the world—fully possessing the monk's treasure.' Or it's like having a rain shower, a patch of earth, and the growth of ten thousand things, all of various sizes and assorted sweetness and bitterness. You can't say that the earth is more important or the rain is more important. Thus, it is said that in the part, the part is revealed, and in the totality, the totality is revealed. How can it be explained?

"The Dharma has no distortion or straightness. When it is revealed to you in whatever way you observe it, it is called 'manifested in form.' Do you see it this way? If you don't, then don't waste time as you sit!"

A monk asked, "Why did the First Ancestor come from the west?"
Xingyan said, "I don't deal with that question."

A monk asked, "How can I sit in meditation like the ancestors did, so that there is no right or wrong?"
Xingyan said, "How are you sitting?"

Xingyan heard a dove call and said, "What's that sound?"
The monk said, "A dove's call."
Xingyan said, "If you don't want to give rise to limitless evil karma, then don't slander the true Dharma of the Tathagatas."

The governor of Jiangnan constructed the Baoci Monastery and called on Xingyan to assume the abbacy and expound the wisdom of the sect. [At the opening ceremony] a crowd of over two thousand gathered, and they had previously never heard Master Xingyan's name.

Xingyan entered the hall and addressed the crowd, saying, "Today, heroes and eminencies have gathered here—a great crowd. Nothing has been left undone for the sake of the Buddhadharma. If you could see all this as mirroring [Buddha's truth], then there would be no need for a speech. And yet, although fundamentally there is nothing to speak of, how can I remain silent?

"The myriad forms of the universe, the expansive source of all the buddhas—when revealed clearly, this is the ocean-seal of shining purity. Obscured, it is impassioned delusion and self-deception.

"Despite the demand for edification by the distinguished guests here, and the requests of those present of high standing, how dare I, in the midst of this dusty world, presume to expound on the most sublime; roll out things and forms; lay out and gather in phenomena; reveal birth and nonbirth; set out annihilation and nonannihilation; completely penetrate birth and death; and speak about eternal truth?

"If I speak falsely then shadows will be cast on a thousand paths. If I speak the truth, then the content of my talk will be empty, without any traces. Only by speaking in that way can I try to expose existence and nonexistence, birth and annihilation."

Chongshou Qizhou

Chongshou Qizhou (d. 992) was a disciple of Fayan Wenyi and a Dharma heir of the Fayan lineage. Chongshou came from Quanzhou.

Chongshou entered the hall and ascended the seat.

A monk asked, "Everyone seeks to witness the first principle. What is the first principle?"

Chongshou said, "Why trouble to ask again?"

Then he also said, "If everyone wants to comprehend buddha nature, then look at temporal causation. What is temporal causation? When you monks go out of here today, will you have it or not? If not, then what makes you leave? If you have it, what is the first principle?

"Monks, the first principle is evident, so why belabor looking for it? The eternal light of buddha nature is in this manner clearly revealed, and all dharmas eternally abide. If you see that dharmas eternally abide, that is still not their true source. What is the true source of dharmas? Have you monks not heard that the ancients said, 'A single person realizes truth and returns to the source, then the emptiness in the ten directions is extinguished'? Then is there a single dharma left to be understood? If the ancients thus put forth the alpha and omega of the great matter, then just act in accordance with it. Why belabor it with endless chatter? If anyone in the congregation doesn't understand this, then say so."

———— ❖ ————

A monk asked, "The lamp of the Dharma eye is like personally seeing the Ju River. Today the empress dowager begs for her life. What is the lamp of Fayan [Dharma eye]?"[159]
Chongshou said, "Ask another question."

———— ❖ ————

A monk asked, "The ancients did not all see the same place. Please, Master, resolve this question."
Chongshou said, "What place did the ancients see that wasn't the same?"

———— ❖ ————

A monk asked, "What is Buddha?"
Chongshou said, "What is Buddha?"
The monk asked, "What is understanding?"
Chongshou said, "Understanding is not understanding."

TIANTAI DESHAO

TIANTAI DESHAO (891–972) was the principal disciple and Dharma heir of Fayan Wenyi. He was a native of Longchuan in Chu Province.[160] He began his monastic life at Longgui ("Returning Dragon") Temple, in his home province. At the age of eighteen he traveled to Kaiyuan Temple in Xinzhou, where he received ordination.

As a young man, Tiantai practiced the observances of Huayan Buddhism. At around the age of thirty, he went traveling to visit various eminent Buddhist masters of the era. Among others, he visited the aged student of Dongshan Liangjie, Zen master Longya Judun.

Upon meeting Longya, Tiantai asked, "Why can't the people of today reach the level of the ancient worthies?"
Longya said, "It's like fire and fire."
Tiantai said, "If suddenly there's water, then what?"
Longya said, "Go! You don't understand what I'm saying."

Tiantai also asked Longya, "What is the meaning of 'the sky can't cover it, the earth can't contain it'?"

Longya said, "It's just like that."

Tiantai asked repeatedly, but each time Longya gave the same answer.

Finally, when he asked again, Longya said, "I've already spoken, now you go find out on your own."

Pressing on with his travels, one day Tiantai was bathing when the meaning of Longya's words finally occurred to him. Lighting incense and bowing in the direction of Longya, he said, "Had you told me then, I'd be reviling you today."

Continuing his travel and study, Tiantai eventually came to Fayan's temple in Linchuan. Fayan immediately recognized the young priest as a great Dharma vessel. One day, as Fayan presided in the hall, a monk asked him, "What is a single drop of the Cao source?"

Fayan said, "A single drop of the Cao source." The monk dejectedly retreated.

Later, as Tiantai reflected on this exchange while meditating, he suddenly experienced great enlightenment, with the "obstructions of everyday life flowing away like melting ice." Tiantai went to Fayan with news of this event. Fayan is reported to have said, "Later you will be the teacher of kings. I won't compare with the brilliance of your attainment of the ancestral way."

Tiantai traveled to reside at the home of Tiantai Buddhism, a temple named Baisha ("White Sands") on Mt. Tiantai. There he found that the records of the Tiantai school were largely lost or in a state of disrepair because of the social upheaval accompanying the end of the Tang dynasty. Tiantai assisted with the retrieval of lost Tiantai doctrinal texts from Korea, thus restoring that school in China. The king of the kingdom of Wuyue invited Tiantai to reside and teach at the famous lake city of Hangzhou and honored him with the title "National Teacher."[161]

A monk asked Tiantai Deshao, "In the teaching there is the phrase, 'the mind is clear and pure, and thus the dharmadhatu is clear and pure.'[162] What is 'clear and pure'?"

Tiantai said, "The kalavinka bird."[163]

The monk said, "Are mind and dharmadhatu one thing or two things?"

Tiantai said, "You ask this. Others ask this."

Tiantai went on to say, "The great way is vast. It encompasses the past and present. It is nameless and formless. It is custom and practice. The virtue that flows from the dharmadhatu is limitless. Mind is also boundless. It is not worldly affairs or what is seen. It is not speech or what is apparent. If it is understood, then this is called 'revealed wisdom.'[164] It is the ultimate principle and the limit of truth. It is mountains, rivers, the great earth, and the myriad things of the universe, like a vast wall of tile and stones not containing the slightest breech. There's nothing more to say."

After a long pause, Tiantai said, "Take care."

———— ◆ ————

Tiantai Deshao addressed the monks, saying, "From time immemorial the Dharma gates of all the buddhas can be likened to a great ocean with innumerable billowing waves. It has never, even for a moment, remained still. It has never been of the realm of existence or nonexistence. Immeasurably vast, it is incandescently manifested. The three realms fit into the point of a feather, and everything from ancient times down to the present is perfectly realized in a single moment. You must completely realize enlightenment—without having a single question remain, nor remembering a single idea, and without resorting to clever talk. The wind, clouds, rivers, and moon—all the myriad things are themselves the Buddhadharma. Don't deceive yourselves! Oh monks! All of your efforts are meaningless! If you really understand, then it can't be hidden. There are no worlds that are hidden. There is no dust not revealed. Common persons stand together with all buddhas. Not using a bit effort, in a single moment you can grasp it. There's nothing more to say. Take care!"

———— ◆ ————

A monk asked, "The mountains, rivers, and the great earth—from where did all of these things come forth?"

Tiantai said, "From where did this question come forth?"

Late in life, Tiantai returned to the mountain that gave him his name. He passed away there at Guoqing ["Clear Country"] Temple.

Tianping Congyi

Tianping Congyi (n.d.) was a disciple of Qingxi Hongjin. He lived and taught in Xiangzhou (a region near modern Anyang City in Hebei Province).

A monk asked Zen master Tianping Congyi, "How does someone leave the three worlds?"

Tianping said, "When the three worlds arrive, then you will leave them."

❖

The monk asked, "What is the style of the Master's house?"
Tianping said, "Revealing earth."

❖

A monk asked, "What is Buddha?"
Tianping said, "Not pointing at heaven or earth."
The monk asked, "Why not point at heaven or earth?"
Tianping said, "I alone am the honored one."

❖

A monk asked, "What is Tianping?"
Tianping said, "Eight dips and nine bumps."

❖

A monk asked, "How do those who drink the deep clear waters of Qingxi [literally, 'clear creek'] not rise or fall?"
Tianping said, "What will you dream of next?"

❖

A monk asked, "The great congregation has assembled. What do you say to them?"
Tianping said, "Where the incense smoke rises, heaven and earth may be seen."

Seventeenth Generation

SHISHUANG CHUYUAN   DAYU SHOUZHI

LANGYE HUIJUE   FUSHAN FAYUAN

TOUZI YIQING   XINGYANG QINGPOU

TIANYI YIHUAI   CHENGTIAN CHUANZONG

YONGMING YANSHOU

SHISHUANG CHUYUAN, "ZHIMING"

SHISHUANG CHUYUAN (986–1039) was a disciple of Fenyang Shanzhao, the famous literary Zen master of the Linji lineage. Shishuang came from the city of Qingxiang in Chuanzhou (located in modern Guangxi Province). He left home at the age of twenty-two, and was ordained at Yinjing Temple. Later, he traveled to Luoyang City with his companions Dayu Shouzhi and Guquan.[165] Hearing that Fenyang Shanzhao had an unsurpassed Zen style, the group proceeded to Fenzhou to study with that master. Two years of severe frustration followed, as Fenyang would not even allow Shishuang into his room for an interview. On each occasion that Shishuang met his teacher he was subjected to a scolding. Fenyang seemed to hurl abuse everywhere, and his training appeared to Shishuang to be little more than a stream of vulgarity.

Making no apparent progress, Shishuang finally poured out his frustration to Fenyang.

"I've been here for two years and you haven't given me any instruction! You've just increased the world's vulgarity, dust, and toil, while the years and months fly away. Even what I knew before is no longer clear, and I've lost whatever good came from leaving home."

But before Shishuang could finish speaking, Fenyang glared at him fiercely and cursed him, saying: "What you know is vile! How dare you sell me short!" So saying, Fenyang picked up his staff to drive Shishuang away. Shishuang tried to plead with him, but Fenyang covered Shishuang's mouth with his hand. At that moment, Shishuang realized great enlightenment.

He then exclaimed, "It's knowing the extraordinary emotion of Linji's way!"

After this event, Shishuang remained as Fen-yang's attendant for seven years.

Shishuang taught in and around ancient Tan-zhou. He gained his mountain name at Shishuang Temple, the temple founded earlier by Zen master Shishuang Qingzhu.

Shishuang entered the hall and addressed the monks, saying, "All of the bud-dhas, and all of the buddhas' anuttara-samyaksambodhi, come forth from this sutra." He then raised his staff upright and said, "This is the Nanyuan Temple staff. Where is the sutra?"

After a long pause he said, "The text is long. I'll give it to you later."

Then, with a shout, he got down from the seat.

◆

Shishuang entered the hall and said, "If a teacher of our school can snatch a jewel off of the clothes of an impoverished man, then he can be said to have reached the stage of 'person.' If not, then he's a mud and water fellow."

After a pause, Shishuang said, "If you meet a swordsman on the road, show him the jeweled sword. If he's not a poet, don't offer him a poem."

Shishuang shouted.

◆

Shishuang entered the hall and said, "I have a word that cuts off thinking and leaves cause and effect behind. But even clever people can't speak it! It may only be transmitted by way of mind. There is another word that may only be directly expressed. What is the word that can only be directly expressed?"

After a pause, Shishuang drew a circle in the air with his staff. Then he shouted.

◆

A monk said, "I'm confused. What should I study?"

Shishuang said, "Xuansha saw Xuefeng arrive."

The monk said, "What does that mean?"

Shishuang said, "In an entire lifetime, never leaving the mountain."

◆

Shishuang addressed the monks, saying, "The more medicine that is used, the worse the disease becomes. The finer the fishing net mesh, the more fish that escape."

Shishuang then left the hall.

———— ✦ ————

A monk asked, "When someone goes on a pilgrimage but doesn't meet a teacher with whom he finds affinity, then what?"

Shishuang said, "The fishing line twists in the water."

———— ✦ ————

A monk asked, "I don't ask about the leaves picked off the branches. What is the actual root?"

Shishuang said, "A willow-wood staff."

The monk said, "What does that mean?"

Shishuang said, "When a monk goes traveling he carries his clothes with it on his shoulders. When he sits, he holds it in his hand."

———— ✦ ————

Shishuang entered the hall and said, "Those persons of nonaction with nothing to do—they still have the problem of the golden lock."

Then, with a shout, he got down from the seat.

———— ✦ ————

Case 46 of the *Gateless Gate* features a famous kōan posed by Shishuang.

Master Shishuang said, "How does one step forward from the top of a hundred-foot pole? An ancient worthy said, 'Although a person sitting atop a hundred-foot pole has gained entry, he has still not reached the truth. From the top of a hundred-foot pole, he must step into the complete universal body in the ten directions.'"

———— ✦ ————

Shishuang received honors from Emperor Ren Zong, and during the return trip to his temple he said to his attendant, "I feel a paralyzing wind."

Shishuang's mouth became crooked.

His attendant stopped and said, "What should we do? You've spent your whole life cursing the buddhas and reviling the ancestors. So now what can you do?"

Shishuang said, "Don't worry. I'll straighten it for you."

He then used his hand to straighten his mouth.

Then Shishuang said, "From now on I won't play any more jokes on you."

The next year, on the fifth day of the first month, the master passed away.

During a relatively short life, Shishuang taught at several different temples and is said to have had fifty Dharma heirs. His famous students, Yangqi Fanghui and Huanglong Huinan, each established distinctive branches of the Linji Zen line. Besides teaching at Chongsheng Temple on Mt. Shishuang, he is known to have taught at the famous Zen mountains Dong Shan, Gui Shan, and Heng Shan. He received the posthumous name "Zen Master Compassionate Clarity."

DAYU SHOUZHI, "CUIYAN"

DAYU SHOUZHI (n.d.) was a disciple of Fenyang Shanzhao. He came from ancient Taiyuan (located in modern Shanxi Province). According to the *Chan Lin Seng Bao Zhuan*, Dayu left home at a young age and entered Chengtian Temple in Luzhou (now the city of Changzhi in Shanxi Province).[166] There, he gained great prominence for his understanding and exposition of the *Lotus* and *Diamond* sutras. On one occasion the great Linji lineage Zen master Fenyang Shanzhao appeared nearby, and Dayu went to listen to him speak. After this event, Dayu sincerely opened to Fenyang's teaching, embraced the way of Zen, and received Dharma transmission in the Linji lineage. He later traveled south to reside and teach at Gao'an.

A monk asked, "What is the style of the house of Dayu?"

Dayu said, "A single uttered word can't be pursued, even by a team of horses."

❖

A monk asked, "What is the buddha within the city?"

Dayu said, "A stone banner at the main intersection."

❖

A monk asked, "How can *it* be expressed without words?"

Dayu said, "The universe three feet too long. The cosmos six feet too short."

The monk said, "I don't understand what you mean."

Dayu said, "All samsaric ground is excessive or lacking."

❖

A monk asked, "Formerly, at the assembly at Vulture Peak, what was it that the Second Ancestor witnessed?"

Dayu said, "Do you remember?"

The monk remained silent for a long while.

Dayu then struck the meditation platform and said, "After so many years, you've forgotten!"

Then Dayu said, "Stop! Stop! If you try to grasp the function from within the words, it will be like seeing shadows when you're dizzy. If you speak of the ancient vehicle, it's like talking in your sleep. Although it is thus, officially, not a single needle can be inserted into it, but privately a cart and horse can pass through it. But if you allow a road there, it will be a place of creepers and reeds."

Dayu then struck the meditation platform again and said, "'The three worlds,' 'all the buddhas,' these phrases are all just a headache. What I say to you all is, can you avoid it? Is there a single person who can avoid it by finding a place where it doesn't exist? Not avoiding it, the ocean-seal radiates brilliantly."

Dayu then raised his whisk and said, "This is the seal. Where is the light? This is the light. Where is the seal? The function flashes, yet you students stand around and think about it! Do you understand? I am speaking a dream, yet what do you say is to be seen in this dream. If you still don't understand, then listen to this verse.

"Mt. Sumeru suspended in the Big Dipper,
The tip of the staff upholds the sun and moon.
Forests and springs conversing,
The waning summer cleaved by the autumn wind.

"Take care!"

◆

Dayu ascended the seat. Displaying a lighted stick of incense to his disciples, he said, "When the brightness comes, unite with the brightness. When the darkness comes, unite with the darkness. When the Way is attained, the world is ordered. When the Way is not attained, the world is disordered."

The following passages are taken from the *Chan Lin Seng Bao Zhuan*.

A monk asked, "The innumerable dharmas are like illusory reflective bubbles. Would the master please bring forth a matter of substantial truth?"

Dayu said, "If two sections are not the same, the text is long."

The monk then asked, "The whole body is the Dharma eye. Where is the mouth?"

Dayu said, "Three leaps."

The monk drew close and said, "I don't understand."

Dayu said, "At the end of the essay are the words, 'In autumn finished, songs and verses are renewed in the spring.' Among the great numbers of monks, one stands out above the rest. It's like the verse by Yang Danian in this era that says,

"For the one who walks within the eight-sided millstone,
Even Manjushri's lion is a cur.
If you plan to conceal yourself within the Northern Dipper,
Then clasp your hands behind the Southern Cross."[167]

Dayu then said, "If you want to understand, then know that a single verse spreads in all directions, obstructing and cutting off the words of patch-robed monks."

Dayu also said, "When Luzu saw a monk approach he faced the wall. Nanquan said, 'You must comprehend what is before the Buddha appears in the world.' But until now there hasn't been a single one, or even a half of one, who understands. I say to you emphatically that if you do not realize your nature that existed before the womb, then you will be chopped in two at the waist."

⸻ ◆ ⸻

The official Mi Jianli of Nanchang invited the master to become the abbot of a temple at Cuiyan ["Emerald Crag"] on West Mountain. At his first lecture in the new hall, Dayu addressed the sacred Buddhist images, saying, "The profound affair is promulgated, the Dharma wheel is again turned." [He then said to the assembly] "Speaking of the Dharma wheel, what is it that turns? Do you understand? You must, at the very top, laugh out, and pivot yourself. But you just come in the hall and cross your legs. Ha, ha, ha. What's that? The food is in the basket, but you sit starving. You must be at ease in the mud and water. Who will you be with? When nobles hear it they are happy and at peace. When commoners hear it they are unselfish."

Langye Huijue, "Kaihua Guangzhao"

Langye Huijue (n.d.) was a disciple of Fenyang Shanzhao. He came from ancient Xiluo. Case 100 of the *Book of Serenity* states that Langye's father was the governor of Hengyang (a city in southern Hunan Province). His father died there, and Langye, fulfilling his filial obligation, carried his father's casket back to their native home. While passing through Lizhou (the modern Li County in Hunan Province), Langye climbed up Mt. Yao to see the ancient monastery there. He was surprised to find that the monastery seemed completely familiar, as though he'd lived there before. Because of this, he left home to become a monk. He studied under Zen master Fenyang Shanzhao and became his Dharma heir. Later, he lived at Chuzhou (the modern Chu County of Anwei Province) where he spread the influence of the Linji school of Zen. His teachings, along with those of his Zen contemporary Xuedou Chongxian (Mingjue), were jointly called "the two gates of sweet dew."[168]

A monk asked Langye, "What is Buddha?"
Langye said, "Copper head, iron forehead."
The monk said, "What does that mean?"
Langye said, "Bird beak, fish gills."

A monk asked, "How is it before the lotus comes out of the water?"
Langye said, "The cat wears a paper hat."
The person asked, "How about after the lotus comes out of the water?"
Langye said, "The dog runs when it sees the whip."

Langye entered the hall and addressed the monks, saying, "Hearing about enlightenment and wisdom, these are the cause of life and death. Hearing about enlightenment and wisdom, that itself is the root of liberation. It's as if a lion were staggering around in every direction with no place to live. If you don't understand, don't let yourself forsake old Shakyamuni! Hey!"

The following passage is provided from the *Book of Serenity*.

A monk asked Langye Jue, "The fundamental purity, how does it suddenly give rise to mountains, rivers, and the great earth?"

Langye said, "The fundamental purity, how does it suddenly give rise to mountains, rivers, and the great earth?"

FUSHAN FAYUAN, "YUANJIAN"

FUSHAN FAYUAN (991–1067), also known as "Yuanjian" ("Perfect Mirror"), was a disciple of Shexian Guixing. He came from ancient Dengzhou (in Henan Province). As a youth he left home to live as a novice monk in a temple headed by a teacher named Sanjiao Song. Fushan attained enlightenment upon hearing his teacher answer another monk's question about Zhaozhou's cypress tree in the courtyard. After taking the monk's vows he traveled widely. A great Zen adept, Fushan received Dharma transmission from both Shexian Guixing and Fenyang Shanzhao.

Zen master Fushan Fayuan entered the hall and addressed the monks, saying, "Dead trees of the Ru Sea blossom, but they do not take on the colors of spring."[169]

A monk asked, "What is Buddha?"
Fushan said, "The big ones are like elder brothers. The small ones are like younger brothers."

A monk asked, "Why did the First Ancestor come from the west?"
Fushan said, "Bones piled up on a broad plain."

Zen master Fushan entered the hall and addressed the monks, saying, "I won't speak any more about the past and the present. I just offer the matter before you now in order for you to understand."
A monk then asked, "What is the matter before us now?"
Fushan said, "Nostrils."
The monk then asked, "What is the higher affair?"
Fushan said, "The pupils of the eye."

Fushan entered the hall and addressed the monks, saying, "When heaven attains unity there is great clarity. When the earth attains unity there is great peace. When a king attains unity he rules the entire land. When a patch-robed monk attains unity, then trouble and catastrophe are at hand."

Fushan then struck the meditation platform, got down, and left the hall.

Among his accomplishments, Fushan is remembered as the Linji lineage monk who saved the Caodong Zen line from extinction. This remarkable episode occurred when Dayang Jingxuan, at the age of eighty, could find no successor to carry on the teachings of the Caodong school. He then entrusted Dongshan's teaching to Fushan along with the following verse:

> The grass atop Wide Poplar Mountain,
> Relies on you 'til the time.
> Its wayward sprouts are borne to fertile ground,
> And the fathomless mystery takes ethereal root.

Fushan protected the sprouts of the Dongshan school for ten years, finally passing the Caodong Dharma to Touzi Yiqing.

In the manner of Dongshan Liangjie's "five ranks," Fushan used a unique metaphysical framework to expound his Dharma teaching. This framework contained nine principles and was called "Fushan's Nine Teachings."

During his final years, Fushan retired to Hui Shengyan. There he expounded the deepest principles of the buddhas and ancestors. One day, he taught about the "nine teachings." He repeated each of them, saying, "The teaching of the true Buddhadharma eye; the teaching of the Buddhadharma treasure; the teaching of the penetration of principle; the teaching of the penetration of things; the teaching of the opposition of principle and things; the teaching of the winding path [of a bodhisattva]; the teaching of uniting with the wondrous time; the teaching of the golden needle and two locks [going beyond the opposition of principle and things]; and the teaching of the immediacy of reality."

The monks repeated the "nine teachings" back to Fushan.

Fushan then said, "But the perfect and ultimate Dharma gate is actually composed of ten teachings. All of you have just recited the nine teachings, but there is one more. Do you see it? If you clearly understand it and are intimate with it, then I invite you to come forward and speak to the assembly so that we can witness your understanding. If you can clearly explain this, then I'll concede that you have penetrated the prior nine teachings and possess the perfectly clear eye of the Way. But if we see that you're not really intimate with this teaching, that what you say doesn't meet with what's required, and that your understanding is just based on what I have said, then we'll know that what you have is just a spurious Dharma. Have you all reached this?"

None of the monks spoke.

Zen master Fushan sighed and passed away.

TOUZI YIQING

TOUZI YIQING (1032–83) was the Caodong Zen school Dharma heir, but not the direct student, of Dayang Jingxuan. He came from ancient Qingshe (near the modern city of Yanshi in Henan Province). According to the *Wudeng Huiyuan*, he left lay life at the age of seven to live at Miaoxiang Temple. Initially, he studied the "hundred dharmas doctrine" of the Consciousness-Only school of Buddhism. One day he said, "(This doctrine) is obscure and extensive. Of what advantage is all of this difficulty?" Later he undertook the practices of the Huayan school, but upon reading the words "Mind is self-nature," he had an insight, saying, "Dharma is not found in the written word, and how can one speak of it?" He then went traveling to find and study under a Zen teacher.

At that time, Zen master Yuanjian [Fushan Fayuan] was staying at Sacred Peak. One night he saw a blue eagle in a dream and took it as an omen.[170] The next morning, Touzi arrived and Yuanjian received him ceremoniously.

Now, because a non-Buddhist once asked the Buddha, "I don't ask about that which may be spoken of, and I don't ask about what may not be spoken of...," after three years Yuanjian asked Touzi, "Let's see if you remember your *huatou*."

Touzi began to answer when Yuanjian suddenly covered Touzi's mouth with his hand. Touzi then experienced enlightenment. He bowed.

Yuanjian said, "Have you awakened to the mysterious function?"

Touzi said, "Were it like that I'd have to spit it out."

At that time an attendant standing to one side said, "Today Qing Huayan [Touzi] is sweating as if he were ill!"

Touzi turned to him and said, "Don't speak insolently! If you do so again I'll vomit!"

After three more years, Yuanjian revealed to Touzi the essential doctrine passed down from Dongshan and Touzi grasped it entirely. Yuanjian presented Touzi with Dayang's portrait, sandals, and robe. He then instructed him to "carry on the method of this school in my behalf, so that it will not end here. Well and befittingly sustain and preserve it."

Yuanjian then wrote a verse and presented it to Touzi.

Mt. Sumeru stands in the great void.
It supports the spinning sun and moon.
Upon it countless peaks do rest,
The white clouds there transformed.

The Shoalin wind sows a forest.
The Caodong screen rolled up.
A golden phoenix lives in a dragon's nest.
Imperial moss is crushed by a wagon.

❖

Zen master Fayuan sent Touzi to study with Zen master Yuantong Shen. But when Touzi arrived at Yuantong's place, rather than going for an interview with that teacher at the appointed time, he remained sleeping in the monk's hall.

The head monk reported this to Yuantong, saying, "There is a monk who's sleeping in the hall during the day. I'll go deal with it according to the rules."

Yuantong asked, "Who is it?"

The head monk said, "The monk Qing."

Yuantong said, "Leave it be. I'll go find out about it."

Yuantong then took his staff and went into the monk's hall. There he found Touzi in a deep sleep. Hitting the sleeping platform with his staff, he scolded him, "I don't offer any 'leisure rice' here for monks so that they can go to sleep."

Touzi woke up and asked, "How would the master prefer that I practice?"

Yuantong said, "Why don't you try practicing Zen?"

Touzi said, "Fancy food doesn't interest someone who's sated."

Yuantong said, "But I don't think you've gotten there yet."

Touzi said, "What point would there be in waiting until you believed it?"

Yuantong said, "Who have you been studying with?"

Touzi said, "Fushan."

Yuantong said, "No wonder you're so obstinate!"

They then held each other's hands, laughed, and went to talk in Yuantong's room.

From this incident Touzi's reputation spread widely.

Touzi first taught on White Cloud Temple in Jianzhou. He later moved to the

Shengyin Monastery in Shuzhou (located on Mt. Qian in Anwei Province).

Zen master Touzi Yiqing entered the hall and addressed the monks, saying, "To speak of this affair is like a phoenix soaring into the heavens, not leaving a trace behind. It's like a ram whose horns are entangled in a tree [and thus does not touch the ground]. Where will you find any tracks? A golden dragon in not concealed in a cold swamp. A jade rabbit nests in the moonlight. In order to establish the guest and host, you must stick your head out beyond the noisy world. If you answer my questions properly, you're singing at the edge of the mysterious road. But in that case, you're still only halfway there. If you're still staring in miscomprehension, don't belabor what you see!"

❖

Zen master Touzi Yiqing entered the hall and addressed the monks, saying, "Don't stop in a run-down shack in an isolated village. Go through the mountain pass of the buddhas and ancestors. You are all like Su Taichu, always hitting barriers, never finding your way home.[171] You're like Lord Xiang when he reached the Niao River.[172] Where can you escape your tortured life? All Zen worthies who have reached this state—if they go forward, they fall into the hands of the celestial demons. If they retreat, they slip into the way of the hungry ghosts. If they go neither forward nor backward, then they drown in the dead water. All of you! Where will you find peace?"

After a pause, Touzi said, "Even three feet of snow can't crush a one-inch spiritual pine."

❖

When Touzi was near death, he composed a poem:

As the abbot of two temples,
I couldn't assist the Buddha way.
My parting message to you all,
Don't go seeking after something.

Touzi then put down the brush and passed away.

Upon his death, Touzi received the posthumous name "Zen Master Complete Compassion."

XINGYANG QINGPOU

XINGYANG QINGPOU (n.d.) was a disciple of Dayang Jingxuan. He lived and taught on Xingyang Mountain in ancient Yingzhou. Although he was a prominent successor of Dayang, he unfortunately did not outlive his teacher, nor did he have any Dharma heirs to carry on the Caodong line.

The *Wudeng Huiyuan* records an event that occurred when Xingyang worked as the head gardener at Mt. Dayang.

> When Xingyang was chief gardener he was tending the melons. Dayang asked him, "When will the sweet melons be ripe?"
>
> Xingyang said, "Now they're already very ripe."
>
> Dayang said, "Pick the sweet ones and take them away."
>
> Xingyang said, "To whom shall I give them?"
>
> Dayang said, "Give them to someone who hasn't been in the garden."
>
> Xingyang said, "Do you think that people who haven't been in the garden will eat them?"
>
> Dayang said, "Do you know these people or not?"
>
> Xingyang said, "Although I don't know them, I can't help but provide for them."
>
> Dayang laughed and went off.

After becoming the abbot of a temple, Xingyang entered the hall and addressed the monks, saying, "The principle of the great way that came from the west cuts off the hundred negations. Words that accord with the essential teaching go on without end. But what benefit could there be in just arduously submitting to the teachings of our school? Although it's like this, there are many different affairs to deal with. But in the teaching of our school, there is only one path that passes through. Everyone discuss this!"

A monk asked Xingyang Qingpou, "When the Sagara Dragon emerges from the sea, the entire universe shudders.[173] At just such a time, how is this expressed?"

Qingpou said, "The Garuda King confronts the universe! Among you here, who can come forth?"

The monk asked, "If suddenly someone comes forth, then what?"

Qingpou said, "It's like a falcon striking a pigeon. You don't believe me. If you can experience it behind your skull, then you'll at last realize the truth."

The monk said, "In that case, I'll just fold my hands on my chest and retreat three steps."

Qingpou said, "The tortoise that upholds Mt. Sumeru won't tolerate another one going back with a dot on its forehead!"[174]

<hr />

A monk asked Qingpou, "Where have all the ancient saints gone?"

Qingpou said, "The moon peacefully shines on the thousand rivers. Its solitary light illuminates to the bottom of the sea."

<hr />

Zheng Jinbu asked, "At what time did you go into the hall [begin teaching]?"

Qingpou said, "I do not enter the hall as one of a succession of monks. Rather, I enter the hall and speak before the sun and moon were born."

<hr />

When Qingpou was ill in bed, Dayang said to him, "The body is an illusion, and within this illusion affairs are carried out. If not for this illusion, the great matter would have no place from which to be undertaken. If the great matter is undertaken, it is seen to be an illusion. What do you say?"

Qingpou said, "There is still this matter here."

Dayang said, "And what is that matter?"

Qingpou said, "Encircling the earth, the lustrous crimson orb. At ocean bottom, not planting flowers."

[Qingpou paused and closed his eyes.]

Dayang smiled and said, "Are you awake?"

Qingpou said, "I've forgotten what I was about to say."

He then passed away.

TIANYI YIHUAI

TIANYI YIHUAI (993–1064) was a student of Xuedou Chongxian in the Yunmen school. He came from the coastal city of Leqing in what is now Zhejiang Province. The son of a fisherman, Tianyi infuriated his father when he jumped out of the fishing boat rather than kill fish. As a youngster he entered Tiantong Monastery as a novice monk.[175] Around the year 1027, after passing scriptural examinations, Tianyi set off to live and practice at various temples.[176] During this period he developed doubts about his faith and practice. An old monk named Fahua admonished him, "Go to Yunmen and Linji!"

Thus, Tianyi traveled on to Cuifeng Temple in Suzhou, where he met the great Zen teacher, Xuedou Chongxian.

At their first encounter, Xuedou said, "What is your name?"

Tianyi said, "Yihuai."

Chongxian said, "Why isn't it Huaiyi?" [Reversing the order of the two characters of this name creates the Chinese word "doubt."]

Tianyi said, "The name was given to me."

Chongxian said, "Who gave you this name?"

Tianyi said, "I received it at my ordination nearly ten years ago."

Chongxian said, "How many pairs of sandals have you worn out since you set out traveling?"

Tianyi said, "The master shouldn't deceive people!"

Chongxian said, "I haven't said anything improper. What do you mean?"

Tianyi remained silent.

Chongxian then hit him and said, "Strip off the silence and there's a fraud! Get out!"

Later, when Tianyi was in Chongxian's room for an interview, Chongxian said, "Practicing like this you won't attain it. Not practicing like this you won't attain it. This way or not this way, neither way will attain it."

Tianyi began to speak but Chongxian drove him out of the room with blows. This unpleasant scene repeated itself four times. Some time later, while Tianyi fetched water from the well and carried it with a shoulder pole back to the temple, the pole suddenly broke. As the bucket crashed to the ground Tianyi was suddenly enlightened. He then composed the following verse that Xuedou greatly praised:

One, two, three, four, five, six, seven,
Alone atop the 80,000-foot peak,
Snatching the pearl from the jaws of the black dragon,
A single word exposes Vimalakirti.

---------- ❖ ----------

Zen master Tianyi Yihuai entered the hall to address the monks. When everyone was settled he said, "If I just get up here and say, 'Hello everyone,' it's like spending a thousand taels of gold. If I just get down from here and say,

'Take care,' it's like enjoying the support of all the world. But if I talk about the Buddhadharma, then even a single drop of water can't be consumed. And if I have some idle, pointless discussion, then it's like putting cinders in your eyes. So what shall I do?"

After a long pause he said, "Do you understand? Take care!"

<hr>

Tianyi addressed the monks, saying, "A distinguished teacher of our sect said, 'You must drive away the ox from the plowman, grab away the starving man's food, regard the mean as noble, and regard the noble as mean. If you drive the ox away, then the plowman's crop will be abundant. If you snatch away the food, then you will forever end the starving man's hunger and thirst. Taking the mean as noble, a handful of dirt becomes gold. Taking the noble as mean, you change gold into dirt.'

"But as for me, I don't drive away the plowman's ox. Nor do I steal the starving man's food. Why is that? Because what use do I have for the plowman's ox? How could I eat that food? Moreover, I don't turn a handful of dirt into gold, or gold into dirt. And why is this? Because gold is gold; dirt is dirt; jade is jade; stone is stone; a monk is a monk; and a layperson is a layperson.

"Since antiquity there have existed heaven and earth, sun and moon, mountains and rivers, people and their relationships. This being so, how many of the deluded can break through the San Mountain Pass and meet Bodhidharma?"[177]

<hr>

A monk said, "I have just arrived here. I ask the master to expound the Dharma."

Tianyi said, "The birds call in the forest. The fish swim in the deep water."

<hr>

Tianyi addressed the monks, saying, "Patch-robed monks who prattle on about this don't realize the highest wisdom-eye Dharma gate."

A monk once asked, "What is the highest wisdom-eye Dharma gate?"

Tianyi said, "When the clothes are tattered, skin and bones show through. When the house collapses, then sleep looking at the stars."

<hr>

Tianyi addressed the monks. "'The green creeper spreads and reaches up to the top of the pine tree. The white clouds appear in the midst of empty space.' How does speaking in this manner compare to saying, 'The clouds rise up at

South Mountain; the rain falls on North Mountain'? If you understand this, it's a sweet melon that is sweet to the bottom. If you don't understand, it's a bitter gourd that is bitter to the root."

⸻ ❖ ⸻

Once, Zen master Tianyi said to a monk, "A handless man can use his fist. A tongueless man can speak. If suddenly a handless man strikes a tongueless man, what does the tongueless man say?"

CHENGTIAN CHUANZONG

CHENGTIAN CHUANZONG was a disciple of Xuedou Chongxian. Little is known of his life or teaching. He taught at Chengtian Temple in Quanzhou. The temple was regarded as one of the three great temples of ancient Fuzhou.

A monk asked Zen master Chengtian Quanzong, "When the great function is manifested without hindrance or restriction, what then?"
Chengtian said, "Today at Chengtian the flag was raised and lowered."
The monk then shouted.
Chengtian said, "A descendant of Linji."
The monk shouted again.
Chengtian hit him.

⸻ ❖ ⸻

A monk asked Chengtian Chuanzong, "What is the essence of prajna?"
Chengtian said, "Clouds basket the blue peaks."
The monk said, "What is the function of prajna?"
Chengtian said, "The moon in a clear pool."

YONGMING YANSHOU

YONGMING YANSHOU (904–75) was a disciple of Tiantai Deshao. He came from ancient Yuhang (located near Hangzhou City in Zhejiang Province). A brilliant and devoted practitioner of Buddhism, Yongming is honored as the third ancestor of the Fayan lineage of Zen, as well as the sixth ancestor of Chinese Pure

Land Buddhism. He left home at the relatively late age of thirty to study under Zen master Cuiyan Lingcan at Longce Temple.[178] Later, he undertook intensive Zen meditation practices under National Teacher Deshao on Mt. Tiantai, becoming his Dharma heir in the Fayan Zen lineage. The *Wudeng Huiyuan* relates that Yanshou remained so still during a ninety-day meditation session that a bird built a nest in the folds of his motionless clothing. Sometime later, Yanshou moved to nearby Guoqing Temple, where he undertook the Pure Land practice of chanting and other austerities.[179]

Yongming assumed his first position of abbot at Mt. Xuedou. Later, he moved to Hangzhou, where he restored Lingyin Monastery, a major temple that remains a national attraction in China. At the invitation of the ruler, Yanshou then moved to Yongming Monastery on the south shore of Hangzhou's West Lake. He remained there for fifteen years, receiving the mountain name by which he is remembered.

Yongming, as the occasion required, taught using both Zen and Pure Land methods of instruction. Like the Fayan school's founder, Fayan Wenyi, Yongming's syncretic method of instruction presaged the wide dilution of Zen with other Buddhist schools that occurred as the Song dynasty proceeded. A huge congregation gathered around him, and in his own era he was called an incarnation of Maitreya Bodhisattva. He worked closely with leaders of the Faxiang, Huayan, and Tiantai Buddhist sects to assemble the records and writings of more than two hundred famous Indian and Chinese Buddhist teachers.[180] The king of Korea paid tribute to these texts by sending Yongming various gifts. He also dispatched thirty-six monks to Hangzhou to study under this eminent teacher. Each of these foreign monks is said to have received Yanshou's Dharma seal and then returned to Korea, extending the teachings of the Fayan school into that country.

Zen master Yongming Yanshou addressed the monks, saying, "This place, Xuedou, has erupted eight thousand feet into the air and the earth has turned into slippery grain, stacked in a freakish 80,000-foot peak. You have absolutely nothing firm upon which to stand. In what direction will you step forward?"

---◆---

A monk asked Yongming, "How can one walk upon the path of Xuedou?"
Yanshou said, "Step by step through the wondrous cold landscape; words entirely frozen."

---◆---

Yongming recited the following verse:

"Amidst the high peaks a forlorn ape cries down to the moon.
The recluse chants while half the night candle burns.
Who comprehends this place and time?
At a place deep within white clouds, a Zen monk sits."

A monk asked, "What is Yongming's wondrous mystery?"
Yanshou said, "Add more incense."
The monk said, "Thank you, Master, for your instruction."
Yanshou said, "So you're satisfied and don't want to delve deeper?"
The monk bowed.
Yanshou said, "Listen to this verse.

"If you desire to know Yongming's mystery,
Before the gate is the lake's surface.[181]
The sun illuminates all life.
The wind arises and waves come up."

A monk asked, "This student has long been here at Yongming. Why can't I understand the style of the Yongming House?"
Yongming said, "You can understand the place you don't understand."
The monk said, "How can I understand what I don't understand?"
Yongming said, "An ox gives birth to an elephant. The blue sea gives rise to red dust."

A monk asked, "Our tradition has the saying, 'All the buddhas and their teachings come forth from this scripture.' What is 'this scripture'?"
Yongming said, "Without intention or sound it is endlessly recited."
The monk asked, "How does one receive and uphold it?"
Yongming said, "Those who want to receive and uphold it must look and listen."

A monk asked, "What is the great perfect mirror?"

Yongming said, "A broken dish of sand."

———————— ❖ ————————

During the twelfth month of [the year 975], Yongming became ill. Two days later he bade the monks farewell. Sitting cross-legged in an upright position, he passed away. His stupa was placed on Dazi ["Great Compassion"] Mountain.

Eighteenth Generation

HUANGLONG HUINAN

YANGQI FANGHUI

CUIYAN KEZHEN

CHANGSHUI ZIXUAN

FURONG DAOKAI

HUANGLONG HUINAN

HUANGLONG HUINAN (1002–69) was a disciple of Shishuang Chuyuan. He came from Xinzhou (located east of the modern city of Nanchang in Jiangxi Province). He founded the Huanglong branch of Linji Zen, whose successive generations of teachers resided on Mt. Huanglong for more than 150 years until the line died out.[182] Despite the relatively short existence of the school, its influence on Chinese society was widespread. The Japanese monk Myōan Esai, who is often regarded as the founder of Zen in Japan, studied with this school while visiting China.

According to the *Wudeng Huiyuan*, Huanglong first studied under a Zen master named Letan Chenggong, a teacher of the Yunmen school.

Huanglong was traveling with Zen master Yunfeng Yue. One night they were talking about Yunmen's Dharma and Yunfeng said, "Although Chenggong came after Yunmen, his Dharma is different."

Huanglong asked, "What's different about it?"

Yunfeng said, "Yunmen's Dharma is like making cinnabar with nine turns of the grinder, or touching iron and turning it to gold. But Chenggong's medicine is old hat to the disciples, and if you stick it in the forge it melts away."

Huanglong grew angry and threw a cushion at Yunfeng.

The next day Yunfeng apologized and said, "Yunmen's bearing is like that of a king. Are you willing to die beneath his words? Chenggong also imparts a Dharma to people. Death words. But these death words, can they also give people life?"

Yunfeng then turned to leave, but Huanglong pulled him back, saying, "If that's so, then what teacher now lives up to your meaning?"

Yunfeng said, "Shishuang Chuyuan's methods are known everywhere and all the disciples can see that he's unsurpassed." Huanglong thought to himself, "Master Yue is a student of [Dayu Zhi], but he's sending me to see Shishuang. How can this be?"

Huanglong then went to seek out Shishuang. While on the way he heard that Shishuang was not taking students, so he went instead to Mt. Heng, where he visited the teacher Fuyan Xian. Fuyan gave Huanglong the job of temple secretary. Shortly thereafter Fuyan died, and the governor appointed Shishuang to replace him.

When Shishuang arrived, he disparaged everything at the temple, ridiculing everything he saw as wrong. Huanglong was deeply disappointed with Shishuang's manner.

When Huanglong visited Shishuang in his abbot's room, Shishuang said, "Chenggong studied Yunmen's Zen, so he must surpass Yunmen's teaching. When Yunmen spared Dongshan Shouchu three blows with the staff, did Dongshan suffer the blows or not?"

Huanglong said, "He suffered the blows."

Shishuang said fiercely, "From morning till night the magpies cry and the crows caw, all of them in response to the blows they've suffered."

Shishuang then sat in a cross-legged position, and Huanglong lit incense and bowed to him.

Shishuang later asked, "Zhaozhou said, 'The old lady of Mt. Tai—I'll go check her out for you.' But where was the place he checked her out?"

Huanglong sweated profusely but he couldn't answer.

The next day, Huanglong went to Shishuang's room again. Shishuang berated him unceasingly. Huanglong said, "Is cursing a compassionate way of carrying out the teaching?"

Shishuang yelled, "Try cursing and see!"

At these words Huanglong experienced a great awakening. He then wrote the following verse:

The eminent adept Zhaozhou
Had his reasons for checking out the old lady.
Now the four seas are like a mirror,
And a pilgrim no longer hates the road.

The *Yuxuan Yulu*, a Zen text dating from the Qing dynasty period (1644–1908), offers the following story involving Huanglong Huinan:

A monk was standing and waiting to speak with Huanglong in an interview.[183] Huanglong observed him for a long while, and then said, "There are a million samadhis and limitless gates [by which to enter the Way]. If I tell you something will you believe it?"

The monk said, "The master is sincere. How dare I not believe it?"

Huanglong pointed to his left and said, "Come over here."

The monk then moved to that spot.

Huanglong cried out, "You're following sound and chasing form!"

When the monk's time was up he went out. Later, a different monk entered who knew what had transpired in the previous meeting.

Huanglong asked the monk the same question he had asked the previous monk. The monk responded by saying, "I dare not believe you."

Huanglong again pointed to his left and said, "Come over here."

The monk stood fast and didn't move.

Huanglong cried out, "You come to confide in me and yet you don't obey me! Get out!"

The following passages are from *The Record of [Huanglong] Huinan:*

Huanglong entered the hall and addressed the monks, saying, "The dharma-kaya is formless, but is revealed in things. Prajna wisdom is without knowledge, but it shines in conditional existence."

Huanglong then lifted his whisk and said, "When I lift up the whisk, it is called the dharmakaya. But here it is not revealed in a thing. When I bring the whisk down, it is called prajna wisdom. But here it does not shine in conditional existence."

Huanglong then laughed out loud and said, "If somebody came up here and grabbed me, spit on me, gave me a slap, knocked over the meditation bench and dragged me down to the floor, then I really couldn't blame them!

"Saying these things is like gnawing on the feet of pigs and dogs. What a state I've fallen to!"

◆

Huanglong addressed the monks, saying, "Before I came up here to speak there was nothing in my mind. But now that I've come up here there are a lot of questions. I dare to ask you whether the great vehicle of our school is found in such questions and answers. If it were to be found in such speech, then doesn't the scriptural canon have questions and answers? Yet it is said that [the way of Zen] is transmitted outside of the scriptural teachings. It is transmitted to individuals who are great Dharma vessels. If it can't be found in words, then even if you ask all sorts of excellent questions, what, after all, is the point of doing so? People on pilgrimages should open their eyes. Don't do something you'll regret later.

"If you want to talk about it, then you can say that it can't be realized through mystical perception or self perfection. Nor may it be said to be a result of some all-encompassing understanding. The buddhas of the three worlds have only said you must know yourself. In the entire canon of scripture this can't be explained. In the ancient meeting at Vulture Peak, a vast multitude assembled there, but it was only Mahakashyapa who understood.

"The Fifth Ancestor, Huangmei, had an assembly of seven hundred monks, but he passed the robe and bowl of transmission only to the pilgrim Lu [Huineng].

"How about the likes of you gathered here who are still clinging to delusive greed and ignorance? Can you overcome these things and carry forth our school? Those who leave home must have heroic resolve, cut off the two heads, and practice in seclusion in the house of the self. Afterwards they must throw open the door, get rid of the possessions of that self, and then receive and meet whatever comes, giving aid to any in need. In this way the deep compassion of Buddha can be in some small measure repaid. Aside from acting in this manner, there is nothing else."

Huanglong then struck the meditation platform with his whisk and left the hall.

⸻ ◆ ⸻

Huanglong quoted a saying by Yunmen to the congregation, saying, "'Across the broad plain are innumerable corpses. Those who pass through the forest of thorns are true adepts.'"

He then lifted his whisk and said, "You in the assembly! If you truly call it a broad plain covered with corpses, and you don't call it a whisk, then you haven't yet passed through the forest of thorns!"

Huanglong then got down and left the hall.

⸻ ◆ ⸻

Huanglong addressed the monks, saying, "Great surging waves, vast and expansive, their billowing whitecaps fill the sky! The ones who pass through them and reach the other shore, they have righteously shed worldly concerns. They have left the solitary oarsman behind and their eyebrows are no longer knit with anxiety. If I were to ask for a single phrase from someone who has quieted the wind and pacified the waves, what would it be? Is there anyone here who can speak it? If there's no one who can speak then I'll do it for you."

After a long pause, Huanglong said, "The fisherman hums a carefree song. The woodsman sings a high melody!"

◆

Huanglong addressed the monks, saying, "The sun comes up in the east. The moon goes down in the west. Coming up; going down. From ancient times until today, all of you have completely understood this; completely observed this. It is Vairochana Buddha; limitless and fathomless…. The myriad things of our daily lives all exist in accordance with conditions. All of you! Why don't you see? It's concealed from you by your countless emotions. If you look deeply into causation, then you will not miss what is sacred, nor will you transcend the shadows and traces…. If, in clarity, not a single thought is born, you will be akin to the shining sun and moon, and at one with the revolving firmament. Then the Great Jailer God will give your brains an evil poke that obliterates them!"

◆

Huanglong addressed the monks, saying, "This is the first day of the interval between practice periods. Worthy monks of the congregation! Practice the Way joyfully! At night on the long meditation platform, you can stretch your legs and fold them again whenever you please—not according to someone's instructions. When the sun comes up you get out of bed and eat some breakfast cakes. When you've eaten your fill you can relax.

"At just such a time, what you are doing cannot be called ancient or contemporary. It cannot be considered good or evil. Demons and gods can't find a trace of it. The myriad dharmas are not its partner. Earth can't contain it and heaven can't cover it. Although it's like this, you still must have pupils in your eyes and blood in your veins. Without pupils in your eyes how do you differ from a blind person? Without blood in your veins, how do you differ from a dead person? Thirty years from now, you won't be able to blame me!"

When he finished speaking, Huanglong got down from the seat and left the hall.

◆

Huanglong, while addressing the monks, quoted a teaching by the monk Daju, saying, "'When body, speech, and mind are pure, what is called Buddha appears in the world.[184] When body, speech, and mind are impure, what is called Buddha is extinguished.'

"What a wonderful message! The ancients, according to circumstances, offered expedient means. They talked about a method for each of you here to find an entrance. Since you have an entrance, you must also find an exit. When you climb the mountain you must reach the top. When you go into the sea you must reach the bottom. If you climb a mountain but don't reach the top, then you can't know the vastness of the universe. If you enter the sea but don't reach the bottom, then you can't know the depth of the sea. When you know the vastness of the universe and the depth of the sea, then with one kick you can knock over the four seas.[185] With one shove you can push over Mt. Sumeru. And when you let go, no one, even in your own family, can recognize you.

"The sparrow sings and the crow caws in the willow tree!"

The story of Huanglong's death is narrated in the *Wudeng Huiyuan*.

One day, Huanglong entered the hall and addressed the monks, saying, "This mountain monk has little talent and sparse virtue, yet I've borne the task of being a teacher. So, not being blind to original mind, not deceiving the ancestors, not avoiding birth and death, I now avoid birth and death. Due to not leaving the wheel, I now leave the wheel. That which is not cast off is thus now cast off. That not realized is now completely realized. Thus the light of Buddhism that has passed down from the World-Honored Great Enlightened One is that not a single Dharma can be obtained. What is it that was transmitted to the Sixth Ancestor in the dead of night at Huangmei?"

Huanglong then recited the following verse:

"Attaining not attaining,
Transmitting not transmitting,
How can one speak of
Returning to the root and attaining the essence?
Recalling the leaks in her old dwelling,
To what house does the new bride travel?"

The next day at noon, Huanglong assumed a cross-legged sitting posture and passed away. His memorial stupa was placed on the hill before the temple. He received the posthumous title "Zen Master Universal Enlightenment."

Yangqi Fanghui

Yangqi Fanghui (992–1049) was a disciple of Shishuang Chuyuan. He is known as the founder of the Yangqi branch of the Linji school. All of the Linji Zen schools in the world today are spiritual descendants of this branch. Yangqi's home was the city of Yichun in Yuanzhou (now in Jiangxi Province). As a child he was clever and well spoken. As a young man he is reported to have run afoul of authorities in his job as a tax administrator and was forced to flee into obscurity. He later became a monk at Jiufeng in Duanzhou (west of modern Guangzhou City). Traveling to the region of ancient Tanzhou, he studied under the eminent teacher Shishuang Chuyuan and became his Dharma heir. Later, he gained his mountain name while serving as abbot at the Putong Monastery at Mt. Yangqi. In the year 1046, Yangqi moved to Haihui Temple in Tanzhou.

Yangqi taught the principle that Zen is manifested in everyday events, and the great way of emancipation is to be sought in the common activities of people's lives.

> When Shishuang Chuyuan moved from Nanyuan to Mt. Dao Wu, and then to Shishuang, Yangqi followed him, performing administrative affairs in each place. Although Yangqi remained with Shishuang for a long time, he never attained enlightenment. Each time he would have an interview, Shishuang would say, "There are a lot of administrative affairs requiring attention. Go do them."
>
> On one occasion when Yangqi went to see Shishuang [for instruction on practice], Shishuang said, "Director! Someday your descendants will cover the earth. Why are you in a hurry?"
>
> One day, Shishuang had just gone out when it suddenly began to rain. Yangqi spied his teacher walking on a small path, chased him down, and grabbed him, saying, "You've got to talk to me now, or else I'm going to hit you!"
>
> Shishuang said, "Director! You already completely know how to take care of things, so that's enough!"
>
> Before Shishuang had finished speaking, Yangqi experienced great enlightenment. He then kneeled and bowed to Shishuang on the muddy path.

The *Zeng Ding Fozu Dao Ying* offers a different passage related to Yangqi's spiritual maturity.[186]

Yangqi asked Shishuang, "How is it when the great dark bird cries 'na! na!' and flies down from the clouds into the chaotic mountain peaks?"

Shishuang said, "I walk in wild grasses. You rush into the village."

Yangqi said, "When the senses have no room for even a needle, still there is another question."

Shishuang then shouted.

Yangqi said, "Good shout."

Shishuang shouted again.

Yangqi also shouted.

Shishuang then shouted twice.

Yangqi bowed.

Shishuang said, "This affair concerns one person taking up and carrying a lotus."

Yangqi shook his sleeves and went out.

When Shishuang passed away, Yangqi left and went to live at Pingmai on Jiu Peak. Many monks and lay persons came to Jiu Peak to request that he assume the abbacy at Mt. Yangqi.

At that time, Marquis Qin didn't know Yangqi.

He exclaimed in surprise, "Does Monastery Director Hui understand Zen?"

Upon accepting the invitation to teach, Yangqi met with the congregation to answer questions. At the end of the meeting he said, "Are there any more questions? If so, come forth with them. Today my life is in the hands of each and every one of you, and is dependent on your support. Why is this? An abbot's authenticity is clearly judged by the congregation. It can't be hidden away and obscured like a submerged water plant. It must be tested now before the congregation. Can anyone else come forward to test it? If not, then it is my own loss."

When he finished speaking, Yangqi got down from the seat.

Just then Marquis Qin grabbed him and said, "I'm happy that today I've finally gotten a fellow practitioner."

Yangqi said, "What do you mean by 'fellow practitioner'?"

Marquis Qin said, "Yangqi guides the ox. Marquis Qin pushes it."

Yangqi said, "At this moment, is Yangqi in the front, or is Jiufeng in the front?"

Marquis Qin was unable to answer.

Yangqi then pushed him away and said, "Before I thought we were fellow practitioners, but actually we're not!"

Because of this incident, Yangqi's reputation spread widely through the land.

Yangqi said, "Fog fills the sky and the wind blows wildly. The foliage and the trees, like a great lion's roar, expound the *Mahaprajnaparamita* scripture. All of the buddhas of the three worlds turn the great wheel of Dharma under the heels of each of you! If you understand this, then your wisdom is not wasted. If you don't understand, then don't say that the terrain of Mt. Yangqi is dangerous, because in front of you there is still the highest mountain to climb!"

One day, three monks arrived at the monastery.

Yangqi said to them, "Three people traveling together must have one wisdom."

Yangqi then picked up a cushion and said, "Practitioner, what do you call this?"

The monk said, "A cushion."

Yangqi said, "Really?"

The monk said, "Yes."

Yangqi then again asked, "What do you call it?"

The monk again said, "A cushion."

Yangqi then looked to the left and right and said, "This practitioner possesses the eye."

Yangqi then said to the second monk, "If you want to travel a thousand miles, you must start with the first step. What is the first phrase?"

The monk said, "Arriving here at the master's place, how dare I extend my hand?"

Yangqi then used his hand to draw a circle in the air.

The monk said, "Complete."

Yangqi then extended both of his hands.

When the monk started to speak, Yangqi said, "Complete."

Yangqi then asked the third monk, "From where have you recently departed?"

The monk said, "From Nanyuan."

Yangqi said, "Today, you monks have discovered Yangqi. Please sit and have some tea."

Yangqi entered the hall and said, "The single word of Yangqi is complete and perfect everywhere. If you try to grasp it, it's inconceivable."

A monk asked, "In order to escape the vexations of the mind, one must see the ancient teaching. What is the ancient teaching?"

Yangqi said, "The clear moon of the universe. The clear wave of the blue ocean."

The monk then asked, "If someone doesn't yet understand this, how can he do so?"

Yangqi said, "Beneath the heels."

Yangqi addressed the monks, saying, "There is no great meaning on Yangqi. What you sow you'll reap! Old Shakyamuni was talking in a dream. Where will you find any trace of it now?"

Yangqi then struck the meditation platform and shouted, "Practice!"

Yangqi asked a monk who had just arrived, "The fog is thick and the road is obscured, so how did you get here?"

The monk said, "The sky does not have four walls."

Yangqi said, "How many straw sandals did you wear out coming here?"

The monk shouted.

Yangqi said, "One shout. Two shouts. After that, then what?"

The monk said, "I meet you, Master, but you're quite busy."

Yangqi said, "I don't have my staff. Sit and have some tea."

When another monk arrived, Yangqi said to him, "The leaves fall and the clouds gather. Where did you come from today?"

The monk said, "From Kwan Yin."[187]

Yangqi asked, "How would you say one word from beneath Kwan Yin's heels?"

The monk said, "I've just arrived to see you."

Yangqi said, "What is it that you've seen?"

The monk didn't answer.

Yangqi said to a second monk who had also come, "You! Can you say something for this practitioner?"

The second monk didn't answer.

Yangqi said, "Here are a couple of dumb horses."

Yangqi left thirteen Dharma heirs.

CUIYAN KEZHEN

CUIYAN KEZHEN (d. 1064) was a disciple of Shishuang Chuyuan of the Linji lineage. He came from the ancient city of Changxi in Fuzhou. By some accounts he gained enlightenment when his teacher Shishuang, while lecturing, suddenly pointed at and tapped on Cuiyan's chest. Cuiyan then gained the moniker "Truth Tap Chest." He later resided in Hongzhou, as well as on Mt. Dao Wu in Tanzhou. The following account is provided in the *Wudeng Huiyuan*.

Zen Master Cuiyan Kezhen was from Fuzhou. He studied under Ziming [Shishuang Chuyuan], and because of this spent a summer with Jinlong and attendant Shan. Shan was Ziming's highest ranking student, followed by Daowu Zhen and Yangqi Shanhui.[188] Cuiyan wished to see [attain the level of] Shishuang. Shan laughed at him, saying that in the entire world there was no one who could do so. Shan then questioned Cuiyan and determined that he had not yet penetrated the truth.

As they traveled together on a summer pilgrimage, Shan verbally challenged Cuiyan. Shan picked up a tile, set it on a rock and said, "If you can provide a turning phrase for this, I'll concede that you've seen Ziming." Cuiyan glanced around and started to respond. Shan instantly derided him, saying "Halting the thoughts, stopping the function! Feeling and perception won't penetrate it; what are you dreaming?" Cuiyan was deeply intimidated. They then returned to Shishuang. Ziming saw them coming and called out, "Anyone on pilgrimage must make good use of his time! What's the matter? The summer isn't over yet, so why have you already come back here?"

Cuiyan said, "My mind has been poisoned by elder brother Shan. He hinders people. It's for this reason I've come to see you, Master."

Shishuang suddenly asked him, "What is the ultimate meaning of our school?"

Cuiyan said, "No clouds upon the peaks, the moon sheds waves of mind."

Shishuang looked at him angrily and yelled, "Gray-haired and clever, yet you still have this sort of understanding! When will you cast off life and death?"

Cuiyan was embarrassed and appealed to Ziming for instruction.

Shishuang said, "You ask me."

Cuiyan then asked Shishuang the question that the teacher had asked him moments before. Shishuang shouted at him, saying, "No clouds upon the peaks, the moon sheds waves of mind!"

At these words Cuiyan experienced great enlightenment.

Later, when he resided as abbot on Cui Bluff, a monk asked him, "What is Buddha?"

Cuiyan said, "The same earthen dam, no different dirt."

A monk asked, "Why did Bodhidharma come from the west?"

Cuiyan said, "Plow deeply, plant seeds shallow."

The monk asked, "What is the place where the student's body turns?"

Cuiyan said, "A single wall, a hundred walls."

The monk asked, "What is the place where the student is empowered?"

Cuiyan said, "A thousand days chopping wood, but burning it all in a single day."

A monk asked, "What is the Way?"

Cuiyan said, "Go out the door and look."

The monk said, "What is a person of the Way?"

Cuiyan said, "A manacled prisoner is accused."

Cuiyan, addressing the congregation, quoted a passage by Zen master Longya, saying, "'Studying the Way is like making fire with a drill. You can't stop when you see smoke. You must keep at it until there are flames. Then you've reached your goal.'"

Cuiyan then quoted Zen master Shending, who said, "Studying the Way is easier than drilling for fire, for as soon as you see smoke you can quit. Before the flames arise it has already burned you from head to foot."

Then Zen master Cuiyan said, "From the 'sudden enlightenment' point of view, Longya's statement stops halfway. From the 'gradual enlightenment' point of view, Shending's statement still lacks realization. How would you deal with this question?

"Monks! This year many leaves have fallen. How many of them can you sweep up?"

Cuiyan addressed the monks, saying, "During the Lin Chen rebellion, there were brave army commanders who did not fear life and death. There are courageous hunters who enter the mountains, unmindful of ferocious tigers. There are brave fishermen who never fear water snakes and dragons.

"What is it that Zen monks are courageous about?"

Cuiyan then raised his staff and said, "This is the staff. If you can raise it, hold it, and shake it, then the ten thousand worlds all move in the same moment. If you can't raise it, hold it, and shake it, then for you Manjushri is just Manjushri and 'dropping the self' is just 'dropping the self.'"

When Cuiyan died in the year 1066, Prime Minister Wang Gong mourned at his memorial stupa, crying out, "Truly one of great virtue!"

CHANGSHUI ZIXUAN

CHANGSHUI ZIXUAN (n.d.) was a disciple and Dharma heir of Langye Huijue. He came from Jiaxing. According to the *Wudeng Huiyuan,* as a young man he cut off his hair and continuously recited the *Surangama Sutra.*

Changshui gained a profound insight when he heard the Buddhist teacher Hongmin say, "The demeanor of the bodhisattva is manifestly unproduced."

Changshui then said to Hongmin, "Tapping emptiness, [but instead] striking the bamboo, one still falls into the trap. Raising the eyes and arching the eyebrows, already there's intent. Leaving aside these two paths, realizing the essence." Hongmin approved this as evidence of Changshui's understanding.

Changshui set off to "seek out the source of Zen." Hearing that Langye Huijue's teaching was unsurpassed, he hastened to that teacher's congregation. According to the account in the *Wudeng Huiyuan,* Changshui is the monk who poses to Langye the question about original purity that is cited in case 100 of the *Book of Serenity.*

Changshui stepped forward and asked, "The fundamental purity, how does it suddenly give rise to mountains, rivers, and the great earth?"

Langye said, "The fundamental purity, how does it suddenly give rise to mountains, rivers, and the great earth?"

Changshui thereupon had realization. He said, "I wish to serve as towel and pitcher."

Langye said, "This style will not be long-lived. You should resolutely safeguard it and repay Buddha's kindness. Do not regard any other teaching as greater than this."

Then, as he was instructed, Changshui again bowed and left.

—————— ◆ ——————

On the day when Changshui began his appointment as abbot he addressed the monks, saying, "The Way is not attained by speech or form, nor is it known through design or deliberation. The essence can only be [directly] grasped. It has never been otherwise realized."

Because he was respected by the two schools [Zen and scriptural], and because of his commentary on the *Surangama Sutra*, he became widely known.

Furong Daokai

FURONG DAOKAI (1043–1118) was a disciple of Touzi Yiqing. Furong came from ancient Yizhou (now the city of Linyi in southern Shandong Province). As a young man he practiced certain Taoist arts, including fasting, with the aim of gaining immortality. He later abandoned such practices and studied with a Zen teacher at Shutai Temple, located near the old capital city of Changan. There he passed the scriptural examination to enter the clergy. He subsequently studied with Touzi, becoming his Dharma heir and a link in the historical chain of the Caodong lineage.

Furong asked Touzi, "The words of the buddhas and ancestors were about everyday things such as drinking tea or eating rice. Besides this, does the teaching have anything special for people or not?"

Touzi said, "You speak the Cosmic Emperor's edict. Are you pretending to be Yao, Shun, Yu, and Tang or not?"[189]

Furong wanted to continue speaking but Touzi raised his whisk and placed it over Furong's mouth, saying, "If you have some intention, then you already deserve thirty hits with the stick!"

Furong then experienced enlightenment. He bowed and turned to leave.

Touzi said, "Come back! Your Reverence!"

Furong ignored him.

Touzi said, "Have you come to the place of no doubt?"

Furong then covered his ears with his hands.

Another recorded dialogue between Furong and his teacher also shows Touzi's deep concern about the succession question.

One day Touzi and Furong were walking in the vegetable patch. Touzi came up to Furong and handed him his staff. Furong took it, then walked behind Touzi.

Touzi said, "Is this in accordance with principle?"

Furong said, "Carrying the master's shoes or staff for him, it can't be otherwise."

Touzi said, "There's one walking with me."

Furong said, "Who's not learning from you?"

Touzi went back.

When evening came, he said to Furong, "The matter we spoke of earlier isn't finished."

Furong said, "Master, please speak your mind."

Touzi said, "The morning gives birth to the sun. The evening gives birth to the moon."

Furong then lit the lamp.

Touzi said, "Your comings and goings, none of it is like that of a disciple."

Furong said, "Taking care of the master's affairs, this is in accordance with principle."

Touzi said, "Servants and slaves, what household doesn't have them?"

Furong said, "The master is advanced in years. Neglecting him is unacceptable."

Touzi said, "So this is how you apply your diligence!"

Furong said, "One should repay kindness."

———— ◆ ————

After Furong became abbot, a monk asked him, "The song of the foreigner does not have the five tones [of the musical scale]. Its melody goes beyond the heavens. I ask the master to sing it!"

Furong said, "The wooden cock crows in the night. The iron phoenix sings clearly through the heavens."

The monk said, "In that case, a single phrase of this song includes a thousand old melodies. The itinerant monks that know this tune fill the hall!"

Furong said, "A tongueless child can carry the tune."

The monk said, "You are a great teacher, possessing the celestial eye of humanity."

Furong said, "Quit flapping your lips."

In the year 1080 Furong became the abbot of the Zhaoti Temple and Chongning Baoshou Zen Monastery on Mt. Dayang. There he "propagated the way of the Caodong school, with disciples as numerous as clouds."

One day Furong entered the hall and said, "By day, entering Jetavanavihara Park, a lustrous moon is in the sky. By night, ascending Vulture Peak, the sun fills the eyes.[190] Crows swarming like the snow; a solitary goose becomes a flock; an iron dog barks and rises to the clouds; a water buffalo struggles and enters the sea. Just when it's like this, the ten directions converge, and then what separates self and other? In this place of ancient buddhas, beneath the gate of the ancestors, all of you extend a hand and receive the worthies that have arrived. All of you, can you speak about what you've attained?"

After a long pause Furong said, "Plant an abundance of formless trees for those who come later to see."

———— ❖ ————

Zen master Furong Daokai addressed the monks, saying, "I don't ask about the last thirty days of the twelfth month. I just want to know about the great matter of the twelfth month. Everyone! At that moment, Buddha can't help you, Dharma can't help you, the ancestors can't help you, all the teachers on earth can't help you, I can't help you, and the King of Death can't help you. You must settle this matter now! If you settle it now, the Buddha can't take it from you, the Dharma can't take it from you, the ancestors can't take it from you, all the teachers in the world, and the King of Death can't take it from you.

"Speak out! What is the lesson of this very moment? Do you understand? Next year there'll be a new shoot growing. The annoying spring wind never ceases."

———— ❖ ————

A monk asked, "What is Tao?"

Furong said, "When night comes, a hornless ox rushes into its pen."

Furong said, "When the karmic sounds of bells and drums are not heard, a single sound awakens the one in the dream. Perfect eternal stillness has no extra affairs. Who says Kwan Yin offers some other gate?"

After a long pause, Furong said, "Do you understand? Don't ask the guest on Putuo Mountain.[191] When the eagle cries, the clouds around the island peaks are dispersed!"

Furong entered the hall to address the monks. He held up his staff and said, "Here you see it, the affair of all the buddhas. Even if you can freely 'rise in the east and sink in the west,' 'gather it in and roll it out,' you still don't fundamentally comprehend the affair that predates the seven buddhas.[192] You must realize that there is a person who is not realized through others, who does not receive teachings from others, and who does not fall into stages. If you see this person, the Zen practice of an entire lifetime is concluded."

Furong then suddenly yelled at the monks, "If you have any more doubts, you don't need to see me about them!"

Furong entered the hall and said, "The green mountains are always walking. The stone woman gives birth to a son at night."

A monk asked, "What is the style of the master's house?"
Furong said, "Everyone can see it."

In the year 1104 the emperor Hui Zong heard of Furong's reputation and presented him with the honored purple robe and the title "Zen Master Samadhi Illumination." Furong refused the robe as being inappropriate and incurred the emperor's wrath. The emperor demanded that Furong take up residence in Zizhou [a place in modern Shandong Province]. Furong refused to submit to this as well. Eventually the emperor had a change of heart and honored Furong, building a temple for him at Furong. Furong moved to that location, assumed its mountain name, and remained there, teaching a great number of students, for the rest of his life.

On the fourteenth day of the eighth lunar month in [the year 1118], Furong asked for a brush and paper. He then wrote this verse:

I'm seventy-six years old,
My causational existence is now completed.
In life I did not favor heaven,
In death I don't fear hell.
Hands and body extend beyond the three realms.
What stops me from roaming as I please?

Soon after writing this verse the master passed away.

Nineteenth Generation

YUNAN KEWEN   HUITANG ZUXIN

BAIYUN SHOUDUAN   BAONING RENYONG

DAGUI MUCHE   DANXIA ZICHUN

BAOFENG WEIZHAO

YUNAN KEWEN, "ZHENJING," "BAOFENG"

YUNAN KEWEN (1025–1102), also known as Baofeng, was a disciple of Huanglong Huinan. Baofeng came from ancient Jiafu (now known as Jia County in Henan Province). He is recorded to have been a scholar, learned in non-Buddhist as well as Buddhist disciplines. He received ordination at the age of twenty-five. When he first studied under Huanglong, he failed to gain the import of his teaching. He then traveled to Xiangcheng, where he studied under a monk named Shun. That teacher posed to him the same words that Baofeng had heard previously from Huanglong, whereupon he finally grasped Huanglong's meaning and gained enlightenment. He then returned to Huanglong and became his Dharma heir. Later in his life, Baofeng assumed the abbacy at Mt. Dong, and later founded a new temple at Bao Peak in Longxing (near modern Nanchang City).

> While spending the summer at Mt. Gui, Baofeng heard the story of a monk who asked Yunmen, "Isn't the Buddhadharma like the moon reflected in water?"[193]
>
> Yunmen said, "The clear wave does not penetrate the Way."
>
> Baofeng, hearing this story, gained a great insight.
>
> Baofeng later went to study under Huanglong, but he couldn't grasp his teaching.[194] Baofeng said, "I have some good points, but this old fellow doesn't acknowledge them." He then went to Xiangcheng, where he met with the monk Shun.
>
> Shun asked, "Where did you come from?"
>
> Baofeng said, "I came from Huanglong."
>
> Shun said, "What did Huanglong say recently?"
>
> Baofeng said, "Recently the provincial governor asked Huanglong to assume

the abbacy of Huangbo, and Huanglong thereupon offered this teaching: 'Chanting adulation above the bell tower, planting vegetables below the plat-form. Someone offers turning phrases, then assumes the abbacy.' And when he ascended the seat, he said, 'A ferocious tiger sits on the road. A dragon goes to reside at Huangbo.'"[195]

Without hesitating Shun said, "Assuming the seat, he offered a single turn-ing phrase, and then he assumed the abbacy of Huangbo. But as for the Bud-dhadharma, he doesn't even see it in his dreams."

At these words Baofeng realized great enlightenment and finally understood Huanglong's meaning. He then returned to Huanglong.

Huanglong said, "Where have you come from?"

Baofeng said, "I've come especially to pay you my respects."

Huanglong said, "Right now I'm not here."

Baofeng said, "Where have you gone?"

Huanglong said, "To do communal work at Mt. Tiantai. To go hiking on Mt. Nanyue."

Baofeng said, "In that case, this student is in charge."

Huanglong said, "Where have the sandals beneath your feet come from?"

Baofeng said, "Bringing the texts of seven hundred fifty songs from Mt. Lu."

Huanglong said, "How did you get to be in charge?"

Baofeng pointed at his sandals and said, "How could I not be in charge?"

Huanglong was startled.

———— ◆ ————

On the day he assumed the abbacy [at Bao Peak], Zen master Baofeng offered incense to the sacred figures.

[Later] he halted the questioning from the congregation, saying, "Stop the questions! You are just asking about Buddha and Dharma, but you don't know the source of Buddha and Dharma. Where do you say they come from?"

Baofeng then dropped one foot off of the dais and said, "Formerly, Huanglong himself put forth a command, and all the buddhas in the ten directions dared not oppose it; all the generations of ancestors and all the saints dared not contravene it. The innumerable Dharma gates, all of the sublime mysteries, the seal on the tongue of every teacher in the world, [all of these things] don't dare deviate from it. But leaving aside 'not deviating from it,' where is the seal? Do you see it? If you can see it, then there is no such thing as 'monk' and 'lay person,' no 'universal' and no 'particular.' Everything partakes of it. If you don't see it, then I'll take it back."

Baofeng then withdrew his leg, shouted, and said, "A soldier drills with the (military) seal. A general marches with the military colors. If you ask about Buddha's hand or a donkey's foot or some old country teacher, then you'll get thirty painful strikes from the staff. Is there not something unpleasant in the hall today? If there is, then don't obstruct it. If there isn't, then this old monk is deceiving you. Therefore, our Great Enlightened World-Honored One, in former times in the country of Magadha, on the eighth day of the twelfth month, upon the appearance of the morning star, suddenly was enlightened to the great Way, and the great earth and all beings in one moment became Buddha. Now, Shakyamuni's disciples are in the eastern country of China in the city of Yunyang of the great Song dynasty, on the thirteenth day of the sixth month. When the bright sun appears, will there be another enlightenment?"

He then moved his whisk in a circle and said, "I don't dare deceive you! You are all Buddha!"

The following passages are from *The Record of Kewen*.

Zen master Yunan Kewen said to the congregation, "Everyone! Has your self-belief gone far enough? If you've reached the zenith of belief in self, then you know that self-nature is fundamentally Buddha. When you thus realize no belief in self, then you've become a Buddha. But because of ancient delusion, when a person hears this, it's difficult for him to forsake his belief [in self]. The speech and words of the virtuous, from ancient times down to the present, throughout the current of Zen, have been nothing but the buddha nature of the saints flowing out and being set forth. But what flowed forth was just the branch. Buddha nature is the root.

"These days many people seek the branch but reject the root, forgetting the true and falling into the false, they have harmed the Buddhadharma. What an annoyance it is for them that they should remember that the words and phrases of the ancients were for the sake of Zen and the Way! If not for Bodhidharma's coming from the west, there'd be no Zen to be passed on. It was all for the sake of beings to individually realize their own self-nature and become buddhas, for beings to personally bring forth the entire Buddhadharma. Moreover, it was for the transformation of the universal spirit, whereby all beings are seen to be, in themselves, complete and perfect, and without the need to falsely seek anything outside of themselves.

"If people today seek something outside of themselves, then they cover up the root and will never gain awakening. If one always acts as guest, whereby the countless treasures belong to others, then it is just delusive thinking, and ultimately the flowing cycle of birth and death can't be avoided."

Zen master Baofeng entered the hall and addressed the monks, saying, "What a beautiful snowfall! It's like white rice ashes covering everything! Those of you who are cold—go gather around the stove and get warm. Those of you who are tired—go pull your bed cover up over your head and sleep.

"Good brothers! You who have just come down from the monks hall—turn around and go back!"

Baofeng then shouted, got down from his seat, and left the hall.

Baofeng addressed the monks, saying, "Time passes quickly. What about that matter? Though it's like this, I dare not make deceptions here amongst you, because you are all buddhas. Some old awakened one said, 'All hindrances are complete enlightenment.'"

Baofeng suddenly lifted his staff and said, "They are not complete enlightenment!"

He then threw down the staff and said, "Throwing it back and forth. Where's the hindrance?"

He then shouted and got down from his seat.

Baofeng is recorded to have had thirty-eight Dharma heirs. His words have been passed down in *The Record of the Snow Hut*. Upon his death, he received the posthumous title "True Purity."

HUITANG ZUXIN, "HUANGLONG"

HUITANG ZUXIN (1025–1100) was a disciple of Huanglong Huinan. He came from Guangdong Province. He left home at the age of nineteen to live at Mt. Long's Huiquan Temple. His first Zen teacher was named Yunfeng Wenyue.[196] After studying for three years, the young monk had achieved no breakthrough, so he advised Yunfeng of his desire to leave. Yue said, "You must go see Zen master Huinan at Huangbo." Huanglong then went to study under that teacher, but after four years he still hadn't gained clarity. He then departed and returned to Yunfeng.

Huitang discovered that Wenyue had passed away, and so he stayed at Shishuang. One day he was reading a lamp record when he came upon the passage, "A monk asked Zen master Duofu, 'What is Duofu's bamboo grove?' Duofu replied, 'One stalk, two stalks slanted.' The monk said, 'I don't understand.' Duofu then said, 'Three stalks, four stalks crooked.'" Upon reading these words Huitang experienced great awakening and finally grasped the teaching of his previous two teachers.

Huitang returned to see Huanglong Huinan. When he arrived there and prepared to set out his sitting cushion, Huinan said, "You've already entered my room."

Huitang jumped up and said, "The great matter being thus, why does the master teach kōans to the disciples and study the hundred cases [of the kōan collections]?"

Huinan said, "If I did not teach you to study in this manner, and you were left to reach the place of no-mind by your own efforts and your own confirmation, then I would be sinking you."

------ ◆ ------

A monk asked, "What was it before you ascended the Dharma seat?"
Huitang said, "There weren't any affairs."
The monk asked, "How about after you ascended the seat?"
Huitang said, "Lifting my face toward the sky, I don't see the sky."

------ ◆ ------

Huitang said, "Those who want to understand the source of life and death must first clearly understand their own selves. Once they're clear about this, then afterward they can act appropriately according to circumstances, never missing the mark.

"Before the sword appears, there is no 'positive' or 'negative.' But when it comes forth, then there are the five elements, mutually giving rise to or overcoming one another. The alien and familiar are manifested, and the four natures come into abiding. Everything becomes pigeonholed, and the sword of 'yes' and 'no' arises.

"But this leads to that which is true and false not being distinguished, to water and milk not being separated. When a disease enters into the solar plexus of a person, how can he be saved? If a weary and lost traveler doesn't have the bright sun to assist him, he won't find his way back home. When a person truly beholds the great function, then all delusional views are immediately forgotten. When all views are forgotten, the mist and fog are not created. When great wisdom is understood, then there is nothing else. Take care!"

Huitang entered the hall and addressed the monks, saying, "'It's not the wind that moves. It's not the flag that moves.' A clear-eyed fellow can't be fooled. But you worthies' minds are moving slowly. Where will you look to see the ancestral teachers?"

Huitang then threw down the whisk and said, "Look!"

Huitang addressed the monks, saying, "If someone understands the self without understanding what is before the eyes, then this person has eyes but no feet. If he only awakens to what is before his eyes without understanding the self, then this person has feet, but no eyes. Throughout all hours of the day these two sorts of people possess something that is located in their chests. When this thing is in their chests, then an unsettled vision is always before their eyes. With this vision before their eyes, everything they meet gives them some hindrance. So how can they ever find peace?

"Didn't the ancestors say, 'If anything is grasped or lost, one enters the heretical path. When things are left as they are, the body neither goes nor stays'?"

Huitang entered the hall. Striking the meditation platform with his staff, he said, "When a single speck of dust arises, the entire earth fits inside it. A single sound permeates every being's ear. If it is like a lightning swift eagle, then it's in accord with the vehicle. But in stagnant water, where the fish are lethargic, it's hard to whip up waves!"

Huitang entered the hall and said, "Before the appearance of skilled craftsmen, jade could not be separated from stone. Without skilled metallurgists, gold can't be removed from sand. Can someone gain enlightenment without a teacher or not? Come forward and let's check you out."

Huitang then raised his whisk and said, "Tell me, is it gold or is it sand?"

After a long pause, he said, "Don't think of it as here before you. Imagine it a thousand miles away."

Huitang entered the hall and recited a verse:

"Not going,
Not leaving,
Thoughts of South Mountain and Mt. Tiantai,
The silly white cloud with no fixed place,
Blown back and forth by the wind."

———— ◆ ————

Huitang, when interviewing a monk in the abbot's quarters, would often raise a fist and say, "If you call it a fist I'll hit you with it. If you don't call it a fist you're being evasive. What do you call it?"

————— ◆ —————

Before he died, Huitang ordered that his funeral be conducted by his disciples and by [his student] Wang Tingjian, the local governor. During the cremation ceremony, Linfeng tried to light the pyre with a candle on behalf of the governor. The pyre would not light.

Governor Wang then spoke to Huitang's senior disciple, Sixin, saying, "The master is waiting for our senior brother to light the fire."

Sixin ritually refused Wang's request, but the governor urged him to take the candle.

Finally, taking the candle, Sixin raised it before the assembly and said, "What evil have I committed that brings me to this? A great crime is hard to absolve! [Then facing the pyre, Sixin said,] Now, Master, you go on foot into emptiness. If you can't ride an ox, please use a donkey!"

Sixin then drew a circle in the air with the candle, saying, "Here, all defilement is purified!"

He then threw the candle onto the pyre, which instantly erupted into flames.

Huitang's remains were interred on the east side of the "Universal Enlightenment Stupa." The master received the posthumous title "Zen Master Precious Enlightenment."

BAIYUN SHOUDUAN

BAIYUN SHOUDUAN (1025–72) was a disciple of Yangqi Fanghui. He came from Hengyang (a city in Hunan Province). As a youth, he was skilled at scholarly arts. He received ordination at age twenty from a Zen master named Chaling You. He later traveled to study with Yangqi Fanghui, the great teacher of the

Linji lineage, with whom he attained enlightenment. After spending a long period as Yangqi's attendant, Baiyun traveled and taught at a number of different temples, everywhere gathering large crowds of students. He eventually lived and taught at Baiyun Mountain (located seventy kilometers east of Tongcheng County in Anwei Province). The *Wudeng Huiyuan* offers an account of Baiyun's awakening.

One day Yangqi suddenly asked Baiyun, "Under what teacher were you ordained?"

Baiyun said, "Master Chaling You."

Yangqi said, "I heard that he stumbled while crossing a bridge and attained enlightenment. He then composed an unusual verse. Do you remember it or not?"

Baiyun then recited the verse:

"I possess a lustrous pearl
Long locked away by dust and toil.
Now the dust is gone and a light shines forth,
Illuminating myriad blossoms with the mountains and rivers.".

Yangqi suddenly laughed out loud and jumped up. Baiyun was shocked [by this behavior] so much that he hardly slept that night.

Early the next morning Yangqi questioned Baiyun about what had happened the night before. He asked, "Did you witness an exorcism last night?"

Baiyun said, "Yes."

Yangqi said, "You don't measure up to *it*."

This startled Baiyun. He asked, "What do you mean?"

Yangqi said, "*It* enjoyed someone's laughter. You fear someone's laughter."

[Upon hearing these words] Baiyun experienced great enlightenment.

Baiyun then served as Yangqi's attendant for a long period of time. He (later) took leave of Yangqi and traveled to Yuantong Temple where, at the recommendation of [the abbot] Zen master Yuantong Na, he then assumed the abbacy of and taught at Chengtian Temple.[197] There his reputation became widely known.

———— ◆ ————

Zen master Baiyun Shouduan entered the hall and addressed the monks, saying, "In former times there was an assembly at Vulture Peak where the World-Honored One held up a flower, and Mahakashyapa smiled. The World-Honored One said, 'I have *The Treasury of the True Dharma Eye*. I pass it to Mahakashyapa.' This was then passed on in succession down to the present day.

"I say to this assembly that if it was really the true Dharma eye, then old Shakyamuni didn't have it, and so how could he have passed it on? How could it have been transmitted? How can such a thing be said?

"In fact, each of you possesses the treasury of the true Dharma eye. But every day after you get out of bed, there's 'yes, yes,' and 'no, no,' dividing up 'south' and 'north,' and other acts of bifurcation, all of which taken together are the light of the treasury of the true Dharma eye.

"When this eye opens, the entire universe and the great earth, the sun, moon, stars, and constellations, the myriad forms of the universe, though all right before your eyes, do not manifest a single bit of form. Before the eye opens, it is extinguished in the eyes of all people.

"Today it has already opened, and it is not limited to this place. But as to those of you for whom the eye has not opened; I don't lack the ability, so I'll open it and let you see."

Baiyun then raised his hand with two fingers extended vertically and said, "Look! Look! If you can see it then it's the same as I've said. If you can't see *it*, then I'll have to recite another verse:

"The Treasury of the True Dharma Eye *of each of you,*
Cannot be matched by the thousand sages,
The line passes through you,
Brilliantly filling the great Tang.

"*Mt. Sumeru walks into the sea,*
In June a cold frost descends,
Though I speak of it thus,
No words can describe it.

"Monks! I've spoken a mouthful. So why is it that no words can describe it?"
Baiyun then shouted and said, "Each of you has two places to see it!"

⸻ ◆ ⸻

Baiyun said, "Old Shakyamuni recited four great vows, which were:

Though the myriad beings are numberless, I vow to save them;
Though defilements rise endlessly, I vow to end them;
Though Dharma gates are innumerable, I vow to study them;
Though Buddha's way is unsurpassed, I vow to embody it.

"I also have four great vows. They are:

"*When I'm hungry, I eat;*
When it's cold, I put on more clothes;
When I'm tired, I stretch out and sleep;
When it gets warm, I like to find a cool breeze."

◆

Zen master Shouduan addressed the monks, saying, "The ancients have passed down a few words, and before we penetrate them they are like an iron wall. Suddenly, one day, after we see through it, we know that we ourselves are an iron wall. What can be done to see though this question?"

Master Shouduan also said, "An iron wall! An iron wall!"

◆

Zen master Shouduan addressed the monks, saying, "If you go all out and really work up a sweat, then when you see a single stalk of grass a jade palace is revealed. But if you don't put forth this type of effort, then even if you have a jade palace, a single stalk of grass will confound you. How can you really work up a sweat like this? As long as your two hands are tired, you'll never dance gaily in the three palaces."[198]

◆

A monk asked Baiyun, "What is Buddha?"
Baiyun said, "A hot soup pot has no cool spot."

◆

A monk asked, "What is the great meaning of Buddhism?"
Baiyun said, "Push the gourd beneath the water."

◆

A monk asked, "Why did Bodhidharma come from the west?"
Baiyun said, "Birds fly, rabbits walk."

◆

A monk asked, "Praying to the holy ones, believing in one's self—these are not the concerns of a monk. What are the concerns of a monk?"
Baiyun said, "Dead water does not conceal a dragon."

The monk said, "And when it's like that, then what?"

Baiyun said, "Gain kills you."

BAONING RENYONG

BAONING RENYONG (n.d.) was a disciple of Yangqi Fanghui. He came from Siming (a place now in Zhejiang Province). As a young man he possessed a remarkably dignified appearance as well as extraordinary intelligence. He excelled at the study of Tiantai Buddhism. He later studied under the great Yunmen lineage teacher Xuedou Chongxian. Xuedou recognized the young man's wonderful potential as a vessel for the Dharma, but offended Baoning by addressing him with a title akin to the English phrase "academic schoolmaster." Baoning left Xuedou's mountain with the vow, "I will continue in this life to travel on a pilgrimage to study Zen, and if I don't find a teacher who surpasses Xuedou, I vow to never return home."

Baoning traveled until he came to Yangqi Fanghui's temple on Mt. Yungai. It is recorded that at their first meeting, Yangqi did not complete even a single sentence before Baoning attained the "mind-seal of illuminated awakening" (complete enlightenment).

After spending time at Mt. Yungai, Yangqi died, and Baoning set off to travel extensively with his Dharma brother and close friend Baiyun Shouduan. Eventually he settled and taught at the Baoning Temple at Jinling.

> Zen master Baoning Renyong entered the hall to address the monks. The attendant lit incense [to present to the Buddha].
>
> Baoning pointed to the attendant and said, "The attendant has already expounded the Dharma for all of you!"

———— ◆ ————

Baoning addressed the monks, saying, "For more than twenty years I carried a pack and bowl, traveling everywhere within the four seas, studying with more than ten different Zen adepts. But I never caught a glimpse of my own house, and I was just like a senseless stone. All the worthies I practiced with couldn't provide me a single positive benefit. During that entire time I didn't learn a thing. But fortunately, my pitiable life was suddenly blown by the karmic winds into Jiangning, where, jostled by the crowd, I was pushed into an old run-down temple on a busy intersection. There, I just served as a 'porridge vendor,' receiving and helping everyone who came along. My duties never let up. There was sufficient salt and vinegar and there was enough gruel and rice. I passed some time in this fashion. I previously never imagined, even in a dream, that I would realize the Buddhadharma in this way."

◆

Baoning addressed the monks, saying, "Look! Look! I've fallen into 'Plucking Tongue Hell' [a hell where persons who have spoken deceptively have their tongues yanked out]!"

Baoning then pinched his own tongue and cried out, "Aiya! Aiya!"

◆

Baoning said, "There's no Maitreya Buddha up in heaven and there's no Maitreya Buddha in the earth. Why is it that even if you bust open emptiness you still can't find him?"

Baoning then hung a foot down off of his seat and said, "Everyone! Where are you going?"

◆

Baoning said, "If you say that the Buddhadharma supports all beings, you won't avoid having your eyebrows fall out. If you say that the worldly dharmas support all beings, you shoot straight into hell like an arrow.

"But aside from these two ways of speaking, what can I say today? There's no use for the three-inch tongue. The two empty hands can't make a fist!"

◆

A monk asked Baoning Renyong, "What is Buddha?"
Baoning said, "Add wood to the fire."
The monk asked, "What is the Way?"
Baoning said, "There are thorns in the mud."
The monk asked, "Who are people of the Way?"
Baoning said, "Those that hate walking there."

◆

A monk asked, "An old worthy said, 'Though the cold wind withers the leaves, it is still a joy when an ancient returns.' Who is an 'ancient'?"
Baoning said, "Master Yangqi is long gone."

The monk said, "Right here and now, is there someone who can comprehend this?"

Baoning said, "The eyeless old villager secretly taps his head."

A monk asked, "What is Buddha?"

Baoning said, "You're not aware of the stink of your own shit."

Baoning recited a verse to the monks:

A cold autumn wind.
The wind drones in the pines.
The wayward traveler
Thinks of his home.

Then Baoning said, "Who do you say is the traveler? Where is his home?"

A monk asked, "What is Baoning's domain?"

Baoning said, "The king of the mountain falls down."

The monk asked, "What is a person in Baoning's domain?"

Baoning said, "One can't have a single nostril."

A monk asked, "What is Buddha?"

Baoning said, "An iron mallet with no holes."

The monk then asked, "What is the great meaning of the Buddhadharma?"

Baoning said, "A hot soup pot has no cold place."

A monk asked, "Lingshan pointed to the moon. The Sixth Ancestor spoke of the moon. But I, as yet, don't know what is beneath Baoning's gate."

Baoning yelled, "Ah!"

The monk said, "There are flowers stuck to your face."

Baoning shouted.

The monk asked, "I don't ask about picking leaves or seeking branches. I just ask, 'What is it that directly cuts off the source root?'"

Baoning said, "A mosquito on an iron ox."

The monk said, "For those who are clear about cutting off the source, how do you point out the flow?"

Baoning said, "The stone man's back streams with sweat."

Dagui Muche, "Guishan Zhe"

Dagui Muche (d. 1132) was a disciple of Cuiyan Zhen. He came from Linchuan in Fuzhou.

A monk asked Dagui, "What is the meaning of Zhaozhou's cypress tree in the garden?"

Dagui said, "The solitary guest, already cold, felt the piercing sensation of the night wind."

The monk said, "My previous teacher did not speak in this manner. What do you mean?"

Dagui said, "The pilgrim finally knows suffering."

The monk said, "Ten years in the red dust, but today the solitary body is revealed."

Dagui said, "Frost on top of the snow."

❖

A monk asked, "What is the buddha within the city?"

Dagui said, "In the ten-thousand-person crowd, not leaving signs."

The monk asked, "What is the buddha in the village?"

Dagui said, "A muddy pig. A scabby dog."

The monk asked, "What is the buddha in the mountain?"

Dagui said, "Stopping people's coming and going."

❖

A monk asked, "How was it before Niutou met the Fourth Ancestor?"

Dagui said, "Cold hair standing straight."

The monk asked, "After seeing him, then what?"

Dagui said, "Sweat streaming from the forehead."

❖

Dagui addressed the monks, saying, "Not using thought, it is known. Not employing considerations, it is resolved. Luling rice is expensive. Zhenzhou turnips are big."

—————— ◆ ——————

Dagui entered the hall and addressed the monks, saying, "An ancient buddha said, 'Formerly at Varanasi I turned the Dharma wheel of the Four Noble Truths.'[199] [This was] diving into the pit or jumping into the moat. Today I again turn the most sublime, unsurpassed, great wheel of Dharma, adding mud to the ground. If there were no ladder of historical development leading down to this time, then how could one transcend objects?"

Dagui then paused from speaking. After some time he said, "Pop your head out beyond heaven and see! Who is the one at the middle?"

—————— ◆ ——————

Dagui addressed the monks, saying, "Grasping empty forms, chasing echoes—it belabors your spirit. Wake up from your dream and the dream is gone. Then what other matter is left? Old Deshan is on all of your eyebrows and eyelashes, do you all feel him? If you've experienced this then you've awakened from your dream and the dream is gone. If you haven't experienced this, then you are grasping empty forms and chasing echoes. This will go on without end."

—————— ◆ ——————

During [the year 1132], Dagui, though not ill, recited the following verse:

"Last night three times,
Sudden wind and thunder,
The clouds dispersed and left vast space.
The moon sets beyond the river."

He then sat silently for a long while, then suddenly bade the monks farewell and passed away.

Danxia Zichun

Danxia Zichun (1064–1117) was a disciple of Furong Daokai. He came from the ancient city of Zitong (now in Sichuan Province). He was ordained at the age of twenty.

Danxia entered the hall and addressed the monks, saying, "Within the cosmos, inside the universe, at the very center, there is a jewel concealed in form mountain. Dharma master Zhao says that you can only point at tracks and speak of traces of this jewel, and that you cannot hold it up for others to see. But today I split open the universe, break apart form mountain and hold it forth for all of you to observe! Those with the eye of wisdom will see it."

Danxia hit the floor with his staff and said, "Do you see? A white egret stands in the snow, but its color is different. It doesn't resemble the clear moon or the water reeds!"

❖

Danxia entered the hall and said, "Deshan spoke as follows, 'My doctrine is without words and phrases, and truthfully, I have no Dharma to impart to people.' You can say Deshan knew how to 'go into the grass' to save people. But he didn't 'soak the whole body in muddy water.' If you look carefully you see he has just one eye. But as for me, my doctrine has words and phrases, and a golden knife can't cut it open. It is deep, mysterious, and sublime. A jade woman conceives in the night."

❖

Danxia entered the hall and said, "At high noon it still lacks half. In the quiet night it is still not complete. Households haven't known the intimate purpose, always going and coming before the clear moon."

❖

Danxia entered the hall and said, "The precious moon streams its shining light, spreading out vast and clear. The water reflects, but does not absorb its essence, nor does the moon rend its shining mind. When water and moon are both forgotten, this may be called 'cut off.' Therefore it is said, 'Things rising to heaven must fall back to earth. What is fully completed is inevitably lacking.' Cast off the desire for reputation and don't look back. If you can do this, you can then walk in the fantastic diversity. And when you have reached this place, have you seen it all?"

After a long pause Danxia said, "If you are not devoted to walking among people, then you fall into the dirt and mud wearing feathers and horns!"[200]

⸻ ◆ ⸻

A monk asked, "What was it before Niutou met the Fourth Ancestor?"

Danxia said, "When the golden chrysanthemum blooms, the bees contend to grasp it."

The monk said, "After he saw him, what then?"

Danxia said, "Blossoms sprout on a dead tree. They wither, unsustainable."

⸻ ◆ ⸻

Danxia died in the spring [of the year 1117]. A monument and the master's complete remains were placed in a stupa south of Mt. Hong [a location in the modern city of Wuhan in Hubei Province].

BAOFENG WEIZHAO

BAOFENG WEIZHAO (n.d.) was a disciple of Furong Daokai. His home was in ancient Jianzhou (near the modern city of Jianyang in Sichuan Province). As a youth he is said to have led an unruly life. One day while reading a book, he was startled by the phrase, "One's self-nature is near, but realizing it is remote." He then said, "The mundane and the sacred are of one body, but because of habit and circumstances they are differentiated. I know this to be true." He then hastened to the city of Chengdu and studied under the teacher Luyuan Qingtai, receiving ordination at the age of nineteen.

Tai tried to instill in Baofeng a faith in the teaching of "great compassion," but Baofeng was indifferent to this idea. When Tai questioned him about this he said, "Just proclaiming a belief in the Mahayana, how can these words have any effect?" He then dejectedly went traveling, intending to visit Furong Daokai at Da Hong.

One night as he sat on a road a thunderous snowstorm occurred. He heard someone call out "Thief!" and thereupon experienced a realization. He immediately went on to find Furong.

Furong's place at Da Hong was difficult to find. While Baofeng was traveling in a cart from Sanwu to Yishui, the driver became lost. Baofeng, in anger, raised his staff to strike the driver when he suddenly experienced vast enlightenment, exclaiming, "Is the earth not a great tortoise mountain?" Upon arriving at

Yishui, Furong observed him and happily exclaimed, "The heir of my Dharma! There will be many generations to follow!"

❖

Baofeng entered the hall and addressed the monks, saying, "An ancient buddha said, 'When I first gained complete awakening I personally saw that all beings of the great earth are each fully endowed with complete and perfect enlightenment.' And later he said, 'It's a great mystery. No one can fathom it.' I don't see anyone who understands this. Just some blowhards." He then got down from the seat.

❖

Baofeng entered the hall and addressed the monks, saying, "All the buddhas of bygone ages have already entered nirvana. You people! Don't be nostalgic about them. The buddhas of the future have not yet appeared in the world. All of you, don't be deluded! On this very day who are you? Study this!"

❖

Baofeng addressed the monks, saying, "The fundamental self is unborn, nor is it annihilated in the present. It is undying. But to be born in a certain place, and to die someplace else, is the rule of being born in a life. Great persons must position themselves in this flow of life and death. They must lie down in the thorny forest. They must be pliable and able to act according to circumstances. If they are thus, then immeasurable expedients, grand samadhis, and great liberation gates are instantly opened. But if they are not yet this way, then defilements, all toilsome dust, and mountains loom before them and block the ancient road."

❖

When Baofeng died, his cremated remains were like jewels and pearls, and his tongue and teeth were undamaged by the flames. His stupa was placed on the western peak near the temple.

Twentieth Generation

JUEFAN HUIHONG   DOUSHUAI CONGYUE

SIXIN WUXIN   WUZU FAYAN

ZHENXIE QINGLIAO

HONGZHI ZHENGJUE

JUEFAN HUIHONG, "DEHONG," "QINGLIANG"

JUEFAN HUIHONG (n.d.) was a student of Yunan Kewen. He came from Benchun in Jiangxi Province. He was not only one of the great Zen teachers of the Linji/Huanglong lineage, but was a pivotal figure in an era when Zen literature reached its zenith. He authored and compiled a large number of classic Zen commentaries and biographies, including the *Treasured Biographies of the Monks of the Zen Monasteries* (in Chinese, *Chan Lin Seng Bao Zhuan*) and a volume of *Biographies of Eminent Monks* (in Chinese, *Gao Seng Zhuan*).

At the age of nineteen, Juefan received ordination at the Celestial Kings Temple in Luoyang, where he received his first Dharma name, Huihong ("Vast Wisdom"). Juefan reportedly possessed a photographic memory and the ability to remember a book completely after one reading. He wrote poetry under the pen name "Hongdong Jinghua." A Buddhist scholar and philosopher, he thoroughly mastered the "consciousness-only" doctrine of Buddhist thought. The *Wudeng Huiyuan* provides a brief account of his life.

When Qingliang was fourteen, his mother and father died. He then lived as a novice monk under Zen master Sanfeng Qing. Every day he learned several thousand words [of the sutras]. Qingliang mastered a great number of books and completely attained his teacher's Dharma. At the age of nineteen he passed his examinations and entered the clergy at Tianwang Temple in Luoyang, receiving ordination there. He then learned the Madhyamika and consciousness-only doctrine from the monk Xuanmi.

After four years, he stopped studying sutras, and proceeded to study under Master Zhenjing at Guizong. When Zhenjing moved to Shimen, Juefan followed him there. Zhenjing feared that Qingliang suffered from the illness of being too erudite. Whenever Zhenjing spoke of Xuansha's situation before his enlightenment, he would engender doubts in Qingliang. Whenever Qingliang would say something, Zhenjing would say, "Is what you are saying in accord with the Way?"

One day, Qingliang suddenly lost all his doubts. He then composed this verse:

When Lingyun saw them once, he never looked again,
Those branches adorned in red and white did not reveal blossoms.
The wretched fisherman who caught nothing from his boat,
Has returned to net fish and prawns on dry land.

Zhenjing was delighted with Qingliang's verse, declaring it to be of the highest order. Not long after this, Qingliang went on to visit many other famous teachers. They all praised him highly, and because of this he became famous throughout the many Zen monasteries.

The official Xian Mozhu invited Qingliang to become abbot of Beijingde Temple in Fuzhou. Later, he moved to Qingliang Temple [in Nanjing].

Qingliang said to the monks, "In the *Surangama Sutra*, the Tathagata said to Ananda, 'When you smell the fragrance of the sandalwood log that burns in this hearth, the fragrance appears to come from a single sandalwood log, yet everywhere within forty li of the city of Shravasti it may be perceived at the same time. What do you say about this? Does this fragrance arise from the sandalwood; does it arise from your nose; or does it arise in the air?

"Ananda! If you say it arises in your nose, then it could be said to be created by your nose. In that case it would come forth from your nose. There is no sandalwood within your nose. So how is there the scent of sandalwood in your nose? If you say that you smell the fragrance, such that it enters your nose, and that within your nose the fragrance is created, then to say that "you smell" the fragrance is illogical. If the fragrance arises in the air, then because the nature of the air is permanent, the fragrance would always be present. So why then would we need to burn this sandalwood log in the hearth? If the fragrance exists in the wood, then the material of this fragrance would be reduced to smoke when the wood is burned. If the nose were thought to be smelling the smoke of this fragrance, then when the smoke rushed into the sky, it could not travel too far. How could it be smelled at a distance of forty li?

"For this reason, it may be said that the fragrance, the nose, and the perception of the fragrance, all have no abode. Thus, the smelling and fragrance are both empty illusions, fundamentally linked to causality, and having no self-nature.'"

Zen master Qingliang then said, "Enter this perception of the nose. Closely observe for yourself that it is unborn!"

[Qingliang then raised an example from the *Mahaprajnaparamita Sutra*, wherein] the Buddha asked, "What is it that hears? Does 'hearing' employ the ears to hear? Is it 'hearing consciousness' that hears? It may be proposed that it is the ears that hear, but the ears do not have consciousness, so they cannot hear. If it is proposed that it is 'hearing consciousness' that hears, then does not such consciousness exist only in a moment of thought? Thus it would not be able to differentiate [different sounds], and would therefore not be able to hear. If it is proposed that it is consciousness itself that hears, then I say it cannot do so. Why is this? The five senses perceive the five objects of the senses. Thereafter, consciousness perceives consciousness. Consciousness cannot simultaneously perceive the five objects of the senses. It can only perceive these objects as existing in the past or in the future. If consciousness were able to perceive the manifestation of the five objects of the senses, then even someone blind and deaf would be able to perceive sound. Why is this? It is because consciousness is indivisible."

Qingliang then said, "It is this 'perception of the objects of the senses' that accords with the fundamental mystery. It gives evidence to what is unborn and accords with the fundamental mystery. What, after all, is this state?"

After a long pause, Qingliang said, "The white ape has long since called across the thousand cliffs. Blue ropes enmesh the furnace of words!"

◆

In the second year of the Jiangyan era of the Song dynasty [1128], Juefan died at Tongan. As a result of a petition to the emperor by the official Kuo Tianmin, Juefan received the posthumous name "Precious Enlightenment Perfect Clarity."

DOUSHUAI CONGYUE

DOUSHUAI CONGYUE (n.d.) was a disciple of Yunan Kewen. He came from ancient Ganzhou (a place in modern Jiangxi Province). He resided and taught at Doushuai Monastery in Longxing Prefecture (now a district in Nanchang City).

Congyue was the head monk at Daowu Monastery, and on one occasion he led a group of monks on a journey to visit Zen master Yungai Zhi. After only a few sentences of conversation, Zhi knew that Congyue possessed special ability.

Zhi laughed and said, "I observe that your breath is unusual. Why is it that when you speak your breath is like that of a drunkard?"

Congyue's face became flushed and he broke out in a sweat, and he said, "I hope the master won't spare your compassion."

Zhi continued to talk to Congyue, goading him. Congyue was flustered and didn't understand. He asked to have a private interview with Zhi.

In the abbot's room, Zhi asked Congyue, "Have you ever seen Zen master Fachang Diyu?"

Congyue said, "I've read the record of his talks. I understood it all, so I don't want to see him."

Zhi said, "Have you seen Zen master Dongshan Wenhe?"

Congyue said, "Guanxi's disciples don't have any brains. If you put on a cotton garment that smells like piss, what good is it?"

Zhi said, "You should go and practice at that place that smells like piss."

Following Zhi's instructions, Congyue went and practiced with Zen master Wenhe and deeply realized his great teaching. Later Congyue returned to see Zen master Zhi.

Zhi said, "Now that you've seen Guanxi's disciples, what about the great matter?"

Congyue said, "Had it not been for your instruction, It would have slipped past me my entire life."

Congyue then bowed in gratitude.

❖

Zen master Doushuai Congyue entered the hall and addressed the monks, saying, "When a person's eyes and ears are clear, then he resides in a remote mountain valley. The autumn wind rustles the ancient pines and the autumn moon reflects from the cold waters. A patch-robed monk who reaches that place must go still further to realize the truth, for this is still just two apes with four tails hanging down."

After saying this the master shouted.

❖

Doushuai addressed the monks, saying, "I can't differentiate anything. I see a hard-shelled turtle and I mistakenly call it soft-shelled. I can't talk any wondrous talk, or speak about truth. I just flap my lips and drum my tongue. When all the monks in the world see me, they laugh so hard in derision that their tears turn to blood. Don't I turn their derision to happiness? Are you laughing at me now?"

After a pause, the master said, "I blow a light-hearted tune on my flute and it causes people to forget a lifetime of troubles."

———— ◆ ————

Doushuai addressed the monks, saying, "First comes the new spring, and then it's the beginning of summer. The four seasons pass like an arrow. The sun and moon move like a shuttle. Before you know it, a red-faced babe has turned into an old white-hair. You must truly exert yourself and use extraordinary effort. Cultivate your own field, and don't steal someone else's seedlings. Applying yourself in this way, your cultivation will certainly result in finally seeing the white ox on snow mountain."

········· ◆ ·········

In [the year 1091], after bathing, the master assembled the monks and recited this verse:

"*After forty-eight years,*
Sacred and mundane are completely killed off.
Although not heroic,
The Longan road is slippery."[201]

The master suddenly passed away. In accordance with his wishes, his disciples wanted to scatter his cremated remains in the river. However, before his Dharma heirs could do this, an emissary from the master's lay disciple, Duke Zhang, arrived to pay tribute and said, "The old master forcefully expounded the way of the ancestral gate. Those who come to honor him must have a place to do so." He then ordered the construction of a stupa on Luan Peak at Longan. It was named "True Stillness."

SIXIN WUXIN, "HUANGLONG WUXIN"

SIXIN WUXIN (1044–1115) was a disciple of Huitang Zuxin. He came from Shaozhou. According to a legend related in the *Wudeng Huiyuan*, Sixin was born with purple skin on his shoulders and right side, giving him the appearance of wearing a monk's robe. As a young man, he entered Fotuo ("Buddha") Monastery where he gained ordination. He later traveled to visit the teacher Huanglong Zuxin of the Linji Zen lineage.

Huanglong raised his fist and asked, "If you call it a fist you have erred. If you don't call it a fist then you've avoided the question. What do you call it?"

Sixin didn't know what to do. He spent two years working on this question before he arrived at a solution. But when he then went to discuss the matter with Huanglong, his teacher didn't pay any attention and instead became highly agitated. As Sixin tried to explain his insight, Huanglong suddenly yelled, "Stop! Stop! Can you feed people by talking about food?"

This startled and distressed Sixin, who said, "I don't want to be in this place of broken bows and spent arrows. I appeal to the master's compassion. Please direct me to a paradise."

Huanglong said, "A single dust mote flies and heaven is concealed. A mustard seed falls and earth is overturned. Paradise still torments you with confusion. You must completely die so that for unlimited eons to come, with total mind, you can hear."

Sixin left quickly.

One day, as Sixin was talking with a pilgrim monk named Zhishi Chui, there was a sudden flash of lightning and a loud thunderclap. Sixin was instantly enlightened. He rushed to see Huanglong. Forgetting custom he enthused, "Everyone on earth has attained Zen, but they haven't awakened to it."

Huanglong laughed and said, "A practitioner of the first rank! How can I face you?" It was as a result of these events that he received the name Sixin ["Dead Mind"].

Sixin entered the hall and addressed the monks, saying, "It's deep, obscure, distant, and no person can go there. Did Shakyamuni go there or not? If he went there, why can't anyone else? If he didn't go there, who says it's obscure and distant?"

Sixin addressed the monks, saying, "The mind-seal of the ancestors—its appearance is like the function of an iron ox. When it makes an impression it seals. When it seals the seal is lost. It's as though it doesn't disappear, nor does it remain. So does it make a seal or not? At early dawn a monkey picked the golden fruit. At late dusk a phoenix carried away the jade flower."

◆

Sixin addressed the monks, saying, "Great monks on pilgrimage open their cloth bags and take out their bowls and cloths, and thus remove all delights and vexations. They must know the place of 'person.' They must reach the place of 'half person.' And they also must intimately see the place of 'no person.'"

◆

Near death, Sixin recited a verse:

"When speaking, everything is overturned.
When silent, a second thing falls, a third thing falls.
I say to Zen practitioners everywhere,
Sovereign mind is where practice ceases."

The master's stupa was built north of the abbot's room at Huitang Monastery.

Wuzu Fayan, "Qingyuan"

Wuzu Fayan (1024–1104), also known as "Qingyuan," was a disciple of Baiyun Shouduan. He came from Baxi City in Mianzhou (now the city of Mianyang in Sichuan Province). A great transmitter of the Yangqi line of Linji Zen, Wuzu's teaching exerted profound influence on subsequent generations of Zen teachers and on wider Song dynasty society. Leaving home to become a monk at the relatively late age of thirty-five, he traveled to Chengdu to study the doctrines of the Consciousness-Only school of Buddhism. However, Wuzu was troubled by the proposition that when a bodhisattva enters the Way, wisdom and principle are eclipsed, and though environment and mind are reportedly realized as fully united, no evidence can be offered to affirm the truth of this unity.

With this doubt in mind, Wuzu made inquiries to a Tripitaka master about the nature of knowledge.[202] To his question he received the reply, "If a person drinks water, he personally knows hot and cold."

While this helped to clarify Wuzu's understanding, he still said, "Then hot and cold can be known, but what about knowledge of the self?"

Wuzu then asked (the teacher) Zhiben Jiang, "If one does not know the self, how can one understand principle?" But Jiang did not answer, and merely told him, "If you want to be clear on this, then go to the South and attach yourself to a teacher of the buddha mind doctrine." Wuzu then left to seek out such a teacher.

Wuzu's arduous journey led him to seek out Zen masters Yuanzhao and Fushan Fayuan, but neither of these teachers brought Wuzu to a full awakening.[203] Before Fushan died, he directed Wuzu to travel to Baiyun Shouduan's temple to gain instruction.

Upon meeting Baiyun, Wuzu inquired to him about a story concerning Nanquan and the Mani Jewel.[204] Just when he finished asking this question, Baiyun shouted at Wuzu, causing him to instantly attain enlightenment. Wuzu then thanked Baiyun by offering the following verse:

> Before the mountain spreads the plain.
> Repeatedly, with folded hands, I asked the elders.
> They sold to me so many times, and yet I purchased more,
> Just to know that pine and bamboo bring forth the cloudless wind.

Wuzu's fame as a teacher spread widely and students gathered from throughout China to study under him. He first taught at Simian Shan ("Four Face Mountain"), and then moved to Mt. Baiyun. Later he moved to the Dongchan ("East Zen") Temple on Wuzu Mountain.[205] Among Wuzu's twenty-two Dharma heirs were the acclaimed "Three Buddhas," the monks Foyan Qingyuan, Foguo Keqin, and Fojian Huiqin. The following passages appear in *The Record of Fayan*.

A monk asked Zen master Wuzu Fayan, "What is one drop of Baiyun?"

Fayan said, "Pounding. Grinding."

The monk asked, "How about those who drink it?"

Fayan said, "I teach of a place where no face appears."

A monk asked, "Baiyun cut off the tongues of everyone beneath heaven. But as for Baiyun's tongue, who will cut it off?"

Wuzu said, "Old Wang in East Village."

Wuzu then said, "It's nothing other than ordinary affairs. But according to your thinking it's something different. If you think you can understand through speech, then know you haven't penetrated the truth. If you think you can't understood through speech, then your head and mind are like a raging fire. So, just pass through Zhaozhou's gate and cut off Baiyun's tongue yourself. Don't betray the ancient sages' compassion."

Fayan entered the hall. He recited the example of when a monk asked Baling Haojian, "Is the meaning of the ancestors and the meaning of the scriptures the same or different?" Baling said, "The cold fowl flies up into the tree. The cold duck dives into the water."

Fayan said, "Old Baling! He only said one-half. Baiyun didn't go along with his answer. Hold the water in your hands and possess the moon. Brush against the flowers and the fragrance fills your clothes."

Wuzu addressed the monks, saying, "Yesterday when I went into town I noticed a puppet show going on. I couldn't help going over there and taking a look. The puppet was really something to see! At first sight it seemed to move its limbs, walk around, and sit down all on its own. But when you looked closer, you could see that there was someone behind the blue curtain.

"I couldn't help but call out, 'Sir! What's your name?'

"The man replied to me, 'Honored Priest! Just watch the show. Why ask for names?'

"Brethren! When I heard him say this, I didn't have a single word to say in reply, nor a single idea to espouse. Can any of you say anything in my place? Yesterday, that single instance of embarrassment has uprooted all my ideas now."

Wuzu addressed the monks, saying, "When hearing is shallow, the realization is deep. When hearing is deep, there's no realization. What can be done? What can be done? Making a true offering to Buddha doesn't mean giving more incense."

Fayan brought up for consideration the story of when a monk asked Yunmen, "What is the talk that is beyond the buddhas and ancestors?" Yunmen replied, "Cake."

Fayan said, "I don't answer that way. If someone suddenly asks me, 'What is the speech that is beyond the buddhas and ancestors?' I'd just reply to him, 'Donkey shit is like horse shit.' Or I'd say, 'Worn-out reed sandals.' Or I might say, 'The Tortoise God drags his tail.' So now I ask you, are my answers the same or different than Yunmen's? Consider this question."

A monk asked Wuzu Fayan, "What was the meaning of Bodhidharma's facing the wall?"

Wuzu said, "It still hasn't been calculated."

The monk asked, "What about when the Second Ancestor stood in the snow?"

Wuzu said, "An error is an error."

A monk asked, "At the top of a hundred-foot pole, how does one go forward?"

Wuzu said, "Quick, try it and see!"

A monk asked, "What is the affair of the Linji school?"

Wuzu said, "Five rebels hear thunder."

The monk asked, "What is the affair of the Yunmen school?"

Wuzu said, "The red flag is brilliant."

The monk asked, "What is the affair of the Caodong school?"

Wuzu said, "Riding books you won't get home."

The monk asked, "What is the affair of the Guiyang school?"

Wuzu said, "A broken monument across the ancient road."

The monk then bowed.

Wuzu said, "Why don't you ask about the Fayan school?"

The monk said, "I leave it to the master."

Wuzu said, "A thief in the night!"

The *Wudeng Huiyuan* offers an account of Fayan's death.

On the twenty-fifth day of the sixth month of [the year 1104], Wuzu entered the hall and bade the monks farewell, saying, "Zhaozhou had some final words. Do you remember them? Let's see if you can recite them."

When no one responded, Wuzu then recited Zhaozhou's words:

"Fortune few among the thousand,
But one has countless pains and sorrows."

Then Wuzu said, "Take care."

Later that night Wuzu died. It is recorded that a great rock fell down nearby Mt. Xi, creating a sound heard for forty miles.

Zhenxie Qingliao, "Changlu"

Zhenxie Qingliao (1089–1151) was a student of Danxia Zichun. He came from Anchang (in the area of modern Sichuan Province). Zhenxie entered monastic life at the age of eleven and passed his scriptural examinations on the *Lotus Sutra* at the age of eighteen. He then traveled to Jingzi Monastery in Chengdu, where he continued scriptural study. Later, he set off traveling and visited various famous teachers and sacred mountains, including Mt. Emei and Mt. Wutai.

Danxia asked Zhenxie, "What is the self before the empty eon?"

When Zhenxie began to answer, Danxia stopped him and said, "You're disturbed now. Go!"

Later, Zhenxie went traveling to an area of modern Shanxi Province and visited Shaolin Temple. He then went to nearby Boyu Peak, the site of the Second Ancestor's hut, and, while visiting that site, he suddenly experienced enlightenment.

Upon returning to see Danxia, his teacher immediately knew what had transpired.

Before Zhenxie could speak, Danxia slapped him, saying, "You were going to tell me what you know!"

Zhenxie bowed.

The next day, Danxia went into the hall and said to the monks,

"The sun shines on a solitary green peak.
The moon reflects in the cold creek water.
The sublime mystery of the ancestors
Is not found in the small mind."

Danxia then got down from the seat.

Zhenxie came forward and said, "A talk like you gave today won't deceive me again."

Danxia said, "Then explain it to me and we'll see if you understand."

Zhenxie was silent.

Danxia said, "I'll say you caught a glimpse of it."

Zhenxie then went out.

Later, Zhenxie resided at Changlu Temple where he served as attendant to the abbot, a monk named Zuzhao. Zuzhao subsequently became gravely ill and retired from his position, naming Zhenxie as his successor. Zhenxie served as abbot of Changlu until the years of social unrest accompanying the downfall of the Northern Song dynasty (around 1127). He then traveled to a series of places, including Snow Peak in Fujian and Mt. Jing in Hangzhou.

The dowager empress, Zi Ning, ordered the construction of a temple to honor her ancestors. At the opening ceremony Zhenxie lectured to the assembled crowd, saying: "My previous teacher slapped me and all of my cleverness vanished. I was unable to open my mouth to speak. Was that like all of these fast-talking but shallow fellows we see today? If not, [then let them] take the iron bit in their mouths and suffer the whip, then let's see what each of them can say."

———— ◆ ————

Zhenxie entered the hall and addressed the monks, saying, "Climbing to some mountain top, crossing some bridge, rushing about like this is how people these days travel to places high and low. But if they've really penetrated it, then without leaving their room their body pervades the ten directions. Not entering any gate, they are always in their room. But if someone doesn't understand this, then when he feels a draught he goes and hauls a big load of firewood."

———— ◆ ————

Zhenxie addressed the monks, saying, "Looking everywhere it can't be found. There's just one place you can't search, and there it is attained. What place is that?"
After a long pause, Zhenxie said, "The thief's body is already exposed."

———— ◆ ————

Zhenxie said, "Is there anyone who hasn't been stained by Xuansha? Even if you dip this stain in the four seas, you won't be able to wash it out."

———— ◆ ————

A monk asked, "What is the self before the empty eon?"
Zhenxie said, "A white horse enters the flowers and reeds."

———— ◆ ————

A monk asked Zhenxie, "All the buddhas in the three worlds have turned the great wheel of Dharma into the flames. Has this ceased or not?"
Zhenxie laughed out loud and said, "I have doubts about it."

The monk said, "Master, why do you have doubts about this?"

Zhenxie said, "The wild flowers' fragrance fills the road. The secluded bird does not know it's spring."

<hr/>

A monk asked, "Without letting go of wind and color, is it still possible to pivot oneself or not?"

Zhenxie said, "Where the stone person walks, there's no other activity."

<hr/>

One day, Zhenxie went into the kitchen and saw a pot of boiling noodles. Suddenly, the bottom fell out of the pot.

The monks there were crestfallen, saying, "Oh, what a waste!"

Zhenxie said, "An overturned bucket is a joy. Why are you disturbed?"

A monk said, "The master can take delight in it."

Zhenxie yelled, "Really, it's a shame to waste a pot of noodles!"

<hr/>

Zhenxie died in [the year 1151]. His stupa, named "Flowering Paulownia Island," was placed west of the temple. He received the posthumous name "Zen Master Enlightened Emptiness."

HONGZHI ZHENGJUE, "TIANTONG"

HONGZHI ZHENGJUE (1091–1157) was a disciple of Danxia Zichun. He came from ancient Xi Province (now the area of Xi County in Shanxi Province). A brilliant young scholar, he excelled at studying the Confucian classics. Throughout his adult life, Hongzhi lived and taught in ancient Mingzhou, the area around modern Ningbo city in Zhejiang Province. His nickname, Tiantong, is derived from a famous Buddhist mountain monastery of that place. Tiantong was one of the "Five Mountains," five principal Zen monasteries that served as administrative centers for the Zen monastic system during the Song dynasty.[206]

Hongzhi's father practiced Zen under a teacher named Fotuo Xun. One day the Zen master pointed at the young Hongzhi and said to his father, "This child's harmony with the Way is extraordinary. He's not a person of the dusty world. If he 'leaves home' he will be a Dharma vessel."

At age eleven, Hongzhi left home to enter a monastery. He was but fourteen when he received ordination at Ziyun ("Compassion Cloud") Temple. At eighteen he departed to roam as a yunshui, taking a vow to his ancestors to not return until he had resolved the "great affair" of life and death.

Traveling to Xiangshan ("Fragrant Mountain") in Ruzhou, Hongzhi studied with a Zen master and previous student of Danxia Zichun named Kumu Facheng.[207] The name "Kumu" means "tree stump." The term was earlier used to describe the students of Zen master Shishuang Qingzhu, who sat day and night in meditation like "tree stumps." Facheng received this name by following in Shishuang Qingzhu's footsteps, maintaining devotion to zazen as central to Zen practice. This practice greatly influenced Hongzhi's personal outlook and practice. Later, Hongzhi became widely known as the proponent of "silent illumination Zen." The phrase refers to the manifested buddhahood of sitting in silent meditation. This approach to practice attracted hundreds of monks to Tiantong Temple, which thus grew in size and stature. In this way, the practices of Zen master Qingzhu that occurred centuries before on Mt. Shishuang directly influenced and shaped the practice of the Caodong school of Zen.

One day as the monks on Mt. Xiang chanted the *Lotus Sutra*, Hongzhi was instantly enlightened upon hearing the phrase, "Your eye that existed before your parents' birth sees everything in three thousand realms." He then went to the abbot [Facheng] to declare his awakening.

Facheng pointed to a box of incense and said, "What is the thing inside?"

Hongzhi said, "What do you mean?"

Facheng said, "What is in the place of your awakening?"

Hongzhi used his hand to draw a circle in the air and then made the gesture of throwing it behind him.

Facheng said, "What limit is there for old fellows making mud balls?"

Hongzhi said, "Wrong."

Facheng said, "You've attained it when you don't see others."

Hongzhi said, "Yes. Yes."

Hongzhi then traveled on to practice with Danxia Zichun.

Danxia asked, "What is the self that exists before the empty kalpa?"

Hongzhi said, "A frog at the well bottom swallows the moon. Despite the night, three times the window blind was illuminated."

Danxia said, "Don't say any more."

Hongzhi started to speak, but Danxia hit him with his whisk and said, "Don't say it!"

Upon hearing these words Hongzhi was liberated. He then bowed.

Danxia said, "Can't you say something?"

Hongzhi said, "Today I've been robbed and lost my money."

Danxia said, "Without rest I've hit you. Now it's finished."

Hongzhi is remembered as the compiler and verse writer for the collection of one hundred kōans known as the *Book of Serenity*. That classic collection, which is a favorite text of the Caodong Zen school, was re-edited and annotated by the monk Wansong in the thirteenth century.

Once, when Hongzhi's Dharma brother Zhenxie Qingliao assumed the abbacy of Changlu Monastery, Hongzhi made the long trip to the opening ceremonies on foot. As he approached the temple, Zhenxie's attendants noticed that his clothes and shoes were ragged and worn. Quickly they obtained a new pair of sandals for him, and when he arrived they welcomed him by presenting them to him as a gift.

Hongzhi said, "Did I come for shoes?"

The monks, impressed by Hongzhi's modesty and selfless sentiment, asked him to give a lecture on Dharma and take the most honored seat at the ceremony.

The following two passages are from *The Extensive Record of Zen Master Hongzhi*.

Hongzhi Zhengjue addressed the monks, saying, "If on some distant embankment you see horns, then you know for sure there's an ox there. If on some distant mountain you see smoke, then you know for sure there's a fire there. But what is it that all of you here know for certain? Do you understand? When the bird calls from its roost, then morning comes. When you smell the plum blossoms, it means spring has arrived."

———— ◈ ————

Hongzhi addressed the monks, saying, "When the buddhas talk about Dharma, they're just using yellow leaves to stop babies from crying. When the ancestors transmit the teaching, they're just making empty-handed threats. When you reach this point, you must [attain] self-cessation, self-realization, and self-clarity. The Buddha is realized in each individual person, and the Dharma can't be passed to you by someone else. If you understand in this manner, then you are a great adept, a true patch-robed monk, and you have successfully completed the great affair.

"Brethren! How, after all, will you finally find peace? Just wait for the snow to melt and naturally spring will arrive."

◆

A monk asked Hongzhi, "What of the ones who have gone?"

Hongzhi said, "The white clouds rise to the top of the valleys, the blue peaks lean high into the void."

The monk asked, "What of the ones who return?"

Hongzhi said, "Head covered in white hair, leaving the cliffs and valleys. In the dead of night descending through the clouds to the market stall."

The monk asked, "What of the ones who neither come nor go?"

Hongzhi said, "The stone woman calls them back from the three realms dream. The wooden man sits upon and collapses the six gates. In these words the ancestors' way is clearly seen. Understanding the ancestors' way is difficult."

After a long pause, Hongzhi said, "Do you understand? The frozen cock does not announce the house woods dawn.[208] The hidden pilgrims traverse the snowy mountain."

◆

In the ninth month of [the year 1157], Hongzhi visited [various personages of the region] and bade them farewell. On the seventh day of the tenth month he returned to the mountain [Tiantong]. In the early hours of the next morning, the master bathed and changed his clothes. He then sat in an upright position and bade farewell to the monks. He asked his attendants for a brush, and then wrote a letter to [Zen Master] Dahui of Ayuwang Temple, asking him to take care of his final affairs.

He then wrote a verse:

Empty flowers of an illusory dream,
Sixty-seven years,
A white bird disappears in the mist,
Autumn waters touch the sky.

He then threw down the brush and passed away. Enshrined for seven days, his complexion was still lifelike. His entire body was placed in a stupa in the eastern valley. He received the posthumous name "Vast Wisdom." The stupa was named "Divine Light."

Twenty-first Generation

YUANWU KEQIN

TAIPING HUIQIN

FOYAN QINGYUAN

KAIFU DAONING

TIANTONG ZONGJUE

YUANWU KEQIN, "FOGUO," "SHAOJUE"

YUANWU KEQIN (1063–1135) was a disciple of Wuzu Fayan. He came from Chongzhu City in Pengzhou.[209] A gifted youth who thoroughly studied the Confucian classics, he is said to have written one thousand words every day. During a visit to Miaoji Monastery he observed some Buddhist scriptures and was surprised by a strong feeling that he had previously possessed them. He then left home and studied under a Vinaya master named Zisheng and a scriptural teacher named Yuanming.

Foguo once became deathly ill. He realized that his scriptural study and chanting of Buddha's name was insufficient, saying, "The true path of nirvana of all the buddhas is not found in words. I've used sounds to seek form, but it's of no use for dealing with death." After he recovered he set off to seek instruction from the Zen school.

Foguo first studied under a Zen master named Zhenjiao Sheng in Sichuan. During one of their discussions, Sheng pricked his arm and bled a few drops of blood.

Sheng showed it to Foguo and said, "This is a drop of Cao Creek."

This startled Foguo, and only after some time he responded, saying, "Is it really?"

Foguo then left Sichuan and traveled to several teachers, including Dagui Muche and Huanglong Zuxin. Everywhere he went his teachers said that he was to be a great vessel for the Dharma. Huitang declared, "Someday, the entire Linji school will be his disciples."

Finally, Foguo met the great teacher Wuzu. However, Foguo felt that their first meeting was a failure because Wuzu seemed aloof and unsympathetic.

Foguo became angry and began to walk away. As he left, Wuzu called after him, "Wait until you become feverishly ill, then think of me!"

Foguo went to Jinshan.[210] There he became extremely ill. Remembering Wuzu's words, he pledged to return to study with him when he recovered.

When Wuzu saw Foguo return he laughed and told him to go to the practice hall. Foguo then took the position of Wuzu's attendant.

An official of the exchequer named Tixing retired and returned to Sichuan, where he sought out Wuzu to learn about Zen. Wuzu said to him, "When you were young, did you read a poem by Xiaoyan or not? There were two lines which went something like, 'Oh these trinkets mean nothing, for I only want to hear the familiar sounds of my lover.'"

Tixing said, "Yes, I read them."

Wuzu said, "The words are well crafted."

Just then, Foguo came in attendance. He asked, "I heard the master mention the poem by Xiaoyan. Does Tixing know it or not?"

Wuzu said, "He just knows the words."

Foguo said, "'I only want to hear the familiar sounds of my lover.' If he knows the words, why doesn't he understand it?"

Wuzu said, "Why did Bodhidharma come from the west? The cypress tree in front of the garden!"[211]

At these words Foguo was suddenly enlightened. He went outside the cottage and saw a rooster fly to the top of a railing, beat his wings and crow loudly. He said to himself, "Is this not the sound?"

Foguo then took incense [to light in gratitude] and went back into Wuzu's room. There he revealed his attainment and offered this verse:

The golden duck vanishes into the gilt brocade.
With a rustic song, the drunkard returns in the woods.
A youthful love affair
Is known only by the young beauty.

Wuzu then said, "The great matter of the Buddha ancestors is not sought by inferior vessels. I share your joy."

Wuzu then informed the prominent elders of the temple, saying, "My attendant has attained the goal of Zen practice." Because of this, Foguo was promoted to the position of head monk.

Another story of Foguo's early experience under his teacher Wuzu Fayan is recorded in the classical Zen text, *Fozu Lidai Tongzai* (*Complete Historical Record of the Buddha Ancestors*).[212]

When [Yuanwu's teacher] Fayan first came to Wuzu Temple, Yuanwu was working there as temple manager. At that time a new kitchen was to be built in an area where a beautiful tree stood.

Fayan said, "Although the tree is in the way, don't cut it down."

Yuanwu cut down the tree anyway.

Fayan reacted furiously, and picking up his staff he chased after Yuanwu as if to strike him. Yuanwu began to run away to avoid the beating, but then suddenly experienced great enlightenment and cried out, "This is the way of Linji!"

He then grabbed the staff away from Fayan and said, "I recognize you, you old thief!"

Fayan laughed and went off.

From this time forward, Fayan allowed Yuanwu to lecture the Dharma to the other monks.

 During the Chongning era (1102–06), Foguo assumed the abbacy of Zhaojue Temple.[213] He later moved to Xingzhou, where a famous contemporary teacher by the name of Zhang Wujin paid him a visit to discuss the doctrines of Zen and Huayan Buddhism. From this event, Foguo's fame spread widely. Foguo then resided at Blue Cliff Temple on Mt. Jia.[214]

There his students appended Foguo's spoken commentaries to an earlier manuscript known as the *Odes on the Hundred Cases*, a collection of kōans and added verses by Xuedou Chongxian. The resulting text, called the *Blue Cliff Record,* has served as a preeminent volume of kōans for subsequent generations of Zen students. Gaining wide popularity during Foguo's lifetime, the *Blue Cliff Record* received both praise and condemnation. To some it represented the highest standard of Zen literature. To others it represented a subversion of Zen's tradition of pointing directly at mind and shunning the study of written words as a vehicle for liberation. Foguo's famous Dharma heir, Dahui Zonggao, was so alarmed by the success of his teacher's book that he attempted to destroy as many copies as possible. However, the book's circulation was, for better or worse, beyond Dahui's ability to stop it.

Among Foguo's admirers was the high government official Deng Zi, who presented to Foguo the ceremonial purple robe and the name that accompanied him to posterity.[215] Emperor Gao Zong summoned Foguo, and conferred upon him the name Zen Master Yuan Wu ("Perfect Enlightenment").

Foguo entered the hall and addressed the monks, saying: "The eye cannot see the pervasive Buddha body. The ear cannot hear the pervasive Buddha body. Speech cannot describe the pervasive Buddha body. The mind cannot imagine the pervasive Buddha body. Even if you can behold the entire great earth, not missing a trace, then you've gone only half-way. And if called on to do so, how could you describe it? Within its boundaries the sun and moon are suspended— the universal clear emptiness—the endless source of spring."

◆

Foguo entered the hall and addressed the monks, saying, "Fifteen days before, a thousand oxen can't drag it back. Fifteen days later, even the swift falcon can't chase it. Just at fifteen days; the sky serene; the earth serene; equally clear; equally dark. The myriad realms are not revealed here. It can swallow and spit out the ten voids. Step forward and you step across an indescribable fragrant-water ocean. Step back and you rest upon endless miles of white clouds. Stepping neither forward nor back, there is the place where the worthies don't speak, where this old monk doesn't open his mouth."

Raising his whisk he said, "Just when it's like this, what is it?"

◆

Foguo addressed the monks, saying, "Great waves arise on the mountain tops. Dust rises from the bottom of a well. The eyes hear a thunderclap. The ears see a great brocade. The three hundred sixty bones [of the human body] each reveal the incomparably sublime body. The tips of eighty-four thousand hairs display the chiliocosm sea of worlds of the Treasure King. But this is not the pervasive numinous function. Nor is it the manifested Dharma. If only the thousand eyes can suddenly open, then you'll be sitting throughout the ten directions. If you could describe this in a single surpassing phrase, what would you say? To test jade it must be passed through fire. To find the pearl, don't leave the mud."

The following passages are taken from *The Record of Foguo*.

Foguo entered the hall.

A monk asked him, "In all of the great canon of scripture, what is the most essential teaching?"

Foguo said, "Thus I have heard."

Then Foguo said, "This was what Ananda said. What do you say?"

———◆———

Foguo entered the hall.
A monk asked him, "What is the true host?"
Foguo said, "The myriad streams return to the sea. A thousand mountains honor the essential doctrine."

———◆———

Yuanwu Keqin ascended the seat and said, "The heat of a fire cannot compare with the heat of the sun. The cold wind cannot compare with the coldness of the moon. A crane's legs are naturally long and a duck's legs are naturally short. A pine tree is naturally tall and straight, while brambles are crooked. Geese are white. Crows are black. Everything is manifested in this manner. When you completely comprehend this, then everywhere you go you'll be the host. Everything you meet will be the teaching. When you carry this pole, you'll be prepared to fight anywhere. Do you have it? Do you have it?"

———◆———

Foguo entered the hall and said, "Zen is without thought or intention. Setting forth a single intention goes against the essential doctrine. The great Way ends all meritorious work. When merit is established, the essential principle is lost. Upon hearing a clear sound or some external words, do not seek some meaning within them. Rather, turn the light inward and use the essential function to pound off the manacles of the buddhas and ancestors. Where Buddha is, there is also guest and host. Where there is no Buddha, the wind roars across the earth. But when the mind's intentions are stilled, even a great noise becomes a soothing sound. Tell me, where can such a person be found? Put on a shawl and stand outside the thousand peaks. Draw water and pour it on the plants before the five stars."[216]

———◆———

"All the desires of my original mind are fulfilled by the treasury that is naturally here before me. The sky is up above. Down below is the earth. To the left is the kitchen, and to the right is the monk's hall. Before me is the Buddha hall and temple gate, and behind me is the dormitory and abbot's quarters. So where is the treasury? Do you see it? If we stand and sit in a dignified manner, and listen and speak clearly, then brilliant light floods our eyes and there is limitless peace. All sacred and mundane affairs are extinguished and all confining views are dropped away. The Yang-tse River is nectar and the great earth is gold. If from within one's chest a single phrase were to flow forth, what would be said? 'Since ancient times it has streamed like white silk.' 'Upon the horizon are seen the blue mountains.'"

———— ❖ ————

Yuanwu said to the monks, "There is a bright road that the buddhas and ancestors knew. You are facing it, and what you see and hear is not separate from it. The myriad things cannot conceal it and a thousand saints can't embody it. It is vibrant. It can't be carried. It is clearly exposed. It is without impediment. Even if you undergo blows from the staff like rain, and shouts like thunderclaps, you're still no closer to the ultimate principle. What is the ultimate principle? Blind the eyes of the saints and strike me dumb! When the bell strikes at midday, look south and see the Northern Dipper!"

The master then got down and left the hall.

············· ❖ ·············

Yuanwu said, "The sword that kills. The sword that gives life. These are artifices of the ancients, and yet they remain pivotal for us today. Trying to understand from words is like washing a dirt clod in muddy water. But not using words to gain understanding is like trying to put a square peg in a round hole. If you don't use some idea you've already missed it. But if you have any strategy whatsoever, you're still a mountain pass away from it. It's like the sparks from struck flint or a lightning flash. Understanding or not understanding, there's no way to avoid losing your body and life. What do you say about this principle? A bitter gourd is bitter to the root. A sweet melon is sweet to the base!"

The master then got down and left the hall.

Late in August in the year 1135, Foguo appeared to be slightly ill. He sat upright and composed a farewell verse to the congregation. Then, putting down the brush, he passed away. His cremated remains were placed in a stupa next to Zhaojue Temple.

Taiping Huiqin, "Fojian"

Taiping Huiqin (1059–1117) was a disciple of Wuzu Fayan. He came from Shuzhou (now the city of Qianshan in Anwei Province). As a young man he was an accomplished scholar and an adept at the study of Buddhist scriptures. According to the *Wudeng Huiyuan* he "got a taste" of insight when, while reading the *Lotus Sutra*, he encountered the phrase, "There is only this reality. Any other is not the truth." Fojian then set off to study under the famous Zen masters of his era. He eventually came to the great teacher Wuzu.

> One day Fojian heard Wuzu relate the following story, "A monk asked Zhaozhou, 'What is the master's family style?' Zhaozhou said, 'This old monk is deaf. Ask your question again louder.' The monk asked his question again. Zhaozhou said, 'You asked about my family style, but what I see is your family style.'"
>
> Fojian, suddenly seized by doubt, then said to Wuzu, "I ask the master to offer instruction about the ultimate principle."
>
> Wuzu said, "The phenomena of the universe and the ten thousand forms, these are the seal of the one Dharma."
>
> Fojian then prostrated himself before Wuzu. Wuzu thereafter allowed Fojian to be in charge of writing materials.
>
> Later, when Fojian was speaking with Yuanwu [a Dharma brother and the chief monk under Wuzu], Fojian brought up for discussion a story in which the monk Dongsi asks Yangshan about "the lustrous pearl of causation in the Zhen Sea."
>
> Fojian said, "This lustrous pearl is in a place where principle does not reach."
>
> Yuanwu agreed and said, "If it is said to be obtained, then the pearl is concealed. Thus it is said that no words can respond to it and no principle can reach it."
>
> Fojian could say nothing to Yuanwu in response. But the next day, Fojian said to Yuanwu, "Dongsi revealed a pristine pearl. Beneath it Yangshan tipped over a basket."
>
> Yuanwu deeply approved this statement and said to Fojian, "You should go see the old master."
>
> The next day, Fojian went to see Wuzu, but before he could speak Wuzu suddenly cursed him. Angry and frustrated Fojian returned to his cottage and slammed the door, filled with resentment.
>
> Later Yuanwu knocked on the door.
>
> Fojian called "Who is it?"
>
> "Me," said, Yuanwu. "What happened when you saw the old master?"

Fojian said, "I actually didn't see him. You've tricked me! He only swore at me!"

Yuanwu laughed loudly and said, "Remember what you said last night?"

Fojian said, "What?"

Yuanwu said, "You said that Dongsi revealed a pristine pearl and Yangshan tipped over the basket."

These words caused Fojian to finally understand. Yuanwu then took Fojian to see Master Wuzu. When Wuzu saw them coming he suddenly said, "Brother Qin [Fojian], how joyous that the great matter is finally resolved."

Fojian later received formal Dharma transmission from Wuzu and assumed the abbacy of the Taiping Xingguo Monastery on Mt. Zhong.[217] In the year 1111, he became abbot of the Zhihai Temple in Bianjing.[218] Five years later he returned to Mt. Zhong to reside at Jiankang Temple.

Among Fojian's patrons was a high official of the imperial court named Deng Zi. He presented Fojian with the ceremonial purple robe and the name Fojian ("Buddha Mirror"), by which he is remembered.[219]

Upon receiving the robe of transmission from Wuzu, Fojian held it up with both hands and showed it to the congregation, saying, "In former times Shakyamuni Buddha, with a ten-foot gold-trimmed robe, cloaked the entire thousand-foot Buddha body. The Buddha body was not too tall, nor was the robe too short. Do you understand? It's just like this. It's not some other way."

———— ◆ ————

A monk asked, "Why did Bodhidharma come from the west?"

Fojian said, "If you taste vinegar then you know sour. If you taste salt then you know saltiness."

———— ◆ ————

A monk asked, "I've heard that you personally saw Master Wuzu. Is that so?"

Fojian said, "The iron ox grazed in the golden grass."

The monk said, "Then you personally saw Wuzu?"

Fojian said, "Did I give you an offensive answer?"

The monk said, "Was [your meeting with Wuzu] like when Bodhidharma met Emperor Wudi?"

Fojian said, "Foreign speech is easy to understand, but Chinese is difficult to comprehend."

———— ◆ ————

A monk asked, "Putting aside 'Mind is Buddha,' what is the meaning of 'No mind, no Buddha'?"

Taiping said, "Yesterday a monk asked me this. I didn't answer him."

The monk said, "I don't understand whether this is much different from 'Mind is Buddha.'"

Taiping said, "It's as close as 10,000 miles away. It's as far as a gap that a hair can't fit into."

The monk said, "If I suddenly cut off the two heads and 'returned home' to sit in seclusion, then what?"

Taiping said, "Where is your home?"

The monk said, "It's a liberated body within the ten thousand worlds."

Taiping said, "You haven't reached your home yet. Speak again."

The monk said, "When I reach this place, I don't differentiate anything. There's no difference between north and south."

Taiping said, "Just so."

———— ◆ ————

Zen master Taiping entered the hall and addressed the monks, saying, "Attaining the Way is not difficult. Just disdain picking and choosing. The peach blossoms are red and the plum blossoms are white. Who says it's all mixed up to be one color? The sparrow chirps. The oriole sings. Who says that birds make only one sound?

"Those of you who haven't penetrated the essential connection with the ancestors; just let the mountains and rivers be your eye!"

———— ◆ ————

Taiping Huiqin kept six wooden dice in his abbot's quarters. On each side of every die was a single dot. When a monk would enter for an interview, Taiping would throw the dice and say, "Do you understand?" If the monk hesitated, Taiping would drive him from the room with blows.

In the month of August in [the year 1117], Fojian entered the hall and addressed the monks, saying, "The mind-seal of Wuzu is like the great function of an iron ox. The seal was laid down and then destroyed. It may be said that it has neither gone nor remained, nor is it at a place to which a monk may take a pilgrimage. And, after all, what is a place to which a monk may take a pilgrimage? Wait until about October and I'll show you."

On the eighth day of the following month, Fojian bathed, put on his robe and then sat cross-legged in an upright position. With a brush and paper he wrote a few words of farewell. Then, laying down the brush, he passed away. His cremated remains were placed in a stupa by the temple.

FOYAN QINGYUAN, "LONGMEN"

FOYAN QINGYUAN (1067–1120) was a disciple of Wuzu Fayan. He came from the city of Linqiong (near the modern city of Chengdu in Sichuan Province). He is one of three illustrious students of Wuzu Fayan who were known as the "three buddhas."[220]

At the young age of fourteen, Foyan accepted the Buddhist precepts. He then proceeded to study the Buddhist scriptures and practice the tenets of the Vinaya. In the *Lotus Sutra*, he read a passage that said, "It is the Dharma that cannot be discerned by thinking that can be attained." He asked his Vinaya teacher for an explanation of the passage, but received no answer. Foyan sighed and said, "Doctrinal study can't resolve the great matter of life and death."

Foyan "traveled south" and began study at the Dharma seat of a Zen master named Taiping Yan of Shuzhou.[221] One day as he was begging for alms in Luzhou during a rainstorm, Foyan slipped and fell to the ground. In the midst of this predicament he overheard two men arguing fiercely nearby. One of them said, "You're still defiling yourself!" At these words Foyan had an insight. He returned to the temple to question Master Yan about it, but Yan would only say, "I'm not you. You can do it yourself," or "I don't understand. I can't compare to you." This merely increased Foyan's uncertainty, so he went to the head monk, named Yuan Li, and tried to pose his question.

Yuan Li grabbed Foyan's ear and pulled him in a circle around the stove, saying, "You already understand!"

Foyan demanded, "I wanted you to help me. Why are you playing a game?"

Yuan Li said, "Later you'll be enlightened, and then you'll know why today's song bends your ears."

❖

One cold night as he sat up alone, Foyan poked deep in the ashes of a dwindled fire and saw the embers flare up. He suddenly exclaimed, "Poke deeply and you'll find it. Life is like this!"

Foyan then picked up and read some lamp records about a former teacher, Suddenly he "penetrated the bottom of the stove." He then composed a verse.

"In the forest of knives a bird sings out.
Wrapped in a cloak and sitting up late,
Poking the fire and awakening to ordinary life,
The great gods are overturned and smashed.
In the glistening world are the self-deluded.
Who will sing a colorless song?
Realized once, it is not forgotten.
The gate is open, but few pass through it."

Yuanwu [Foyan's younger Dharma brother] visited Foyan's room. He inquired to Foyan about Zen master Qinglin's "hauling soil."

Yuanwu said to Foyan, "From ancient times until today, no one has been able to 'go out.' What do you say about this?"

Foyan said, "What's difficult about it?"

Yuanwu said, "What about Qinglin's phrase, 'The Iron Wheel Emperor at the center of the universe'?"

Foyan said, "What I say is, in the middle of the palace of heaven, all script is discarded."

Yuanwu left, and thereafter told people, "It's wonderful. Elder brother Foyan has life-giving words."

Foyan forcefully expounded the style of the Linji heritage. He taught at Tianning[222] Temple in Shuzhou and Baochan Temple at Mt. Longmen.

Foyan entered the hall and addressed the monks. Holding his staff upright he said, "Know with perfect clarity. It does not come from thought. If you have died you can speak. Dive into the pit. Jump into the moat. After all, what is it?"

Foyan addressed the monks, saying, "'A leaf falls, and throughout the world it is springtime.' 'When there is no road for pursuing thoughts, your laugh kills people.' 'Down below is heaven. Up above is the earth.' This speech does not enter the flow of time. 'South is north.' 'East is west.' 'Movement is stillness.' 'Joy is sorrow.' 'A snake's head or a boreworm's tail both measure up.' 'Sparrows live in the wild tiger's mouth.'

"What sort of speech is this? Go back to the hall!"

Foyan entered the hall and addressed the monks, saying, "Su Wu tended sheep, not submitting to an insult. Li Ling, when meeting a friend, would forget about going home.[223] Those things happened in a foreign country.[224] In this country, among all the Buddhist adepts, some leap over a hole with both feet. Some bury their bodies in dung heaps. Some revile the river gods. It's their spirit of practice, their wondrous function. It's even raising their feet and stamping the ground or striking the meditation benches with their staff. Muzhou always slammed the door. Luzu faced the wall until the end. Was it for the sake of people? Was it for people or not?"

The following two passages are taken from *The Record of the Venerable Ancients.*

Foyan said, "I say there are but two types of sickness. One is to ride a donkey to look for the donkey. The other is riding the donkey and not letting yourself get off of it. Don't you see that riding a donkey to find a donkey is a fatal disease? This old mountain monk is telling you, don't seek it! Clever people understand right where they are. They give up the 'seeking' disease and the crazy, thought-pursuing mind. Once you've seen the donkey, not allowing yourself to get off—now that is a disease that's most hard to cure! This old mountain monk is telling you, Don't ride it!

"You are the donkey. The great earth is the donkey. How are you going to ride it? If you continue to ride it you'll never cure this disease. If you don't ride it, then all the worlds in the ten directions are opened to you. If you can get rid of both of these diseases at once, then there's nothing left in your mind and you're called a person of the Way. What could trouble you?

"Therefore, Zhaozhou asked Nanquan, 'What is the Way?' And Nanquan answered, 'Everyday mind is the Way.'"

◆

Foyan said, "The great practice must be apart from thought. And within the gate of this practice the emphasis is on giving up effort. If only a person can give up emotional thoughts and recognize that the three worlds are empty, then he can realize this practice. Any other practice besides this will be terribly difficult.

"Have you heard the old story of the Vinaya monk? He upheld all the precepts all of his life. When he was walking at night he stepped on something that made a loud noise. He thought it was a toad, and inside of this toad were countless toad eggs. The monk was scared out of his wits and passed out from fright. He dreamed that hundreds of toads were coming after him, demanding their lives. The monk was utterly terrified. When dawn came around he saw that he had just stepped on a dried-out eggplant. The monk, realizing the unreliable nature of his thoughts, then ceased such thinking, and realized the empty nature of the three realms. After this he could begin doing genuine practice.

"Now, I ask you all, was the thing that the monk stepped on in the night a toad? Or was it an eggplant? If it was a toad, then in the morning how was it an eggplant? And if it was an eggplant, there still seemed to be toads who demanded their lives. Have you rid yourself of all these visions? I'll check to see if you understand. If you've gotten rid of the fear of the toads, do you still have the eggplant there? You must have no eggplant either!

"The noon bell has been struck. You've stood here long enough!"

The following selections are from *The Record of Zen Master Foyan*.

Foyan entered the hall and said, "To realize the Dharma of all the sages, just recognize that their Dharma is none other than the Dharma of ordinary people. Completely understand that mundane and holy are not two different things. If you get to the bottom of enlightenment right now, then you have gotten to the bottom of all future delusion. If you get to the bottom of delusion right now, then you have reached the bottom of all future enlightenment. Completely understand that enlightenment and delusion are not two different things. Why should delusion go on being covered up?

"So what is it that all the enlightened ones have realized? It's that when you penetrate 'common,' 'sacred,' 'enlightenment,' and 'delusion,' then you clearly see the source. I dare to ask you all, what is the original person? Teachers and monks everywhere have said, 'Where can the original person not be seen? Mr. Donkey Lips is a great holy man from Si Province.' They have also said, 'It doesn't have a face, so where would you meet it?' Distant water won't put out a nearby fire!

"Apart from these two paths, what is the original person?"

After a long pause, Foyan said, "But even if you understand what I'm saying, how do you realize it yourself?"

———————— ◆ ————————

Foyan entered the hall. He nodded his head to the assembly.

A monk came forward and said, "Today I encountered something…"

Foyan said, "Don't speak foolishness!"

Foyan also said, "Every day all of you do a thousand or ten thousand things. There's nothing you don't try to do. So why is it you don't understand? It's because your faith isn't sufficient. If your faith were sufficient, then even if you did nothing, you'd arrive at it. If you don't give a thought to all the affairs of the world in the ten directions, then you'll realize it.

"Every day you all say a thousand or ten thousand things. There's nothing you don't say. So why is it you don't yet understand? It's because your faith isn't sufficient. If your faith were sufficient, then you'd need say nothing at all. If you didn't give a thought to what has been said by all the tathagatas of the three worlds, then you'd understand in a moment.

"Everyone! Have you reached the field of which I speak? This gate of mine can only be spoken of in terms of authentic realization, not in terms of understanding. If it is to be for the sake of those who experience life and death, then it must be intimately realized. If you are someone who studies self and other, then you won't suffer ridicule. But if you go seeking some special understanding, looking for it in form or words, then you will substitute form for the authentic seal. The result will be, 'If you try to exterminate the tribes, they will arise in rebellion.' If you teach others you'll just harm them!

"In this gate of mine there are no affairs. Do you understand? When a deaf person plays the reed flute, good and evil are nowhere heard!"

One day in [the year 1120], Foyan finished eating, then sat upright in a cross-legged posture and addressed his disciples, saying, "All of the ancient worthies, when they were about to leave the world, composed a verse. May I bid the world good-bye and just quietly go on?"

He then placed his palms together and peacefully passed away.

KAIFU DAONING

KAIFU DAONING (1053–1113) was a disciple of Wuzu Fayan. He came from ancient Wuyuan (located near the border between modern Anwei and Jiangxi Provinces). According to the *Wudeng Huiyuan*, as a young man he visited a temple to bathe and happened to hear a recitation of the *Diamond Sutra*. Momentarily forgetting where he was, his foot slipped into boiling water, the sensation giving him insight about the nature of self. He left home and entered a temple on Mt. Jiang near Nanjing to study under a Zen master named Xuedou Laoliang. Later, Kaifu went traveling and studied under various noted Zen masters of the day.

Finally, Kaifu came to study under Wuzu. It is recorded that Kaifu awakened to the source of Dharma upon hearing Wuzu expound on the two famous kōans "Zhaozhou's Mu" and "Nanyang's Water Pitcher" at the White Lotus Temple.

In the year 1109, the governor of Tanzhou invited Kaifu to assume the abbacy of Kaifu Temple. Students were said to follow him there "like a shadow."

Through Kaifu Daoning the Linji transmission followed a path leading to the great teacher Wumen Huikai, compiler of the *Gateless Gate*, and then on to Japan by way of the Japanese monk, Shinchi Kakushin.

Kaifu entered the hall and addressed the monks, saying, "All the worlds have never been concealed. The entire Buddha body is formless. Meet with the great, undisturbed ignorance. For endless kalpas up to the present there has been no artifice. No artifice. Few people know. The great give up their flesh and bones. Why stand close to the mirror and paint the eyebrows?"

———— ◆ ————

A monk asked, "What is it before the lotus comes out of the water?"
Kaifu said, "People and gods *gassho*."[225]
The monk asked, "What about after it comes out of the water?"
Kaifu said, "Nothing's stopping you from seeing for yourself."

———— ◆ ————

A monk asked, "What does it mean when the words arrive but the meaning does not arrive?"
Kaifu said, "The Rui grass fundamentally has no roots.[226] Believers make use of it."
The monk asked, "What does it mean when the meaning arrives but the words do not arrive?"
Kaifu said, "Receiving the barbed point, not reading the balance scale."
The monk asked, "What is it when meaning and words both arrive together?"
Kaifu said, "The Mahakaruna does not extend its hands.[227] The entire Buddha body is a clear eye."
The monk asked, "What is it when neither meaning nor words arrive?"
Kaifu said, "You go to Xiexiang. I go to Tai."

———— ◆ ————

On the fourth day of the eleventh month of [the year 1113], Kaifu washed his hair and bathed. The following day he gave a talk in the afternoon in which he urged the monks to continue their practice of the Way. He offered them all a sincere farewell. As the sun went down he sat in a cross-legged posture and passed away. His disciples recovered the master's relics and placed them in a stupa.

TIANTONG ZONGJUE

TIANTONG ZONGJUE (n.d.) was a disciple and Dharma heir of Zhenxie Qingliao. He came from Hezhou.[228] Zongjue left home at the age of sixteen and gained ordination two years later. He first studied Zen under Zuzhao Daohe, a master of the Yunmen lineage. After Zuzhao retired from teaching, Zongjue proceeded to study under the Caodong teacher Qingliao, becoming his Dharma heir and a transmitter of the Caodong lineage. In 1132, Zongjue became abbot of Yuelin Temple.[229] He remained at Yuelin for twenty-three years before becoming abbot at Mt. Xuedou. Four years later [1159], he moved to Tiantong Monastery, where he obtained his mountain name and forcefully expounded the Dharma for three years until his death in 1162.

> A monk asked Tiantong Zongjue, "What is the Way?"
> Tiantong said, "Stop making signposts at the crossroads."

———— ◆ ————

Zongjue entered the hall and addressed the monks, saying, "Across the empty eon, the single body extends beyond the world. Uniting with the ultimate is not attained through meaning, nor can its genuine sign be transmitted through words. It is found in unperturbed empty stillness; the white clouds breaking across cold mountains; the ethereal light penetrating the darkness; the lustrous moon that follows the arrival of night. When it is thus, how does one walk the path? Right and wrong have never departed from the fundamental standpoint. Through the length and breadth of the universe, why need one speak of causation?"

Twenty-second Generation

DAHUI ZONGGAO

HUGUO JINGYUAN

ZHU'AN SHIGUI

YUE'AN SHANGUO

XUEDOU ZHIJIAN

DAHUI ZONGGAO, "FORI"

DAHUI ZONGGAO (1089–1163) was a disciple of Yuanwu Keqin (Foguo). He came from Ningguo (located in modern Anwei Province). He left home at the age of seventeen to live at Huiyun ("Wisdom Cloud") Temple on Mt. Dong, and received ordination there the following year.

According to the *Wudeng Huiyuan*, as a young man Dahui happened to encounter a copy of *The Record of Yunmen*. He felt strangely familiar with the text, as though he had previously studied it. Later, he traveled and practiced under various Zen masters, becoming familiar with the prevailing Zen currents of the era.

Dahui ascended Treasure Peak to study under a Zen master named Zhan Tangzhun.[230] Zhan recognized Dahui's unusual ability and assigned him to work as his personal attendant. But Dahui's obstinate personality clashed with his teacher, leading to an exchange in which Zhan ridiculed the young student, saying, "You haven't experienced enlightenment and the problem is your intellectual understanding!"

Later, Zhan became very ill. Calling Dahui to his side before he died, he directed him to seek out Yuanwu Keqin and apply himself diligently as his student.

Soon, Dahui traveled to Yuanwu's residence, Tianning Temple, where he heard the master address the monks.[231]

In his talk, Yuanwu spoke of an incident in which a monk asked Yunmen, "What is the place where all buddhas come forth?" Yunmen answered, "The water on East Mountain flows uphill."

Then someone in the audience asked Yuanwu, "What is the place where all buddhas come forth?"

Yuanwu said, "Warm breezes come from the South, but in the palace there's a cold draught."

Upon hearing these words, Dahui's "past and future were cut off." Although there was movement, forms were unmanifested. He felt himself sitting in a still, barren place.

Yuanwu continued speaking, "It hasn't been easy, but you've made your way to this great field. What a pity if you were now to die and not be able to attain life. It's a great error to rely on words. Without knowing where you'll fall, just let go of the edge of the cliff. Let yourself do it. After you wake up you won't be deceived again. You must believe in this."

Thereafter, Dahui was selected to be an attendant in the wood hall. In this post, each day he accompanied the patrons of the temple when they waited to see and then entered the abbot's quarters for interviews. Yuanwu always said to them, "It's like words without words. Like a creeper held up by a tree."

Once when Yuanwu asked Dahui a question, Dahui started to answer when Yuanwu cut him off by saying, "No! No!"

After six months had passed, Dahui asked Yuanwu, "I've heard that previously you questioned Wuzu about this phrase, but I don't know what he answered."

Yuanwu laughed but did not reply to Dahui's question.

So Dahui said, "At that time you posed this question to everyone. Why not say it again now?"

Yuanwu said, "I said to Wuzu, 'What is the meaning of the phrase, "It is words without words, a creeper held up by a tree"?' Wuzu answered me by saying, 'You can't trace it. It can't be drawn.' I then asked him, 'When the tree has fallen down and the creeper has withered, what then?' Wuzu said, 'See what comes next.'"

At these words Dahui was enlightened. He said, "I understand."

Yuanwu then posed several probing questions at the student, and Dahui replied to each one without hesitation.

Finally Yuanwu said, "At last you know that I didn't deceive you."

Before long, Yuanwu shared his position of honor in the monastery with Dahui. Dahui's reputation as a skilled teacher spread widely, and in the year 1126, when Dahui was only thirty-seven years old, the prime minister presented him with the ceremonial purple robe and the honorific title "Great Teacher Buddha Sun."

In the year 1137, Dahui became abbot of the Nengren Temple.[232] One of Dahui's students, a government official named Zhang Jiucheng, became enmeshed in a political struggle. His opponent, named Chin Gui, gained ascendancy and managed to execute Zhang. Dahui was caught up in the political fallout of this episode and was forced to flee with his monks to Hengyang. While there, he compiled the records of many ancient teachers along with a large number of kōans. The result was a six-volume collection entitled *The Treasury of the True Dharma Eye*.

In the year 1150, Dahui and his monks were forced by social unrest to move again, this time going as far as the southern city of Meizhou in Guangdong Province. There, plague and famine killed more than half of the more than one hundred monks in Dahui's retinue.

By 1158, social conditions improved. Dahui was invited to move to Mt. Jing near Hangzhou and assume the abbacy there. In the years that followed, Dahui emphasized that the goal of all practice is the realization of enlightenment.

Dahui is known to have criticized "silent illumination Zen," which held sway in the Caodong school. The chief proponent of this teaching was Zen master Hongzhi Zhengjue of Tiantong Temple. Despite this, many scholars today point out that mutual respect and cordial relations existed between Dahui and his supposed adversary. Hongzhi requested that Dahui take care of Hongzhi's final affairs after his death.

Dahui entered the hall to address the monks. He raised and lowered his staff, then shouted and said, "Deshan's stick. Linji's shout. Today I present them to you. Heaven is so high. The earth is so vast. So don't be just adding more shit on top of a shit pile. Get rid of your bones and wash out your guts! I'll take three steps back and let you discuss this. Tell me how you will discuss it!"

Dahui then threw down the staff and shouted.

Then he said, "Add a little rouge and she's a respectable girl. But if he has no money he's not a proper suitor!"

❖

Dahui entered the hall and said, "No sooner do we get past the midautumn festival, than it's already the fifteenth day of the ninth month."

He then propped up his staff and said, "It's only this that doesn't change."

He then threw down his staff and said, "All of you! Listen and see!"

A monk asked, "When a single dharma arises, Vairochana Buddha becomes a commoner. When the ten thousand dharmas don't exist, Samantabhadra loses his realm. Leaving aside these two paths, I ask the master to quickly speak."

Dahui said, "Shedding its shell, the turtle flies up to heaven!"

A monk asked, "When mind and Buddha are both forgotten, then what?"

Dahui said, "In the hands of an old woman selling fans, the sun is revealed."

Dahui entered the hall and addressed the monks, saying, "After continuous rain and no break in the clouds, suddenly heaven and earth open up and are clear. Then what use is it to still seek out the ways of the ancestors?"

In the year 1137, the emperor appointed Dahui Zonggao to be abbot of Shuangjing Monastery. One day, news arrived of the death of (Dahui's teacher) Yuanwu Keqin. Dahui personally wrote a eulogy for his late master. That evening during a meeting with the monks, he recited the eulogy.

"A monk asked Changsha, 'When Nanquan died, where did he go?'

"Changsha said, 'In the East Village he's a donkey. In the West Village, he's a horse.'

"The monk said, 'What does this mean?'

"Changsha said, 'If you want to ride him you can ride him. If you want to get off him, you can do that too.'

"As for me, I don't go along with this. If a monk asks me, 'Where did the late master, Yuanwu Keqing, go when he died?' I'd say to him, 'He fell into the Avici Hell.'

"If the monk asked, 'What does this mean?' I'd say, 'Eating molten copper. Drinking molten iron.'

"If the monk asked, 'Is there anyone who can save him or not?' I'd say, 'No one can save him.'

"If he asked, 'Why can't he be saved?' I'd say, 'Because before he died, this was the same food the old fellow ate every day.'"

On the memorial day for Zen master Wushang, Dahui addressed the monks, saying, "Just now, before the drum sounded, Zen master Wushang personally, for the sake of everyone, entered the mud and water. The entangling weeds were thick. I don't want to add more mud to the ground."

❖

Zen master Dahui Zonggao entered the hall and addressed the monks, saying, "Mind is Buddha. There is no other Buddha. It's like a relaxing fist that becomes a hand, or water becoming a wave. A wave is water; a hand is a fist. This mind is not subject to past, future, or present. Since it is not subject to 'internal' or 'external'; 'past,' 'future,' or 'present'; this 'mind' and this 'Buddha' are just false names. If they are just false names, then is everything said in the entire scriptural canon true or not? If it isn't true, then can't we forget about old Shakyamuni's flapping lips and three-inch tongue? So what about it after all? Just know to do what's right. Don't ask about what's gone on before!"

❖

Dahui Zonggao asked a monk, "The Way does not require practice, but it must not be defiled. What is the undefiled way?"
The monk said, "I don't dare answer."
Dahui said, "Why not?"
The monk said, "I'm afraid of defilement."
Dahui said, "Good! Bring in the broom for sweeping shit!"
The monk was flustered.
Dahui drove him out of the room with blows.

❖

A monk came in to see the master.
Dahui said, "Old Shakyamuni's come!"
When the monk came before him, he said, "Oh, it's not him after all."
Then he struck the monk.
The next monk came in, and Dahui said, "Old Shakyamuni's come!"
The monk asked a question and immediately went out.
Dahui said, "Looked like the real thing."

❖

Dahui said, "Every day, persons who study the Way should investigate others' efforts, and they should always examine their own effort. In this manner they cannot help but be successful in practicing the Way. Whether they're joyous, angry, at peace, or troubled, all these occasions are times for examination."

Zen master Dahui was sitting and relaxing in his quarters when he suddenly said, "These days, the brethren gain their understandings with intellect and emotion. Many of them just recall some idle talk or catchy phrases and bring them in here to use as their answers to my questions. It's as if they have a priceless jewel in their hand, and when someone asks them, 'What's in your hand?' they drop it, then pick up a lump of dirt.

"So stupid! If they keep on like this they'll never gain enlightenment!"

Dahui entered the hall and said, "Silently sitting for nine years at Shaolin, suddenly 'breaking through to the divine light.' If right now you can't distinguish jade from stone, then you're just bound in hemp and wrapped in paper. Those people who chatter on about this thing, that thing, or some other thing— if they were clear-eyed people, how could they speak of 'breaking through'? Even today, here on Mt. Jing, we haven't avoided these pretenders. Some of these disciples spread idle talk about the old barbarian's nine years.[233] It's a shame we let them get away with it. These days, there are 'silent illumination' disciples who spend long years sitting in a demon's cave. And as for those who prattle on about this thing, that thing, or some other thing, it's all just wind whistling in the tree tops."

In the year 1163, a falling star fell to the west of the temple with a terrifying flash. Dahui soon became slightly ill. On the ninth day of the eighth month, his disciples inquired about his health. Dahui exerted himself and said in a loud voice, "Tomorrow I'm setting off on a journey." The next day at the fifth hour, he personally wrote his testimonial, and then wrote a farewell letter to [his friend] layman Ziyan. At the request of his monks he then composed a verse in large brushstrokes:

Birth is just so.
Death is just so.
So, as for composing a verse,
Why does it matter?

Dahui then threw down the brush and passed away in a composed manner. The next morning a large snake appeared, coiled next to the housing of the

Dragon King Well. It was colored white at the middle and head, as though in mourning. This was a manifestation of the Dragon King. Monks everywhere lamented, and the emperor was aggrieved at the news of the master's death.

Shangzhi Shizhen said in eulogy, "Birth and annihilation are not annihilated. Eternal abiding does not abide. Perfect enlightenment is empty and clear. It is revealed in everything."

After the prime minister paid his respects, a long line of mourners followed. Dahui's disciples interred his entire body in a stupa at the side of the Clear Moon Pavilion. The master was seventy-five years old and had been a monk for fifty-eight years. By imperial order, the Clear Moon Pavilion was renamed as the Sublime Joy Hermitage. The master received the posthumous name "Universal Enlightenment." The stupa was named "Precious Light." In [the year 1174], the master's complete works were memorialized to the throne, and thereafter widely circulated in the great canon.

Huguo Jingyuan

Huguo Jingyuan (n.d.) was a disciple of Yuanwu Keqin. He came from ancient Yongjia. After entering monastic life as a young man he first studied with a teacher named Xigong on Mt. Ling. After receiving the precepts, he studied Tiantai doctrines for three years, but gave up this pursuit to study under Zen master Yuanwu Keqin.

Jingyuan overheard a monk reading a teaching by Zen master Sixin that said, "Because enlightenment is realized in delusion, in enlightenment one recognizes the delusion within enlightenment and the enlightenment within delusion. When enlightenment and delusion are both forgotten, then one may establish all dharmas from this place that is without enlightenment and delusion." When Jingyuan heard this he experienced doubt. But later, when he was hurrying to the Buddha hall, just as he pushed open the door he suddenly experienced vast enlightenment. He then became Yuanwu's attendant, and during this time his great function and skill as a speaker became apparent. Yuanwu came to regard him as his primary assistant and presented him with a self-portrait, saying, "During my entire life I've only espoused 'intractable Zen.' When someone runs into it, it is like an iron wall. It's like being snared in a trap with one's feet cut off, and with the entire world closing in with pitch-like darkness.

For years [the students] flail about without a knife [to cut their way out], or else they use a diamond hammer to smash birds' nests. Finally, if they see my true face, in an instant they escape from 'self' and 'other.'"

◆

Zen master Jingyuan entered the hall and addressed the monks, saying, "When old Shakyamuni was born, he was really a laughingstock. With one hand he pointed at heaven and with the other he pointed at the earth, and then he said, 'I alone am the honored one.' Later, the great teacher Yunmen said, 'If I had been there and seen that, then for the sake of peace in the world I would have beaten him to death and fed him to the dogs.' There are people who don't go along with that. But if we are going to honor the ancestors then we certainly honor Yunmen, right? So, what is it we honor about Yunmen? Not the killing part, right? Aren't we glad he couldn't do that?

"Today, assuming the abbacy here at Nanming, I must be lenient. If I'm not lenient, then people across the great earth will all have to beg for their lives. If the great matter before us cannot be grasped, then I'll go with you all up to the Buddha hall and we'll all take turns giving him a beating! Why? Because if you don't hear the true Way, then acting against the rules is not a transgression."

◆

The master became ill. He invited Zen master Ying Anhua to come from the Western Hall Monastery and act as head monk. He gave him instructions about temple affairs as though everything was normal. He then formed his hand into a fist and passed away. After his cremation, it was found that among his sacred relics the flames did not consume his teeth, his tongue, and his right fist. His stupa was placed east of the temple in front of Liuyuan Cave. He was fifty-three years of age.

ZHU'AN SHIGUI

ZHU'AN SHIGUI (1083–1146) was a disciple of the great teacher Foyan. He came from the city of Chengdu, Sichuan Province. As a young man he entered Dazi ("Great Compassion") Temple in Chengdu under a Buddhist teacher named Zongya. There he studied the *Surangama Sutra*. After five years, he set off as a yunshui, studying under various Buddhist teachers of his time. Eventually he came to Mt. Longmen, where he met Foyan. Shigui, already an experienced

Zen student, demonstrated his understanding to his new teacher. Foyan advised him, "Your grasp of mind is thorough, but you must open your eyes and ears." Shigui then assumed a temple post as director of the monks' hall.

When Shigui was serving as Foyan's attendant, he said, "What is it when questions and answers stop?"

Foyan said, "It's like when you strike the hammer on the sounding board at the monk's hall."

Shigui didn't understand what Foyan meant. That evening Foyan went to Shigui's quarters and spoke with him. In the course of this conversation Shigui brought up their earlier conversation.

Foyan said, "Empty talk."

Upon hearing this, Shigui experienced great enlightenment.

Around the year 1115, Shigui began teaching in Tianning. He remained there until about the year 1135, when, at the invitation of the emperor, he assumed the abbacy of Nengren Temple.

Shigui addressed the monks, saying, "Ten thousand years—a single thought. A single thought—ten thousand years. Rolling in the mud with your clothes on, washing your feet, and climbing into bed to sleep. The affairs of an eon are here before you. When the ocean surges with billowing waves, fools try to measure how big they are."

Then, lifting his staff upright, Shigui said, "All of you here, you don't have an entrance. You must have an entrance. And when you have an entrance, you must begin the path of the revealed body. But what is the path of the revealed body?"

After a long pause, Shigui said, "The heavy snow can't crush the pine. The blowing wind moves not the moon." Shigui then lowered his staff and left the hall.

--------------------- ◆ ---------------------

Shigui entered the hall and addressed the monks, saying, "Before the ten thousand things come forth—your eyes see form. Your ears hear sounds—a talk in the hall. Above your head there is the bright sky. Your feet walk upon the ground. All of you only know that today is the first day of the fifth month. You really don't know that the golden bird scurried away at midnight, or that the jade rabbit has climbed the sky east of the sea."

Shigui then struck the meditation platform with his whisk, got down from the seat, and left the hall.

Shigui entered the hall and addressed the monks, saying, "Vast clarity, no awakening. If there are dharmas there is delusion. None of you can stand in that place. None of you can live in that place. If you stand there then there is danger. If you live there it is reckless. Grasping the meaning does not end the mystery. Speaking the words does not end the meaning. Using it does not end the function. If you're clear on these three things, then wherever you are you'll have no need for control, for everything will naturally reveal itself. You will have no need for concern, for everything will be naturally understood. But although it is thus, there is still a higher matter you must know. How long the rain before the sky clears? Ha!"

A monk asked Shigui, "What is the first principle?"
Shigui said, "What you just asked is the second principle."

A monk asked, "Does a dog have buddha nature? Zhaozhou said, 'Wu.' What did this mean?"
Shigui said, "Just once bitten by a snake, and thereafter afraid of a broken rope in a well."

A monk asked, "What is the meaning of 'wordless words, a creeper clinging to a tree'?"
Shigui said, "A thief's heart is empty."

In [the year 1146] Shigui called together the congregation, elders, and persons of the order to give them final instructions. The next day he bathed, sounded the bell to assemble the monks, and sat down. He then quietly passed away. On the day of his cremation, his pallbearers each received a portion of his sacred relics. The rest were placed in a stupa on Mt. Gu.

Yue'an Shanguo, "Dagui"

Yue'an Shanguo (n.d.) was a disciple of Kaifu Daoning. He came from ancient Xinzhou (an area in what is now Jiangxi Province). He lived and taught at Moon Hermitage on famous Mt. Gui. Yue'an transmitted the Dharma seal of Yangqi Zen to Wumen Huikai, the compiler of the *Gateless Gate*.

Yue'an posed a kōan to his students, which was later included by Wumen Huikai as case eight in the *Gateless Gate*, entitled "Xi Zhong's Cart."[234]

Master Yue'an asked a monk, "If you disconnected each end of the hundred spokes on Xi Zhong's cart, and removed the axle, what principle would be clearly revealed?"

The *Wudeng Huiyuan* indicates that Master Yue'an's narrative did not stop with this question, but continued as follows:

Upon speaking thus, Yue'an used his staff to draw a circle in the air. He then said, "Never fail to recognize the scale's balance!"

He then stood up, got down from the meditation platform, thanked the hall attendant, and went out.

———— ❖ ————

Zen master Yue'an entered the hall and addressed the monks, saying, "An escaped wild tiger has a bell around its neck. It strikes fear in everyone, and they flee in terror. Grabbing the lustrous pearl from the blue dragon's lair! Lighting up heaven and illuminating earth! This old mountain monk speaks before you today, but it's beyond my words of praise. All of you! What are you doing here?"

Yue'an then raised his whisk and said, "My eyebrows! They're falling out again!"

He then threw down his whisk and left the hall.

———— ❖ ————

Yue'an addressed the monks, saying, "When mind is born, dharmas are also born. When mind passes away, all dharmas pass away. When mind and dharmas are all forgotten, a turtle is called the Great Tortoise [that upholds the earth]. Zen worthies! Can you speak or not? If you can speak, then I'll give you the abbot's staff! If you can't speak, then just go back to the monk's hall and drink some tea!"

A monk asked, "Why did Bodhidharma sit facing a wall for nine years?"
Master Yue'an said, "The fish swims in muddy water."

A monk asked, "The Second Ancestor bowed three times. Why did he receive the marrow?"

Yue'an said, "When the ground is fertile the eggplants are big."

A monk asked, "If a flower blooms with five petals, it is naturally complete. What principle does this make clear?"

Yue'an said, "A thief is exposed by his booty."

XUEDOU ZHIJIAN, "ZU'AN"

XUEDOU ZHIJIAN (1105–92) was the Dharma heir of the Caodong lineage teacher Tiantong Zongjue. He came from ancient Chuzhou (located within modern Anwei Province). Information about his life in the lamp records is sketchy.

One day when Zhijian was a boy, his mother noticed a mark on his hands as she washed them. She said, "What is this?"

The boy said, "My hands are like the Buddha's hands [have the marks of the Buddha]."

He first studied under Zen master Zhenxie Qingliao at Changlu. Later he continued study under Zhenxie's Dharma heir, Tiantong Zongjue, who recognized him as a "great vessel of the Dharma."

He subsequently lived in seclusion on Mt. Xiang, where it is recorded that he attained enlightenment late one night despite the appearance of one hundred strange apparitions.[235] He then returned to see Zongjue, who confirmed his awakening and passed to him the Dharma seal of the Caodong school.

In the year 1154, Zhijian became abbot of Xizhen Temple near Hangzhou.[236] In 1184 he moved to Mt. Xuedou, where a large number of students gathered to study with him. During his final years he lived in seclusion in a cottage located east of the temple. He died in 1192, the ongoing transmission of the lineage passing to his most famous student, Tiantong Rujing.

Upon assuming the abbacy, Zhijian recited a verse to the monks in praise of the scriptural passage, "The World-Honored One had a secret word. Mahakashyapa did not conceal it. All night it rained flowers and the city was awash in fragrance."

"My hand was like the Buddha's.
My teachers expounded endlessly.
I concealed myself on Xiang Mountain
And outside walked raging spirits,
But when I connected with Tiantong
The hundred ghosts disappeared.
Bodhidharma didn't see that
The World-Honored One concealed nothing."

Twenty-third Generation

DAHONG ZUZHENG

TIANTONG RUJING

DAHONG ZUZHENG, "LAO NA"

DAHONG ZUZHENG (n.d.) was a disciple of Yue'an Shanguo. He came from Tanzhou. Although Dahong transmitted the Yangqi branch of Linji Zen to later generations, details of his life are lost in history.

Zuzheng addressed the monks, saying, "In the myriad forms, a single body is revealed. How would you speak of the single body principle?"

He then raised his whisk and said, "Traveling throughout the realm, crossing many river banks and mountains."

❖

A monk asked Zuzheng about the following story: "Yunmen asked a monk, '[Is the phrase] "The silent light illuminates worlds as countless as sands in the river Ganges" just flowery speech or not?' The monk answered, 'Yes.' Yunmen then said, 'Speech falls short.' Do you not know where this monk's speech falls short?"

Zuzheng said, "A mudfish climbs the bamboo stalk."

❖

A monk asked, "Without resorting to words, please, Master, point directly at the teaching."

Zuzheng raised his whisk.

The monk said, "Is there still a higher matter?"

Zuzheng said, "Yes."

The monk said, "What is the higher matter?"

Zuzheng said, "Quick, bow three times!"

TIANTONG RUJING

TIANTONG RUJING (1163–1228) was a disciple and Dharma heir of Zu'an Zhijian. Rujing came from the city of Weijiang in ancient Mingzhou (near modern Ningbo City in Zhejiang Province). During his life he lived at a succession of famous temples including Qingliang Temple at Nanjing and Jingzi Temple on the south edge of West Lake in Hangzhou. He eventually resided at Tiantong, where he taught and transmitted the Buddhadharma to the famous Japanese monk Eihei Dogen. *The Record of Rujing* reveals Dogen's teacher to be among the most poetically expressive of all the Zen ancients. He effused his Dharma talks with wonderful natural allusions and poetry of the highest order. The following passages are from *The Record of Rujing*.

Once, when sitting in his abbot's quarters, Zen master Tiantong Rujing said, "Gouge out Bodhidharma's eyeball and use it like a mud ball to hit people!"

Then he yelled, "Look! The ocean has dried up and the ocean floor is cracked! The billowing waves are striking the heavens!"

⸻ ◆ ⸻

Rujing addressed the monks, saying, "This morning is the first day of spring. The poetry of the pomegranate blossoms enters its samadhi. How can such words be expressed?"

Rujing lifted his whisk and said, "Witness a single red speck of the myriad karmic streams! The spring colors that move us need not be many."[237]

⸻ ◆ ⸻

Rujing entered the hall and said, "The willows are adorned with waistbands, and plum blossoms fall onto your sleeves. You catch a glimpse of the orioles. Dance like the great wind!"

Then Rujing said, "Whose realm is this? At the foot of the Jingzi Temple gate—the heads of tuber plants appear."

⸻ ◆ ⸻

Zen worthies from all directions assembled at Qingliang Temple [a temple in Nanjing City where Tiantong then resided as abbot].

Tiantong addressed them, saying, "The great way has no gate! It jumps off the heads of you Zen worthies who have assembled from every direction. Emptiness is without a path. It goes in and out of the nostrils of the host of Qingliang Temple. Attendees here today are the thieving descendants of the Tathagata—the calamitous offspring of Linji!

"Aiyee! Everyone is dancing crazily in the spring wind. The apricot blossoms have fallen and the red petals are scattered on the breeze!"

⬧

Zen master Tiantong Rujing entered the hall. Striking the ground with his staff he said, "This is the realm of vertical precipice."

Striking the floor again he said, "Deep, profound, remote, and distant. No one can reach it."

He struck again and said, "But supposing you could reach this place, what would it be like? Aieee! I smile and point to the place where apes call. There is yet another realm where the numinous traces may be found."

⬧

Tiantong addressed the monks, saying, "Thoughts in the mind are confused and scattered. How can they be controlled? In the story about Zhaozhou and whether or not a dog has buddha nature, there is an iron broom named 'Wu.' If you use it to sweep thoughts, they just become more numerous. Then you frantically sweep harder, trying to get rid of even more thoughts. Day and night you sweep with all your might, furiously working away. All of a sudden, the broom breaks into vast emptiness, and you instantly penetrate the myriad differences and thousand variations of the universe."

⬧

Tiantong addressed the monks, saying, "The clouds mindlessly drift past the mountain cliffs. Four years ago, or just yesterday, is today. In due course, water returns to its source. Four years hence, or just today, is yesterday."

Tiantong then raised his whisk and moved it in a great circle, saying, "If I must present this to you here, then I say that every year is a good year. Every day is a good day. So tell me, how can this be verified? Where clouds and water meet they laugh 'Ha, Ha!' Their laughter spontaneously fills the wind and sunlight."

Twenty-fourth Generation

YUELIN SHIGUAN

YUELIN SHIGUAN

YUELIN SHIGUAN (1143–1217) was a disciple of Dahong Zuzheng. He taught at Wanshou ("Long Life") Temple in Suzhou around the year 1200. Other details of his life are sketchy. He is remembered primarily as the teacher who transmitted the Dharma seal of Linji Zen to the famous priest Wumen Huikai.

Twenty-fifth Generation

WUMEN HUIKAI

WUMEN HUIKAI, "HUANGLONG," "FOYAN"

WUMEN HUIKAI (1183–1260) was a student of Yuelin Shiguan. Huikai came from Hangzhou, the site of West Lake and numerous famous Zen temples. Lamp records indicate that he started his Zen study with the master Yuelin Shiguan of the Yangqi branch in the Linji tradition, who gave him the kōan "Wu" as the focus of his study. Wumen worked with this famous kōan for six years without progress. Finally, he vowed not to sleep until he penetrated the heart of this Zen gate. Finally, as he stood in the Dharma hall, he heard the bell sound for the midday meal and suddenly realized profound enlightenment. He then wrote a verse that included the following:

> *A clear sky and shining sun,*
> *A great thunderclap,*
> *Instantly all beings' eyes are opened,*
> *And the myriad things come together.*

The following day, Wumen entered Yuelin's room to gain confirmation of his experience.
Yuelin said, "Where did you see these gods and devils?"
Wumen shouted.
Yuelin also shouted.
Wumen shouted again.
In this exchange Wumen's enlightenment was confirmed.

Wumen Huikai is particularly remembered for compiling and annotating the famous Zen collection of kōans called the *Gateless Gate*. This collection of forty-eight kōans, published in 1229, has been extensively used in kōan practice from the time of its appearance down to the present. Each kōan is offered with Wumen's commentary.

In 1246, Wumen was appointed by Emperor Li Zong to establish the Huguo Renwang ("Protecting the Country Benevolent Sovereign") Temple. Later, during a drought, the emperor called on Wumen to perform ceremonies to bring rain. Instead, Wumen sat in continuous silent meditation. When an envoy from the emperor asked Wumen what he was doing to bring rain, he replied, "Silently not influencing [anything]." Immediately after this exchange, the rains came and spread throughout the country. As a result, the emperor bestowed on Wumen the honorific name Foyan ("Buddha Eye").

In 1249, *The Record of Zen Master Wumen Huikai* was published in two volumes and widely circulated. The texts are also known as *The Record of Zen Master Foyan*. In the first book are ten Dharma lectures that Wumen gave when he resided at various temples after the year 1217. The second text contains commentaries by Wumen, and his accounts of the buddhas and ancestors.

APPENDIX

Faith in Mind
(attributed to the Third Ancestor, Jianzhi Sengcan)

Attaining the Way is not difficult,
Just avoid picking and choosing.
If you have neither aversion nor desire,
You'll thoroughly understand.
A hair's breadth difference
Is the gap between heaven and earth.
If you want it to come forth
Let there be no positive and negative.
For such comparisons
Are a sickness of the mind.
Without knowing the Great Mystery
Quiet practice is useless.
The great perfection is the same as vast space,
Lacking nothing, nothing extra.
Due to picking up and discarding
You will not know it.
Don't chase the conditioned
Nor abide in forbearing emptiness.
In singular equanimity
The self is extinguished.
Ceasing movement and returning to stillness,
This is complete movement.
But only suppress the two aspects
How can you realize unity?
Not penetrating the one,
The two lose their life.
Reject existence and you fall into it,

Pursue emptiness and you move away from it.
With many words and thoughts
You miss what is right before you.
Cutting off words and thought
Nothing remains unpenetrated.
Return to the root and attain the essence,
For if you chase the light you'll lose the Way.
But if you reflect the light for but a moment,
All previous shadows are dispelled.
All previous shadows are transformed
Because they were all due to delusive views.
It's no use to seek truth,
Just let false views cease.
Don't abide in duality
And take care not to seek,
For as soon as there is yes and no,
The mind is lost in confusion.
Two comes forth from one,
But don't hold even the one,
For when even the one mind is unborn,
The myriad things are flawless
Without flaws, without things.
With no birth, no mind,
Function is lost to conditions,
Conditions perish in function,
Conditions arise from function,
Function is actualized from conditions.
You should know that duality
Is originally one emptiness,
And one emptiness unifies duality,
Encompassing the myriad forms.
Not perceiving refined or vulgar
Is there any prejudice?
The Great Tao is vast,
With neither ease nor difficulty,
If you have biased views and doubts,

And move too fast or slow
Grasping the world without measure,
Then your mind has taken a wayward path,
Let it all naturally drop away
And embody no coming or going,
In accord with your fundamental nature unite with Tao
And wander the world without cares,
Being tied by thought runs counter to Truth,
But sinking into a daze is not good,
Don't belabor the spirit,
Why adhere to intimate or distant?
If you want to experience the one vehicle,
Don't malign the senses.
For when the senses are not maligned
That itself is perfect awakening,
The wise do not move,
But the ignorant bind themselves.
Though one Dharma differs not from another
The deluded self desires each,
Objectifying the mind to realize mind,
Is this not a great error?
Delusion gives rise to quietness or chaos,
But enlightenment has no positive and negative,
The duality of existence
Is born from false discrimination,
Flourishing dreams and empty illusions,
Why try to grab them?
Gain and loss, true and false,
Drop them all in one moment.
If the eyes don't sleep
All dreams disappear.
If the mind does not go astray
The myriad dharmas are but One,
And the One encompasses the Mystery.
In stillness, conditioned existence is forgotten,
And the myriad things are seen equally,

Naturally returning to each one's own nature.
When all dharmas are extinguished
It is immeasurable.
Cease movement and no movement exists,
When movement stops there is no cessation.
Since two are not manifest
How is there even one?
Finally, ultimately,
Principles do not exist,
Bring forth the mind of equanimity
And all activities will be put to rest,
All doubts extinguished.
True faith is upright,
And nothing then remains,
Nothing is remembered,
And the empty brightness shines naturally
Without effort of mind.
There, not a thought can be measured,
Reason and emotion can't conceive it.
In the Dharma realm of true thusness
There is neither other, nor self,
One should hasten to behold it.
Just say, "Not two,"
For in "not two" all things are united,
And there is nothing not included.
The wise ones of the ten directions
Have entered this great understanding,
An understanding which neither hastens nor tarries.
In ten thousand years, a single thought,
Not to be found within "existence and nonexistence,"
But meeting the eye in the ten directions.
The smallest is no different from the largest,
Eliminating boundaries,
The largest is the same as the smallest,
Not seeing divisions,
Existence is but emptiness,

Emptiness, existence.
That which is not of this principle
Must not be preserved.
The one is everything,
Everything, the one.
If your understanding is thus,
What is left to accomplish?
Faith and mind are undivided,
Nonduality is both faith and mind.
The way of words is cut off,
Leaving no past, no future, no present.

Source: *Chan Zong Bao Dian,* published by Hebei Chanxue Yanjiusuo, 1992.

SELECT BIBLIOGRAPHY

Works and authors from Taiwan are offered
with Wade-Giles romanization.

Texts in English

App, Urs. *Master Yunmen*. New York: Kodansha America Inc., 1994.

Chang, Chung-yuan. *Original Teachings of Chan Buddhism*. New York: Vintage Books, 1971.

Chen, Kenneth. *Buddhism in China: A Historical Survey*. Princeton: Princeton University Press, 1964.

Cleary, J.C. *Zen Dawn*. Boston and London: Shambhala, 1986.

Cleary, Thomas. *No Barrier: Unlocking the Zen Koan: A New Translation of the Zen Classic* Wumenguan. New York: Bantam Books, 1992.

de Bary, Theodore, Wing-tsit Chan, and Burton Watson. *Sources of Chinese Tradition*. New York and London: Columbia University Press, 1960.

Dumoulin, Heinrich. *Zen Buddhism: A History*. Vol. 1, *India and China*. New York: Macmillan, 1988.

Kuei-Fêng Tsung-mi. *Inquiry into the Origin of Humanity*. Translation with annotated commentary by Peter N Gregory. Kuroda Institute. Honolulu: University of Hawaii Press, 1995.

Miura, Isshu, and Ruth Fuller Sasaki. *Zen Dust*. Kyoto: The First Zen Institute of America in Japan, 1966.

Ogata, Sohaku. *The Transmission of the Lamp: Early Masters* (the first ten fascicles of the Jingde Era *Transmission of the Lamp* translated into English). Durango: Longwood Academic, 1990.

Powell, William F., trans. *The Record of Tung-shan*. Kuroda Institute. Honolulu: University of Hawaii Press, 1986.

Red Pine, trans. *The Zen Teaching of Bodhidharma*. San Francisco: North Point Press, 1989.

Suzuki, Daisetz Teitaro. *Studies in the Lankavatara Sutra*. Reprint. First Published by Routledge & Kegan Paul Ltd., London: 1930. Published by arrangement with the original publisher. Boulder: Prajna Press, Great Eastern Book Company, 1981.

Wansong. *Book of Serenity*. Translated by Thomas Cleary. Hudson, N.Y.: The Lindisfarne Press, 1990.

Watson, Burton, trans. *The Zen Teachings of Master Lin-chi*. Boston and London: Shambhala, 1993.

Wu, John C. H. *The Golden Age of Zen*. Taipei: United Publishing Center, 1975.

Yampolsky, Philip B. *The Platform Sutra of the Sixth Patriarch*. New York: Columbia University Press, 1967.

Yuanwu Keqin. *The Blue Cliff Record*. Translated by Thomas Cleary and J. C. Cleary. Boston: Shambhala, 1977.

Modern Texts in Chinese

Du Xuwen and Wei Daoru. *Zhongguo Chanzong Tongshi (A Complete History of Chinese Chan)*. Nanjing: Jiangsu Classics Publishing House, 1993.

Ge Zhaoguang. *Zhongguo Chan Sixiang Shi (History of Chinese Chan Thought)*. Beijing: Beijing University Publishing House, 1995.

Hong Pimu. *Xinbian Baihua Chanzong Miaoyu (Wondrous Words of Chan Newly Compiled in Vernacular Chinese)*. Beijing: China United Literature Publishing Company, 1995.

Hong Xiuping. *Zhongguo Chanxue Sixiang Shiwang (Collected History of Chinese Chan Thought)*. Beijing: Beijing University Publishing House, 1994.

Hsü Yun. *Tseng Ting Fo Tsu Tao Ying (Annotated Portraits of the Buddha Ancestors)*. 1946. Reprint, Taipei: Hsin Wen Fêng, 1975.

Jiang Yihua. *Hu Shi Xueshu Wenji (Collected Documents of the Scholarship of Hu Shi)*. Beijing: China Publishing House, 1997.

Jing Hui. *Chanzong Baodian (Treasured Classics of Chan)*. Zhaoxian: Hebei Research Institute for Chan Buddhism, 1992.

Kuan, Shih-ch'ien. *Chung-kuo Ch'an-tsung Shih (China's Chan History)*. Taipei: Great East Book Company, 1991.

Li Shan and Jiang Feng. *Chanzong Denglu Yijie (Interpretations of the Chan Lamp Records)*. Jinan: Shandong Peoples' Publishing House, 1994.

Ma Tianxiang. *Zhongguo Chanzong Sixiang Fazhan Shi (History of the Development of Chinese Chan Thought)*. Changsha: Hunan Educational Publishing House, 1997.

Puji. *Wudeng Huiyuan (Compendium of Five Lamps)*. Translated into modern Chinese by Jiang Zongfu, Li Haixia, and others. Zhongqing: Xinan Normal University Publishing House, 1997.

Wei Daoru. *Songdai Chanzong Wenhua (Song Dynasty Chan Culture)*. Dengzhou: Chongzhou Classics Publishing House, 1993.

Weichi Zhiping. *Baihua Qiannian Zhongguo Gaoseng Zhuan (A Thousand Years of Eminent Monks' Biographies in Modern Vernacular Chinese)*. Wuhan: Huazhong Science and Technology University Publishing House, 1994.

Wu Limin, Yu Sunming, et al. *Chanzong Zongpai Yuanliu (Origins of the Chan Schools)*. Beijing: China Social Science Publishing House, 1998.

Yang Cengwen. *Shenhui Heshang Chanhualu (Record of Chan Discourses by the Monk Shenhui)*. Beijing: China Publishing House, 1996.

Yang, Huinan. *Ch'an Shih Yu Ch'an Ssu (Chan History and Thought)*. Taipei: Great East Book Company, 1996.

Yin Hsün. *Chung-kuo Ch'an-tsung Shih, Ts'ung Yin-tu Ch'an dao Chung-hua Ch'an (Chinese Chan History, from Indian Chan to Chinese Chan)*. Taipei: Cheng Wen Publishing House, 1972.

Yin Hsün. *Fo-chiao Chih Ch'i-yuan Yu Kaizhan (Buddhism's Sources and Development)*. Taipei: Cheng Wen Publishing House, 1982.

Yuan Bing, ed. *Chanzong Yuyan He Wenxian (Chan Language and Documents)*. Nanchang: Jiangxi People's Publishing House, 1995.

———. *Chanyu Yizhu (Translated and Annotated Chan Discourses)*. Beijing: Language Publishing House, 1999.

Yuan Bing. *Zhongguo Chanzong Yulu Daguan (Survey of the Recorded Discourses of Chinese Chan)*. Nanchang: Baihuazhou Wenyi Publishing House, 1994.

Premodern Texts in Chinese

Bodhidharma. *Luebian Dacheng Rudao Sixing Guan (Four Practices for Entering the Way of the Mahayana)*. Recorded by his disciple Tan Lin. Reprinted in *Chanzong Baodian*, Zhaoxian: Hebei Chan Research Institute, 1993.

Ching Chu, comp. *Wudeng Huiyuan Xulue (Continued and Abridged Compendium of Five Lamps)*. Reprint, Taipei: Hsin Wen Fêng Publishing Company, 1978.

Chun Er and Ching, comp. *Tsu T'ang Chi (Ancestral Hall Collection)*. Reprint, Taipei: Hsin Wen Fêng Publishing Company, 1988.

Dao Xuan. *Xu Gao Seng Zhuan (Continued Biographies of Eminent Monks)*. Taisho, vol. 50, no. 2060.

Hui Hong, comp. *Chan Lin Seng Bao Zhuan (Treasured Biographies of Chan Monks)*. Reprint, Taipei: Hsin Wen Fêng, 1974.

Hui Jiao, *Gao Seng Zhuan (Biographies of Eminent Monks)*. Taisho, vol. 50, no. 2059.

Huineng. *Tan Jing (Platform Classic)*. Recorded by his disciple Fahai. Reprinted in *Chanzong Baodian*. Zhaoxian: Hebei Chan Research Institute, 1993.

Huiran, comp. *Zhenzhou Linji Huizhao Chanshi Yulu (Record of Zen Master Linji Huizhao of Zhenzhou)*. Taisho, vol. 47, no. 1985.

Nian Chang, comp. *Fo-tsu Li-tai T'ung-tsai (Extensive Historic Record of the Buddha Ancestors)*. Reprint, Taipei: Hsin Wen Fêng Publishing Company, 1974.

Sengcan. "Xin Xin Ming" (Inscription on *Faith in Mind*). Reprinted in *Chanzong Baodian*. Zhaoxian: Hebei Chan Research Institute, 1993.

Shaolong and others, comp. *Yuanwu Foguo Chanshi Yulu Xu (The Collection of Records of Zen Master Yuanwu Foguo)*. Taisho, vol. 47, no. 1997.

Suwen, comp. *Rujing Heshang Yulu (The Record of the Monk Rujing)*. Taisho, vol. 48, no. 2002.

Ta-ch'uan Ling-yin P'u Chi, comp. *Wu-Teng Hui-yuan (Compendium of Five Lamps)*. Reprint, Taipei: Hsin Wen Fêng Publishing Company, 1990.

Tao Yuan, comp. *Jingde Chuandeng Lu (Record of the Transmission of the Lamp of the Jingde Era)*. Reprint, Taipei: Hsin Wen Fêng Publishing Company, 1994.

Wansong. *Congrong An Lu (Book of Serenity)*. Taisho, vol. 48, no. 2004.

Wumen Huikai. *Wumen Guan (Gateless Gate)*. Taisho, vol. 48, no. 2005.

Yuan-chi Chu-ting. *Hsü Ch'uan Teng Lu (Continuation of the Transmission of the Lamp)*. *Wan Hsü Tsang Ching* vol. 142. Taipei: Hsin Wen Fêng Publishing Company, 1995.

Yuanwu Keqin. *Biyan Lu (Blue Cliff Record)*. Taisho, vol. 48, no. 2003.

Yufeng and others, comp. *Jingling Qingliang Yuan Wenyi Chanshi Yulu (The Record of Zen Master Wenyi of Qingliang Monastery in Jinling)*. Taisho, vol. 47, no. 1991.

Zhi Zhao. *Rentian Yanmu (The Celestial Eye of Humanity)*. Taisho, vol. 48, no. 2006.

Records of Individual Teachers

Fayan Wenyi. *Taisho*, vol. 47, no. 1991, p. 588.

Fenyang Wude. *Taisho*, vol. 47, no. 1992, p. 594.

Hongzhi Zhengjue. *Taisho*, vol. 48, no. 2001, p. 1.

Huanglong Huinan. *Taisho*, vol. 47, no. 1993, p. 629.

Linji Huizhao of Zhenzhou. *Taisho*, vol. 47, no. 1985, p. 495.

Tiantong Rujing. *Taisho*, vol. 48, no. 2002, p. 121.

Wuzu Fayan. *Taisho*, vol. 47, no. 1995, p. 649.

Xuansha Shibei. *Wanxu Zangjing*, vol. 126, p. 407.

Xuedou Chongxian (Mingjue). *Taisho*, vol. 47, no. 1996, p. 669.

Yangqi Fanghui. *Taisho*, vol. 47, no. 1994, p. 640.

Yuanwu Foguo. *Taisho*, vol. 47, no. 1997, p. 713.

Yunmen Wenyan. *Taisho*, vol. 47, no. 1988, p. 544.

Chinese Electronic Texts

The texts listed below are the primary electronic source materials used for this volume. They may be found at the web site shown below for the International Research Institute for Zen Buddhism at Hanazono University, Kyoto:

http://www.iijnet.or.jp/iriz/irizhtml/zentexts.cdtexts.htm

Dachuan Lingyin Puji. *Wudeng Huiyuan*. Urs App, ed. Zhonghua Shuju. Kyoto: IRIZB Website, 1995.

Huihong Juefan. *Chan Lin Seng Bao Zhuan*. Urs App, ed. Dainippon Zokuzokyo, vol. 137, pp. 439–568. Kyoto: IRIZB Website, 1995.

Qing Shizong. *Yuxuan yulu*. Urs App, ed. Dainippon Zokuzokyo, vol. 119, pp. 357–809. Kyoto: IRIZB Website, 1995.

Sengding Shouze. *Guzunsu Yulu*. Urs App, ed. Dainippon Zokuzokyo, vol. 118. Kyoto: IRIZB Website, 1995.

Wumen Huikai. *Chanzong Wumenguan*. Urs App, ed. Dainippon Zokuzokyo, vol. 119, pp. 319–35. Kyoto: IRIZB Website, 1995.

ROMANIZATION TABLES

The following tables list names of the Zen ancestors in alphabetical order in each of three common romanization systems. Names are presented in pinyin, Wade-Giles, and Japanese romaji with the location of each ancestor on the accompanying Lineage Chart of the Zen Ancestors.

Pinyin–Wade-Giles–Romaji

PINYIN (Chinese)	WADE-GILES (Chinese)	ROMAJI (Japanese)	LOCATION
Baiyun Shouduan	Pai-yün Shou-tuan	Hakuun Shutan	C19
Baizhang Huaihai	Pai-chang Huai-hai	Hyakujō Ekai	A9
Baizhang Niepan	Pai-chang Nieh-p'an	Hyakujō Nehan	D10
Bajiao Huiqing	Pa-chiao Hui-ch'ing	Bashō Esei	E13
Baling Haojian	Pa-ling Hao-chien	Haryō Kōkan	I14
Baoci Xingyan	Pao-ts'u Hsing-yen	Hōji Gyōgon	M16
Bao'en Xuanze	Pao-ên Hsüan-tsê	Hōon Gensoku	K16
Baofeng Weizhao	Pao-fêng Wei-chao	Hōhō Ishō	G19
Baofu Congzhan	Pao-fu Ts'ung-chan	Hofuku Jūten	N13
Baoning Renyong	Pao-ning Jên-yung	Honei Ninyū	D19
Baoshou Yanzhao	Pao-shou Yen-chao	Hōju Enshō	B12
Caoshan Benji	Ts'ao-shan Pen-chi	Sōzan Honjaku	J12
Caoxi (see Dajian Huineng)			
Changqing Da'an (see Guishan Da'an)			
Changqing Huileng	Ch'ang-ch'ing Hui-lêng	Chōkei Eryō	O13
Changsha Jingcen	Ch'ang-sha Ching-ts'ên	Chōsha Keishin	J10
Changshui Zixuan	Ch'ang-shui Tzu-hsuan	Chōsui Shisen	E18
Chanti Weizhao (see Baofeng Weizhao)			
Chengtian Chuanzong	Ch'eng-t'ien Ch'uan-tsung	Jōten Denshū	I17
Chongshou Qichou	Ch'ung-shou Ch'i-ch'ou	Sūju Keichū	N16
Chuanzi Decheng	Ch'uan-tzü Tê-ch'êng	Sensu Tokujō	M10
Cizhou Faru	Ts'ü-chou Fa-ju	Jishū Hōnyo	O8
Cuiwei Wuxue	Ts'ui-wei Wu-hsüeh	Suibi Mugaku	O10
Cuiyan Kezhen	Ts'ui-yen K'o-chên	Suigan Kashin	D18
Cuiyan Lingcan	Ts'ui-yen Ling-ts'an	Suigan Reisan	J13

Cuiyan Shouzhi (*see* Dayu Shouzhi)

Daguang Juhui	Ta-kuang Chü-hui	Daikō Kokai	O12
Dagui Muche	Ta-kuei Mu-chê	Daii Botetsu	E19
Dahong Zuzheng	Ta-hung Tsu-Chêng	Daikō Soshō	D23
Dahui Zonggao	Ta-hui Tsung-kao	Daie Sōkō	A22
Dajian Huineng	Ta-chien Hui-nêng	Daikan Enō	I16
Dalong	Ta-lung	Dairyō	

    (not shown; 8th generation under Qingyuan through Deshan Xuanjian)

Daman Hongren	Ta-man Hung-jên	Daiman Kōnin	I5
Damei Fachang	Ta-mei Fa-ch'ang	Daibai Hōjō	E9
Danxia Tianran	Tan-hsia T'ien-jan	Tanka Tenen	O9
Danxia Zichun	Tan-hsia Tzu-ch'un	Tanka Shijun	F19
Danyuan Yingzhen	Tan-yüan Ying-chên	Tangen Ōshin	M8
Daowu Yuanzhi	Tao-wu Yüan-chih	Dōgo Enchi	N10

Daoxin (*see* Dayi Daoxin)

Dasui Fazhen	Ta-sui Fa-chên	Daizui Hōshin	C11

Datong (*see* Yuquan Shenxiu)

Dayang Jingxuan	Ta-yang Ching-hsüan	Taiyō Kyōgen	F16

Dayang Yan (*see* Dayang Jingxuan)

Dayi Daoxin	Ta-i Tao-hsin	Daii Dōshin	I4

Dayu (*see* Gaoan Dayu)

Dayu Shouzhi	Ta-yü Shou-chih	Daigu Shushi	B17
Dazu Huike	Ta-tsu Hui-k'o	Taiso Eka	I2
Deshan Xuanjian	Tê-shan Hsüan-chien	Tokusan Senkan	P11
Deshan Yuanmi	Tê-shan Yüan-mi	Tokusan Emmitsu	J14
Dingzhou Shizang	Ting-chou Shih-tsang	Jōshū Sekisō	P8

Dizang (*see* Luohan Guichen)

Dongshan Liangjie	Tung-shan Liang-chieh	Tōzan Ryōkai	L11
Dongshan Shouchu	Tung-shan Shou-ch'u	Tōsan Shusho	K14
Doushuai Congyue	Tou-shuai Ts'ung-yüeh	Tosotsu Jūetsu	B20

Farong (*see* Niutou Farong)

Fayan Wenyi	Fa-yen Wên-i	Hōgen Bun'eki	L15
Fengxian Daochen	Fêng-hsien Tao-ch'ên	Hōsen Dōshin	H14
Fengxue Yanzhao	Fêng-hsüeh Yen-chao	Fūketsu Enshō	A14
Fenyang Shanzhao	Fên-yang Shan-chao	Fun'yō Zenshō	A16

Foguo (*see* Yuanwu Keqin)

Fojian (*see* Taiping Huiqin)

Fori (*see* Dahui Zonggao)

Foyan Qingyuan	Fo-yen Ch'ing-yüan	Butsugen Seion	C21
Furong Daokai	Fu-jung Tao-k'ai	Fuyō Dōkai	F18
Fushan Fayuan	Fu-shan Fa-yüan	Fuzan Hōen	E17
Gaoan Dayu	Kao-an Ta-yü	Kōan Daigu	H10
Guannan Daochang	Kuan-nan Tao-ch'ang	Kannan Dōjō	F10

Guifeng Zongmi	Kuei-fêng Tsung-mi	Keihō Shūmitsu	
(not shown; student of Suizhou Daoyuan Q11)			
Guishan Da'an	Kuei-shan Ta-an	Isan Daian	C10
Guishan Lingyou	Kuei-shan Ling-yu	Isan Reiyū	E10
Guizong Cezhen	Kuei-tsung Ts'ê-Chên	Kisō Sakushin	L16
Guizong Zhichang	Kuei-tsung Chih-ch'ang	Kisu Chijō	F9
Hai Brother Hai (see Baizhang Huaihai)			
Hangzhou Tianlong	Hang-chou T'ien-lung	Kōshū Tenryū	G10
Hermit of Tongfeng (see Tongfeng Anzhu)			
Heze Shenhui	Ho-tsê Shên-hui	Kataku Jinne	O7
Hongren (see Daman Hongren)			
Hongzhi Zhengjue	Hung-chih Chêng-chüeh	Wanshi Shōgaku	F20
Huangbo Xiyun	Huang-po Hsi-yün	Ōbaku Kiun	A10
Huanglong Huinan	Huang-lung Hui-nan	Ōryū Enan	A18
Huanglong Zuxin (see Huitang Zuxin)			
Huangmei (see Daman Hongren)			
Huguo Jingyuan	Hu-kuo Ching-yüan	Gokoku Keigen	B22
Huguo Shoucheng	Hu-kuo Shou-chêng	Gokoku Shuchō	G13
Huichao (see Guizong Cezhen)			
Huike (see Dazu Huike)			
Huineng (see Dajian Huineng)			
Huitang Zuxin	Hui-t'ang Tsu-hsin	Kaidō Soshin	B19
Huizhao (see Linji Yixuan)			
Iron Grinder Liu (see Liu Tiemo)			
Jianfeng (see Yuezhou Qianfeng)			
Jianzhi Sengcan	Chien-Chih Sêng-ts'an	Kanchi Sōsan	I3
Jiashan Shanhui	Chia-shan Shan-hui	Kassan Zenne	M11
Jingqing Daofu	Ching-ch'ing Tao-fu	Kyōsei Dōfu	K13
Jingzhao Mihu	Ching-chao Mi-hu	Keichō Beiyu	E11
Jingzhong Shenhui	Ching-Chung Shên-hui	Jōshu Jinne	Q9
Jingzhong Wuxiang	Ching-Chung Wu-Hsiang	Jōshu Musō	Q8
Jinhua Juzhi	Chin-hua Chü-chih	Gutei Chikan	I11
Jinshan (see Qingxi Hongjin)			
Jiufeng Daoqian	Chiu-fêng Tao-ch'ien	Kyūhō Dōken	N12
Jiufeng Qin	Chiu-fêng Ch'in	Kyūhō Gon	G16
Juefan Huihong	Chüeh-fan Hui-hung	Kakuhan Ekō	A20
Juzhi "One Finger Zen" (see Jinhua Juzhi)			
Kaifu Daoning	K'ai-fu Tao-ning	Kaifuku Dōnei	D21
Langye Huijue	Lang-yeh Hui-chüeh	Rōya Ekaku	D17
Lazy An (see Guishan Da'an)			
Liangshan Yuanguan	Liang-shan Yüan-kuan	Ryōzan Enkan	F15
Lianhua Fengxiang	Lien-hua Fêng-hsiang	Renge Hōshō	H15
Lingyun Zhiqin	Ling-yün Chih-ch'in	Reiun Shigon	D11
Linji Yixuan	Lin-chi I-hsüan	Rinzai Gigen	A11

Liu Tiemo	Liu T'ieh-mo	Ryū Tetsuma	H11
Longji Shaoxiu	Lung-chi Shao-hsiu	Ryūsai Shōshū	Q15
Longtan Chongxin	Lung-t'an Ch'ung-hsin	Ryūtan Sōshin	P10
Longya Judun	Lung-ya Chü-tun	Ryūge Kodon	H12
Lotus Flower Peak (the Hermit of, *see* Lianhua Fengxiang)			
Luohan Guichen	Lo-han Kuei-ch'ên	Rakan Keichin	M14
Luopu Yuanan	Lo-p'u Yüan-an	Rakuho Gen'an	M12
Luoshan Daoxian	Lo-shan Tao-hsien	Razan Dōkan	P13
Luzu Baoyun	Lu-tsu Pao-yün	Roso Hōun	J9
Magu Baoche (*see* Mayu Baoche)			
Mayu Baoche	Ma-yu Pao-ch'ê	Mayoku Hōtetsu	H9
Mazu Daoyi	Ma-tsu Tao-i	Baso Dōitsu	A8
Mihu (*see* Jingzhao Mihu)			
Mingan Rongxi	Ming-an Jung-hsi	Myōan Eisai	C23
Mingzhao Deqian	Ming-chao Tê-ch'ien	Myōshō Tokken	P14
Moshan Liaoran	Mo-shan Liao-jan	Massan Ryōnen	J11
Muzhou Daoming	Mu-chou Tao-ming	Bokushū Dōmyō	B11
Nanpu Shaoming	Nan-p'u Shao-ming	Nampo Jōmyō	A23
Nanquan Puyuan	Nan-ch'üan P'u-yüan	Nansen Fugan	M9
Nanta Guangyong	Nan-t'a Kuang-yung	Nantō Kōyū	E12
Nanyang Huizhong	Nan-yang Hui-chung	Nan'yō Echū	M7
Nanyuan Huiyong	Nan-yüan Hui-yung	Nan'in Egyō	A13
Nanyue Huairang	Nan-yüeh Huai-jang	Nangaku Ejō	A7
National Teacher Zhong (*see* Nanyang Huizhong)			
Nirvana Master (*see* Baizhang Niepan)			
Niutou Farong	Niu-t'ou Fa-jung	Gozu Hōyū	Q5
Overnight Guest (*see* Yongjia Xuanjue)			
Pangyun (Layman Pang)	P'ang Yün	Hōun	G9
Panshan Baoji	P'an-shan Pao-chi	Banzan Hōshaku	I9
Puji (*see* Songshan Puji)			
Puti Damo	P'u-t'i Ta-mo	Bodai Daruma	I1
Qianfeng (*see* Yuezhou Qianfeng)			
Qinglin Shiqian	Ch'ing-lin Shih-ch'ien	Seirin Shiken	K12
Qingxi Hongjin	Ch'ing-hsi Hung-chin	Seikei Kōshin	P15
Qingyuan Xingsi	Ch'ing-yüan Hsing-ssu	Seigen Gyōshi	L7
Qinshan Wensui	Ch'in-shan Wên-sui	Kinzan Bunsui	G12
Ruiyan Shiyan	Jui-yen Shih-yen	Zuigan Shigen	Q13
Sansheng Huiran	San-shêng Hui-jan	Sanshō Enen	C12
Sengcan (*see* Jianzhi Sengcan)			
Shengshou Nanyin	Shêng-shou Nan-yin	Seijū Nan'in	Q10
Shenshan Sengmi (*see* Mi Shibo)			
Shenxiu (*see* Yuquan Shenxiu)			
Shexian Guixing	Shê-hsien Kuei-hsing	Sekken Kisei	E16
Shishuang Chuyuan	Shih-shuang Ch'u-yüan	Sekisō Soen	A17

Shishuang Qingzhu	Shih-shuang Ch'ing-chu	Sekisō Keisho	N11
Shitou Xiqian	Shih-t'ou Hsi-ch'ien	Sekitō Kisen	L8
Shoushan Xingnian	Shou-shan Hsing-nien	Shuzan Shōnen	A15
Shushan Kuangren	Shu-shan K'uang-jên	Sozan Kyōnin	L12
Sixin Wuxin	Ssü-hsin Wu-hsin	Shishin Goshin	C20
Songshan Puji	Sung-shan P'u-chi	Sūzan Fujaku	P7
Suizhou Daoyuan	Sui-chou Tao-yüan	Suishū Dōen	Q11
Taigu Puyu	T'ai-ku P'u-yü	(Korean) Taigo Pou	B23
Taiping Huiqin	T'ai-p'ing Hui-ch'in	Taihei Egon	B21
Taiyuan Fu	T'ai-yüan Fu	Taigen Fu	L13
Tianhuang Daowu	T'ien-huang Tao-wu	Tennō Dōgo	P9
Tianping Congyi	T'ien-p'ing Ts'ung-i	Tempyō Jūi	P16
Tiantai Deshao	T'ien-t'ai Tê-shao	Tendai Tokushō	O16
Tiantong (see Hongzhi Zhengjue)			
Tiantong Rujing	T'ien-t'ung Ju-ching	Tendō Nyojō	E23
Tiantong Zongjue	T'ien-t'ung Tsung-chüeh	Tendō Sōkaku	E21
Tianyi Yihuai	T'ien-i I-huai	Tenne Gikai	H17
Tongan Daopi	T'ung-an Tao-p'i	Dōan Dōhi	F13
Tongan Guanzhi	T'ung-an Kuan-chih	Dōan Kanshi	F14
Touzi Datong	T'ou-tzü Ta-t'ung	Tōsu Daidō	O11
Touzi Yiqing	T'ou-tzü I-ch'ing	Tōsu Gisei	F17
Wang Yanbin	Wang Yen-pin	Ō Enhin	O14
Wenshu Yingzhen	Wên-shu Ying-chên	Monju Ōshin	J15
Wuben (see Dongshan Liangjie)			
Wufeng Changguan	Wu-fêng Ch'ang-kuan	Gohō Jōkan	B10
Wujiu Youxuan	Wu-chiu Yu-hsüan	Ukyū Yūgen	L9
Wumen Huikai	Wu-mên Hui-k'ai	Mumon Ekai (see note)	D25
Wuzu Fayan	Wu-tsu Fa-yen	Goso Hōen	D20
Xianglin Chengyuan	Hsiang-lin Ch'êng-yüan	Kyōrin Chōon	G14
Xiangyan Zhixian	Hsiang-yen Chih-hsien	Kyōgen Chikan	G11
Xinghua Cunjiang	Hsing-hua Ts'un-chiang	Koke Sonshō	A12
Xingyang Qingpou	Hsing-yang Ch'ing-p'ou	Kōyō Seibō	G17
Xingyang Qingrang	Hsing-yang Ch'ing-jang	Kōyō Seijō	E14
Xita Guangmu	Hsi-t'a Kuang-mu	Saitō Kōboku	D12
Xitang Zhizang	Hsi-t'ang Chih-tsang	Seidō Chizō	B9
Xiushan (see Longji Shaoxiu)			
Xiyuan Siming	Hsi-yüan Ssü-ming	Saiin Shimyō	B13
Xuansha Shibei	Hsüan-sha Shih-pei	Gensha Shibi	M13
Xuedou Chongxian	Hsüeh-tou Ch'ung-hsien	Setchō Jūken	H16
Xuedou Zhijian	Hsüeh-tou Chih-chien	Setchō Chikan	E22
Xuefeng Yicun	Hsüeh-fêng I-ts'un	Seppō Gison	P12
Yang Wuwei	Yang Wu-wei	Yō Mui	I18
Yangqi Fanghui	Yang-ch'i Fang-hui	Yōgi Hōe	C18
Yangshan Huiji	Yang-shan Hui-chi	Kyōzan Ejaku	F11

Yanguan Qi'an	Yen-kuan Ch'i-an	Enkan Seian	D9
Yantou Quanhuo	Yen-t'ou Ch'üan-huo	Gantō Zenkatsu	Q12
Yanyang Shanxin	Yen-yang Shan-hsin	Genyō Zenshin	K11
Yaoshan Weiyan	Yao-shan Wei-yen	Yakusan Igen	N9
Yongjia Xuanjue	Yung-chia Hsüan-chüeh	Yōka Genkaku	N7
Yongming Yanshou	Yung-ming Yen-shou	Yōmei Enju	O17
Yongping Daoyuan	Yung-p'ing Tao-yüan	Eihei Dōgen	E24
Yuanguan (*see* Liangshan Yuanguan)			
Yuanming (*see* Deshan Yuanmi)			
Yuantong Fashen	Yüan-t'ung Fa-shên	Entsū Hōshū	H18
Yuanwu Keqin	Yüan-wu K'ê-ch'in	Engo Kokugon	A21
Yue'an Shanguo	Yüeh-an Shan-kuo	Gettan Zenka	D22
Yuelin Shiguan	Yüeh-lin Shih-kuan	Gatsurin Shikan	D24
Yuezhou Qianfeng	Yüeh-chou Ch'ien-fêng	Esshū Kempō	I12
Yunan Kewen	Yün-an K'o-wên	Un'an Kokubun	A19
Yunju Daoying	Yün-chü Tao-ying	Ungo Dōyō	F12
Yunmen Wenyan	Yün-men Wên-yen	Ummon Bun'en	I13
Yunyan Tansheng	Yün-yen T'an-shêng	Ungan Donjō	L10
Yuquan Shenxiu	Yü-Ch'uan Shên-hsiu	Gyokusen Jinshū	P6
Zhangjing Huaiyun	Chang-ching Huai-yün	Shōkei Eki	C9
Zhaozhou Congshen	Chao-chou Ts'ung-shên	Jōshū Jūshin	K10
Zhenxie Qingliao	Chên-hsieh Ch'ing-liao	Shinketsu Seiryō	E20
Zhimen Guangzuo	Chih-mên Kuang-tso	Chimon Kōso	G15
Zhishen (*see* Zizhou Zhishen)			
Zhongyi Hongen	Chung-i Hung-ên	Chūyū Kōon	K9
Zhu'an Shigui	Chu-an Shih-kuei	Chikuan Shikei	C22
Zifu Rubao	Tsü-fu Ju-pao	Shifuku Nyohō	D13
Zizhou Chuji	Tsü-chou Ch'u-chi	Shishū Shojaku	Q7
Zizhou Zhishen	Tsü-chou Chih-shên	Shishū Chisen	Q6
Zu'an (*see* Xuedou Zhijian)			

Wade-Giles–Pinyin–Romaji

WADE-GILES (Chinese)	PINYIN (Chinese)	ROMAJI (Japanese)	LOCATION
Chang-ching Huai-yün	Zhangjing Huaiyun	Shōkei Eki	C9
Ch'ang-ch'ing Hui-lêng	Changqing Huileng	Chōkei Eryō	O13
Ch'ang-sha Ching-ts'ên	Changsha Jingcen	Chōsha Keishin	J10
Ch'ang-shui Tzu-hsuan	Changshui Zixuan	Chōsui Shisen	E18
Chao-chou Ts'ung-shên	Zhaozhou Congshen	Jōshū Jūshin	K10
Ch'eng-t'ien Ch'uan-tsung	Chengtian Chuanzong	Jōten Denshū	I17
Chên-hsieh Ch'ing-liao	Zhenxie Qingliao	Shinketsu Seiryō	E20
Chia-shan Shan-hui	Jiashan Shanhui	Kassan Zenne	M11
Chien-Chih Sêng-ts'an	Jianzhi Sengcan	Kanchi Sōsan	I3
Ch'ien-fêng (*see* Yüeh-chou Ch'ien-fêng)			
Chih-mên Kuang-tso	Zhimen Guangzuo	Chimon Kōso	G15
Chih-shên (*see* Tsü-chou Chih-shên)			
Ching-chao Mi-hu	Jingzhao Mihu	Keichō Beiyu	E11
Ching-ch'ing Tao-fu	Jingqing Daofu	Kyōsei Dōfu	K13
Ching-Chung Shên-hui	Jingzhong Shenhui	Jōshu Jinne	Q9
Ching-Chung Wu-Hsiang	Jingzhong Wuxiang	Jōshu Musō	Q8
Ch'ing-hsi Hung-chin	Qingxi Hongjin	Seikei Kōshin	P15
Ch'ing-lin Shih-ch'ien	Qinglin Shiqian	Seirin Shiken	K12
Ch'ing-yüan Hsing-ssu	Qingyuan Xingsi	Seigen Gyōshi	L7
Chin-hua Chü-chih	Jinhua Juzhi	Gutei Chikan	I11
Chin-shan (*see* Ch'ing-hsi Hung-chin)			
Ch'in-shan Wên-sui	Qinshan Wensui	Kinzan Bunsui	G12
Chiu-fêng Ch'in	Jiufeng Qin	Kyūhō Gon	G16
Chiu-fêng Tao-ch'ien	Jiufeng Daoqian	Kyūhō Dōken	N12
Chu-an Shih-kuei	Zhu'an Shigui	Chikuan Shikei	C22
Ch'uan-tzü Tê-ch'êng	Chuanzi Decheng	Sensu Tokujō	M10
Chü-chih "One Finger Zen" (*see* Chin-hua Chü-chih)			
Chüeh-fan Hui-hung	Juefan Huihong	Kakuhan Ekō	A20
Chung-i Hung-ên	Zhongyi Hongen	Chūyū Kōon	K9
Ch'ung-shou Ch'i-ch'ou	Chongshou Qichou	Sūju Keichū	N16
Fa-jung (*see* Niu-t'ou Fa-jung)			
Fa-yen Wên-i	Fayan Wenyi	Hōgen Bun'eki	L15
Fêng-hsien Tao-ch'ên	Fengxian Daochen	Hōsen Dōshin	H14
Fêng-hsüeh Yen-chao	Fengxue Yanzhao	Fūketsu Enshō	A14
Fên-yang Shan-chao	Fenyang Shanzhao	Fun'yō Zenshō	A16
Fo-chien (*see* T'ai-p'ing Hui-ch'in)			
Fo-jih (*see* Ta-hui Tsung-kao)			
Fo-kuo (*see* Yüan-wu K'ê-ch'in)			
Fo-yen Ch'ing-yüan	Foyan Qingyuan	Butsugen Seion	C21

Fu-jung Tao-k'ai	Furong Daokai	Fuyō Dōkai	F18
Fu-shan Fa-yüan	Fushan Fayuan	Fuzan Hōen	E17
Hai, Brother Hai (*see* Pai-chang Huai-hai)			
Hang-chou T'ien-lung	Hangzhou Tianlong	Kōshū Tenryū	G10
Hermit of T'ung-fêng (*see* T'ung-fêng An-chu)			
Ho-shan Wu-yin (not shown; student of Chiu-fêng Tao-ch'ien)			
Ho-tsê Shên-hui	Heze Shenhui	Kataku Jinne	O7
Hsiang-lin Ch'êng-yüan	Xianglin Chengyuan	Kyōrin Chōon	G14
Hsiang-yen Chih-hsien	Xiangyan Zhixian	Kyōgen Chikan	G11
Hsing-hua Ts'un-chiang	Xinghua Cunjiang	Koke Sonshō	A12
Hsing-yang Ch'ing-jang	Xingyang Qingrang	Kōyō Seijō	E14
Hsing-yang Ch'ing-p'ou	Xingyang Qingpou	Kōyō Seibō	G17
Hsi-t'a Kuang-mu	Xita Guangmu	Saitō Kōboku	D12
Hsi-t'ang Chih-tsang	Xitang Zhizang	Seidō Chizō	B9
Hsiu-shan (*see* Lung-chi Shao-hsiu)			
Hsi-yüan Ssü-ming	Xiyuan Siming	Saiin Shimyō	B13
Hsüan-sha Shih-pei	Xuansha Shibei	Gensha Shibi	M13
Hsüeh-fêng I-ts'un	Xuefeng Yicun	Seppō Gison	P12
Hsüeh-tou Chih-chien	Xuedou Zhijian	Setchō Chikan	E22
Hsüeh-tou Ch'ung-hsien	Xuedou Chongxian	Setchō Jūken	H16
Huang-lung Hui-nan	Huanglong Huinan	Ōryū Enan	A18
Huang-lung Tsu-hsin (*see* Hui-t'ang Tsu-hsin)			
Huang-mei (*see* Ta-man Hung-jên)			
Huang-po Hsi-yün	Huangbo Xiyun	Ōbaku Kiun	A10
Hui-ch'ao (*see* Kuei-tsung Ts'ê-Chên)			
Hui-k'o (*see* Ta-tsu Hui-k'o)			
Hui-nêng (*see* Ta-chien Hui-nêng)			
Hui-t'ang Tsu-hsin	Huitang Zuxin	Kaidō Soshin	B19
Huizhao (*see* Lin-chi I-hsüan)			
Hu-kuo Ching-yüan	Huguo Jingyuan	Gokoku Keigen	B22
Hu-kuo Shou-chêng	Huguo Shoucheng	Gokoku Shuchō	G13
Hung-chih Chêng-chüeh	Hongzhi Zhengjue	Wanshi Shōgaku	F20
Hung-jen (*see* Ta-man Hung-jên)			
Iron Grinder Liu (*see* Liu T'ie-mo)			
Jui-yen Shih-yen	Ruiyan Shiyan	Zuigan Shigen	Q13
K'ai-fu Tao-ning	Kaifu Daoning	Kaifuku Dōnei	D21
Kao-an Ta-yü	Gaoan Dayu	Kōan Daigu	H10
Kuan-nan Tao-ch'ang	Guannan Daochang	Kannan Dōjō	F10
Kuei-fêng Tsung-mi	Guifeng Zongmi	Keihō Shūmitsu	
(not shown; student of Suizhou Daoyuan Q11)			
Kuei-shan Ling-yu	Guishan Lingyou	Isan Reiyū	E10
Kuei-shan Ta-an	Guishan Da'an	Isan Daian	C10
Kuei-tsung Chih-ch'ang	Guizong Zhichang	Kisu Chijō	F9
Kuei-tsung Ts'ê-Chên	Guizong Cezhen	Kisō Sakushin	L16

Lang-yeh Hui-chüeh	Langye Huijue	Rōya Ekaku	D17
Lazy An (see Kuei-shan Ta-an)			
Liang-shan Yüan-kuan	Liangshan Yuanguan	Ryōzan Enkan	F15
Lien-hua Fêng-hsiang	Lianhua Fengxiang	Renge Hōshō	H15
Lin-chi I-hsüan	Linji Yixuan	Rinzai Gigen	A11
Ling-yün Chih-ch'in	Lingyun Zhiqin	Reiun Shigon	D11
Liu T'ieh-mo	Liu Tiemo	Ryū Tetsuma	H11
Lo-han Kuei-ch'ên	Luohan Guichen	Rakan Keichin	M14
Lo-shan Tao-hsien	Luoshan Daoxian	Razan Dōkan	P13
Lotus Flower Peak (the Hermit of, see Lian-hua Fêng-hsiang)			
Lung-chi Shao-hsiu	Longji Shaoxiu	Ryūsai Shōshū	Q15
Lung-t'an Ch'ung-hsin	Longtan Chongxin	Ryūtan Sōshin	P10
Lung-ya Chü-tun	Longya Judun	Ryūge Kodon	H12
Lo-p'u Yüan-an	Luopu Yuanan	Rakuho Gen'an	M12
Lu-tsu Pao-yün	Luzu Baoyun	Roso Hōun	J9
Ma-ku Pao-ch'ê (see Ma-yu Pao-ch'ê)			
Ma-tsu Tao-i	Mazu Daoyi	Baso Dōitsu	A8
Ma-yu Pao-ch'ê	Mayu Baoche	Mayoku Hōtetsu	H9
Mi-hu (see Ching-chao Mi-hu)			
Ming-an Jung-hsi	Mingan Rongxi	Myōan Eisai	C23
Ming-chao Tê-ch'ien	Mingzhao Deqian	Myōshō Tokken	P14
Mo-shan Liao-jan	Moshan Liaoran	Massan Ryōnen	J11
Mu-chou Tao-ming	Muzhou Daoming	Bokushū Dōmyō	B11
Nan-ch'üan P'u-yüan	Nanquan Puyuan	Nansen Fugan	M9
Nan-p'u Shao-ming	Nanpu Shaoming	Nampo Jōmyō	A23
Nan-t'a Kuang-yung	Nanta Guangyong	Nantō Kōyū	E12
Nan-yang Hui-chung	Nanyang Huizhong	Nan'yō Echū	M7
Nan-yüan Hui-yung	Nanyuan Huiyong	Nan'in Egyō	A13
Nan-yüeh Huai-jang	Nanyue Huairang	Nangaku Ejō	A7
National Teacher Chung (see Nan-yang Hui-chung)			
Nirvana Master (see Pai-chang Nieh-p'an)			
Niu-t'ou Fa-jung	Niutou Farong	Gozu Hōyū	Q5
Pa-chiao Hui-ch'ing	Bajiao Huiqing	Bashō Esei	E13
Pai-chang Huai-hai	Baizhang Huaihai	Hyakujō Ekai	A9
Pai-chang Nieh-p'an	Baizhang Niepan	Hyakujō Nehan	D10
Pai-yün Shou-tuan	Baiyun Shouduan	Hakuun Shutan	C19
Pa-ling Hao-chien	Baling Haojian	Haryō Kōkan	I14
P'ang Yün (Layman P'ang)	Pangyun	Hōun	G9
P'an-shan Pao-chi	Panshan Baoji	Banzan Hōshaku	I9
Pao-ên Hsüan-tsê	Bao'en Xuanze	Hōon Gensoku	K16
Pao-fêng Wei-chao	Baofeng Weizhao	Hōhō Ishō	G19
Pao-fu Ts'ung-chan	Baofu Congzhan	Hofuku Jūten	N13
Pao-ning Jên-yung	Baoning Renyong	Honei Ninyū	D19
Pao-shou Yen-chao	Baoshou Yanzhao	Hōju Enshō	B12

Pao-ts'u Hsing-yen	Baoci Xingyan	Hōji Gyōgon	M16
P'u-chi (see Sung-shan P'u-chi)			
P'u-t'i Ta-mo	Puti Damo	Bodai Daruma	I1
San-shêng Hui-jan	Sansheng Huiran	Sanshō Enen	C12
Sêng-ts'an (see Chien-Chih Sêng-ts'an)			
Shê-hsien Kuei-hsing	Shexian Guixing	Sekken Kisei	E16
Shêng-shou Nan-yin	Shengshou Nanyin	Seijū Nan'in	Q10
Shên-hs'iu (see Yü-Ch'uan Shên-hs'iu)			
Shen-shan Ts'êng-mi (see Mi Shih-po)			
Shih-shuang Ch'ing-chu	Shishuang Qingzhu	Sekisō Keisho	N11
Shih-shuang Ch'u-yüan	Shishuang Chuyuan	Sekisō Soen	A17
Shih-t'ou Hsi-ch'ien	Shitou Xiqian	Sekitō Kisen	L8
Shou-shan Hsing-nien	Shoushan Xingnian	Shuzan Shōnen	A15
Shu-shan K'uang-jên	Shushan Kuangren	Sozan Kyōnin	L12
Ssü-hsin Wu-hsin	Sixin Wuxin	Shishin Goshin	C20
Sui-chou Tao-yüan	Suizhou Daoyuan	Suishū Dōen	Q11
Sung-shan P'u-chi	Songshan Puji	Sūzan Fujaku	P7
Ta-chien Hui-nêng	Dajian Huineng	Daikan Enō	I16
Ta-hui Tsung-kao	Dahui Zonggao	Daie Sōkō	A22
Ta-hung Tsu-Chêng	Dahong Zuzheng	Daikō Soshō	D23
T'ai-ku P'u-yü	Taigu Puyu	(Korean) Taigo Pou	B23
T'ai-p'ing Hui-ch'in	Taiping Huiqin	Taihei Egon	B21
Ta-i Tao-hsin	Dayi Daoxin	Daii Dōshin	I4
T'ai-yüan Fu	Taiyuan Fu	Taigen Fu	L13
Ta-kuang Chü-hui	Daguang Juhui	Daikō Kokai	O12
Ta-kuei Mu-chê	Dagui Muche	Daii Botetsu	E19
Ta-lung	Dalong	Dairyō	
(not shown; 8th generation under Ch'ing-yüan through Tê-shan Hsüan-chien)			
Ta-man Hung-jên	Daman Hongren	Daiman Kōnin	I5
Ta-mei Fa-ch'ang	Damei Fachang	Daibai Hōjō	E9
Tan-hsia T'ien-jan	Danxia Tianran	Tanka Tenen	O9
Tan-hsia Tzu-ch'un	Danxia Zichun	Tanka Shijun	F19
Tan-yüan Ying-chên	Danyuan Yingzhen	Tangen Ōshin	M8
Tao-hsin (see Ta-i Tao-hsin)			
Tao-wu Yüan-chih	Daowu Yuanzhi	Dōgo Enchi	N10
Ta-sui Fa-chên	Dasui Fazhen	Daizui Hōshin	C11
Ta-tsu Hui-k'o	Dazu Huike	Taiso Eka	I2
Ta-t'ung (see Yü-Ch'uan Shên-hs'iu)			
Ta-yang Ching-hsüan	Dayang Jingxuan	Taiyō Kyōgen	F16
Ta-yang Yen (see Ta-yang Ching-hsüan)			
Ta-yü (see Kao-an Ta-yü)			
Ta-yü Shou-chih	Dayu Shouzhi	Daigu Shushi	B17
Tê-shan Hsüan-chien	Deshan Xuanjian	Tokusan Senkan	P11
Tê-shan Yüan-mi	Deshan Yuanmi	Tokusan Emmitsu	J14

T'ien-huang Tao-wu	Tianhuang Daowu	Tennō Dōgo	P9
T'ien-i I-huai	Tianyi Yihuai	Tenne Gikai	H17
T'ien-p'ing Ts'ung-i	Tianping Congyi	Tempyō Jūi	P16
T'ien-t'ai Tê-shao	Tiantai Deshao	Tendai Tokushō	O16
T'ien-t'ung (*see* Hung-chih Chêng-chüeh)			
T'ien-t'ung Ju-ching	Tiantong Rujing	Tendō Nyojō	E23
T'ien-t'ung Tsung-chüeh	Tiantong Zongjue	Tendō Sōkaku	E21
Ting-chou Shih-tsang	Dingzhou Shizang	Jōshū Sekisō	P8
Ti-tsang (*see* Lo-han Kuei-ch'ên)			
Tou-shuai Ts'ung-yüeh	Doushuai Congyue	Tosotsu Jūetsu	B20
T'ou-tzü I-ch'ing	Touzi Yiqing	Tōsu Gisei	F17
T'ou-tzü Ta-t'ung	Touzi Datong	Tōsu Daidō	O11
Ts'ao-shan Pen-chi	Caoshan Benji	Sōzan Honjaku	J12
Tsü-chou Chih-shên	Zizhou Zhishen	Shishū Chisen	Q6
Tsü-chou Ch'u-chi	Zizhou Chuji	Shishū Shojaku	Q7
Ts'ü-chou Fa-ju	Cizhou Faru	Jishū Hōnyo	O8
Tsü-fu Ju-pao	Zifu Rubao	Shifuku Nyohō	D13
Ts'ui-wei Wu-hsüeh	Cuiwei Wuxue	Suibi Mugaku	O10
Ts'ui-yen K'o-chên	Cuiyan Kezhen	Suigan Kashin	D18
Ts'ui-yen Ling-ts'an	Cuiyan Lingcan	Suigan Reisan	J13
T'ung-an Kuan-chih	Tongan Guanzhi	Dōan Kanshi	F14
T'ung-an Tao-p'i	Tongan Daopi	Dōan Dōhi	F13
T'ung-fêng An-chu (not shown; student of Lin-chi I-hsüan)			
Tung-shan Liang-chieh	Dongshan Liangjie	Tōzan Ryōkai	L11
Tung-shan Shou-ch'u	Dongshan Shouchu	Tōsan Shusho	K14
Wang Yen-pin	Wang Yanbin	Ō Enhin	O14
Wên-shu Ying-chên	Wenshu Yingzhen	Monju Ōshin	J15
Wu-ben (*see* Tung-shan Liang-chieh)			
Wu-chiu Yu-hsüan	Wujiu Youxuan	Ukyū Yūgen	L9
Wu-fêng Ch'ang-kuan	Wufeng Changguan	Gohō Jōkan	B10
Wu-mên Hui-k'ai	Wumen Huikai	Mumon Ekai	D25
Wu-tsu Fa-yen	Wuzu Fayan	Goso Hōen	D20
Yang-ch'i Fang-hui	Yangqi Fanghui	Yōgi Hōe	C18
Yang-shan Hui-chi	Yangshan Huiji	Kyōzan Ejaku	F11
Yang Wu-wei	Yang Wuwei	Yō Mui	I18
Yao-shan Wei-yen	Yaoshan Weiyan	Yakusan Igen	N9
Yen-kuan Ch'i-an	Yanguan Qi'an	Enkan Seian	D9
Yen-t'ou Ch'üan-huo	Yantou Quanhuo	Gantō Zenkatsu	Q12
Yen-yang Shan-hsin	Yanyang Shanxin	Genyō Zenshin	K11
Yüan-kuan (*see* Liang-shan Yüan-kuan)			
Yüan-ming (*see* Tê-shan Yüan-mi)			
Yüan-t'ung Fa-shên	Yuantong Fashen	Entsū Hōshū	H18
Yüan-wu K'ê-ch'in	Yuanwu Keqin	Engo Kokugon	A21
Yü-Ch'uan Shên-hsiu	Yuquan Shenxiu	Gyokusen Jinshū	P6

Romaji–Pinyin–Wade-Giles

ROMAJI (Japanese)	PINYIN (Chinese)	WADE-GILES (Chinese)	LOCATION
Banzan Hōshaku	Panshan Baoji	P'an-shan Pao-chi	I9
Bashō Esei	Bajiao Huiqing	Pa-chiao Hui-ch'ing	E13
Baso Dōitsu	Mazu Daoyi	Ma-tsu Tao-i	A8
Bodai Daruma	Puti Damo	P'u-t'i Ta-mo	I1
Bokushū Dōmyō	Muzhou Daoming	Mu-chou Tao-ming	B11
Butsugen Seion	Foyan Qingyuan	Fo-yen Ch'ing-yüan	C21
Chikuan Shikei	Zhu'an Shigui	Chu-an Shih-kuei	C22
Chimon Kōso	Zhimen Guangzuo	Chih-mên Kuang-tso	G15
Chōkei Eryō	Changqing Huileng	Ch'ang-ch'ing Hui-lêng	O13
Chōsha Keishin	Changsha Jingcen	Ch'ang-sha Ching-ts'ên	J10
Chūyū Kōon	Zhongyi Hongen	Chung-i Hung-ên	K9
Daibai Hōjō	Damei Fachang	Ta-mei Fa-ch'ang	E9
Daie Sōkō	Dahui Zonggao	Ta-hui Tsung-kao	A22
Daigu Shushi	Dayu Shouzhi	Ta-yü Shou-chih	B17
Daii Botetsu	Dagui Muche	Ta-kuei Mu-chê	E19
Daii Dōshin	Dayi Daoxin	Ta-i Tao-hsin	I4
Daikan Enō	Dajian Huineng	Ta-chien Hui-nêng	I16
Daikō Kokai	Daguang Juhui	Ta-kuang Chü-hui	O12
Daikō Soshō	Dahong Zuzheng	Ta-hung Tsu-Chêng	D23
Daiman Kōnin	Daman Hongren	Ta-man Hung-jên	I5
Dairyō	Dalong	Ta-lung	

(not shown; 8th generation under Qingyuan through Deshan Xuanjian)

ROMAJI (Japanese)	PINYIN (Chinese)	WADE-GILES (Chinese)	LOCATION
Daizui Hōshin	Dasui Fazhen	Ta-sui Fa-chên	C11
Daruma (*see* Bodai Daruma)			
Dōan Dōhi	Tongan Daopi	T'ung-an Tao-p'i	F13
Dōan Kanshi	Tongan Guanzhi	T'ung-an Kuan-chih	F14
Dōgo Enchi	Daowu Yuanzhi	Tao-wu Yüan-chih	N10
Dōshin (*see* Daii Dōshin)			
Eihei Dōgen	Yongping Daoyuan	Yung-p'ing Tao-yüan	E24
Eka (*see* Taiso Eka)			
Engo Kokugon	Yuanwu Keqin	Yüan-wu K'ê-ch'in	A21
Enkan Seian	Yanguan Qi'an	Yen-kuan Ch'i-an	D9
Enō (*see* Daikan Enō)			
Entsū Hōshū	Yuantong Fashen	Yüan-t'ung Fa-shên	H18
Esshū Kempō	Yuezhou Qianfeng	Yüeh-chou Ch'ien-fêng	I12
Fūketsu Enshō	Fengxue Yanzhao	Fêng-hsüeh Yen-chao	A14
Fun'yō Zenshō	Fenyang Shanzhao	Fên-yang Shan-chao	A16
Fuyō Dōkai	Furong Daokai	Fu-jung Tao-k'ai	F18
Fuzan Hōen	Fushan Fayuan	Fu-shan Fa-yüan	E17

Gantō Zenkatsu	Yantou Quanhuo	Yen-t'ou Ch'üan-huo	Q12
Gatsurin Shikan	Yuelin Shiguan	Yüeh-lin Shih-kuan	D24
Gensha Shibi	Xuansha Shibei	Hsüan-sha Shih-pei	M13
Genyō Zenshin	Yanyang Shanxin	Yen-yang Shan-hsin	K11
Gettan Zenka	Yue'an Shanguo	Yüeh-an Shan-kuo	D22
Gohō Jōkan	Wufeng Changguan	Wu-fêng Ch'ang-kuan	B10
Gokoku Keigen	Huguo Jingyuan	Hu-kuo Ching-yüan	B22
Gokoku Shuchō	Huguo Shoucheng	Hu-kuo Shou-chêng	G13
Goso Hōen	Wuzu Fayan	Wu-tsu Fa-yen	D20
Gozu Hōyū	Niutou Farong	Niu-t'ou Fa-jung	Q5
Gutei Chikan	Jinhua Juzhi	Chin-hua Chü-chih	I11
Gyokusen Jinshū	Yuquan Shenxiu	Yü-Ch'uan Shên-hsiu	P6
Hakuun Shutan	Baiyun Shouduan	Pai-yün Shou-tuan	C19
Haryō Kōkan	Baling Haojian	Pa-ling Hao-chien	I14
Hofuku Jūten	Baofu Congzhan	Pao-fu Ts'ung-chan	N13
Hōgen Bun'eki	Fayan Wenyi	Fa-yen Wên-i	L15
Hōhō Ishō	Baofeng Weizhao	Pao-fêng Wei-chao	G19
Hōji Gyōgon	Baoci Xingyan	Pao-ts'u Hsing-yen	M16
Hōju Enshō	Baoshou Yanzhao	Pao-shou Yen-chao	B12
Honei Ninyū	Baoning Renyong	Pao-ning Jên-yung	D19
Hōon Gensoku	Bao'en Xuanze	Pao-ên Hsüan-tsê	K16
Hōsen Dōshin	Fengxian Daochen	Fêng-hsien Tao-ch'ên	H14
Hōun	Pangyun (Layman Pang)	P'ang Yün	G9
Hyakujō Ekai	Baizhang Huaihai	Pai-chang Huai-hai	A9
Hyakujō Nehan	Baizhang Niepan	Pai-chang Nieh-p'an	D10
Isan Daian	Guishan Da'an	Kuei-shan Ta-an	C10
Isan Reiyū	Guishan Lingyou	Kuei-shan Ling-yu	E10
Jishū Hōnyo	Cizhou Faru	Ts'ü-chou Fa-ju	O8
Jōshu Jinne	Jingzhong Shenhui	Ching-Chung Shên-hui	Q9
Jōshū Jūshin	Zhaozhou Congshen	Chao-chou Ts'ung-shên	K10
Jōshu Musō	Jingzhong Wuxiang	Ching-Chung Wu-Hsiang	Q8
Jōshū Sekisō	Dingzhou Shizang	Ting-chou Shih-tsang	P8
Jōten Denshū	Chengtian Chuanzong	Ch'eng-t'ien Ch'uan-tsung	I17
Kaidō Soshin	Huitang Zuxin	Hui-t'ang Tsu-hsin	B19
Kaifuku Dōnei	Kaifu Daoning	K'ai-fu Tao-ning	D21
Kakuhan Ekō	Juefan Huihong	Chüeh-fan Hui-hung	A20
Kanchi Sōsan	Jianzhi Sengcan	Chien-Chih Sêng-ts'an	I3
Kannan Dōjō	Guannan Daochang	Kuan-nan Tao-ch'ang	F10
Kassan Zenne	Jiashan Shanhui	Chia-shan Shan-hui	M11
Kataku Jinne	Heze Shenhui	Ho-tsê Shên-hui	O7
Keichō Beiyu	Jingzhao Mihu	Ching-chao Mi-hu	E11
Kinzan Bunsui	Qinshan Wensui	Ch'in-shan Wên-sui	G12
Kisō Sakushin	Guizong Cezhen	Kuei-tsung Ts'ê-Chên	L16
Kisu Chijō	Guizong Zhichang	Kuei-tsung Chih-ch'ang	F9

Kōan Daigu	Gaoan Dayu	Kao-an Ta-yü	H10
Koke Sonshō	Xinghua Cunjiang	Hsing-hua Ts'un-chiang	A12
Kōnin (see Daiman Kōnin)			
Kōshū Tenryū	Hangzhou Tianlong	Hang-chou T'ien-lung	G10
Kōyō Seibō	Xingyang Qingpou	Hsing-yang Ch'ing-p'ou	G17
Kōyō Seijō	Xingyang Qingrang	Hsing-yang Ch'ing-jang	E14
Kyōgen Chikan	Xiangyan Zhixian	Hsiang-yen Chih-hsien	G11
Kyōrin Chōon	Xianglin Chengyuan	Hsiang-lin Ch'êng-yüan	G14
Kyōsei Dōfu	Jingqing Daofu	Ching-ch'ing Tao-fu	K13
Kyōzan Ejaku	Yangshan Huiji	Yang-shan Hui-chi	F11
Kyūhō Dōken	Jiufeng Daoqian	Chiu-fêng Tao-ch'ien	N12
Kyūhō Gon	Jiufeng Qin	Chiu-fêng Ch'in	G16
Massan Ryōnen	Moshan Liaoran	Mo-shan Liao-jan	J11
Mayoku Hōtetsu	Mayu Baoche	Ma-yu Pao-ch'ê	H9
Monju Ōshin	Wenshu Yingzhen	Wên-shu Ying-chên	J15
Mumon Ekai	Wumen Huikai	Wu-mên Hui-k'ai	D25
Myōan Eisai	Mingan Rongxi	Ming-an Jung-hsi	C23
Myōshō Tokken	Mingzhao Deqian	Ming-chao Tê-ch'ien	P14
Nampo Jōmyō	Nanpu Shaoming	Nan-p'u Shao-ming	A23
Nangaku Ejō	Nanyue Huairang	Nan-yüeh Huai-jang	A7
Nan'in Egyō	Nanyuan Huiyong	Nan-yüan Hui-yung	A13
Nansen Fugan	Nanquan Puyuan	Nan-ch'üan P'u-yüan	M9
Nantō Kōyū	Nanta Guangyong	Nan-t'a Kuang-yung	E12
Nan'yō Echū	Nanyang Huizhong	Nan-yang Hui-chung	M7
Ōbaku Kiun	Huangbo Xiyun	Huang-po Hsi-yün	A10
Ō Enhin	Wang Yanbin	Wang Yen-pin	O14
Ōryū Enan	Huanglong Huinan	Huang-lung Hui-nan	A18
Rakan Keichin	Luohan Guichen	Lo-han Kuei-ch'ên	M14
Rakuho Gen'an	Luopu Yuanan	Lo-p'u Yüan-an	M12
Razan Dōkan	Luoshan Daoxian	Lo-shan Tao-hsien	P13
Reiun Shigon	Lingyun Zhiqin	Ling-yün Chih-ch'in	D11
Renge Hōshō	Lianhua Fengxiang	Lien-hua Fêng-hsiang	H15
Rinzai Gigen	Linji Yixuan	Lin-chi I-hsüan	A11
Roso Hōun	Luzu Baoyun	Lu-tsu Pao-yün	J9
Rōya Ekaku	Langye Huijue	Lang-yeh Hui-chüeh	D17
Ryōzan Enkan	Liangshan Yuanguan	Liang-shan Yüan-kuan	F15
Ryūge Kodon	Longya Judun	Lung-ya Chü-tun	H12
Ryūsai Shōshū	Longji Shaoxiu	Lung-chi Shao-hsiu	Q15
Ryūtan Sōshin	Longtan Chongxin	Lung-t'an Ch'ung-hsin	P10
Ryū Tetsuma	Liu Tiemo	Liu T'ieh-mo	H11
Saiin Shimyō	Xiyuan Siming	Hsi-yüan Ssü-ming	B13
Saitō Kōboku	Xita Guangmu	Hsi-t'a Kuang-mu	D12
Sanshō Enen	Sansheng Huiran	San-shêng Hui-jan	C12
Seidō Chizō	Xitang Zhizang	Hsi-t'ang Chih-tsang	B9

Seigen Gyōshi	Qingyuan Xingsi	Ch'ing-yüan Hsing-ssu	L7
Seijū Nan'in	Shengshou Nanyin	Shêng-shou Nan-yin	Q10
Seikei Kōshin	Qingxi Hongjin	Ch'ing-hsi Hung-chin	P15
Seirin Shiken	Qinglin Shiqian	Ch'ing-lin Shih-ch'ien	K12
Sekisō Keisho	Shishuang Qingzhu	Shih-shuang Ch'ing-chu	N11
Sekisō Soen	Shishuang Chuyuan	Shih-shuang Ch'u-yüan	A17
Sekitō Kisen	Shitou Xiqian	Shih-t'ou Hsi-ch'ien	L8
Sekken Kisei	Shexian Guixing	Shê-hsien Kuei-hsing	E16
Sensu Tokujō	Chuanzi Decheng	Ch'uan-tzü Tê-ch'êng	M10
Seppō Gison	Xuefeng Yicun	Hsüeh-fêng I-ts'un	P12
Setchō Chikan	Xuedou Zhijian	Hsüeh-tou Chih-chien	E22
Setchō Jūken	Xuedou Chongxian	Hsüeh-tou Ch'ung-hsien	H16
Shifuku Nyohō	Zifu Rubao	Tsü-fu Ju-pao	D13
Shinketsu Seiryō	Zhenxie Qingliao	Chên-hsieh Ch'ing-liao	E20
Shishin Goshin	Sixin Wuxin	Ssü-hsin Wu-hsin	C20
Shishū Chisen	Zizhou Zhishen	Tsü-chou Chih-shên	Q6
Shishū Shojaku	Zizhou Chuji	Tsü-chou Ch'u-chi	Q7
Shōkei Eki	Zhangjing Huaiyun	Chang-ching Huai-yün	C9
Shuzan Shōnen	Shoushan Xingnian	Shou-shan Hsing-nien	A15
Sōsan (see Kanchi Sōsan)			
Sōzan Honjaku	Caoshan Benji	Ts'ao-shan Pen-chi	J12
Sozan Kyōnin	Shushan Kuangren	Shu-shan K'uang-jên	L12
Suibi Mugaku	Cuiwei Wuxue	Ts'ui-wei Wu-hsüeh	O10
Suigan Kashin	Cuiyan Kezhen	Ts'ui-yen K'o-chên	D18
Suigan Reisan	Cuiyan Lingcan	Ts'ui-yen Ling-ts'an	J13
Suishū Dōen	Suizhou Daoyuan	Sui-chou Tao-yüan	Q11
Sūju Keichū	Chongshou Qichou	Ch'ung-shou Ch'i-ch'ou	N16
Sūzan Fujaku	Songshan Puji	Sung-shan P'u-chi	P7
Taigen Fu	Taiyuan Fu	T'ai-yüan Fu	L13
Taihei Egon	Taiping Huiqin	T'ai-p'ing Hui-ch'in	B21
Taiso Eka	Dazu Huike	Ta-tsu Hui-k'o	I2
Taiyō Kyōgen	Dayang Jingxuan	Ta-yang Ching-hsüan	F16
Tangen Ōshin	Danyuan Yingzhen	Tan-yüan Ying-chên	M8
Tanka Shijun	Danxia Zichun	Tan-hsia Tzu-ch'un	F19
Tanka Tenen	Danxia Tianran	Tan-hsia T'ien-jan	O9
Tempyō Jūi	Tianping Congyi	T'ien-p'ing Ts'ung-i	P16
Tendai Tokushō	Tiantai Deshao	T'ien-t'ai Tê-shao	O16
Tendō Nyojō	Tiantong Rujing	T'ien-t'ung Ju-ching	E23
Tendō Sōkaku	Tiantong Zongjue	T'ien-t'ung Tsung-chüeh	E21
Tenne Gikai	Tianyi Yihuai	T'ien-i I-huai	H17
Tennō Dōgo	Tianhuang Daowu	T'ien-huang Tao-wu	P9
Tokusan Emmitsu	Deshan Yuanmi	Tê-shan Yüan-mi	J14
Tokusan Senkan	Deshan Xuanjian	Tê-shan Hsüan-chien	P11
Tōsan Shusho	Dongshan Shouchu	Tung-shan Shou-ch'u	K14

Tosotsu Jūetsu	Doushuai Congyue	Tou-shuai Ts'ung-yüeh	B20
Tōsu Daidō	Touzi Datong	T'ou-tzü Ta-t'ung	O11
Tōsu Gisei	Touzi Yiqing	T'ou-tzü I-ch'ing	F17
Tōzan Ryōkai	Dongshan Liangjie	Tung-shan Liang-chieh	L11
Ukyū Yūgen	Wujiu Youxuan	Wu-chiu Yu-hsüan	L9
Ummon Bun'en	Yunmen Wenyan	Yün-men Wên-yen	I13
Un'an Kokubun	Yunan Kewen	Yün-an K'o-wên	A19
Ungan Donjō	Yunyan Tansheng	Yün-yen T'an-shêng	L10
Ungo Dōyō	Yunju Daoying	Yün-chü Tao-ying	F12
Wanshi Shōgaku	Hongzhi Zhengjue	Hung-chih Chêng-chüeh	F20
Yakusan Igen	Yaoshan Weiyan	Yao-shan Wei-yen	N9
Yōgi Hōe	Yangqi Fanghui	Yang-ch'i Fang-hui	C18
Yōka Genkaku	Yongjia Xuanjue	Yung-chia Hsüan-chüeh	N7
Yōmei Enju	Yongming Yanshou	Yung-ming Yen-shou	O17
Yō Mui	Yang Wuwei	Yang Wu-wei	I18
Zuigan Shigen	Ruiyan Shiyan	Jui-yen Shih-yen	Q13

NOTES

1   Yunshui refers to an itinerant Buddhist monk who travels unbounded like the "clouds and water" to find spiritual teachers.

2   Some scholars call these works "eulogistic."

3   "Zen" is the Japanese pronunciation of the Chinese word *Chan*. The two terms are interchangeable. The latter term is generally used in discussions within the context of Chinese culture. Because the Zen tradition was made known to Westerners largely through the works of Japanese scholars and religious figures such as Daisetz Suzuki, the term "Zen" is widely recognized in the West. For this reason the word "Zen" is used in this book instead of the Chinese word "Chan."

4   "Mahayana," meaning "Great Vehicle," is the name of the dominant East Asian form of Buddhism. Its doctrines emphasize the salvation of all beings and it is thus regarded as the "great vehicle" for the deliverance of beings to nirvana.

5   At this time, China was divided into regional dynasties. Emperor Wu of the Liang dynasty ruled during the period 502–550. His capital was located in ancient Jiankang, now the city of Nanjing, where the conversation with Bodhidharma is believed to have occurred.

6   The *Record of Luoyang's Buddhist Temples: Taisho*, vol. 51, p. 999.

7   The *Wudeng Huiyuan (Compendium of Five Lamps)* is a text compiled by the monk Puji in the late thirteenth century that unified into one volume the essential contents of five earlier lamp records.

8   Akshobhya Buddha (Sanskrit for "Immovable") is a legendary buddha who presides over the eastern paradise. He accumulated merit and ultimately became a buddha by an ancient vow to never feel aversion nor anger toward any being.

9   The Chinese four elements are earth, water, fire, and wind. The Sanskrit word *skandha*, meaning "aggregate," refers to the components of experience. They are (1) form, (2) sensation, (3) perception, (4) mental formations, and (5) consciousness.

10 *Continued Biographies of Monks*, by Dao Heng. *Taisho*, vol. 50, p. 552.

11 A disciple of Bodhidharma named Tan Lin is believed to have recorded this teaching. This translation is taken from the *Chanzong Baodian (Treasured Classics of Zen)*, published by the Hebei Institute for Chan Research, 1993, p. 3.

12 In Buddhism, the "three worlds" are the past, future, and present.

13 The *Transmission of the Lamp*, a record compiled over four hundred years after Huike's birth, indicates that he studied under a Zen teacher named Baojing prior to meeting Bodhidharma. This belies the idea that Chinese tradition does not recognize other Zen teachers before Bodhidharma. Rather, it shows that the "First Ancestor" is remembered as the originator of the surviving schools of subsequent ages.

14 Mt. Song, one of the great Buddhist mountains of China, is located southwest of the modern city of Zhengzhou in Henan Province.

15 The Tiantai Buddhism master Dao Heng wrote the *Continued Biographies of Eminent Monks, Taisho,* vol. 50, p. 425.

16 The "Three Jewels," or "Three Treasures," are (1) Buddha, the awakened one, (2) Dharma, Buddha's truth, and (3) Sangha, the community of followers of Buddha.

17 Located about forty kilometers east northeast of modern Anyang City in Hebei Province.

18 The poem *Faith in Mind (Xin Xin Ming)* is believed by many scholars to have been written after Sengcan's lifetime, perhaps by an individual in the Oxhead Zen school.

19 The Sanlun ("Three Treatises") school of Buddhism based its teaching upon three works written by Nagarjuna and Aryadeva. The Tiantai Buddhist school, founded by Zhiyi (538–97), is based on the teachings of the *Lotus Sutra.*

20 The *Prajnaparamita Sutra (Great Wisdom Sutra)* is a collection of forty smaller sutras, including the well-known *Heart Sutra* and *Diamond Sutra,* that are studied and chanted in the Zen tradition. The teachings of the Mahayana Buddhist tradition draw extensively from the teachings of this sutra.

21 This is a play on words. The Chinese words for "name" and "nature" are homonyms. The boy answered Daoxin's question as if he'd been asked his "nature" rather than his name.

22 The *Discourse on the Highest Vehicle* is a text said to quote Hongren's teaching. Modern scholars debate how much, if any, of the text can be genuinely attributed to Hongren.

23 The "twelve divisions" was a traditional way of classifying the Buddhist canon in ancient India.

24 The *Record of the Lankavatara Masters, Taisho,* vol. 85, p. 1283.

25 *Bodhi* is a Sanskrit term for transcendent wisdom. It is broadly translated as enlightenment or wisdom.

26 This passage is from the *Ancestral Hall Collection,* an early Zen lamp record

compiled and edited by the monks Jing and Yun Ershi in the year 952. Reprinted by Hsin Wen Feng, Taipei, 1986, p. 52.

27 "Expedient words" are words that facilitate the spiritual awakening of those who hear them.

28 In Buddhism, the mind's disease is its natural belief in "self" and "other."

29 In the Chinese Buddhist tradition, the term for "sutra" *(jing)* refers to texts that are the recorded speech of the Buddha or those closely associated with him. Outside the Buddhist tradition, however, the same Chinese word simply means "classic" or "scripture." An example is Laozi's *Dao De Jing* ("Virtuous Way Classic"). The commonly used term *"Platform Sutra,"* therefore, may also be called the *"Platform Classic."*

30 The Chinese term "woods" also carries the meaning "community of Buddhist practitioners," or monastery. This temple, which remains a religious and tourist attraction, is now known as Nanhua Temple. It is located east of the city of Shaozhou in Northern Guandong Province.

31 *Samadhi* (Sanskrit for "establish, make firm") is traditionally defined as a non-dualistic state of mind where there is no experience of subject and object.

32 The "three poisons" of Buddhism are greed, hatred, and delusion. Mara is the king of the sixth heaven of the realm of desire. Prior to Buddha's enlightenment, Mara attacked him with seductive visions to prevent him from learning the truth of the cause of suffering.

33 The Buddha.

34 *Chanzong Baodian,* published by the Hebei Institute for the Study of Chan, 1993.

35 The Vinaya school of Buddhism emphasizes the observance of the rules of conduct for Buddhists believers and the Buddhist clergy. These rules are set forth in a collection known as the Vinayapitaka.

36 Zen master Hui An of Mt. Song was a prominent disciple of the Fifth Ancestor, Daman Hongren. He lived to the age of 128.

37 This refers to Nanyue's student, Zen master Mazu Daoyi. Mazu's name includes the Chinese word for "horse."

38 *Qi,* commonly written as "chi" in English, is sometimes translated as "spiritual essence" or "breath."

39 The four noble truths, said to have constituted the Buddha's enlightenment, are (1) the existence of suffering as an attribute of existence; (2) the cause of suffering, which is desire and attachment; (3) the end of suffering through the final cessation of desire and attachment; and (4) the path for achieving the end of

suffering. After his enlightenment Buddha offered these truths as his first teaching in the city of Varanasi.

40 According to tradition, Bodhidharma's robe and bowl were passed from ancestor to ancestor until their transmission from Hongren to Huineng at Huangmei. Thereafter, competing Zen schools disputed the robe's possession as a symbol of their legitimacy in the line of succession.

41 Zhuji City is located about forty kilometers south of Hangzhou in Zhejiang Province.

42 The dharmakaya is the Dharma body, the embodiment of truth.

43 Vairochana is a legendary buddha who is regarded as the spiritual essence of Buddhist truth.

44 The *Senika* was a doctrine criticized by Shakyamuni Buddha. It proposes that the mind is eternal but form is subject to decay and annihilation.

45 The "two great attributes" are wisdom (in Chinese, *zhihui*) and virtue (in Chinese, *fude*).

46 The four stances are walking, sitting, standing, and lying down.

47 Beijing: China Publishing House, 1996.

48 The words for "lion" and "teacher" in Chinese are homonyms. Thus, Mazu is metaphorically asking, "Are you a teacher?"

49 Lingnan, literally "south of the mountains," is equivalent in Zen jargon to the Southern school of Zen, the spiritual descendants of the Sixth Ancestor.

50 *Shitou* translates as "stone" or "rock."

51 The *Zhao Lun (Zhao Treatise)* is a classical text of commentaries on the sutras by the Chinese monk Seng Zhao (384–414), a disciple of the great translator Kumarajiva.

52 This verse is widely known by its Japanese name, the *Sandokai.*

53 The three Buddhist realms are the worlds of (1) desire, (2) form, and (3) nonform (pure spirit). The six Buddhist realms are (1) hell realm, (2) hungry ghost realm, (3) animal realm, (4) spirit realm, (5) human realm, and (6) heavenly realm.

54 Xinwu was located west of the modern city of Nanchang in Jiangxi Province.

55 Baizhang appears to be making a metaphor, comparing Buddhists who simply chant scriptures with Hindus in India before the appearance of Buddha.

56 This passage is from the *Ancestral Hall Collection.*

57 Now the city of Ningdu in southern Jiangxi Province.

58 This passage is from the *Transmission of the Lamp.*

59 The Three Vehicles (in Sanskrit, *Triyana*) are the vehicles that convey beings across samsara to nirvana. They are the three great sects of Buddhism: the Hinayana, Madhyamayana, and Mahayana.

60 A location in modern Jiangsu Province.

61 Yuquan Temple was located on Yuquan ("Jade Spring") Mountain in what is now Dangyangang County in Hubei Province.

62 Uncertain location. By imperial edict, many temples in China at this time were named "Longxing" ("Rejuvenated Dragon").

63 Guizong Temple is located at the foot of the famous Buddhist mountain named Mt. Lu near Jiujiang City, Jiangxi Province.

64 Kwan Yin (pinyin, "Guanyin"), also named "Kwan Shih Yin," is the Chinese name of the bodhisattva Avalokiteshvara. The name means "hears the cries of the world." Originally a male deity, this bodhisattva evolved from its Indian origins into a female in the Chinese Buddhist pantheon and is regarded as the "Goddess of Mercy."

65 The term "scriptural monk" refers to a follower of a Buddhist sect that takes a sutra as the basis of its teachings. This term is used in contrast with a Zen monk, who does not rely on written teachings.

66 During this era, Zen monks often stayed at temples that were not Zen temples, and thus they earned the common moniker "Zen guests."

67 Tianran's name translates as "natural."

68 Located near the Yang-tse River in southern Anwei Province.

69 Xin Zheng is located in modern Henan Province.

70 The term "Old Teacher" (in Chinese, *Laoshi*; in Japanese, *Rōshi*) remains as an affectionate sobriquet for older Zen teachers.

71 Dipamkara Buddha is a legendary buddha, the first of twenty-four mythical buddhas who existed prior to the historical Buddha, Shakyamuni.

72 The four modes of birth are womb, egg, moisture, and transformation.

73 National Teacher Faqin, a teacher of the Oxhead Zen school, founded a temple on Mt. Jing near Hangzhou in the year 742.

74 Zen master Funiu was a student of Zen masters Faqin and Mazu.

75 "Sacred relics" are the remains of a body after it is cremated.

76 Manjushri is the bodhisattva of wisdom. He is commonly depicted riding a lion, holding a sword in one hand and the *Prajnaparamita Sutra* in the other.

77 Samantabhadra is the bodhisattva of all-pervading good. He is often depicted riding an elephant.

78 The Chinese word *hsiu* means "to cease."

79 Baizhang.

80 The "Min waters" refers to Baizhang's residence on Mt. Huangbo on the coast of Fuzhou.

81 The Zhang River lies between Wanling, where this poem was composed, and Huangbo's previous residence on Mt. Huangbo in Fuzhou.

82 Yuzhou was located near the modern city of Yunlian, bordering the three modern provinces of Sichuan, Guizhou, and Yunnan.

83 Wufeng's name means "five peaks."

84 According to tradition, true monks will encounter Manjushri during their pilgrimage to Mt. Tai.

85 The "four bodies" is one of various ways of describing a buddha. More commonly used is the term "three bodies" (in Sanskrit, *Trikaya*), which include the dharmakaya (the buddha body per se), the Sambhogakaya (the bliss body), and the Nirmanakaya (the transformation body).

86 Zhigong (418–514), also known as Baozhi, was a Buddhist adept well versed in Zen practice.

87 Huang Chao was a bloodthirsty leader of a rebel army in China during this era.

88 Zen Master Guling Shenzan was a disciple of Baizhang Huaihai.

89 The Chinese term *shan zhi shi*, here translated as "Buddhist worthies," comes from the Sanskrit words *kaly amitra*, meaning a person who, like a buddha or bodhisattva, lives to guide others to virtue.

90 This monastery, now named Bailin Temple, has been recently rebuilt on its ancient foundations. Among many other structures are Zhaozhou's refurbished stupa, the Kuan Yin Hall, and the Wumenguan Meditation Hall.

91 *Canqing* is a meeting between a Zen student and his or her teacher where the student asks questions and receives instruction.

92 The city of Jianchang was located about thirty kilometers north of the modern city of Nanchang in Jiangxi Province.

93 Shimen Mountain is located near modern Qingtian City in Zhejiang Province.

94 The dharmakaya is the "Body of the Dharma," or of truth.

95 This passage is from the *Transmission of the Lamp*.

96 Non-action (in Chinese, *wu wei*) is a term often associated with Taoism, but also used frequently in Zen Buddhism.

97 The name "Longtan" means "dragon marsh."

98 Ancient Muzhou was located in the region near Jiande in modern Zhejiang Province.

99 A *cangue* is a torture device used in ancient China.

100 The Consciousness-Only school of Chinese Buddhism evolved from the Vijnanavada school of Indian Buddhism. Its fundamental thesis is that everything exists only in consciousness and there is no independent existence for phenomena.

101 The "Western Paradise" is the heavenly kingdom of Amitabha, the buddha worshiped in the Pure Land sect of Buddhism.

102 The five precepts for lay persons are (1) not killing, (2) not stealing, (3) not misusing sexuality, (4) not engaging in slander, and (5) not taking intoxicants.

103 The West River is an allusion to Sichuan, the area where Dasui lived.

104 An *asura* is a demonlike entity. It is categorized as belonging to one of the six Buddhist realms of existence.

105 This passage is from the *Transmission of the Lamp*.

106 *Sindhava* is an old Zen term taken from Sanskrit that is applied to a Zen adept or skilled Zen student of advanced understanding.

107 *The Record of the Venerable Ancients* (in Chinese, *Guzunsu Yulu*) was compiled by the monk Shouze around the year 1150. It contains the teachings of more than forty Zen ancients, most of whom were not included in the more famous *Transmission of the Lamp*.

108 The Chinese phrase used here by Zihu is a double entendre. One interpretation is "it's transmitted from left and right," and a second interpretation is, "circle left and circle right." While Zihu apparently meant to convey the first meaning, Iron Grinder Liu responded as if to the second meaning.

109 Another pun with the Chinese homonyms "lion" and "master."

110 A river near Shanxin's temple was named Xinxing. The Chinese name means "new refreshing."

111 Liling City is southwest of Changsha in modern Hunan Province.

112 The "four benefits" or "four graces" are the compassionate benefits bestowed on students by their mother and father (who bestow life and support), the Buddha (who bestows the path to enlightenment and to overcoming suffering), and their Dharma teacher (whose teaching efforts leads the student to the realization of

the Way). The three existences include (1) desire-existence, including the six realms of heaven, human, ashura, beast, hungry ghost, and the hells; (2) form-existence, which exists apart from the polluted desire-existence in a state of purity; and (3) non-form-existence, which, although empty in nature, still witnesses cause and effect.

113 The *Anapana Sutra* is a treatise on meditation techniques such as stilling the mind and following the breath.

114 The six senses, as they are traditionally defined in Buddhism, are sight, sound, smell, taste, touch, and ideation.

115 The Qinglong Commentaries were famous Tang dynasty annotated copies of the *Diamond Sutra* authored by the monks Dao Yin and Fengxuan Zongzhao of Qinglong Temple.

116 Part of the meaning of this story comes from a play on the Chinese words "dim sum" (Mandarin, *dian xin*). The words "dim sum" have the generic meaning of any type of small snack. The words also mean "touching mind" or "refreshing mind." One account of the phrase "dim sum" claims that it evolved from its Zen origin to mean "putting something in an empty stomach."

117 These terms describe various doctrinal stages of development toward Buddha-hood.

118 Zen master Dajue, like Xinghua, also studied under Linji, and was thus Xinghua's Dharma brother.

119 In Zen temples at this time, *puqing*, meaning "all invited," was the name applied to a common work session in which everyone, including the abbot, participated.

120 A "wooden goose" was the name applied to a float that was cast out of boats to test the current prior to the boat's proceeding through a treacherous area.

121 In the Zen tradition, before a candidate for the abbacy of a temple can assume that position, he must demonstrate his understanding to the congregation in a manner that meets their approval.

122 The Chinese words *fu chuan* means "overturned boat."

123 It is said that when one speaks inappropriately of the Dharma, one's eyebrows fall out.

124 J. C. Cleary provides an excellent review of Guifeng's views in the introduction of his book *Zen Dawn*. Boston and London: Shambhala, 1986. See also Peter N. Gregory's translation with commentary of Guifeng's *Inquiry into the Origin of Humanity*. Kuroda Institute. Honolulu: University of Hawaii Press, 1995.

125 *The Surangama Sutra* (*Sutra of the Heroic One*, or *Heroic March Sutra*) is a popular and influential sutra in the development of Zen and Mahayana Buddhism.

126 The "six *paramitas*" are six practices that lead to salvation. They are (1) *dana* (charity), (2) *shila* (keeping the precepts), (3) *kshanti* (patience), (4) *virya* (zeal), (5) *dhyana* (meditation), and (6) *prajna* (wisdom).

127 The *pratyupanna samadhi* is a severe practice whereby, for up to ninety days, the practitioner, without rest except for short meals, invokes Amitabha Buddha while walking or standing, and thus absolves all accumulated evil karma. The practice leads to the appearance of all the buddhas to the practitioner.

128 "Family style" refers to the teaching methods or style of a particular house or lineage of Zen.

129 The Hui Chang suppression occurred when the emperor Wu Zong, in the year 845, proscribed Buddhist activities. The suppression of Buddhism was extreme until the emperor died the following year.

130 This passage is an excerpt from the *Extensive Record of Zen Master Yunmen*.

131 "Breaking out" and "breaking in" are from the context of a chick breaking out of an egg and the hen pecking at the egg from the outside to assist the chick. Here when Jingqing asks, "Will you live or not?" he is making an analogy to a chick trying to attain life by getting out of the shell.

132 When dots of ink are applied to create the pupils in the eyes of a picture of a dragon, it is believed to come alive.

133 Min is the ancient name of the area now roughly covered by Fujian Province.

134 "Han" is the traditional name of ethnic Chinese.

135 An *arhat* ("worthy one") is a person who has attained the highest awakening as to the nature of reality. Such a person has not undertaken the great vow to save all beings, and thus has attained salvation only for himself. An arhat is considered to be the ideal of Hinayana ("lesser vehicle") Buddhism. *Tathagata* ("thus come") is one of the ten titles of the Buddha, one who has attained supreme enlightenment.

136 This Mt. Gui is a different mountain from the Mt. Gui associated with the Guiyang school of Zen.

137 *Namufo* is the recitation in praise of Amida Buddha used in the Pure Land school of Buddhism.

138 The Buddha of Supreme Wisdom and Penetration is described in Chapter Seven of the *Lotus Sutra*. He existed in an ancient time, measured before the present by *kalpas* (world ages) equal to the atoms in a chiliocosm. He spent ten kalpas in meditation before becoming a buddha. He had sixteen sons, including (in later rebirths) Amitabha and Shakyamuni buddhas.

139 A play on words. *Su*, here indicated as a surname, also means "common" or

"lay" (nonclerical). Thus, the monk is remarking on the Buddhist view of the world's condition.

140 The term *tihu* refers literally to fine ghee, but also means the goodness of Buddha.

141 The term "rice bag" alludes to a monk who doesn't seriously pursue practice, but merely consumes the monastery's rice each day. A similar term of derision is "clothes hanger."

142 Jiangxi and Hunan are provinces in south central China where a great number of Zen temples existed.

143 To "pull out nails and draw out wedges" means to liberate beings.

144 Avichi is the eighth and deepest Buddhist hell.

145 Luohan's posthumous title may be translated several ways, including "Zen Master Truth Echo" or even "Zen Master True Presence."

146 The "Medicine" or "Healing" Buddha (in Chinese, *Yao Shi Fo*) is often found in Chinese temples sitting at Shakyamuni Buddha's left side.

147 Vulture Peak was the location where the Buddha lectured and passed the first transmission of the Zen school to his disciple Mahakashyapa.

148 Maitreiya Buddha is a buddha that is believed will come in the future to offer salvation.

149 Qicong was a fellow student of Fenyang who studied under Shoushan.

150 "West River" is another name for the district in Fenzhou where Fenyang taught.

151 A "dragon gate adept" refers to a Chinese myth about fish that meet once a year, converging at the rapids in a branch of the Yellow River. There they try to pass upstream through roaring rapids. The fish that manage to pass through the rapids turn into dragons. The fish unable to pass are forced back and receive a mark on their foreheads.

152 Dayang made this change due to a then current taboo on using the word "xuan."

153 See the section on Fushan Fayuan (p. 358), for more information.

154 A person who starts strong but finishes weak.

155 A mythical sword.

156 Zen master Qingfeng Chengyi was a teacher in the Caodong lineage.

157 The Chinese phrase *bing ding tongzi* may also be translated as "fire god." It originally referred to the youth responsible for lighting lanterns in the evening.

158 This passage is from a Song dynasty text entitled *The Celestial Eye of Human-*

ity, compiled by the monk Huiyan Zhishao. The text provides a description of the five houses of Zen.

159 The *Compendium of Five Lamps* uses the term "Dharma eye." The *Transmission of the Lamp* uses the term "Pure Wisdom."

160 Longchuan of Chu Province was located in the area of modern Zhejiang Province.

161 Zhiyi (538–97) founded the Tiantai school of Buddhism on this mountain.

162 The dharmadhatu is everything in the phenomenal and noumenal universe, the myriad dharmas.

163 A bird, said to live in the valleys of the Himalayan Mountains, that possesses a sweet song.

164 The Chinese here is a translation of the Sanskrit word *prajna,* usually translated as "wisdom."

165 Guquan, also known by the name "The Banana Hermit," was a student and Dharma heir of Fenyang Shanzhao.

166 The *Chan Lin Seng Bao Zhuan* is a collection of short biographies and recorded teachings of eighty-one Zen masters who lived during the period 907–1117.

167 Yang Danian (974–1020), also known as Yang Yi , was a literary figure of the Northern Song dynasty era.

168 "Sweet dew" is a traditional phrase of high praise for Buddhist teachings. In old China the phrase also had the meaning "great peace."

169 The "Ru Sea" is a play on words. In classical Chinese, the word *ru* also means "you."

170 The Chinese word *qing,* which occurs in Touzi's name, means "blue."

171 Su Taichu was a political figure during the Warring States period in China who suffered persecution.

172 Lord Xiang was a political-military figure who, being surrounded by enemy troops, killed himself on the banks of the Niao River.

173 This is one of eight mythical dragons that live in the sea, a protector of Kwan Yin Bodhisattva. The mythical Garuda bird eats dragons. However, the Garuda cannot eat this dragon.

174 For an explanation of this passage see note 150.

175 Tiantong is located near modern Ningbo City, Zhejiang Province.

176 During the Tang dynasty the large number of young people wanting to enter the Buddhist clergy caused the government to limit the number of monks by

instituting examinations. One such exam required the candidate to completely memorize and demonstrate an understanding of a number of Buddhist scriptures. This type of examination continued up through the Ming dynasty (1368–1644).

177 The San Mountain Pass is a famous location in the San Mountains in Shanxi Province.

178 Longce Temple was located in Hangzhou.

179 Guoqing Temple is located at the foot of Mt. Tiantai in Tiantai County, Zhejiang Province.

180 The "Faxiang" school is one of several names ascribed to the followers of the Consciousness-Only doctrine.

181 The famous West Lake of Hangzhou was seen from the front gate of Yongming Monastery.

182 Mt. Huanglong ("Yellow Dragon Mountain") is located in modern Xiushui County of Jiangxi Province.

183 The monk was meeting the master in a formal visit commonly known by the Japanese term *sanzen*. These interviews of the monks by their teacher are meant to determine the monk's level of understanding. In the Japanese Sōtō school of Zen these interviews are known by the Japanese term *dokusan*.

184 Daju was a student of Mazu Daoyi.

185 Four seas surrounded the mythical Mt. Sumeru.

186 The *Zeng Ding Fozu Dao Ying (Edited and Amended Portraits of the Buddha Ancestors)* was compiled and edited by Venerable Xuyun and reprinted by Xin Wen Fêng Publishing House, Taipei, 1979.

187 See footnote 64.

188 Yangqi Hui is Yangqi Fanghui, founder of the Yangqi branch of the Linji school of Zen.

189 These are the names of legendary rulers of ancient China.

190 This was a famous park in India where the Buddha taught, a place now in the modern city of Setmahet.

191 Mt. Putuo is the Chinese home of Kwan Yin Bodhisattva.

192 According to Buddhist tradition, the historical Buddha, Shakyamuni, was the seventh buddha to appear in the world.

193 This was probably the temple of Zen master Dagui Huaixiu, a teacher in ancient Fuzhou.

194 The Chinese phrase used here literally means "couldn't accord with him" or, more literally, he "couldn't connect" with his teacher, Huanglong.

195 Huanglong's name means "yellow dragon."

196 A student of Cuiyan Zhi, Yunfeng was a prominent Zen teacher of the Song dynasty who taught at Falun Temple on Mt. Heng. He later lived and taught at Yunfeng.

197 Zen Master Yuantong Na (1010–71), a prominent teacher who resided at Yuantong Temple on Mt. Lu, located south of Jiujiang City in Jiangxi Province. Chengtian Temple is located east of Jiujiang City in Jiangxi Province.

198 This is a reference to three anciently known beautiful palaces in China, located in what is now Henan Province.

199 Varanasi is the former name for the city of Benares, in India.

200 The term "wearing feathers and horns" means to become like a beast.

201 Longan is a place name of where Doushuai lived.

202 The Tripitaka is the complete canon of Buddhist scriptures.

203 A teacher of the Yunmen lineage, Yuanzhao was a student of Tianyi Yihuai.

204 The Mani jewel is a gem or luminous pearl symbolizing the Buddha's teaching.

205 The Dongchan Temple on Wuzu Mountain (also called "East Mountain") is located near the site of the modern city of Huangmei in Hubei Province. "East Zen" refers to the East Mountain school of Zen, the school established on this mountain by the Fifth Ancestor, Daman Hongren.

206 The "Five Mountains" were five leading Zen temples of this era. They included Xingshen Wanshou Zen Temple on Mt. Jing, Lingyin and Jingzi temples in Hanzhou, and Jingde and Guanli temples on mountains near what is now Ningbo City in Zhejiang Province.

207 Kumu Facheng (1071–1128). Mt. Xiang is located near the city of Linru in modern Henan Province.

208 Here the words "house woods" are a double entendre, meaning Zen and the Buddhist community.

209 Chongzhu City in Pengzhou was located in the area of modern Peng County in Sichuan Province.

210 Jinshan Temple is a famous temple located northwest of modern Zhenjiang City in Jiangsu Province.

211 This is a well-known kōan by Zhaozhou.

212 The monk Nian Chang compiled this text during the Yuan dynasty (1206–1333).

213 The Zhaojue ("Luminous Enlightenment") Temple was located in Chengdu City, Sichuan Province.

214 The Blue Cliff Temple was another name for the Ling Quan Monastery on Mt. Jia. Its location is about fifteen kilometers southwest of the modern village of Sanbanqiao in Shimen County, Hunan Province.

215 Foguo means "buddha essence" or "buddha seed."

216 The "five stars" is an ancient Chinese phrase that means "fate."

217 The Taiping Xingguo Yuan ("Great Peace Rejuvenate the Country Monastery") was located on Mt. Zhong near what is now the city of Nanjing.

218 The Zhihai ("Wisdom Ocean") Temple in ancient Bianjing was located near what is now the city of Kaifeng in Henan Province.

219 The Chinese characters of Fojian's name also imply the meanings "Buddha Example," or even "Buddha Precept."

220 Fayan's famous "three buddhas" included Foguo Keqin, Fojian Huiqin, and Foyan Qingquan. The word "Fo" in each of their names means "buddha."

221 This teacher is obscure. Shu Province was an area in the southern part of modern Anhui Province.

222 Tianning Temple is located in Jiangsu Province near the city of Tianning, in Jiangdu County.

223 Su Wu and Li Ling were historical figures who lived in the Western Han dynasty (206 B.C.E–32 C.E.)

224 Foyan here differentiates between acts that are for one's own benefit and the actions of enlightened Buddhist practitioners who work for the benefit of others.

225 To *gassho* is to place palm to palm in a gesture of respect.

226 Rui grass is an auspicious plant.

227 *Mahakaruna* (in Chinese, *dabei*) is a Sanskrit term meaning "great compassion" or "great pity." It refers to the tragedy of the suffering of beings and the mind of compassion that responds to that suffering.

228 Hezhou is the ancient name for He County in Anwei Province.

229 Yuelin Temple is located in Fenghua County in Zhejiang Province.

230 Treasure Peak is located near modern Nanchang City in Jiangxi Province.

231 See note 222.

232 Nengren Temple was located in the city of Nanjing in Jiangsu Province.

233 The "old barbarian," Bodhidharma, sat facing the wall for nine years at Shaolin Temple.

234 Xi Zhong is a legendary Chinese builder of wheeled vehicles who is said to have lived during the ancient Xia dynasty (2205–1766 B.C.E.).

235 Mt Xiang is located on the Yang-tse River in Jiangsu Province.

236 Xizhen Temple was located west of Mt. Wuyun in Hangzhou.

237 Pomegranate blossoms are fiery red.

INDEX

Qinshan Wensui 213–16, 242, 243
Qizhou 75
Quan Province 221
Quanwei 316
Quanzhou 84, 219, 237, 242, 280, 304, 343, 345, 367
Realizing Unity. See Cantongjie
Rebirth of Maitreya Sutra 211
Record of Fenyang Wude 330
Record of Kewen 391
Record of Linji 205
Record of the Monasteries 126
Record of National Teacher Huizhong 53
Record of the True School 126
Record of the Venerable Ancients. See Guzunsu Yulu
Record of Yunmen 439
Record of the Zen Discourses by the Monk Shenhui 60
Record of Zen Master Xuansha Shibei 273
Records of the Lankavatara Masters 31
Renxian 337
Ren Zong, Emperor 353
Rinzai school. *See* Linji school
Rui Cliff 284
Ruiyan Monastery 284
Ruiyan Shiyan 283–85
Ruizhou 178, 234, 337
Rui Zong, Emperor 41
Ru Province 252
Ru Sea 358
Ruzhou 249, 251, 287, 310, 327, 332, 420
Samantabhadra 113, 163, 199, 235, 313, 442
Samaya 302
Sandokai. See Cantongjie
Sanfeng Peak 212
Sanfeng Qing 407
Sanjiao Song 358
Sanlun school 26
Sansheng Huiran 158, 201, 202, 205–6
Sansheng Monastery 205
Santai City 161
Secluded Perch Temple 32
Second Ancestor 16, 20, 23, 24, 48, 151, 272, 355, 416, 417, 450. *See also* Dazu Huike
Sengcan. *See* Jianzhi Sengcan
Shakyamuni 27, 113, 165, 199, 274, 298, 303, 307, 308, 323, 357, 380, 391, 397, 412, 430, 443, 446

Shan, attendant 381
Shanchun 27
Shandong Province 136, 155, 172, 201, 309, 384, 387
Shanghai City 145, 259
Shangzhi Shizhen 445
Shankou, Mount 162
Shanxi Province 107, 327, 354, 417, 419
Shao 103
Shaoguan 166
"Shaojue." *See* Yuanwu Keqin
Shaolin Temple 16, 18, 20, 21, 417, 444
Shaoxing City 316
Shaozhou 39, 45, 166, 411
Shen 280
Shending 382
Shenguang 241
Shengyin Monastery 362
Shenhui. *See* Heze Shenhui
Shenxiu. *See* Yuquan Shenxiu
"Shenzhao." *See* Dasui Fazhen
Shexian Guixing 332–34, 358
Shijiazhuang City 203, 332
Shimen, Mount 71, 142
Shinchi Kakushin 437
Shiqian. *See* Qinglin Shiqian
Shishuang, Mount 151, 192, 354, 420
Shishuang Chuyuan 351–54, 372, 377, 378, 381, 392
Shishuang Qingzhu 98, 190–92, 234, 235, 236, 244, 281, 352, 420
Shishuang Temple 352
Shiting Temple 208
Shitou school 50
Shitou Xiqian 4, 48, 49, 50, 66, 69, 70, 71–75, 94, 107, 108, 110, 111, 113, 114, 168, 319
Shoushan Xingnian 252, 309–12, 328, 329, 332
Shu, Mount 226
Shuangjing Monastery 442
Shuangyan Monastery 307
Shun 389
Shushan Kuangren 178, 226, 258
Shutai Temple 384
Shuzhou 193, 362, 429, 432, 433
Sichuan Province 65, 66, 145, 161, 162, 196, 245, 291, 337, 404, 405, 413, 417, 423, 424, 432, 446

ABOUT WISDOM

WISDOM PUBLICATIONS, a not-for-profit publisher, is dedicated to making available authentic Buddhist works by the world's leading Buddhist scholars. We publish our titles with the appreciation of Buddhism as a living philosophy and with the special commitment to preserve and transmit important works from all the major Buddhist traditions.

If you would like more information or a copy of our mail-order catalog, please contact us at:

Wisdom Publications
199 Elm Street
Somerville, Massachusetts 02144 USA
Telephone: (617) 776-7416 • Fax: (617) 776-7841
Email: info@wisdompubs.org • www.wisdompubs.org

THE WISDOM TRUST

As a not-for-profit publisher, Wisdom Publications is dedicated to the publication of fine Dharma books for the benefit of all sentient beings and dependent upon the kindness and generosity of sponsors in order to do so. If you would like to make a donation to Wisdom, please do so through our Somerville office. If you would like to sponsor the publication of a book, please write or e-mail us for more information.

Thank you.

Wisdom Publications is a non-profit, charitable 501(c)(3) organization and a part of the Foundation for the Preservation of the Mahayana Tradition (FPMT).

LINEAGE CHART OF THE ZEN ANCESTORS

THIS UNIQUE and highly informative chart provides extensive information about 179 of the most famous Zen teachers of ancient China. All five of the traditional schools of Zen are included (in addition to other Zen schools and branches) and are color-coded for easy reference. Included for each ancestor are his or her names in Chinese pinyin and Japanese romaji transliterations, and known birth and death dates. The chart also displays each ancestor according to his or her generation, and the relative seniority between "Dharma siblings." Readers can locate any ancestor quickly using the coordinates provided.

Additional or replacement copies of the chart are available at $4.95 each from Wisdom Publications. Please call 617-776-7416 ext. 24, or write to Wisdom Publications, 199 Elm Street, Somerville, MA 02144 USA.